KARAKURI ODETTE

カラクリ オデット

Vol. 3

Julietta Suzuki

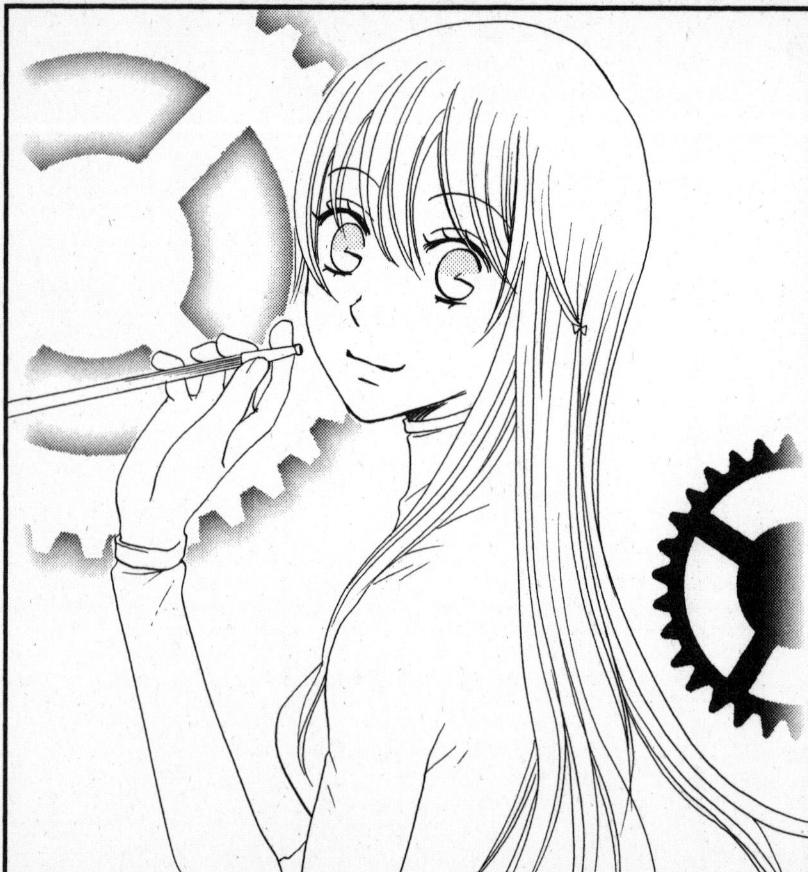

Karakuri Odette Volume 3
Created by Julietta Suzuki

Translation - Aimi Tokutake
Copy Editor - Daniella Orihuela-Gruber
English Adaptation - Peter Ahlstrom
Retouch and Lettering - Star Print Brokers
Production Artist - Rui Kyo
Graphic Designer - Al-Insan Lashley

Editor - Lillian Diaz-Przybyl
Print Production Manager - Lucas Rivera
Managing Editor - Vy Nguyen
Senior Designer - Louis Csontos
Art Director - Al-Insan Lashley
Director of Sales and Manufacturing - Allyson De Simone
Associate Publisher - Marco F. Pavia
President and C.O.O. - John Parker
C.E.O. and Chief Creative Officer - Stu Levy

A  Manga

TOKYOPOP Inc.
5900 Wilshire Blvd. Suite 2000
Los Angeles, CA 90036

E-mail: info@TOKYOPOP.com
Come visit us online at www.TOKYOPOP.com

ISBN: 978-1-4278-1409-8

First TOKYOPOP printing: May 2010
10 9 8 7 6 5 4 3 2 1
Printed in the USA

KARAKURI ODETTE

カラクリ オデット

Vol. 3

by Julietta Suzuki

HAMBURG // LONDON // LOS ANGELES // TOKYO

Contents

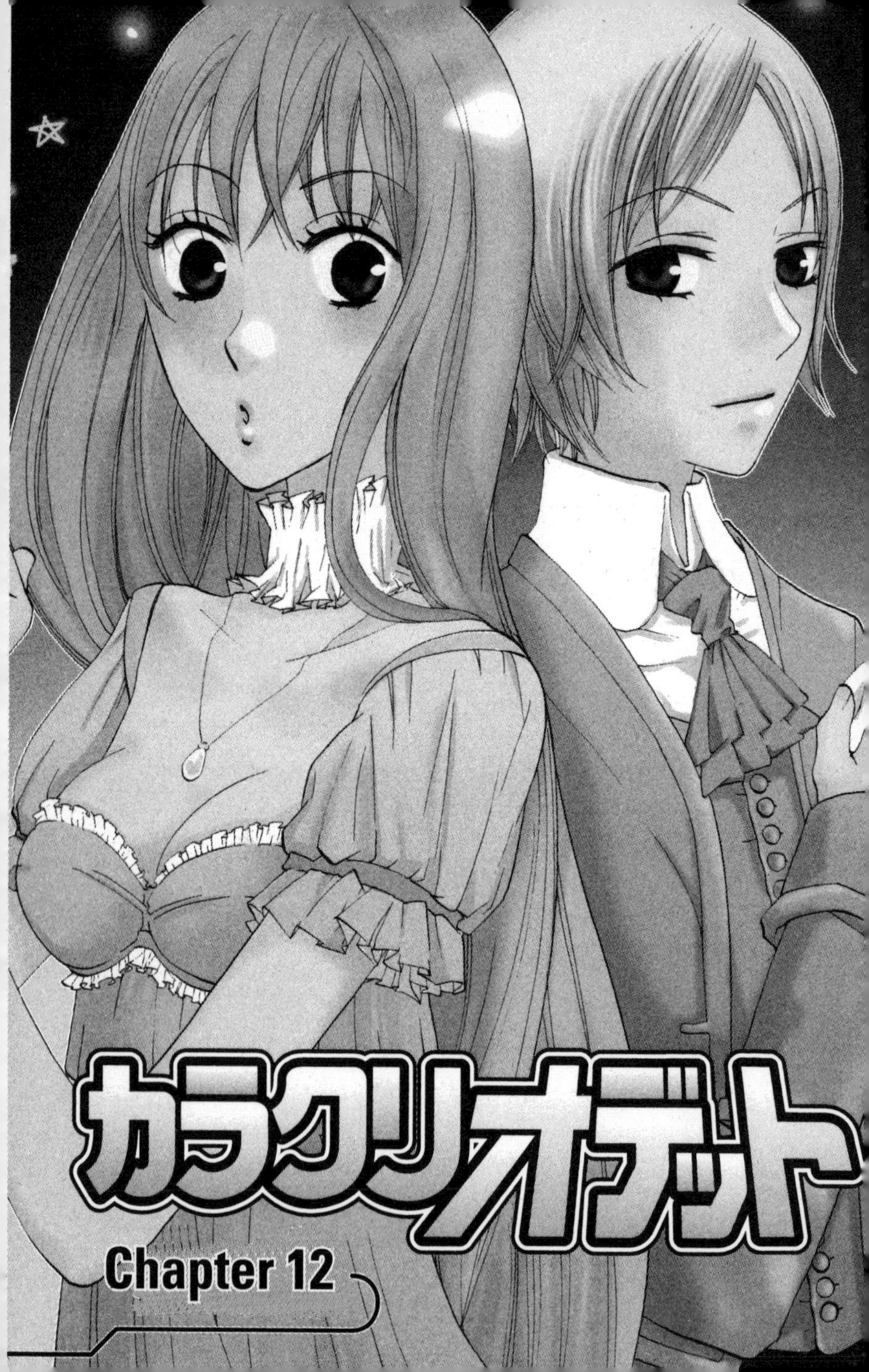
カラクリオデット
Chapter 12

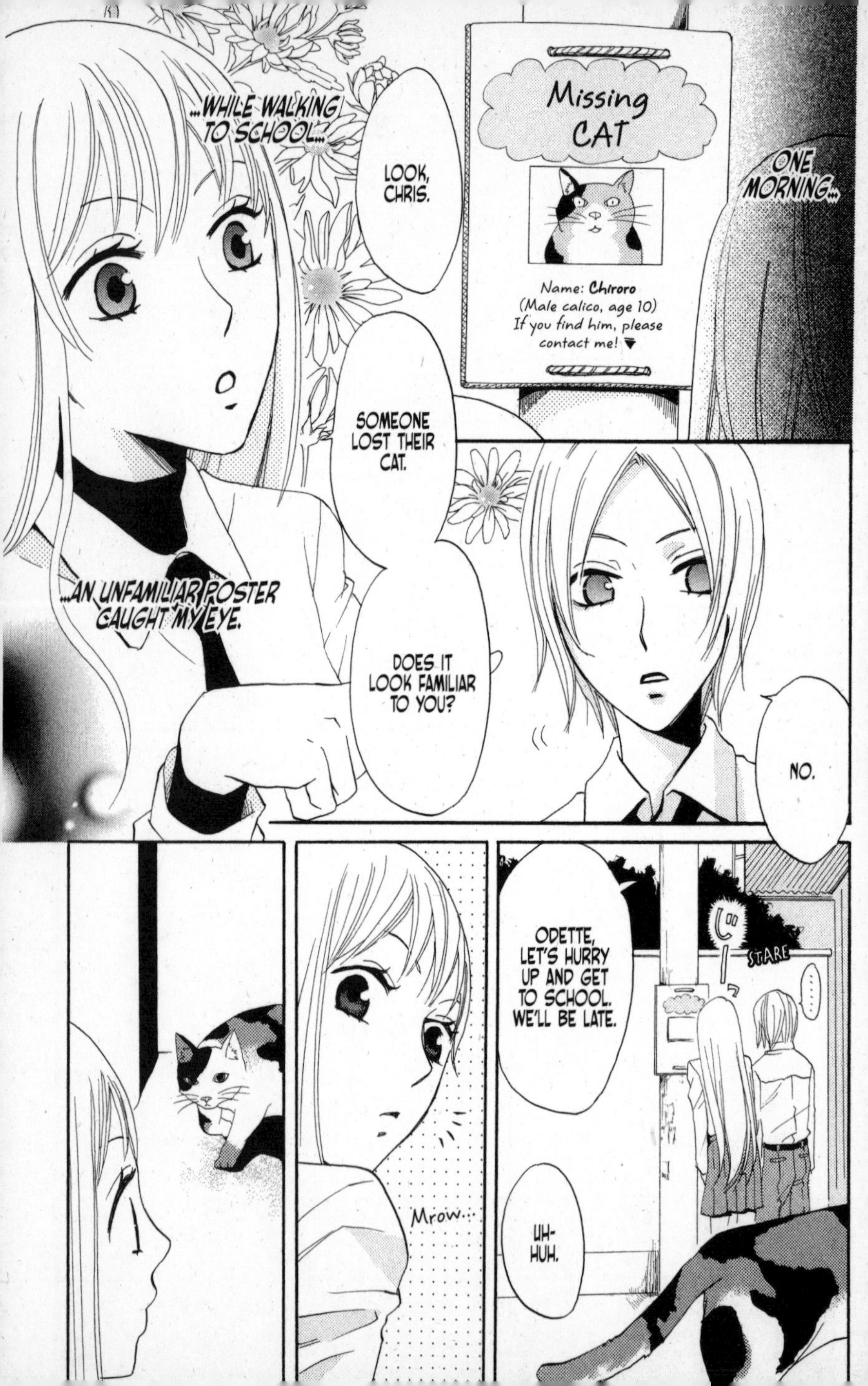
ONE MORNING...
Missing CAT
Name: Chiroro
(Male calico, age 10)
If you find him, please contact me!
...WHILE WALKING TO SCHOOL...
...AN UNFAMILIAR POSTER CAUGHT MY EYE.
LOOK, CHRIS.
SOMEONE LOST THEIR CAT.
DOES IT LOOK FAMILIAR TO YOU?
NO.
ODETTE, LET'S HURRY UP AND GET TO SCHOOL. WE'LL BE LATE.
STARE
...
UH-HUH.
Mrow...

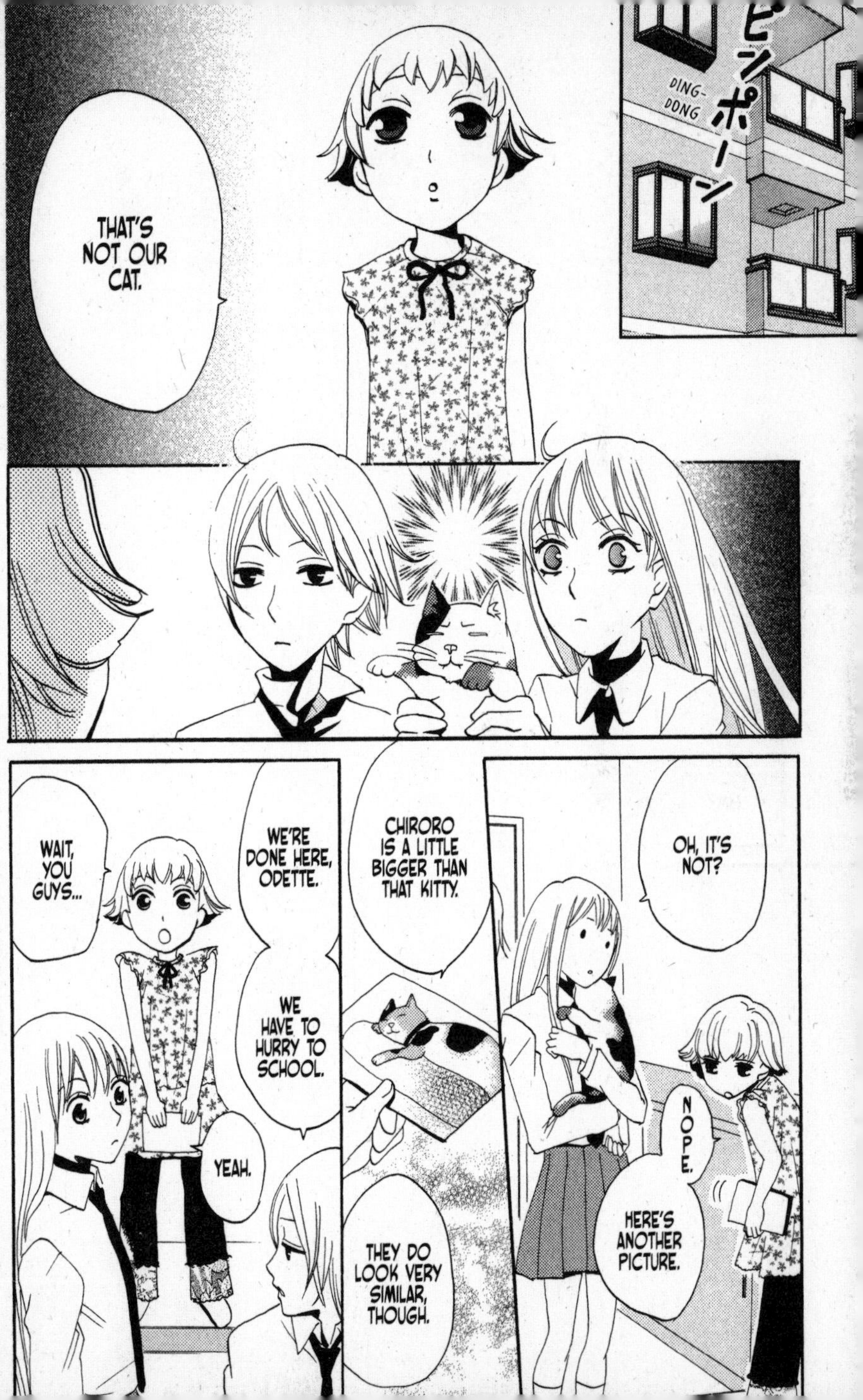
ピンポーン
DING-DONG
THAT'S NOT OUR CAT.
OH, IT'S NOT?
NOPE.
HERE'S ANOTHER PICTURE.
CHIRORO IS A LITTLE BIGGER THAN THAT KITTY.
THEY DO LOOK VERY SIMILAR, THOUGH.
WE'RE DONE HERE, ODETTE.
WE HAVE TO HURRY TO SCHOOL.
WAIT, YOU GUYS...
YEAH.

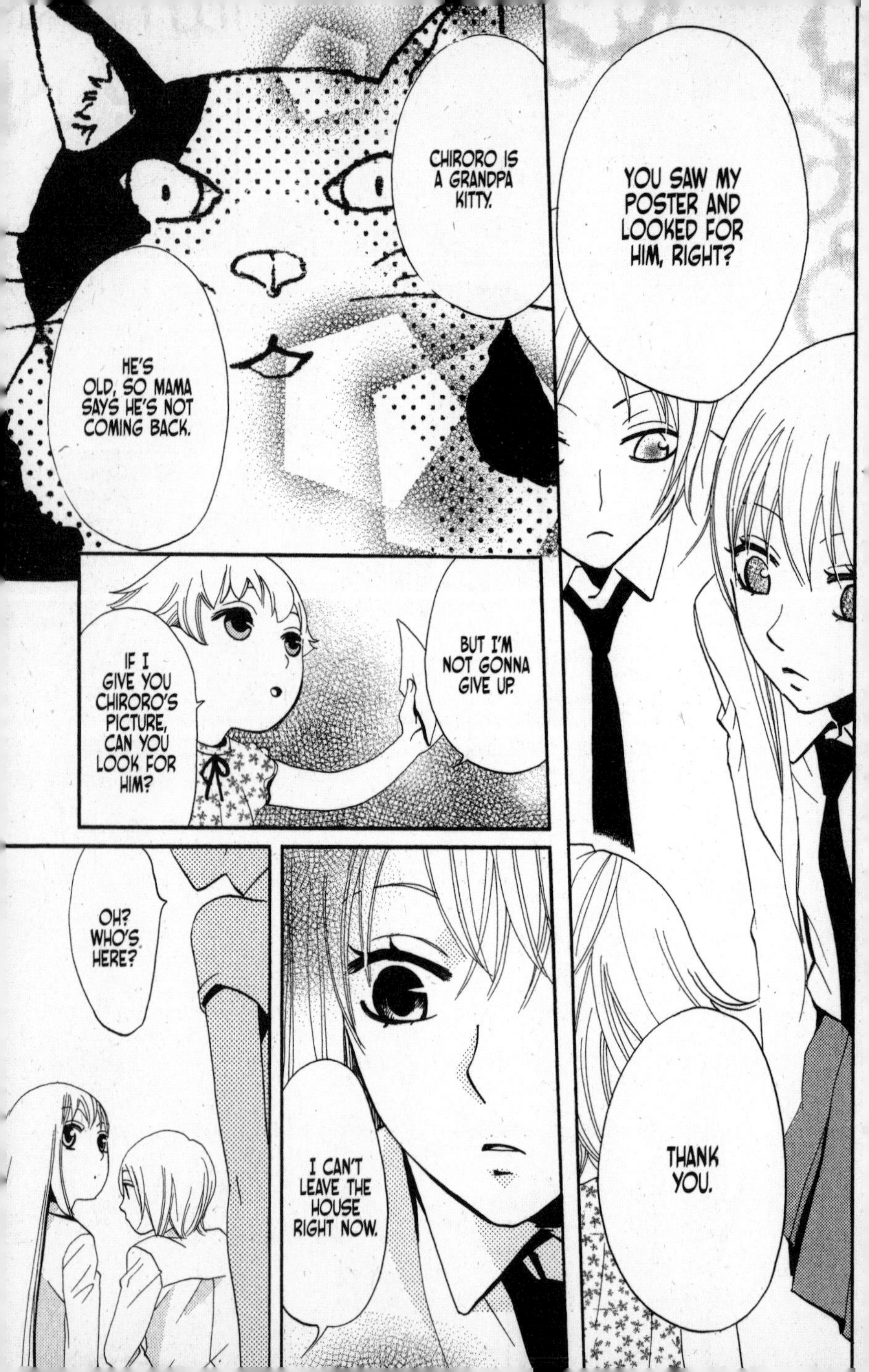
YOU SAW MY POSTER AND LOOKED FOR HIM, RIGHT?
CHIRORO IS A GRANDPA KITTY.
HE'S OLD, SO MAMA SAYS HE'S NOT COMING BACK.
BUT I'M NOT GONNA GIVE UP.
IF I GIVE YOU CHIRORO'S PICTURE, CAN YOU LOOK FOR HIM?
THANK YOU.
I CAN'T LEAVE THE HOUSE RIGHT NOW.
OH? WHO'S HERE?

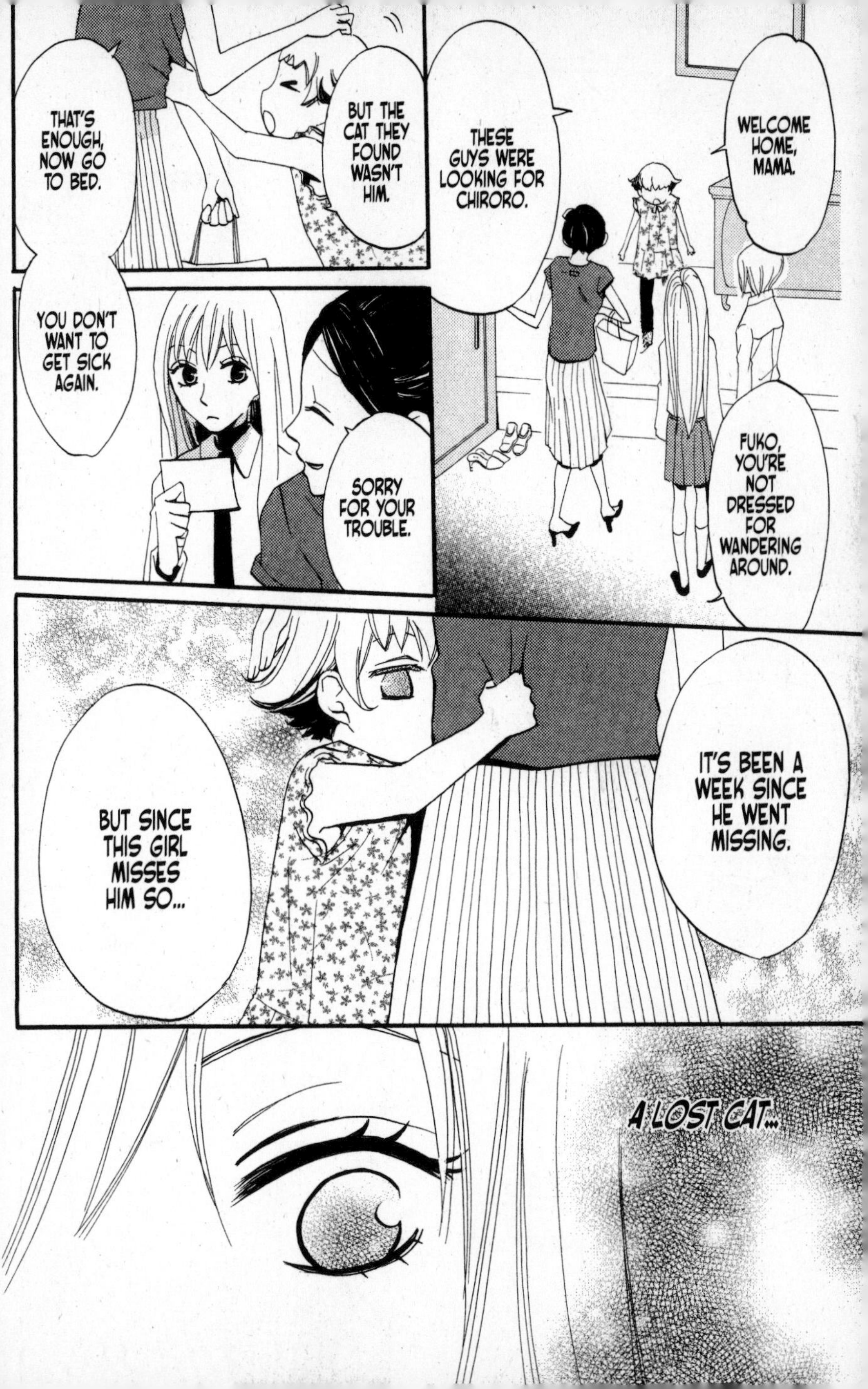
WELCOME HOME, MAMA.
THESE GUYS WERE LOOKING FOR CHIRORO.
FUKO, YOU'RE NOT DRESSED FOR WANDERING AROUND.
BUT THE CAT THEY FOUND WASN'T HIM.
THAT'S ENOUGH, NOW GO TO BED.
SORRY FOR YOUR TROUBLE.
YOU DON'T WANT TO GET SICK AGAIN.
IT'S BEEN A WEEK SINCE HE WENT MISSING.
BUT SINCE THIS GIRL MISSES HIM SO...
A LOST CAT...

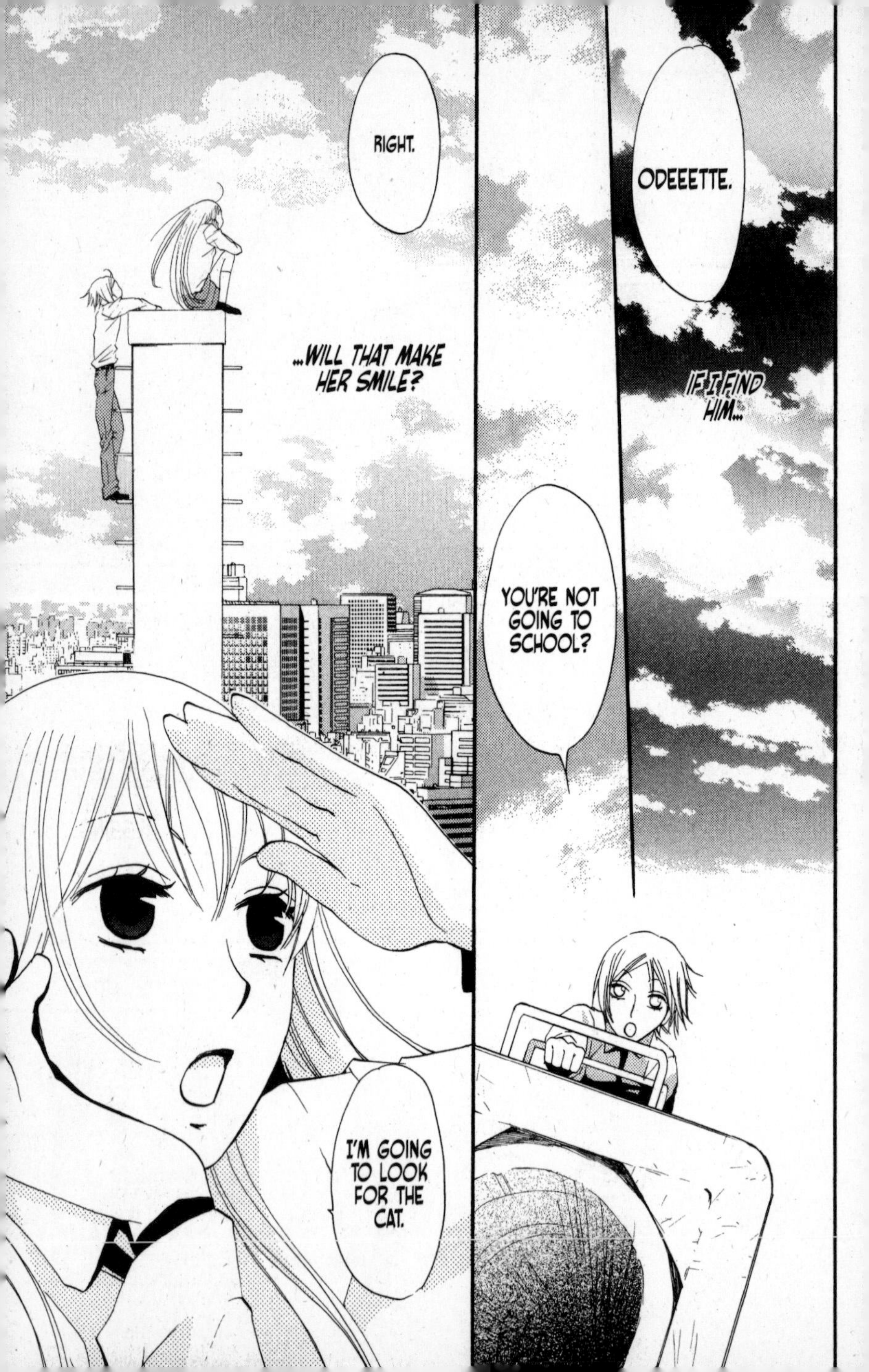
ODEEETTE.
IF I FIND HIM...
YOU'RE NOT GOING TO SCHOOL?
RIGHT.
...WILL THAT MAKE HER SMILE?
I'M GOING TO LOOK FOR THE CAT.

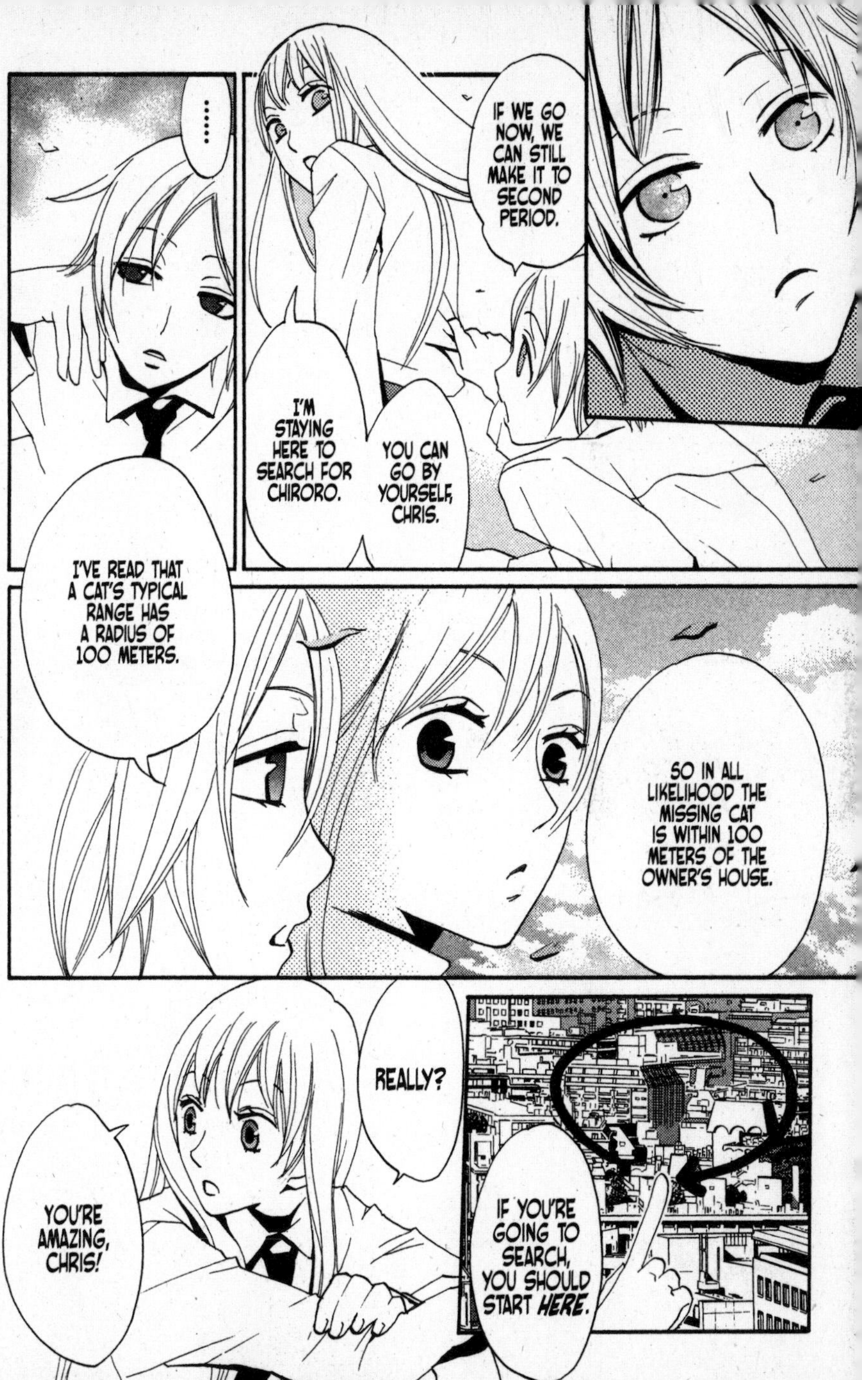
IF WE GO NOW, WE CAN STILL MAKE IT TO SECOND PERIOD.
YOU CAN GO BY YOURSELF, CHRIS.
I'M STAYING HERE TO SEARCH FOR CHIRORO.
......
I'VE READ THAT A CAT'S TYPICAL RANGE HAS A RADIUS OF 100 METERS.
SO IN ALL LIKELIHOOD THE MISSING CAT IS WITHIN 100 METERS OF THE OWNER'S HOUSE.
IF YOU'RE GOING TO SEARCH, YOU SHOULD START *HERE*.
REALLY?
YOU'RE AMAZING, CHRIS!

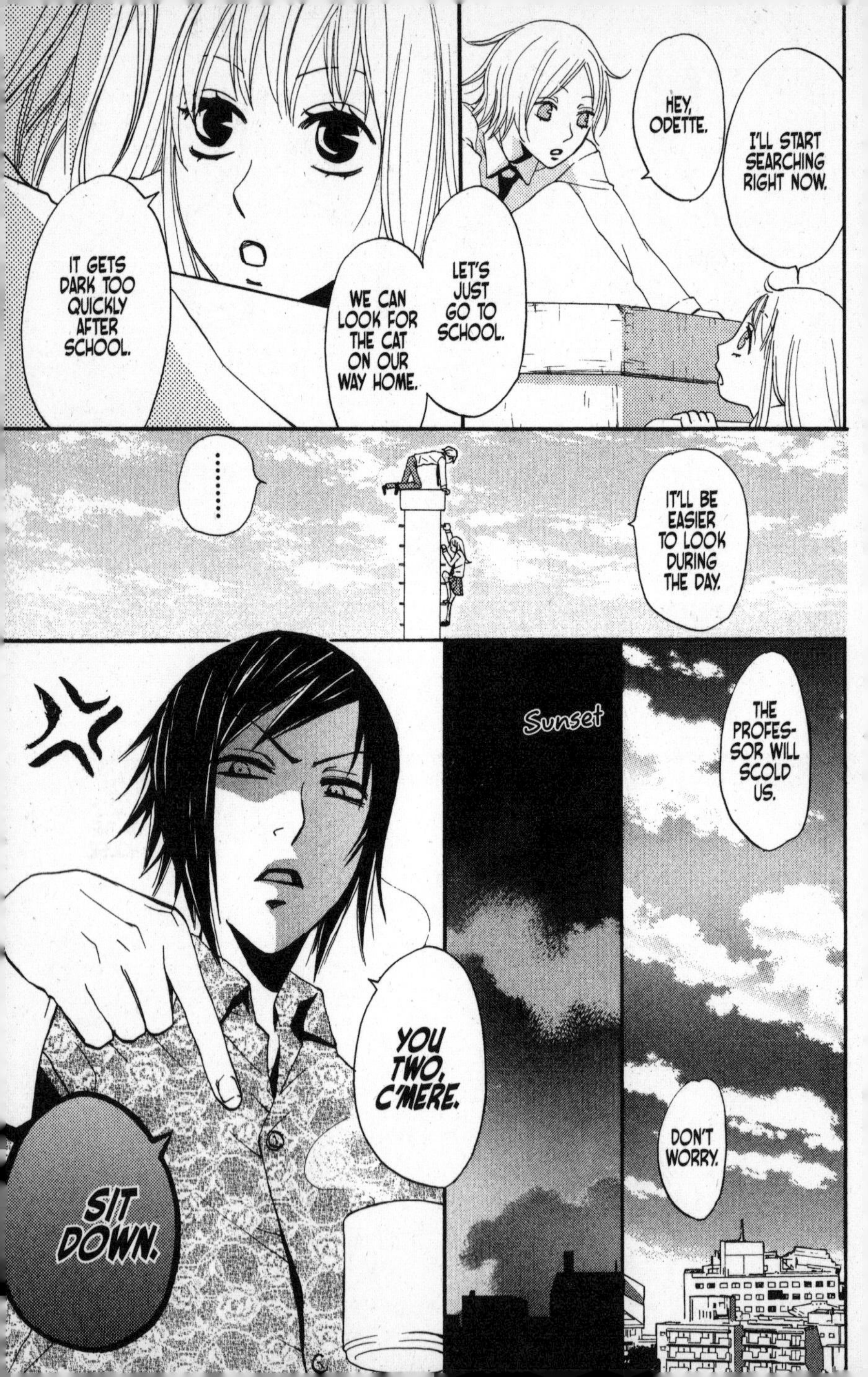
HEY, ODETTE.
I'LL START SEARCHING RIGHT NOW.
LET'S JUST GO TO SCHOOL.
WE CAN LOOK FOR THE CAT ON OUR WAY HOME.
IT GETS DARK TOO QUICKLY AFTER SCHOOL.
IT'LL BE EASIER TO LOOK DURING THE DAY.
....
THE PROFES-SOR WILL SCOLD US.
DON'T WORRY.
Sunset
YOU TWO, C'MERE.
SIT DOWN.

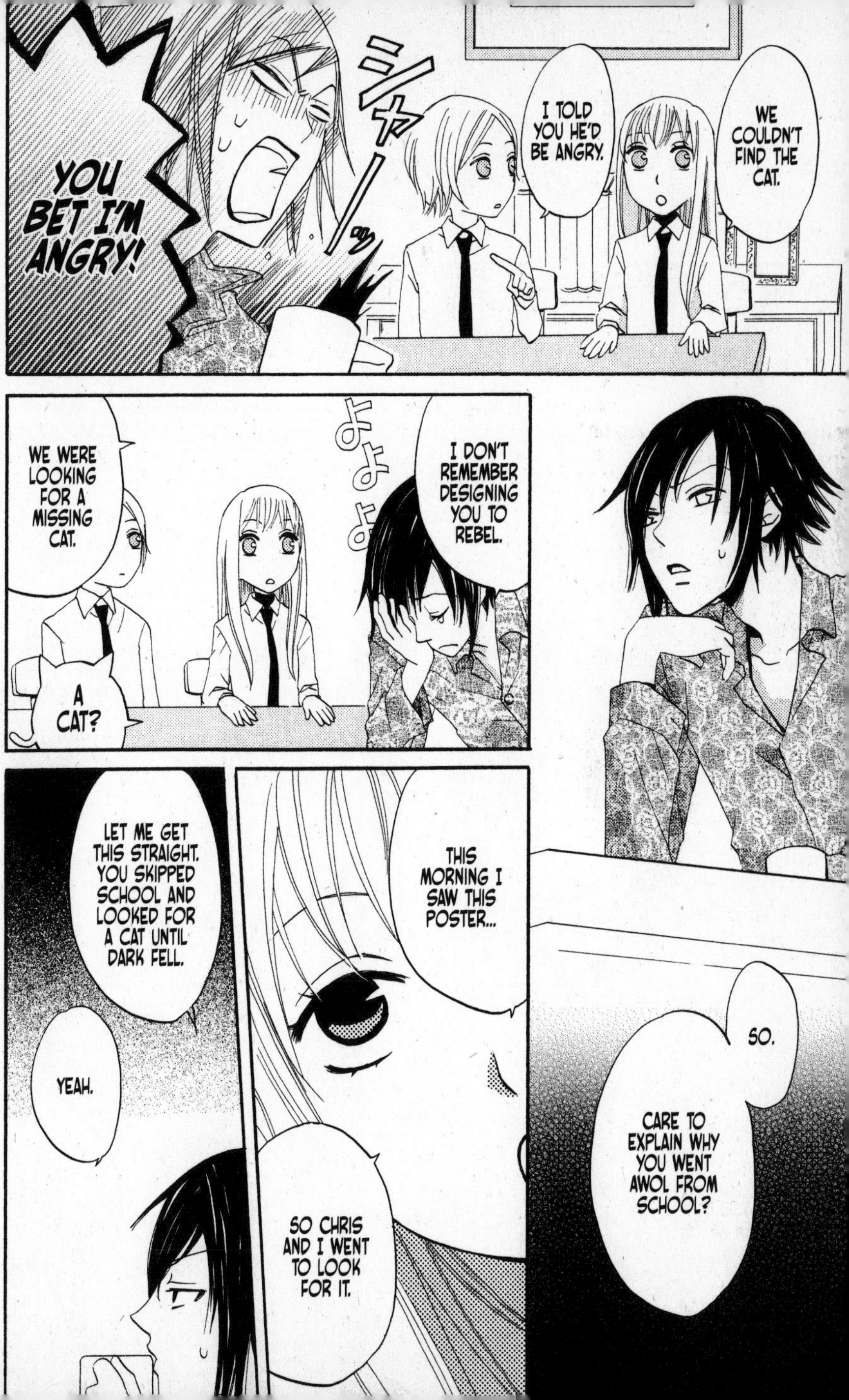
WE COULDN'T FIND THE CAT.
I TOLD YOU HE'D BE ANGRY.
シャー
YOU BET I'M ANGRY!
SO.
CARE TO EXPLAIN WHY YOU WENT AWOL FROM SCHOOL?
I DON'T REMEMBER DESIGNING YOU TO REBEL.
よよよ
WE WERE LOOKING FOR A MISSING CAT.
A CAT?
THIS MORNING I SAW THIS POSTER...
SO CHRIS AND I WENT TO LOOK FOR IT.
LET ME GET THIS STRAIGHT. YOU SKIPPED SCHOOL AND LOOKED FOR A CAT UNTIL DARK FELL.
YEAH.

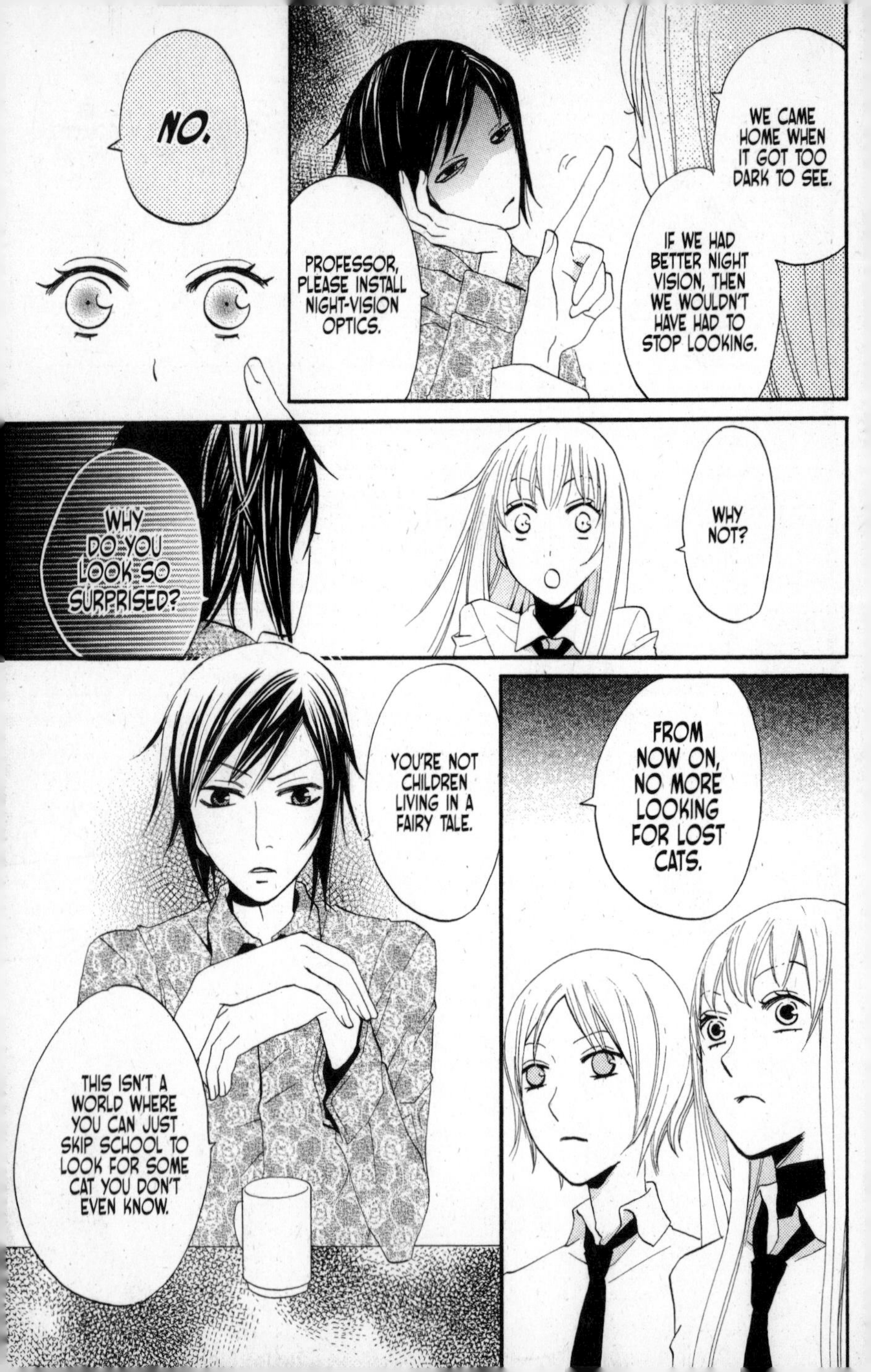
WE CAME HOME WHEN IT GOT TOO DARK TO SEE.
IF WE HAD BETTER NIGHT VISION, THEN WE WOULDN'T HAVE HAD TO STOP LOOKING.
PROFESSOR, PLEASE INSTALL NIGHT-VISION OPTICS.
NO.
WHY NOT?
WHY DO YOU LOOK SO SURPRISED?
FROM NOW ON, NO MORE LOOKING FOR LOST CATS.
YOU'RE NOT CHILDREN LIVING IN A FAIRY TALE.
THIS ISN'T A WORLD WHERE YOU CAN JUST SKIP SCHOOL TO LOOK FOR SOME CAT YOU DON'T EVEN KNOW.

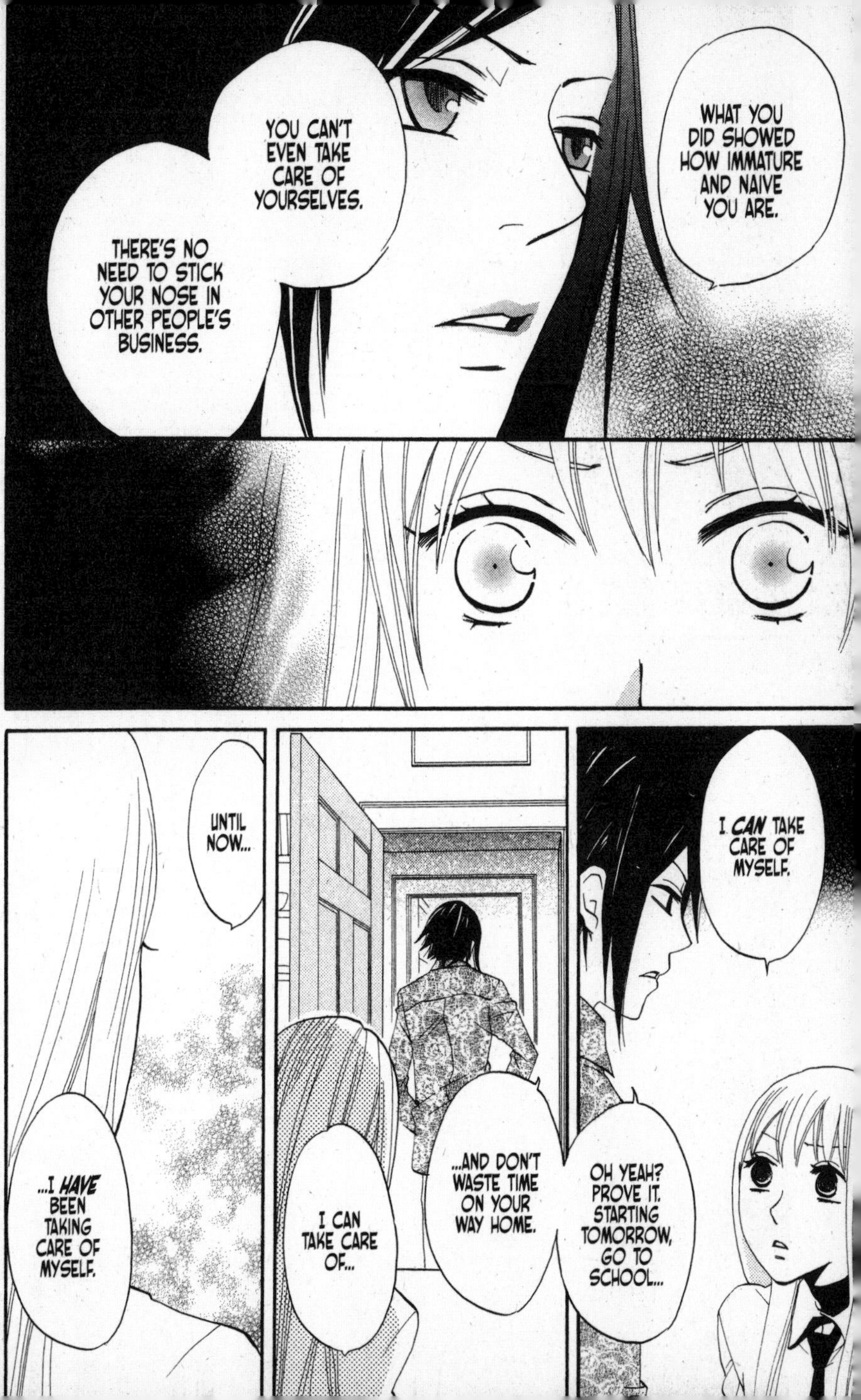
WHAT YOU DID SHOWED HOW IMMATURE AND NAIVE YOU ARE.
YOU CAN'T EVEN TAKE CARE OF YOURSELVES.
THERE'S NO NEED TO STICK YOUR NOSE IN OTHER PEOPLE'S BUSINESS.
I *CAN* TAKE CARE OF MYSELF.
OH YEAH? PROVE IT. STARTING TOMORROW, GO TO SCHOOL...
...AND DON'T WASTE TIME ON YOUR WAY HOME.
I CAN TAKE CARE OF...
UNTIL NOW...
...I *HAVE* BEEN TAKING CARE OF MYSELF.

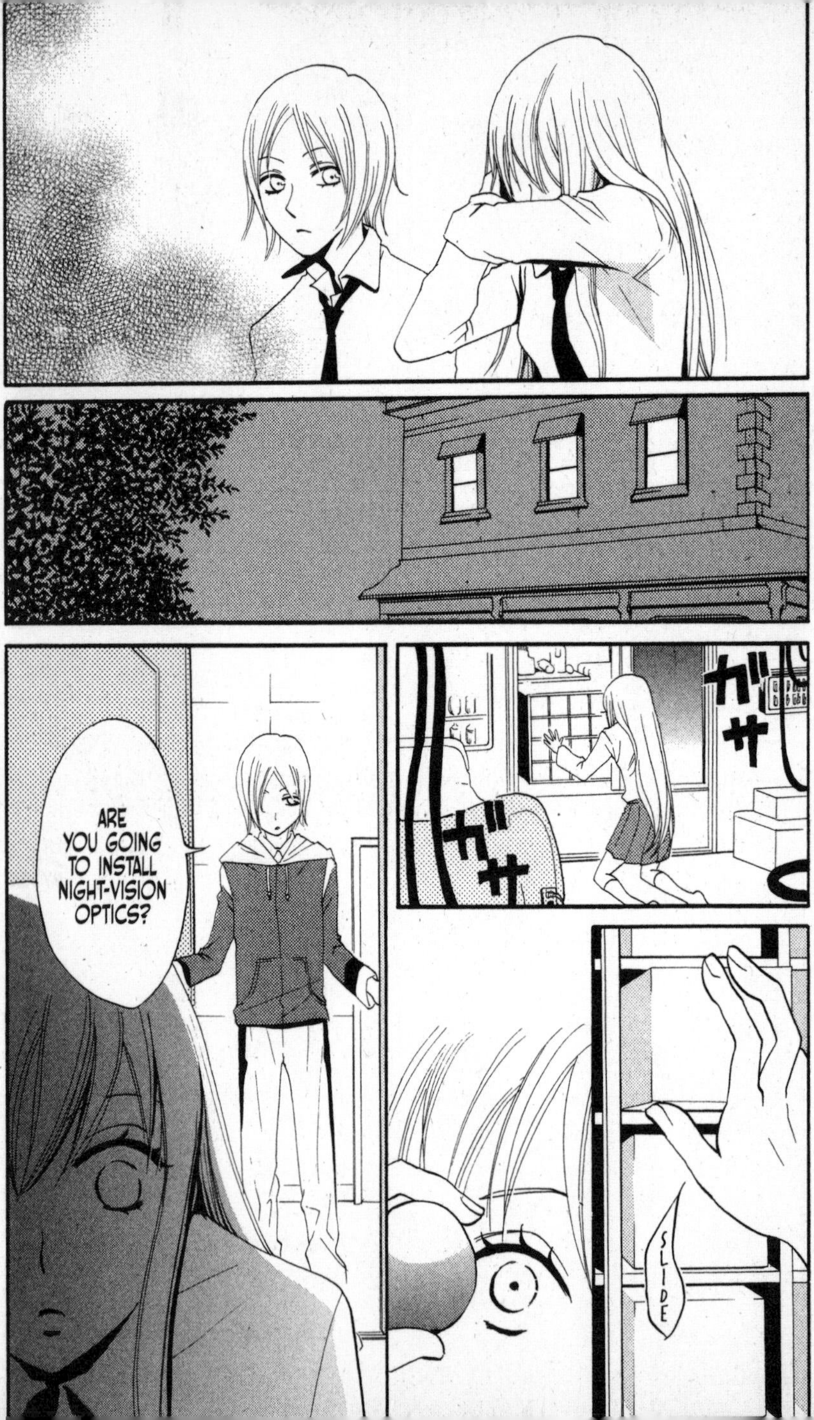
ガサ
ガサ
SLIDE
ARE YOU GOING TO INSTALL NIGHT-VISION OPTICS?

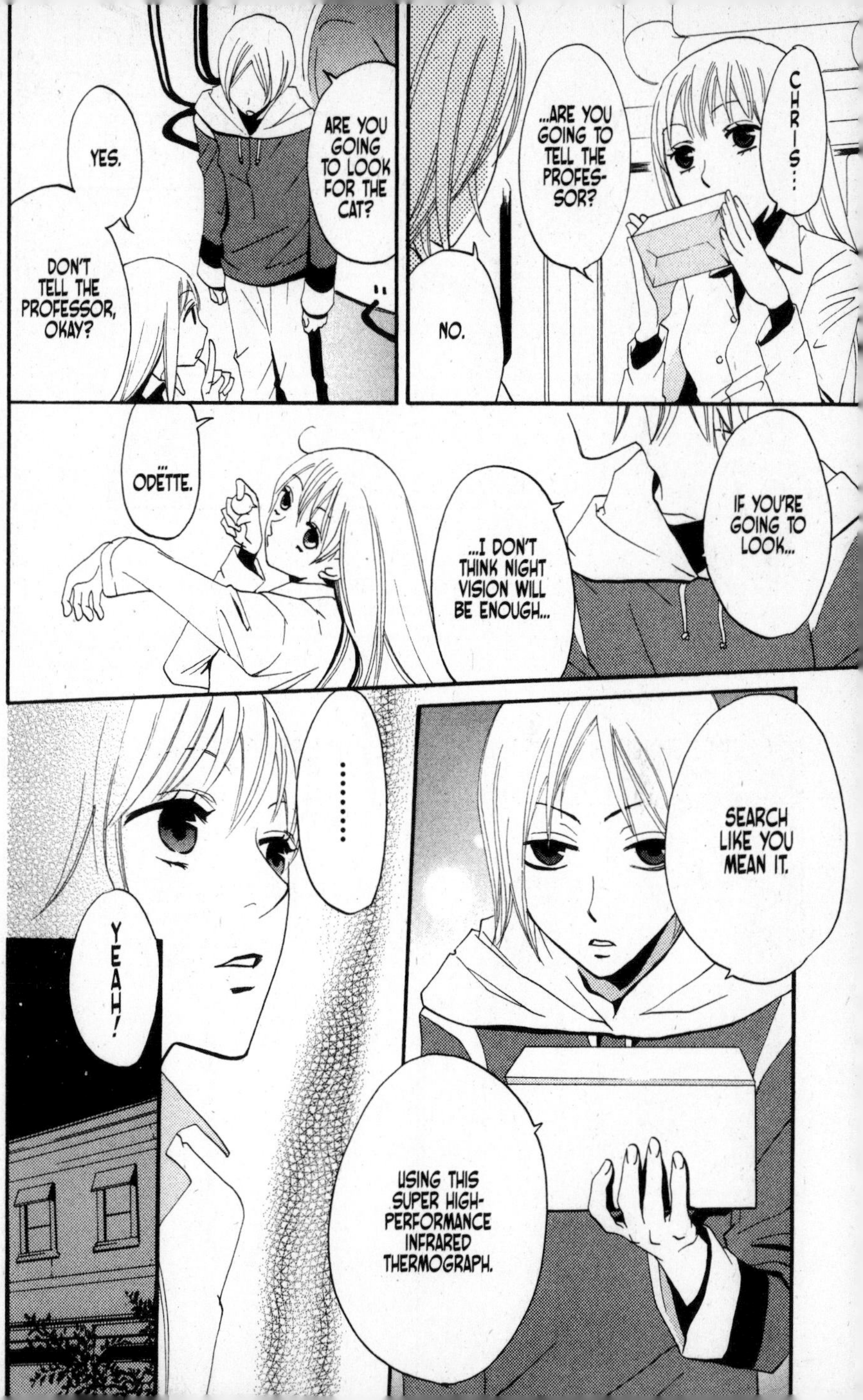
CHRIS...
...ARE YOU GOING TO TELL THE PROFESSOR?
NO.
ARE YOU GOING TO LOOK FOR THE CAT?
YES.
DON'T TELL THE PROFESSOR, OKAY?
IF YOU'RE GOING TO LOOK...
...I DON'T THINK NIGHT VISION WILL BE ENOUGH...
... ODETTE.
SEARCH LIKE YOU MEAN IT.
USING THIS SUPER HIGH-PERFORMANCE INFRARED THERMOGRAPH.
....
YEAH!

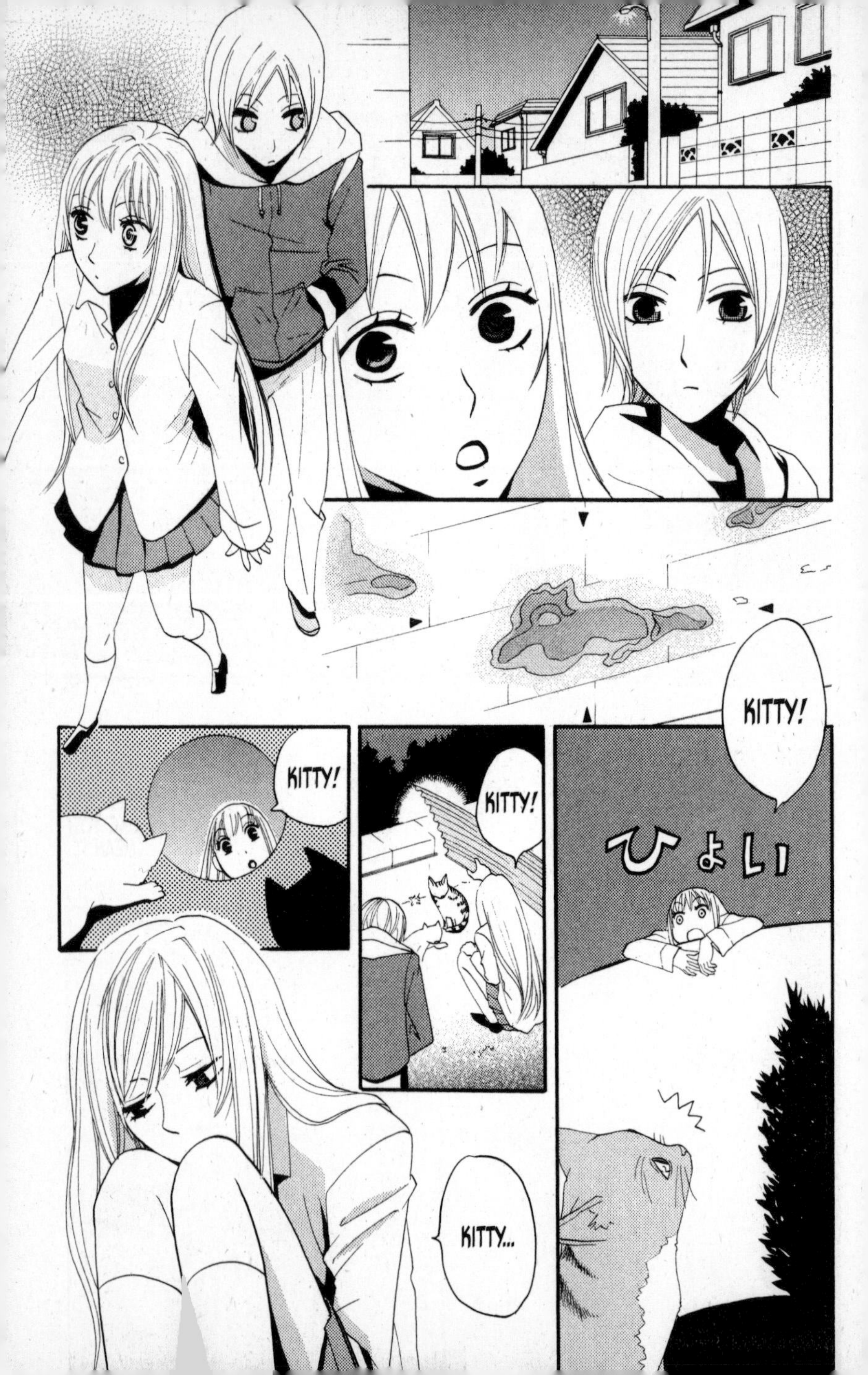
KITTY!
ひょい
KITTY!
KITTY!
KITTY...

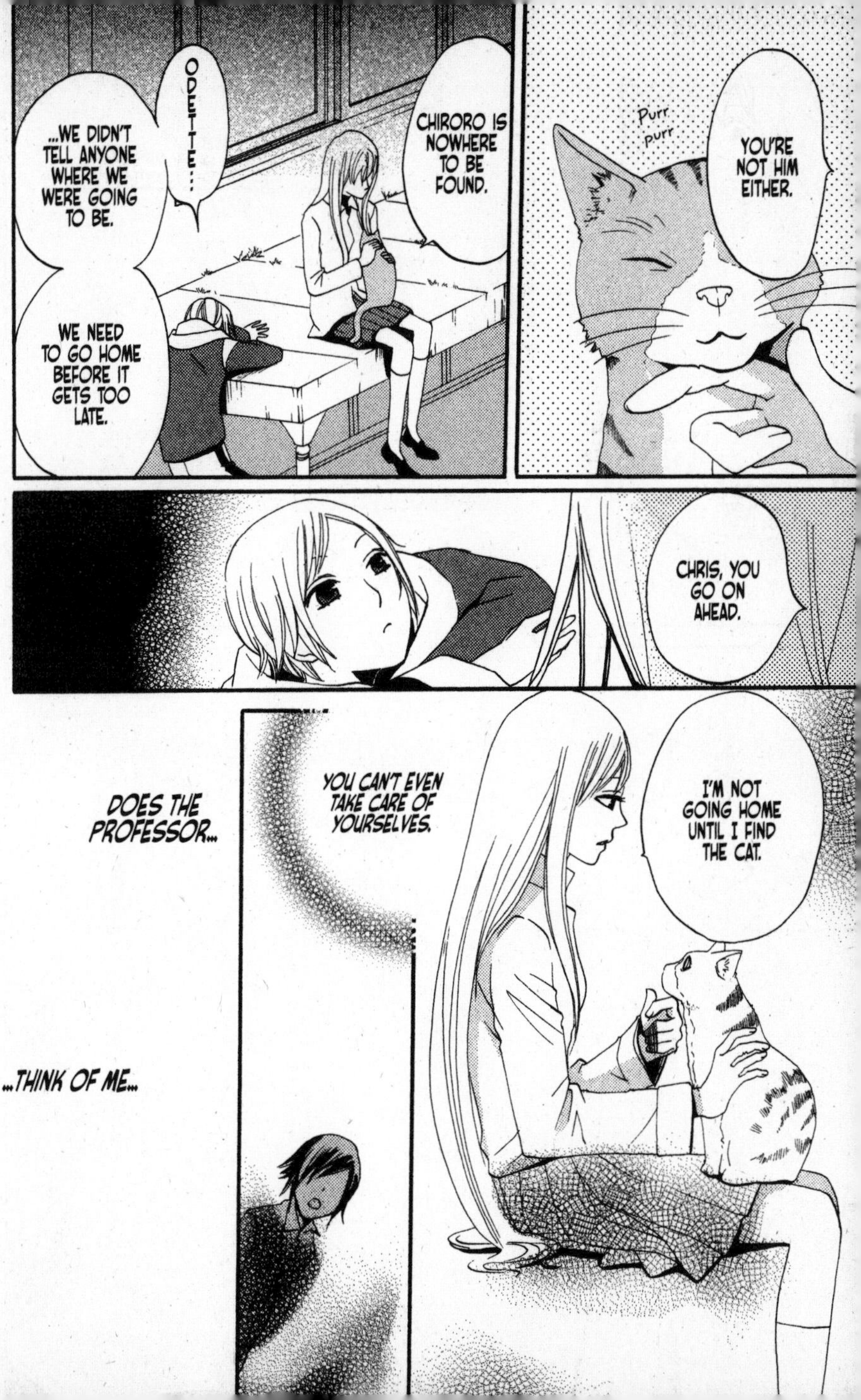
Purr purr
YOU'RE NOT HIM EITHER.
CHIRORO IS NOWHERE TO BE FOUND.
ODETTE...
...WE DIDN'T TELL ANYONE WHERE WE WERE GOING TO BE.
WE NEED TO GO HOME BEFORE IT GETS TOO LATE.
CHRIS, YOU GO ON AHEAD.
I'M NOT GOING HOME UNTIL I FIND THE CAT.
YOU CAN'T EVEN TAKE CARE OF YOURSELVES.
DOES THE PROFESSOR...
...THINK OF ME...

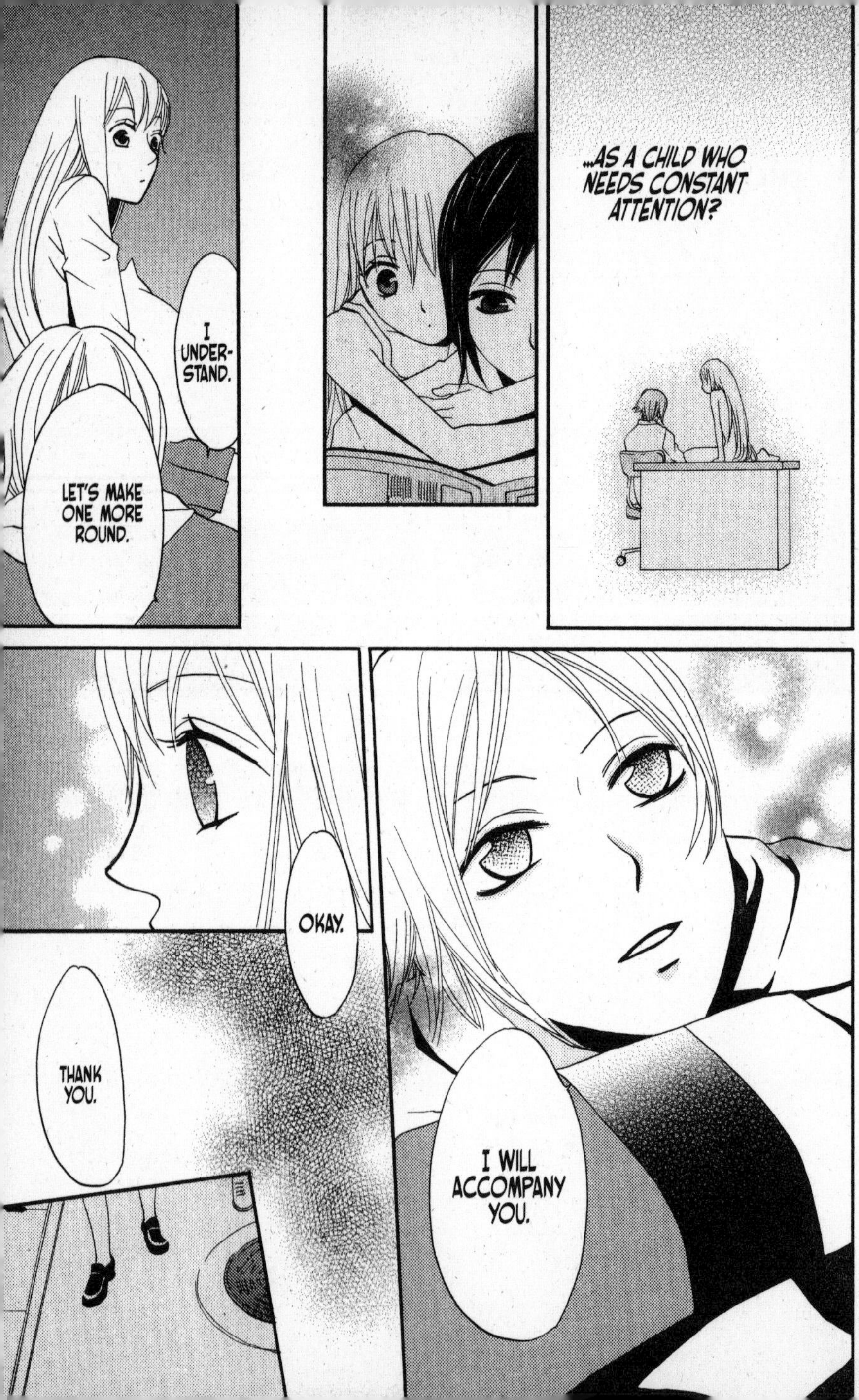
...AS A CHILD WHO NEEDS CONSTANT ATTENTION?
I UNDER-STAND.
LET'S MAKE ONE MORE ROUND.
I WILL ACCOMPANY YOU.
OKAY.
THANK YOU.

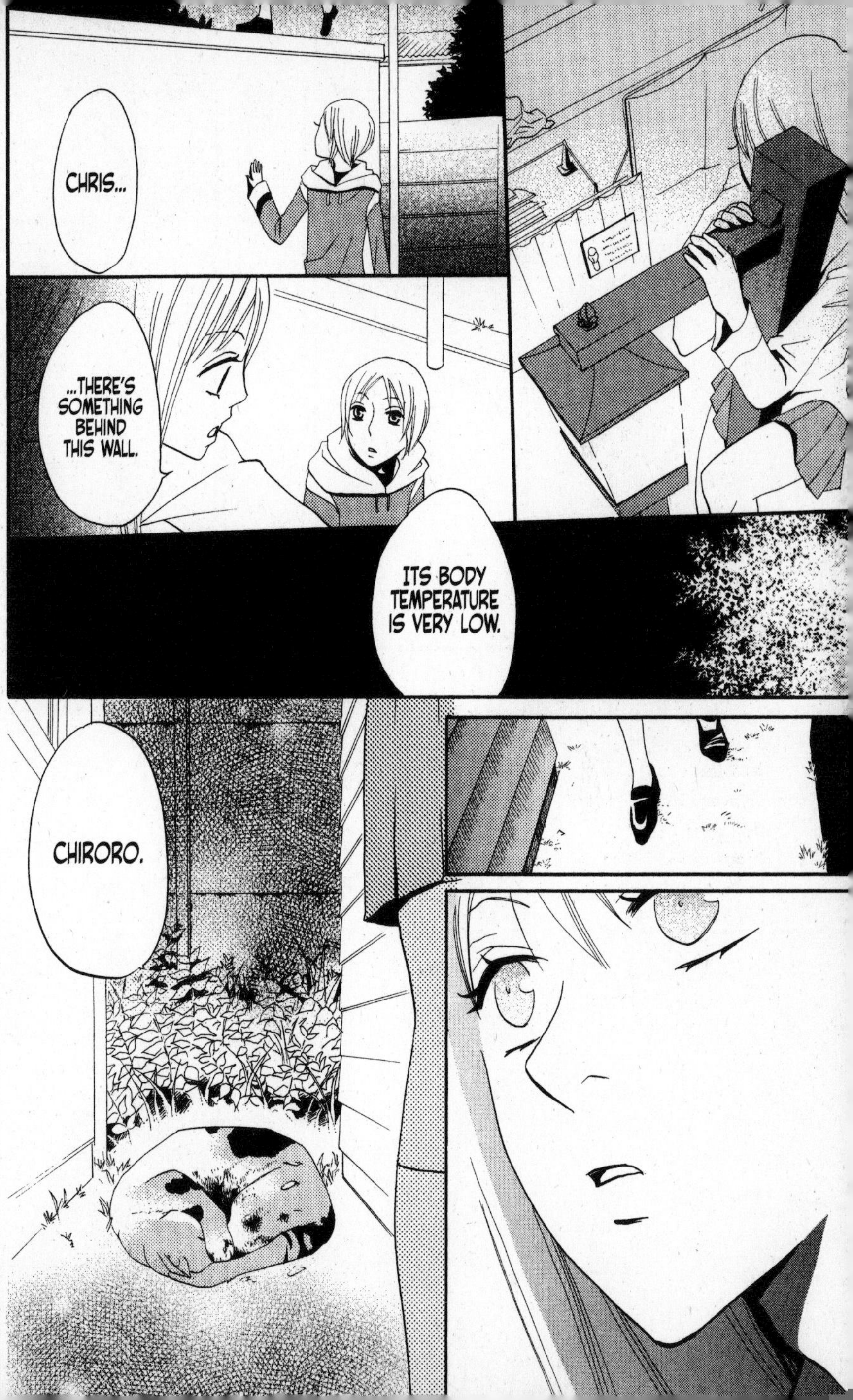
CHRIS...
...THERE'S SOMETHING BEHIND THIS WALL.
ITS BODY TEMPERATURE IS VERY LOW.
CHIRORO.

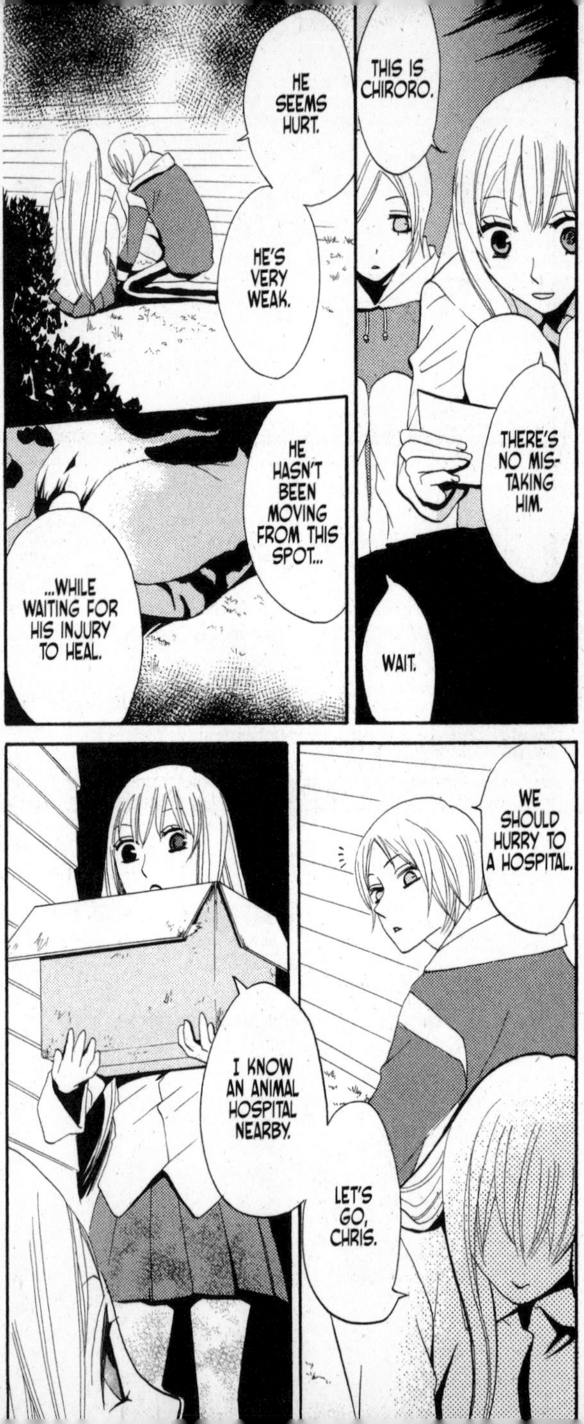
THIS IS CHIRORO.
THERE'S NO MISTAKING HIM.
WAIT.
HE SEEMS HURT.
HE'S VERY WEAK.
HE HASN'T BEEN MOVING FROM THIS SPOT...
...WHILE WAITING FOR HIS INJURY TO HEAL.
WE SHOULD HURRY TO A HOSPITAL.
I KNOW AN ANIMAL HOSPITAL NEARBY.
LET'S GO, CHRIS.

Hello, Juli here. Thank you so much for picking up Karakuri Odette Volume Three!

♥ ♥ ♡ ♥ ♡ ♥

I recently became a cat owner. It's a Scottish Fold ♂ (the kind with folded ears). He came home with me at six weeks, and now he's five months old. So cuuute! ♥ I'm totally gaga over him! ♥ I've always wanted a cat, so every day I'm enjoying my life as a cat owner! He's such a cute kitty!

♡ ♡ ♥ ♡ ♥ ♡

Anyway, I hope you enjoy this volume.

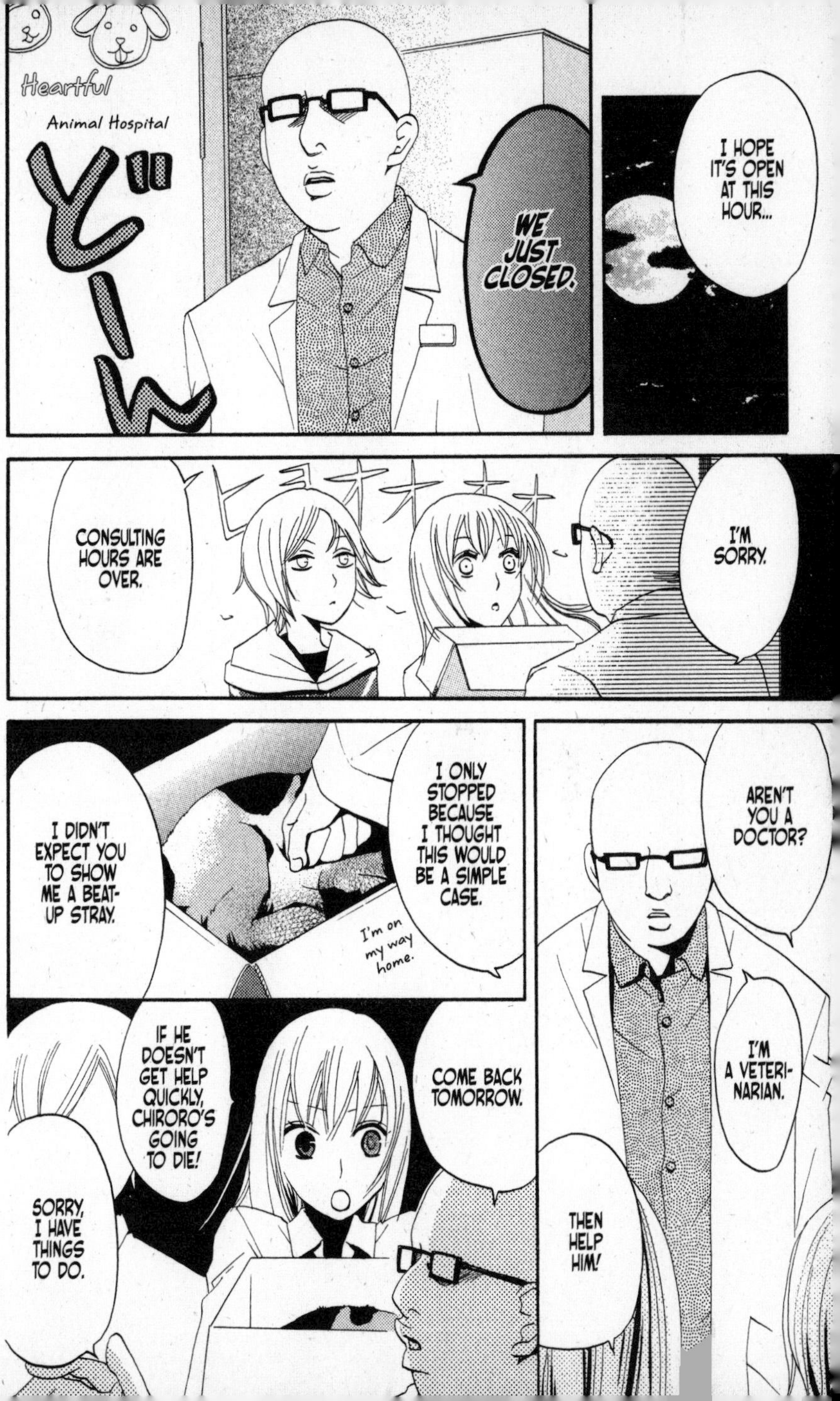
I HOPE IT'S OPEN AT THIS HOUR...
WE JUST CLOSED.
Heartful
Animal Hospital
どーん
I'M SORRY.
ヒョオオオオ
CONSULTING HOURS ARE OVER.
AREN'T YOU A DOCTOR?
I'M A VETERINARIAN.
THEN HELP HIM!
I ONLY STOPPED BECAUSE I THOUGHT THIS WOULD BE A SIMPLE CASE.
I'm on my way home.
I DIDN'T EXPECT YOU TO SHOW ME A BEAT-UP STRAY.
COME BACK TOMORROW.
IF HE DOESN'T GET HELP QUICKLY, CHIRORO'S GOING TO DIE!
SORRY, I HAVE THINGS TO DO.

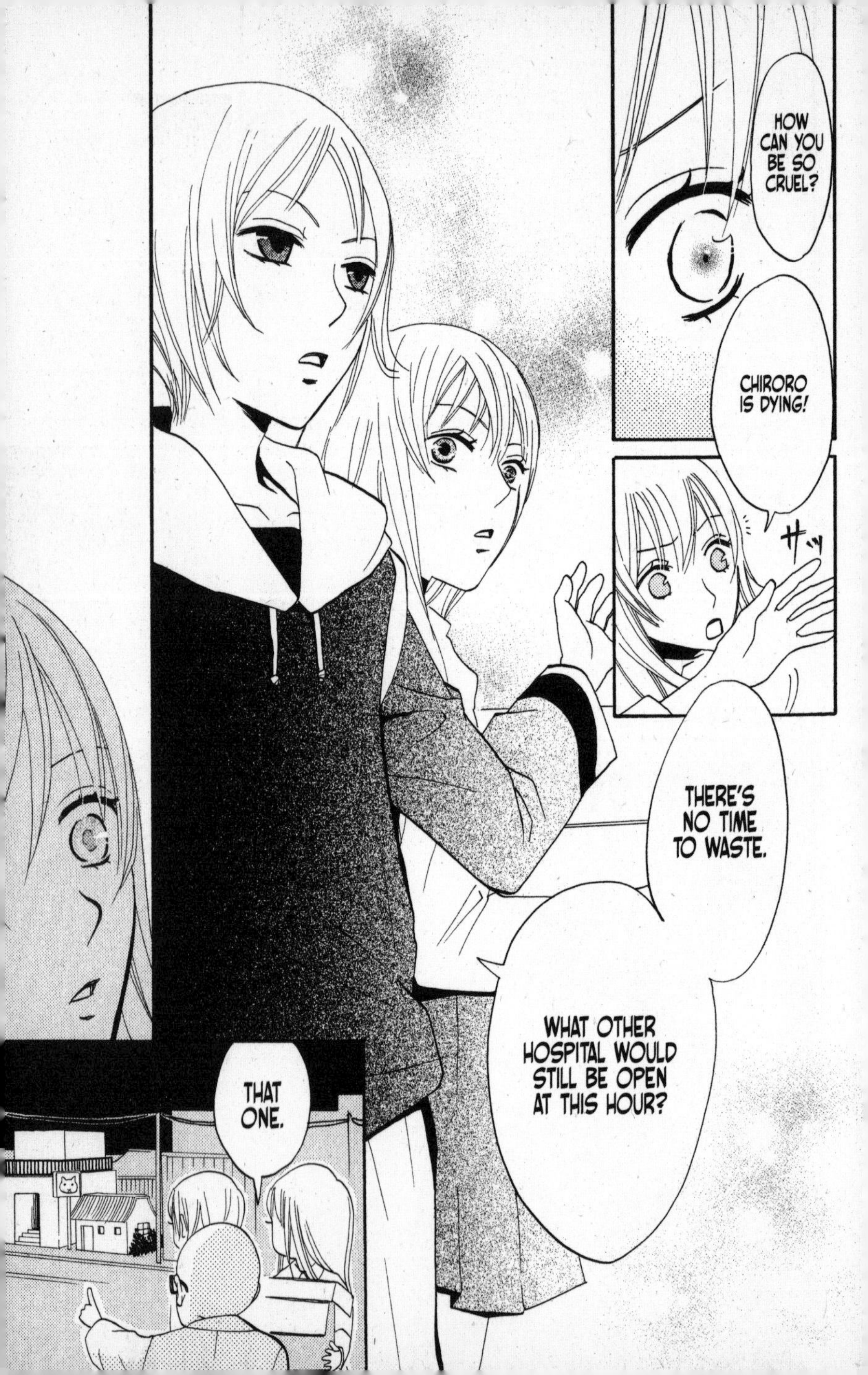
HOW CAN YOU BE SO CRUEL?
CHIRORO IS DYING!
サッ
THERE'S NO TIME TO WASTE.
WHAT OTHER HOSPITAL WOULD STILL BE OPEN AT THIS HOUR?
THAT ONE.

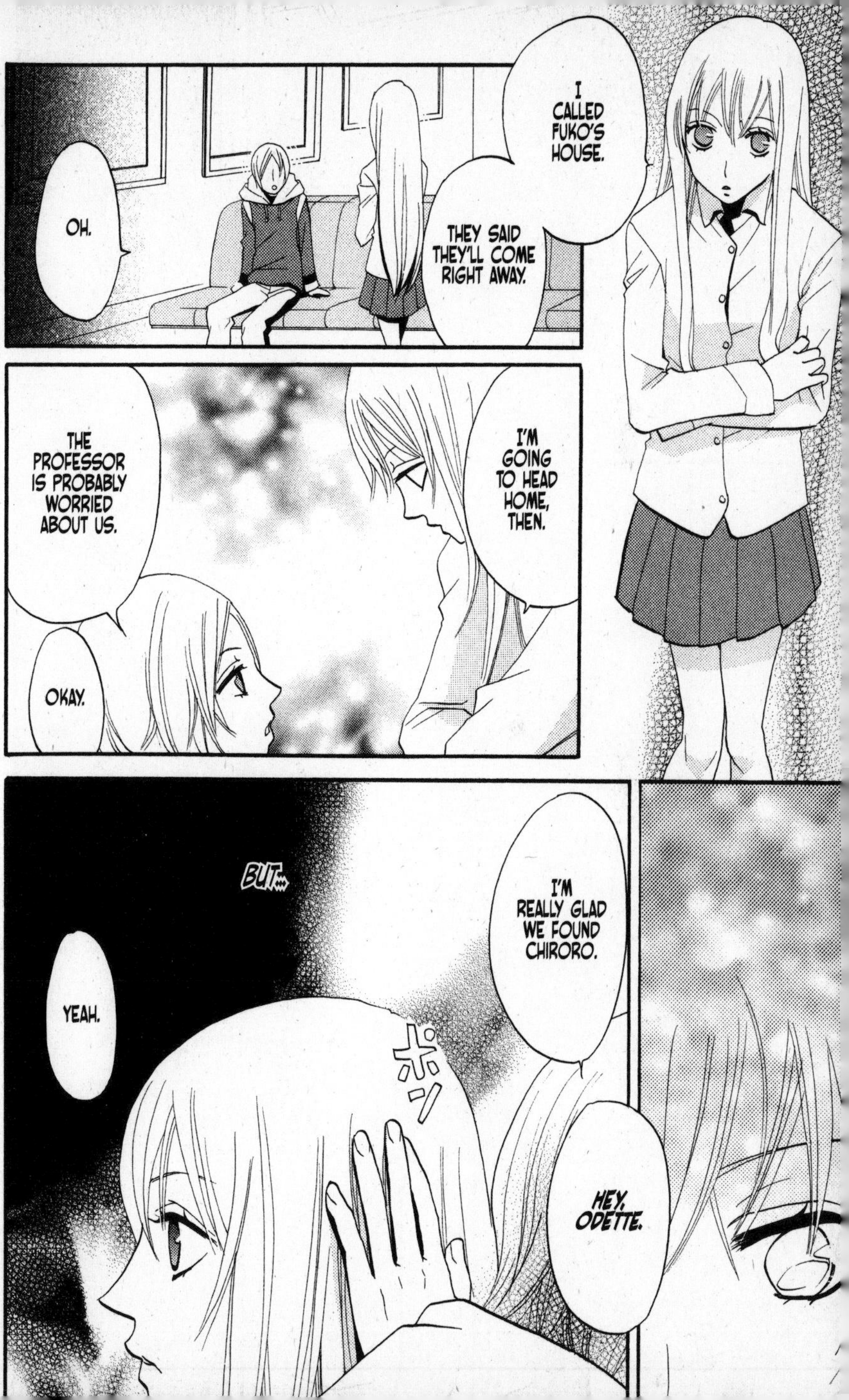
I CALLED FUKO'S HOUSE.
THEY SAID THEY'LL COME RIGHT AWAY.
OH.
I'M GOING TO HEAD HOME, THEN.
THE PROFESSOR IS PROBABLY WORRIED ABOUT US.
OKAY.
HEY, ODETTE.
I'M REALLY GLAD WE FOUND CHIRORO.
ポン
BUT...
YEAH.

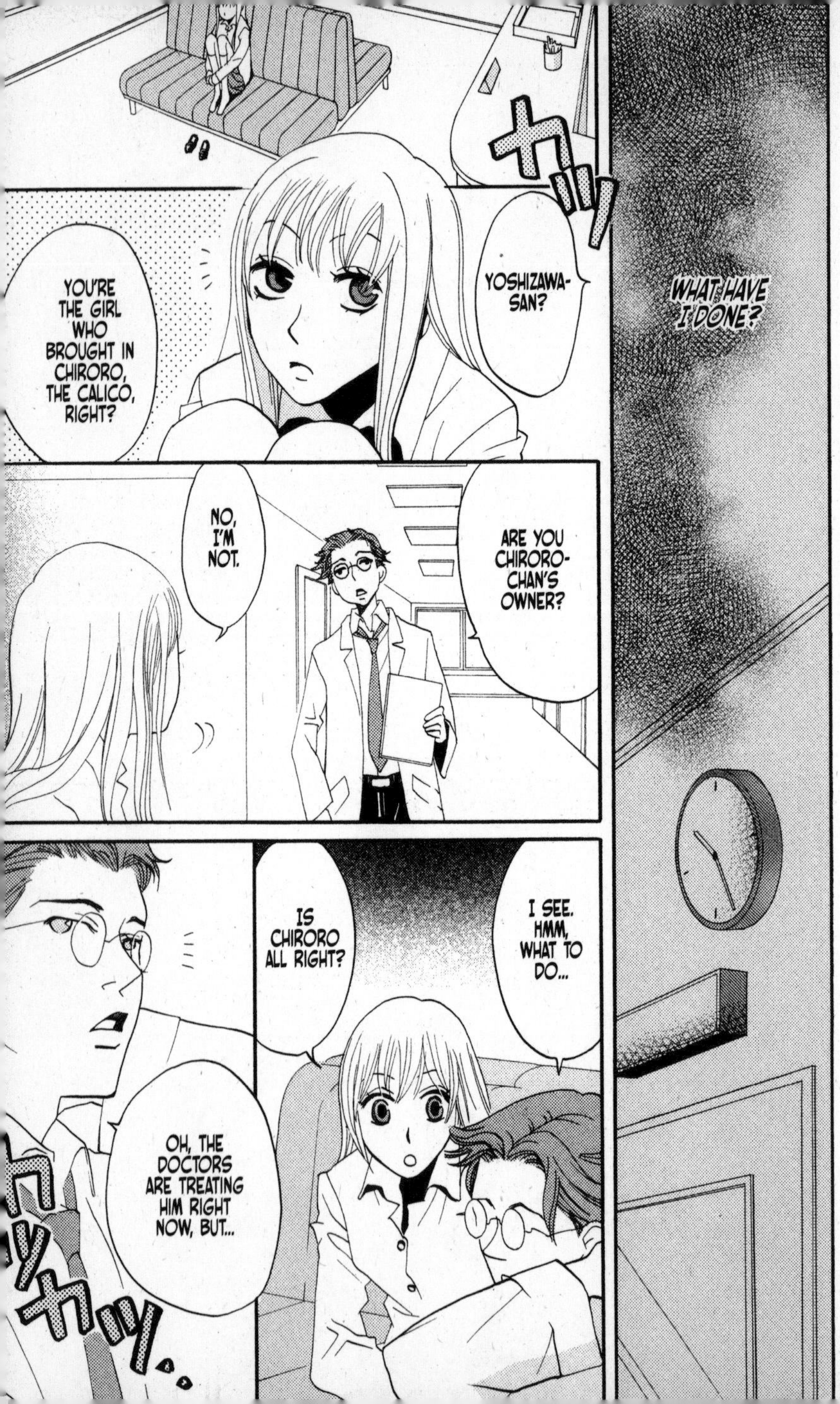
WHAT HAVE I DONE?
カッ
YOSHIZAWA-SAN?
YOU'RE THE GIRL WHO BROUGHT IN CHIRORO, THE CALICO, RIGHT?
ARE YOU CHIRORO-CHAN'S OWNER?
NO, I'M NOT.
I SEE. HMM, WHAT TO DO...
IS CHIRORO ALL RIGHT?
OH, THE DOCTORS ARE TREATING HIM RIGHT NOW, BUT...
カッカッ...

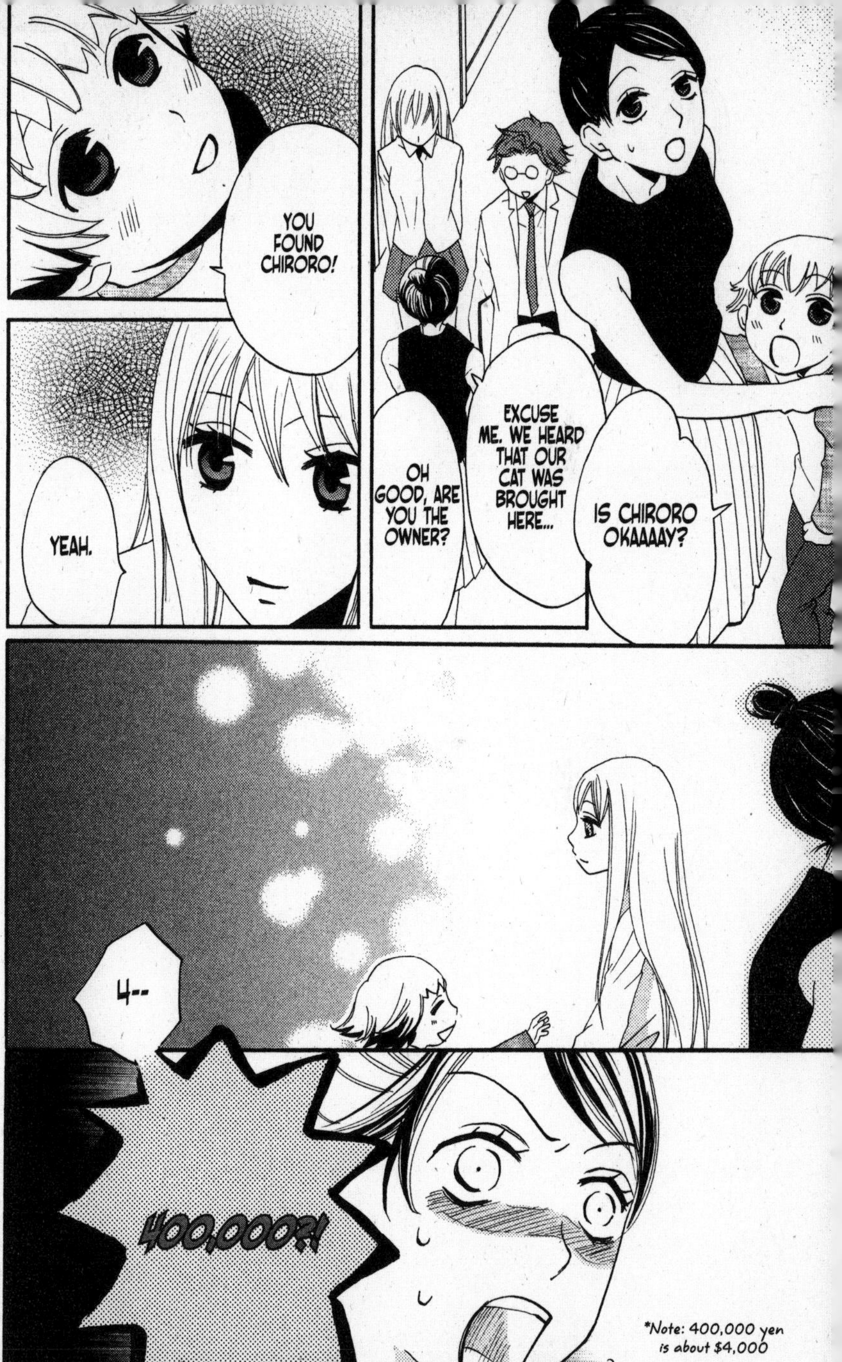
IS CHIRORO OKAAAAY?
EXCUSE ME. WE HEARD THAT OUR CAT WAS BROUGHT HERE...
OH GOOD, ARE YOU THE OWNER?
YOU FOUND CHIRORO!
YEAH.
4--
400,000?!

*Note: 400,000 yen is about $4,000

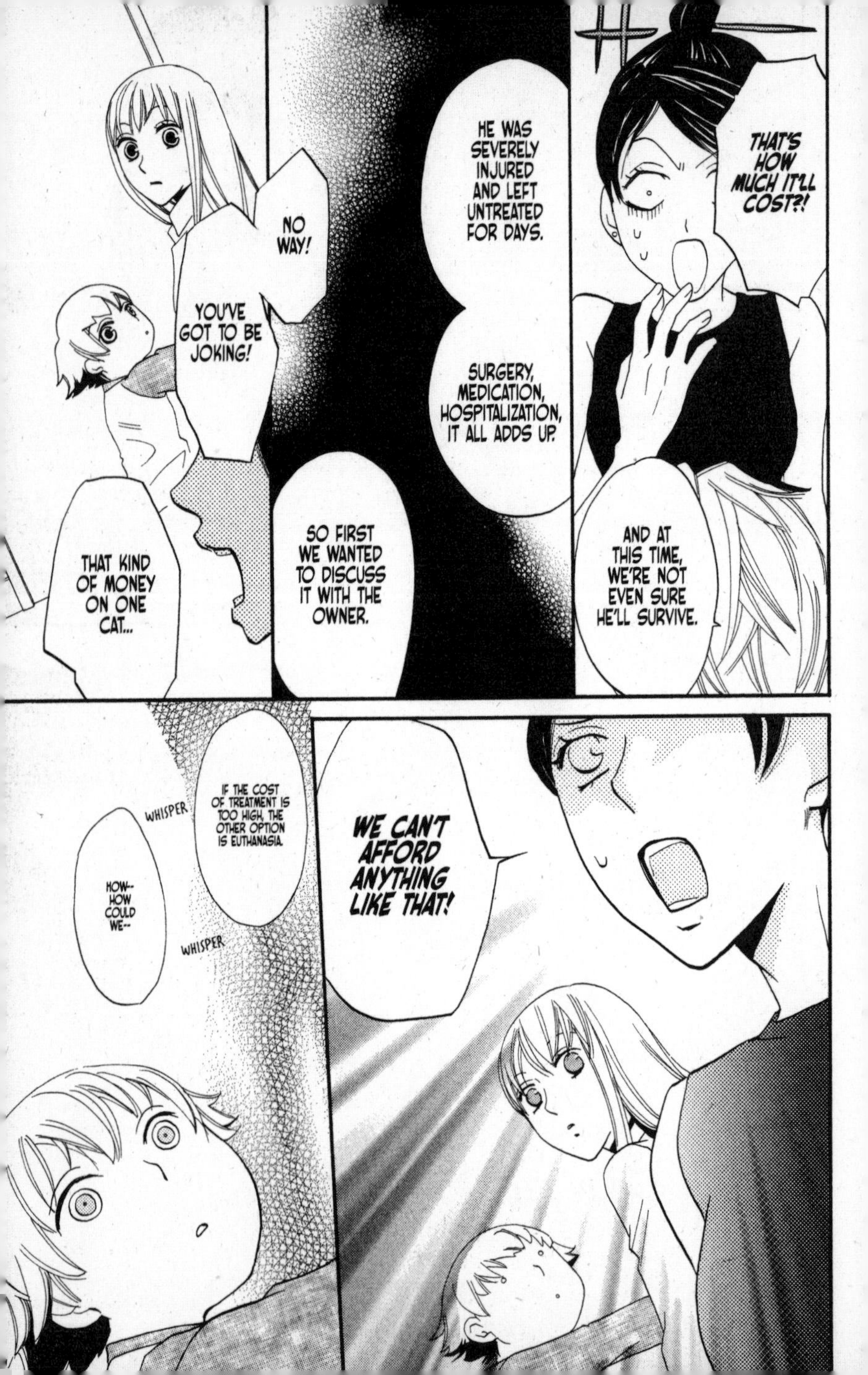
THAT'S HOW MUCH IT'LL COST?!
AND AT THIS TIME, WE'RE NOT EVEN SURE HE'LL SURVIVE.
HE WAS SEVERELY INJURED AND LEFT UNTREATED FOR DAYS.
SURGERY, MEDICATION, HOSPITALIZATION, IT ALL ADDS UP.
SO FIRST WE WANTED TO DISCUSS IT WITH THE OWNER.
NO WAY!
YOU'VE GOT TO BE JOKING!
THAT KIND OF MONEY ON ONE CAT...
WE CAN'T AFFORD ANYTHING LIKE THAT!
IF THE COST OF TREATMENT IS TOO HIGH, THE OTHER OPTION IS EUTHANASIA.
WHISPER
HOW-- HOW COULD WE--
WHISPER

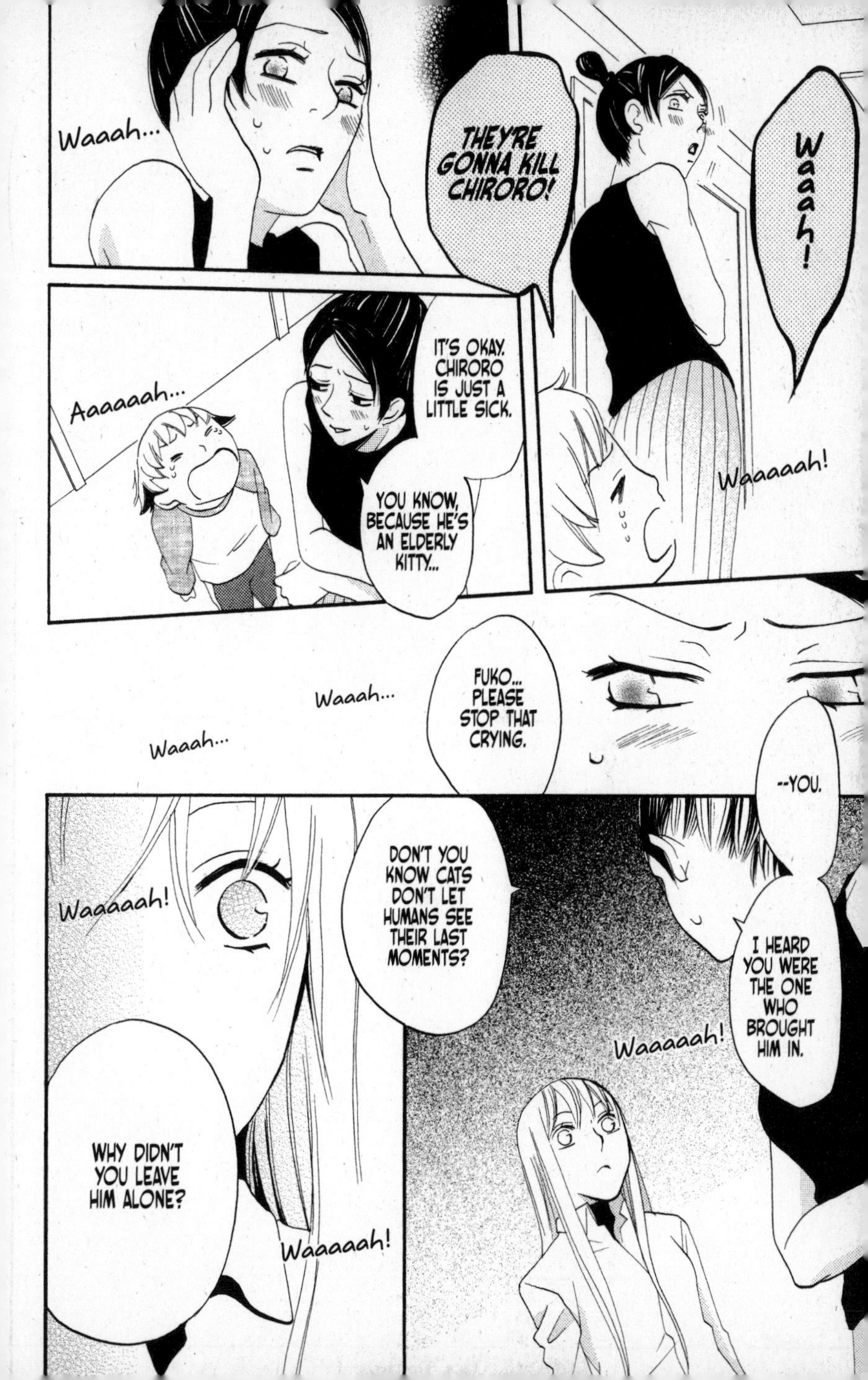
Waaah!
THEY'RE GONNA KILL CHIRORO!
Waaah...
Waaaaah!
IT'S OKAY. CHIRORO IS JUST A LITTLE SICK.
YOU KNOW, BECAUSE HE'S AN ELDERLY KITTY...
Aaaaaah...
FUKO... PLEASE STOP THAT CRYING.
Waaah...
Waaah...
--YOU.
I HEARD YOU WERE THE ONE WHO BROUGHT HIM IN.
Waaaaah!
DON'T YOU KNOW CATS DON'T LET HUMANS SEE THEIR LAST MOMENTS?
Waaaaah!
WHY DIDN'T YOU LEAVE HIM ALONE?
Waaaaah!

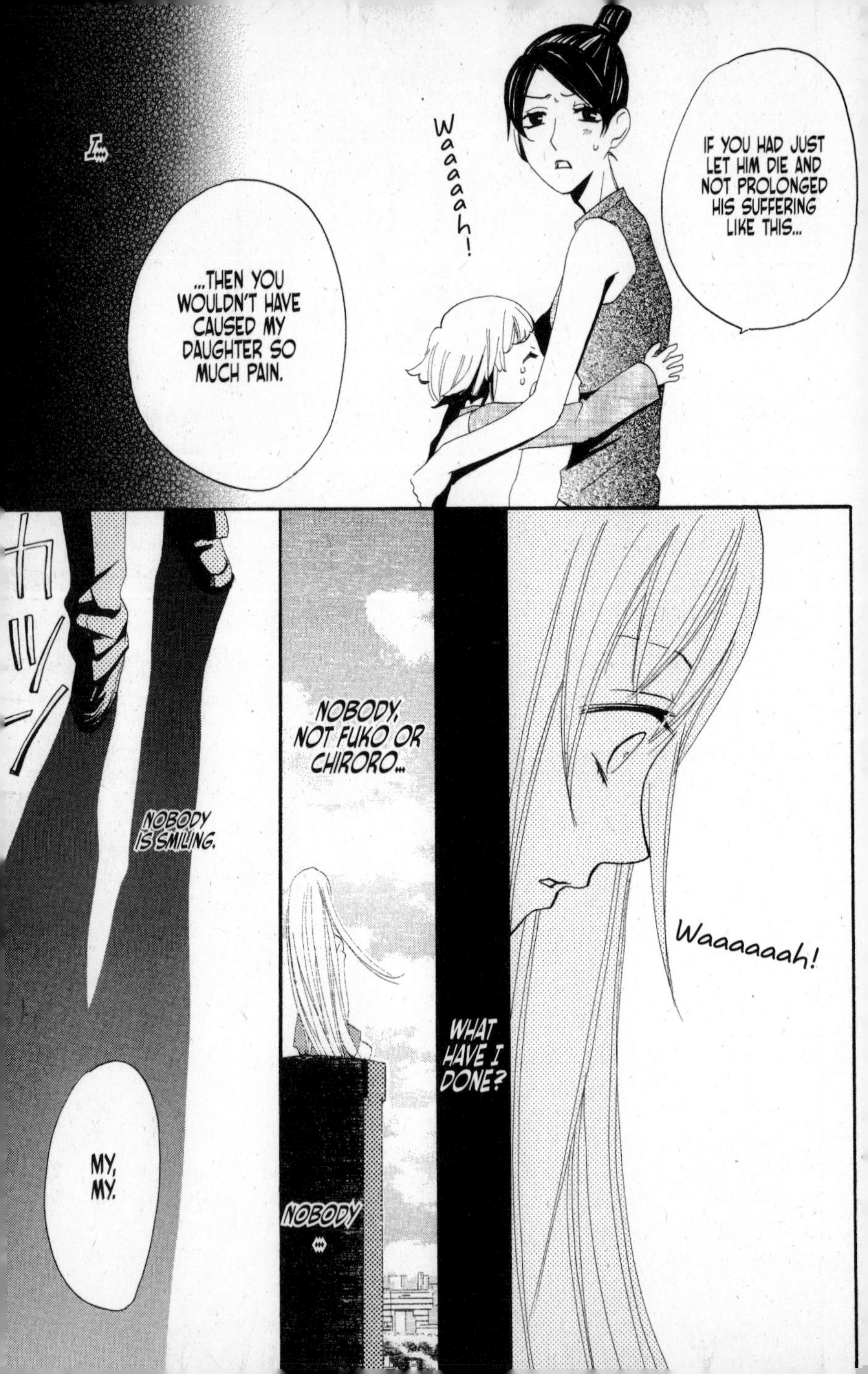
IF YOU HAD JUST LET HIM DIE AND NOT PROLONGED HIS SUFFERING LIKE THIS...
Waaaaah!
...THEN YOU WOULDN'T HAVE CAUSED MY DAUGHTER SO MUCH PAIN.
Waaaaaah!
WHAT HAVE I DONE?
NOBODY. NOT FUKO OR CHIRORO...
NOBODY...
NOBODY IS SMILING.
MY, MY.

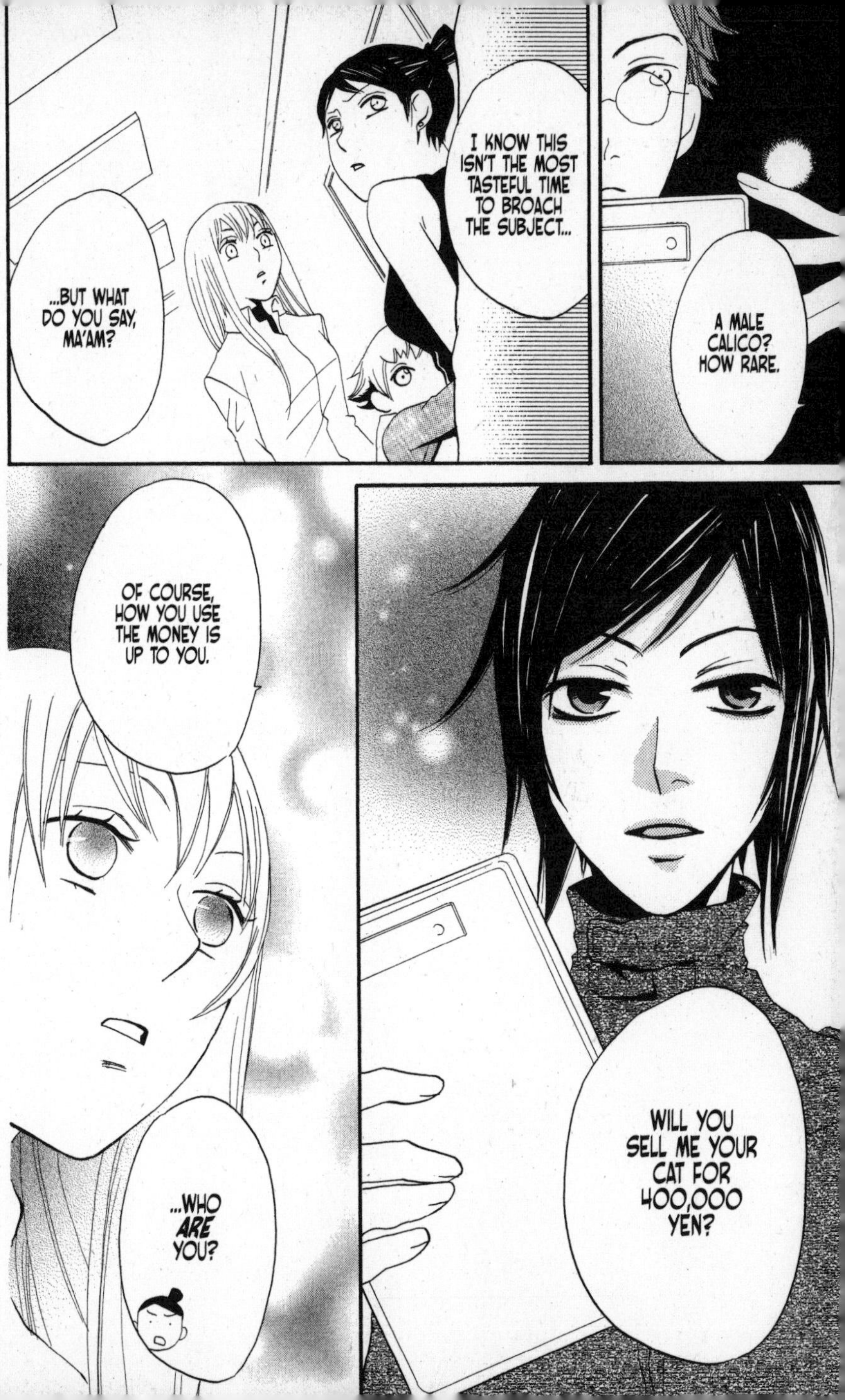
A MALE CALICO? HOW RARE.
I KNOW THIS ISN'T THE MOST TASTEFUL TIME TO BROACH THE SUBJECT...
...BUT WHAT DO YOU SAY, MA'AM?
WILL YOU SELL ME YOUR CAT FOR 400,000 YEN?
OF COURSE, HOW YOU USE THE MONEY IS UP TO YOU.
...WHO *ARE* YOU?

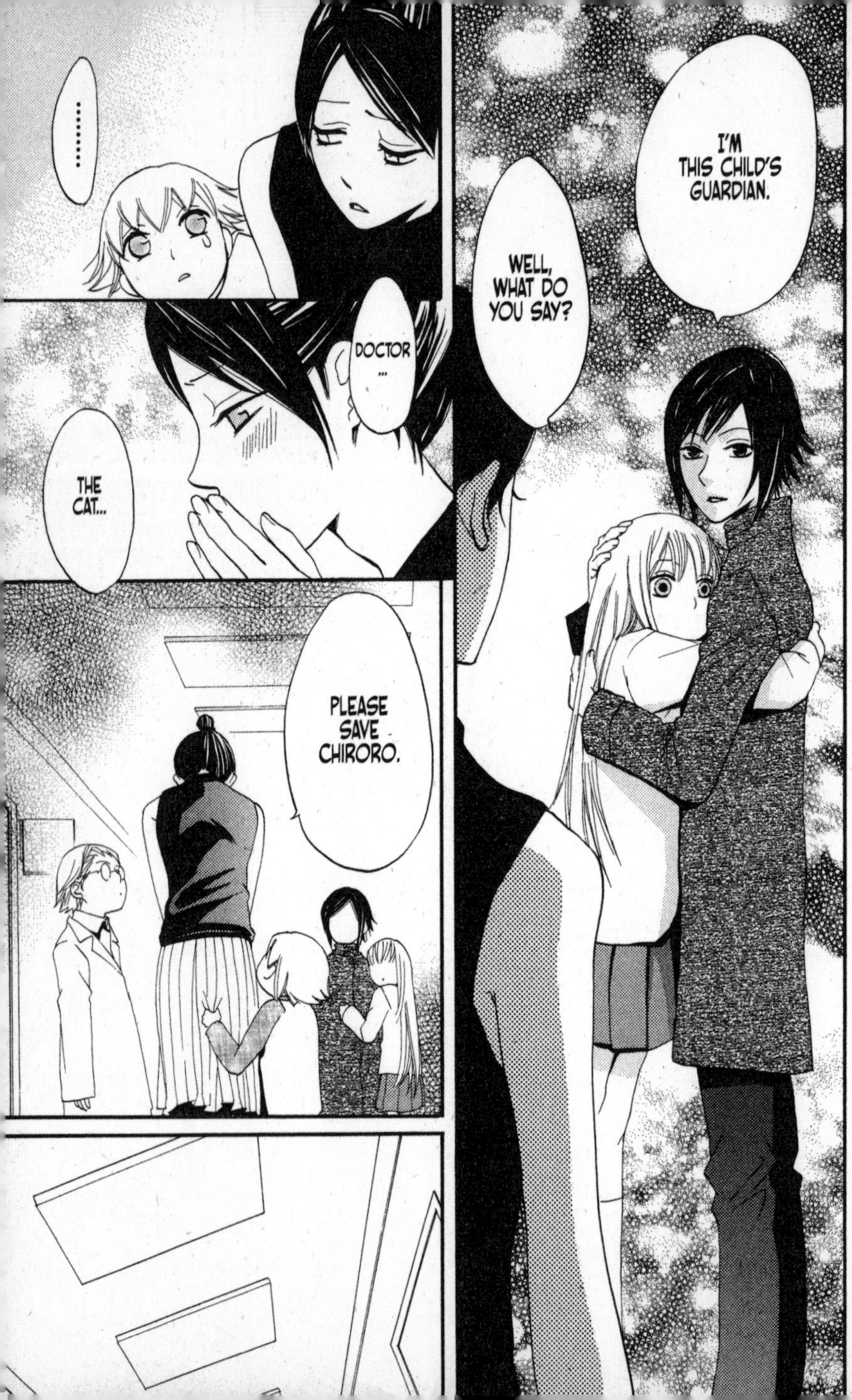
I'M THIS CHILD'S GUARDIAN.
WELL, WHAT DO YOU SAY?
......
DOCTOR ...
THE CAT...
PLEASE SAVE CHIRORO.

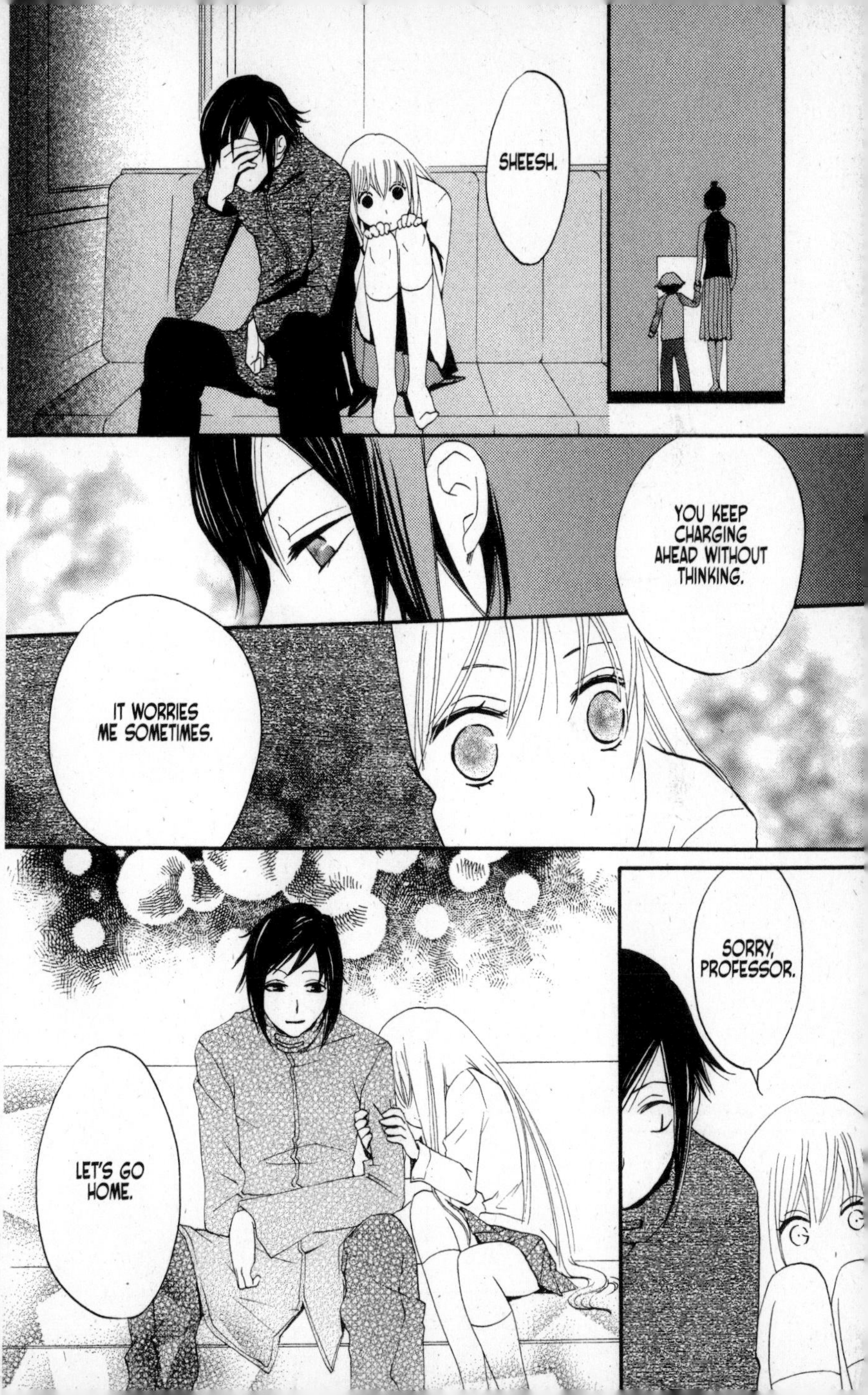
SHEESH.
YOU KEEP CHARGING AHEAD WITHOUT THINKING.
IT WORRIES ME SOMETIMES.
SORRY, PROFESSOR.
LET'S GO HOME.

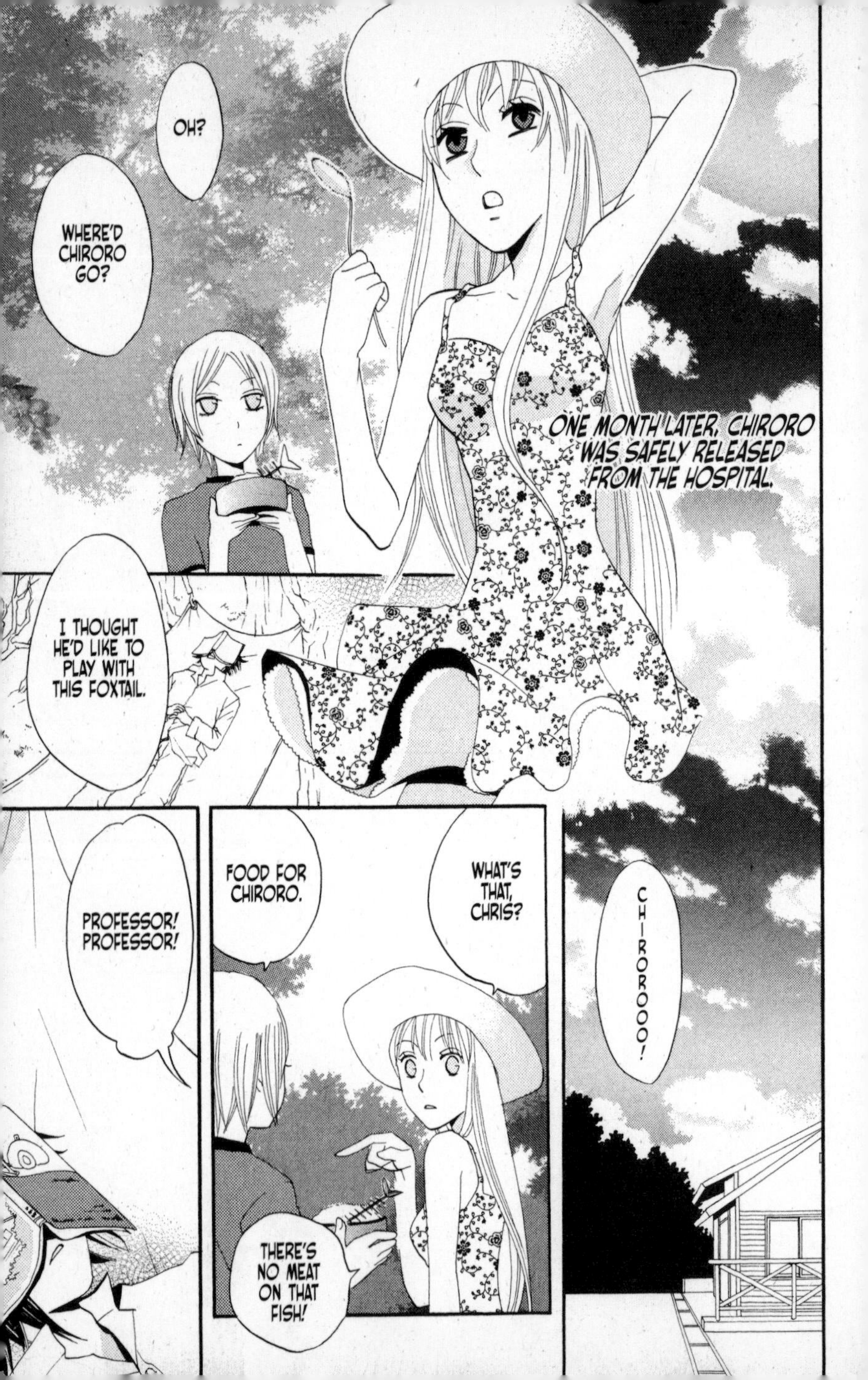
ONE MONTH LATER, CHIRORO WAS SAFELY RELEASED FROM THE HOSPITAL.
CHIROROOO!
OH?
WHERE'D CHIRORO GO?
I THOUGHT HE'D LIKE TO PLAY WITH THIS FOXTAIL.
WHAT'S THAT, CHRIS?
FOOD FOR CHIRORO.
THERE'S NO MEAT ON THAT FISH!
PROFESSOR! PROFESSOR!

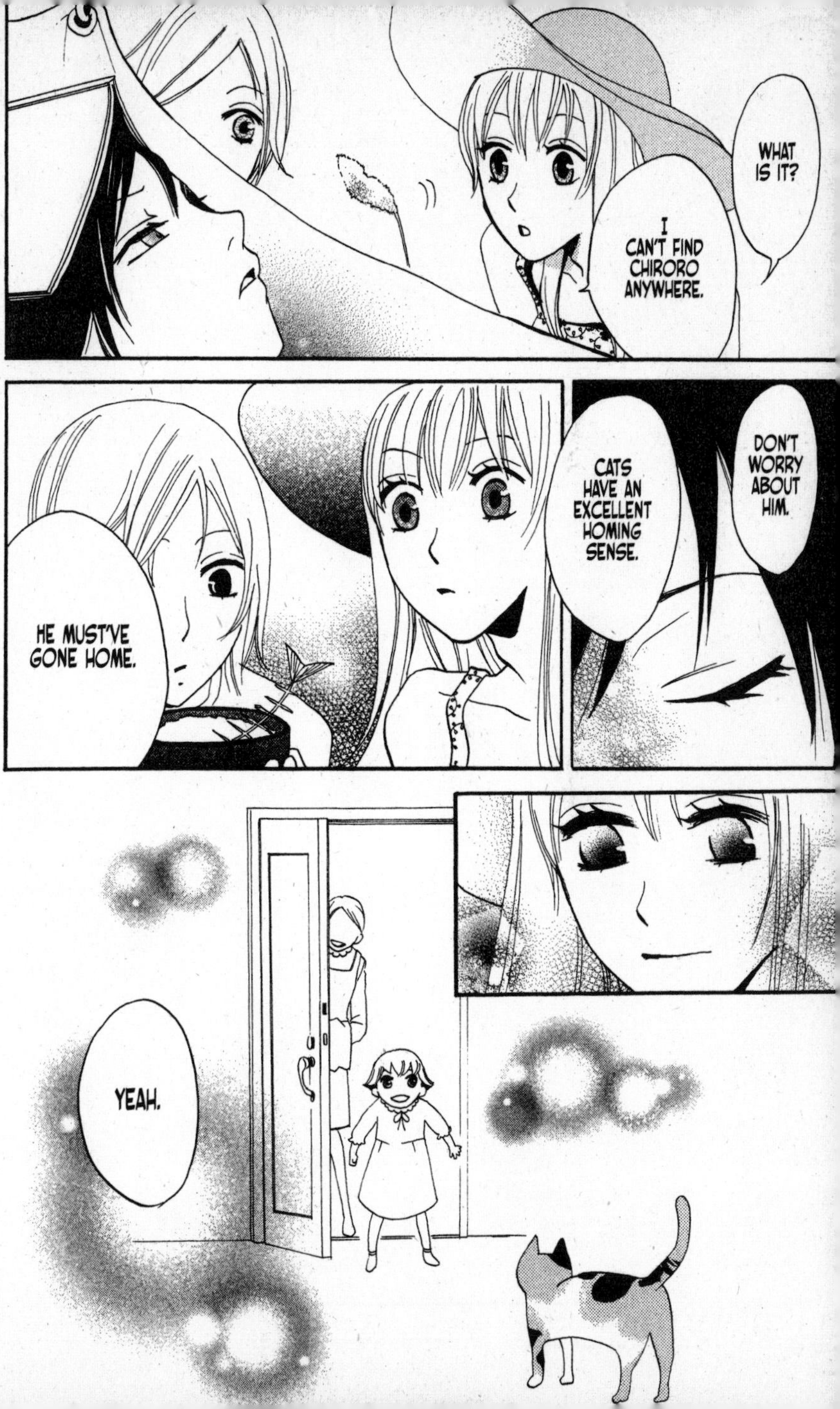
WHAT IS IT?
I CAN'T FIND CHIRORO ANYWHERE.
DON'T WORRY ABOUT HIM.
CATS HAVE AN EXCELLENT HOMING SENSE.
HE MUST'VE GONE HOME.
YEAH.

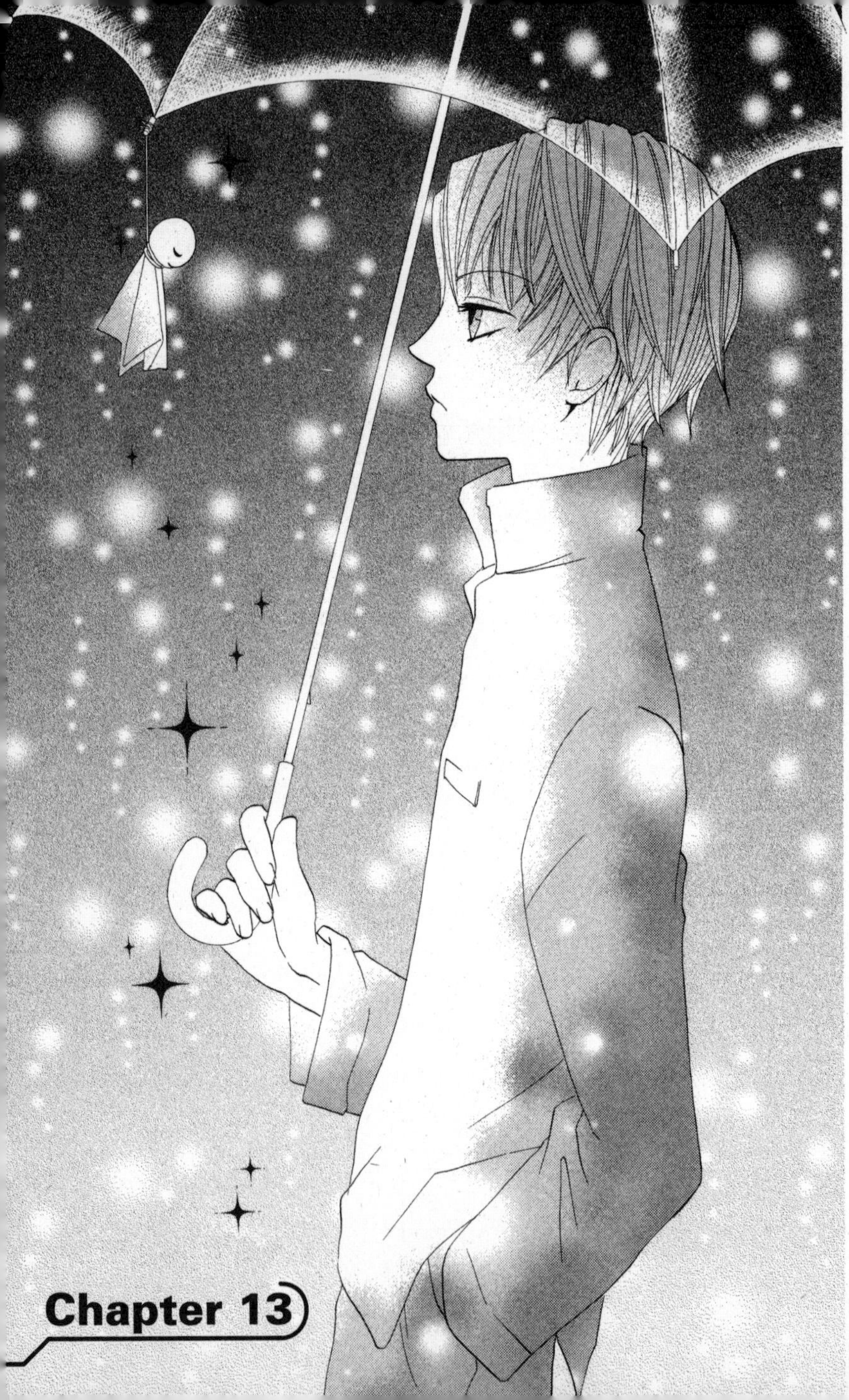
Chapter 13

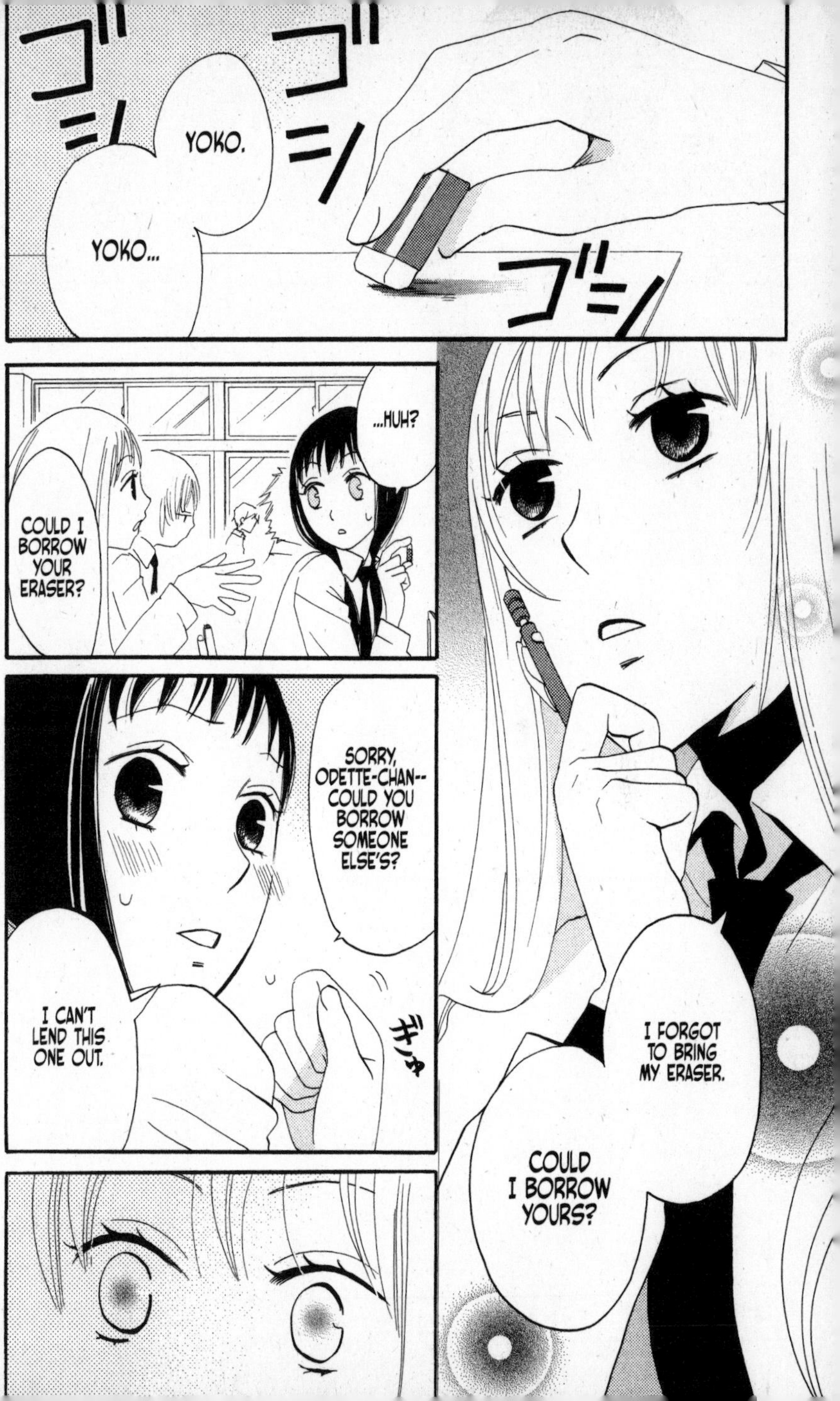
ゴシ
ゴシ
YOKO.
YOKO...
ゴシ
I FORGOT TO BRING MY ERASER.
COULD I BORROW YOURS?
...HUH?
COULD I BORROW YOUR ERASER?
SORRY, ODETTE-CHAN-- COULD YOU BORROW SOMEONE ELSE'S?
ギュ
I CAN'T LEND THIS ONE OUT.

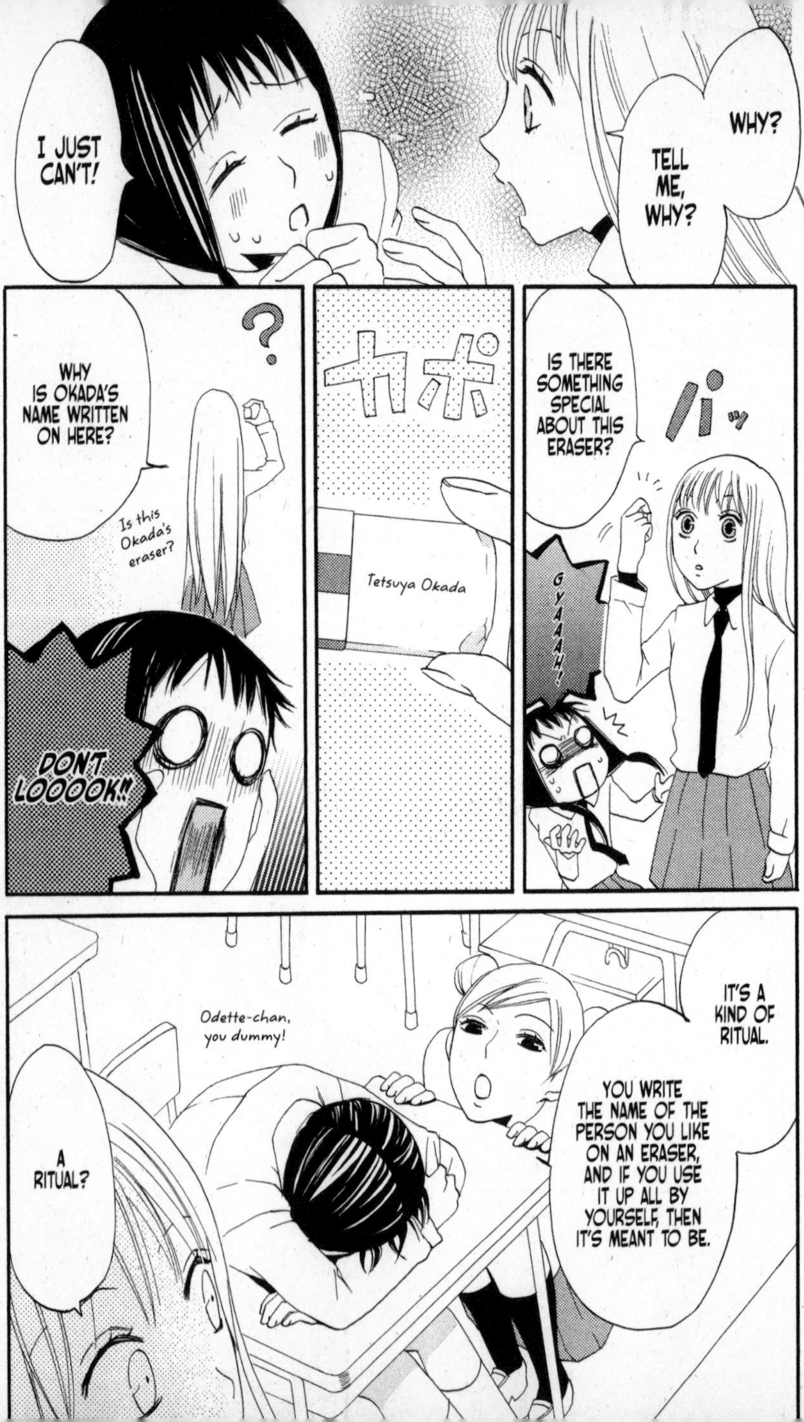
WHY?
TELL ME, WHY?
I JUST CAN'T!
IS THERE SOMETHING SPECIAL ABOUT THIS ERASER?
パッ
GYAAAAH!
カポ
Tetsuya Okada
WHY IS OKADA'S NAME WRITTEN ON HERE?
?
Is this Okada's eraser?
DONT LOOOOK!!
IT'S A KIND OF RITUAL.
YOU WRITE THE NAME OF THE PERSON YOU LIKE ON AN ERASER, AND IF YOU USE IT UP ALL BY YOURSELF, THEN IT'S MEANT TO BE.
Odette-chan, you dummy!
A RITUAL?

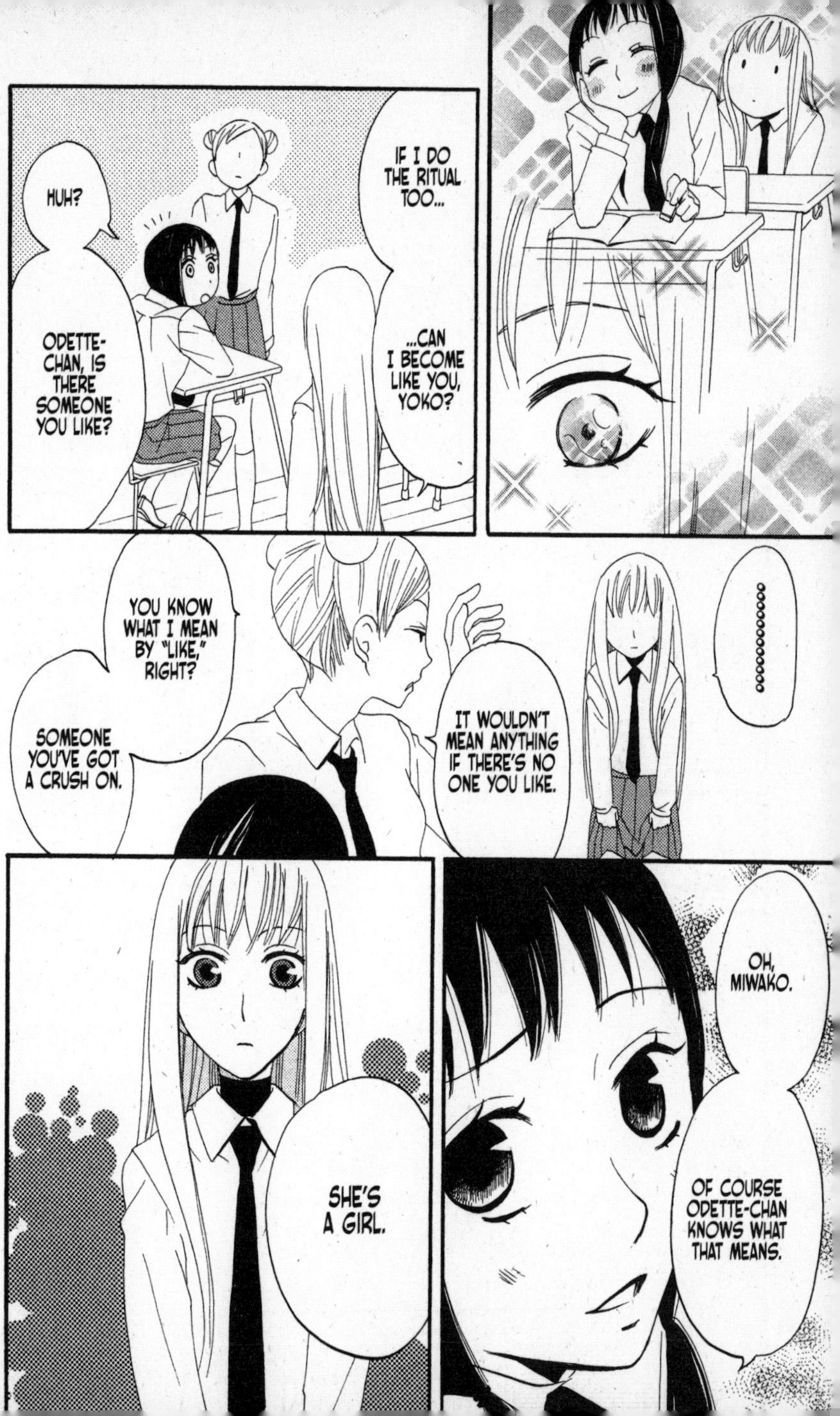
IF I DO THE RITUAL TOO...
...CAN I BECOME LIKE YOU, YOKO?
HUH?
ODETTE-CHAN, IS THERE SOMEONE YOU LIKE?
......
YOU KNOW WHAT I MEAN BY "LIKE," RIGHT?
SOMEONE YOU'VE GOT A CRUSH ON.
IT WOULDN'T MEAN ANYTHING IF THERE'S NO ONE YOU LIKE.
OH, MIWAKO.
OF COURSE ODETTE-CHAN KNOWS WHAT THAT MEANS.
SHE'S A GIRL.

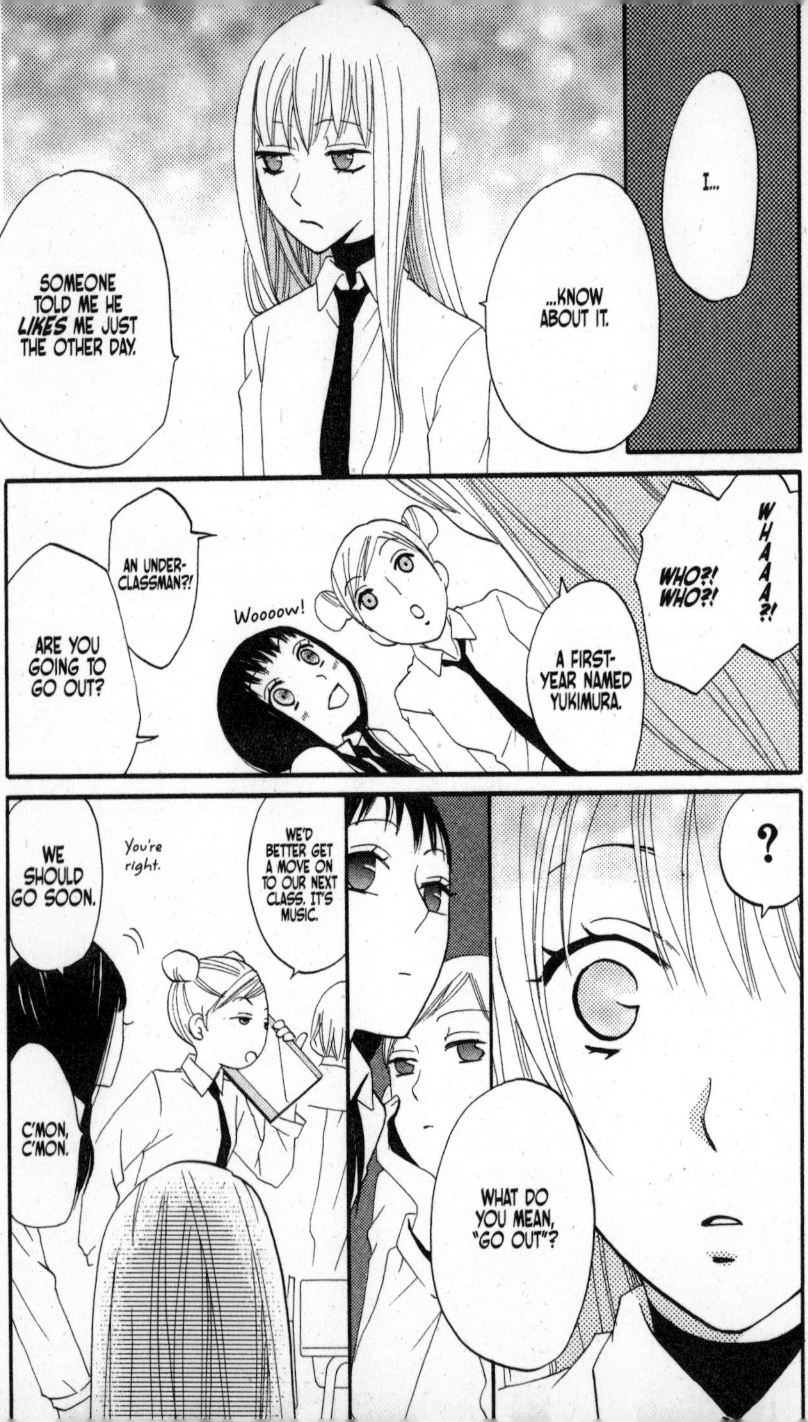
I...
...KNOW ABOUT IT.
SOMEONE TOLD ME HE *LIKES* ME JUST THE OTHER DAY.
WHAAAA?!
WHO?! WHO?!
A FIRST-YEAR NAMED YUKIMURA.
Woooow!
AN UNDER-CLASSMAN?!
ARE YOU GOING TO GO OUT?
?
WHAT DO YOU MEAN, "GO OUT"?
WE'D BETTER GET A MOVE ON TO OUR NEXT CLASS. IT'S MUSIC.
You're right.
WE SHOULD GO SOON.
C'MON, C'MON.

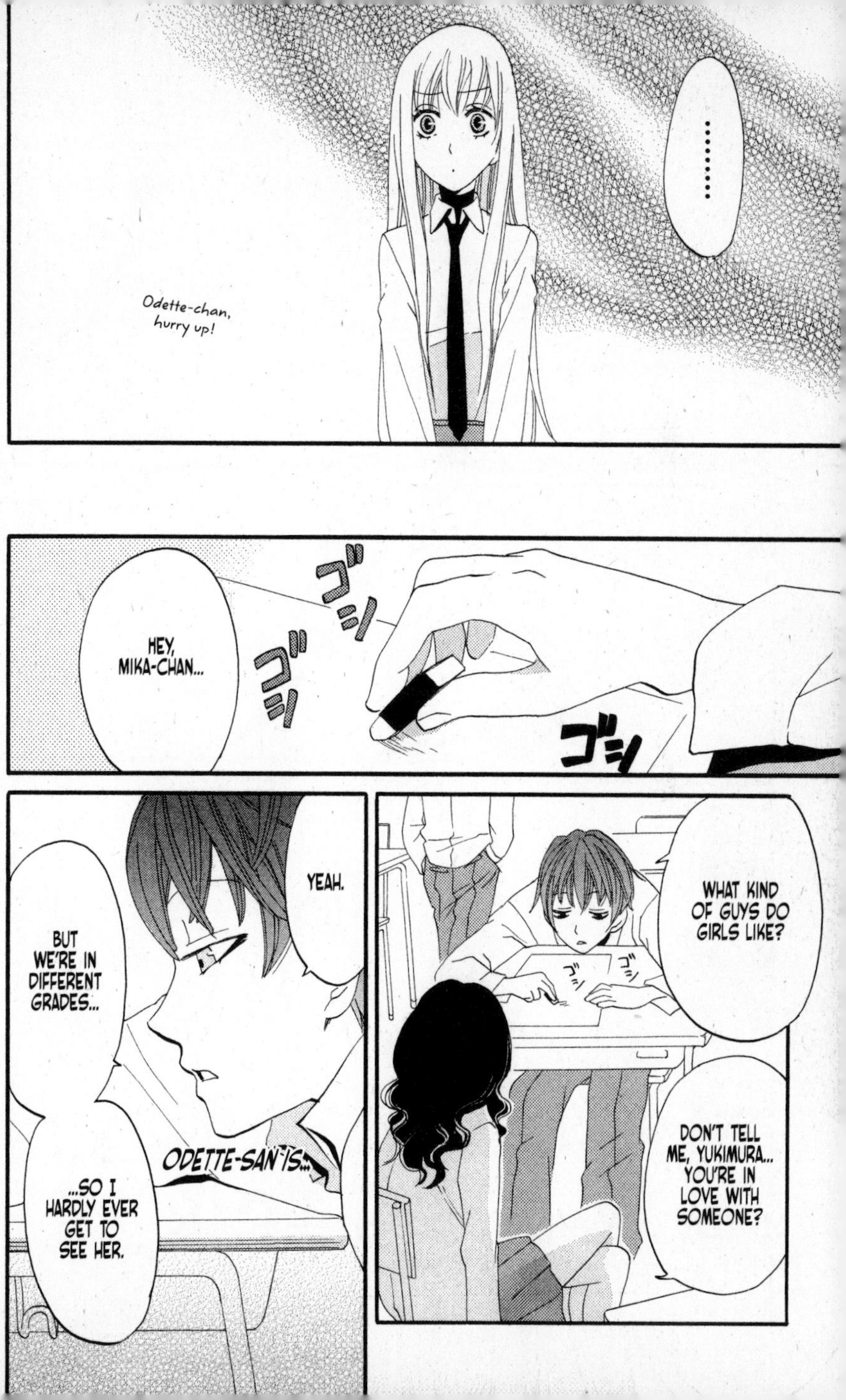

......
Odette-chan, hurry up!
ゴシ
ゴシ
ゴシ
HEY, MIKA-CHAN...
WHAT KIND OF GUYS DO GIRLS LIKE?
ゴシ
ゴシ
DON'T TELL ME, YUKIMURA... YOU'RE IN LOVE WITH SOMEONE?
YEAH.
BUT WE'RE IN DIFFERENT GRADES...
ODETTE-SAN IS...
...SO I HARDLY EVER GET TO SEE HER.

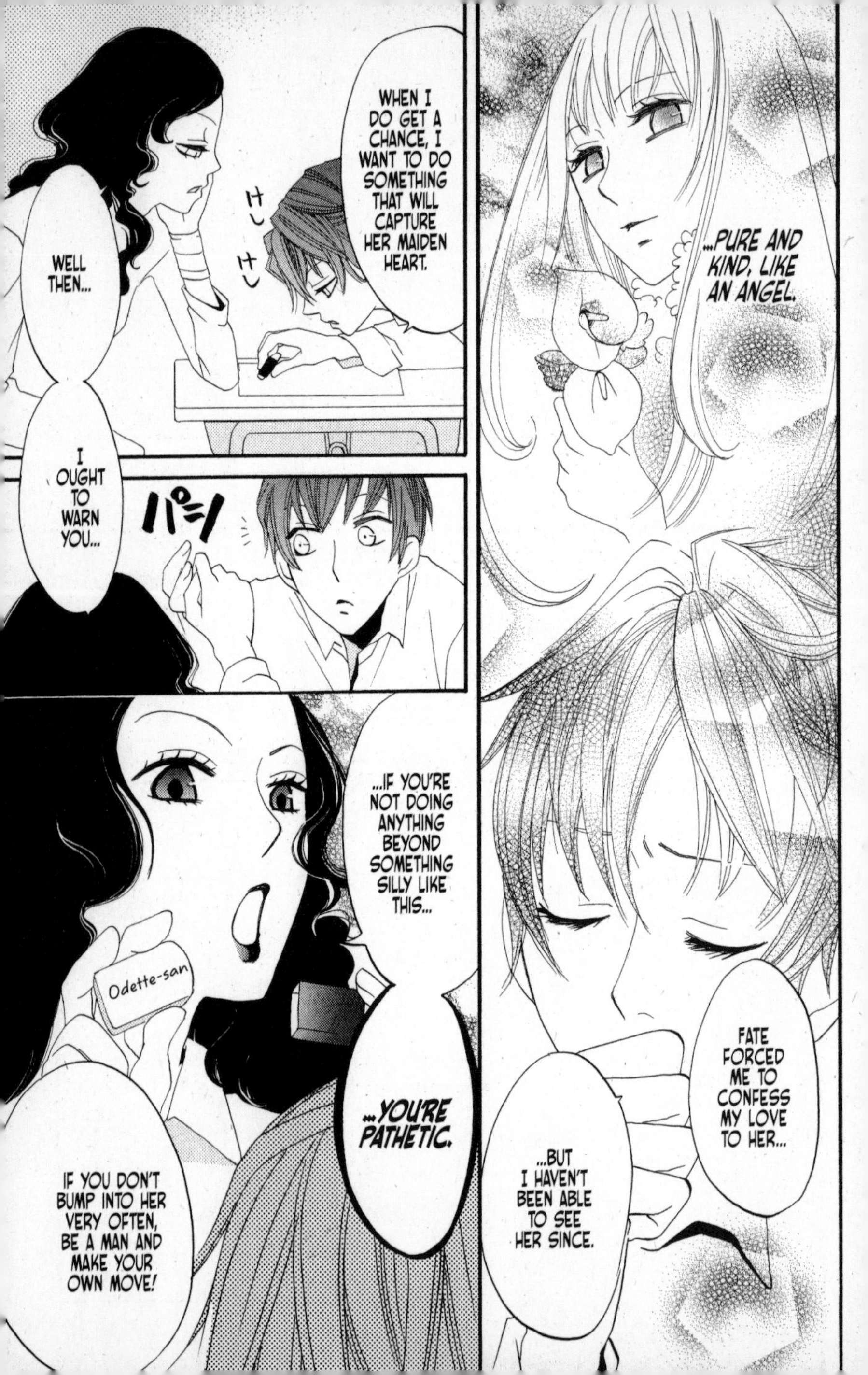
...PURE AND KIND, LIKE AN ANGEL.
FATE FORCED ME TO CONFESS MY LOVE TO HER...
...BUT I HAVEN'T BEEN ABLE TO SEE HER SINCE.
WHEN I DO GET A CHANCE, I WANT TO DO SOMETHING THAT WILL CAPTURE HER MAIDEN HEART.
けし けし
WELL THEN...
I OUGHT TO WARN YOU...
...IF YOU'RE NOT DOING ANYTHING BEYOND SOMETHING SILLY LIKE THIS...
...YOU'RE PATHETIC.
Odette-san
IF YOU DON'T BUMP INTO HER VERY OFTEN, BE A MAN AND MAKE YOUR OWN MOVE!

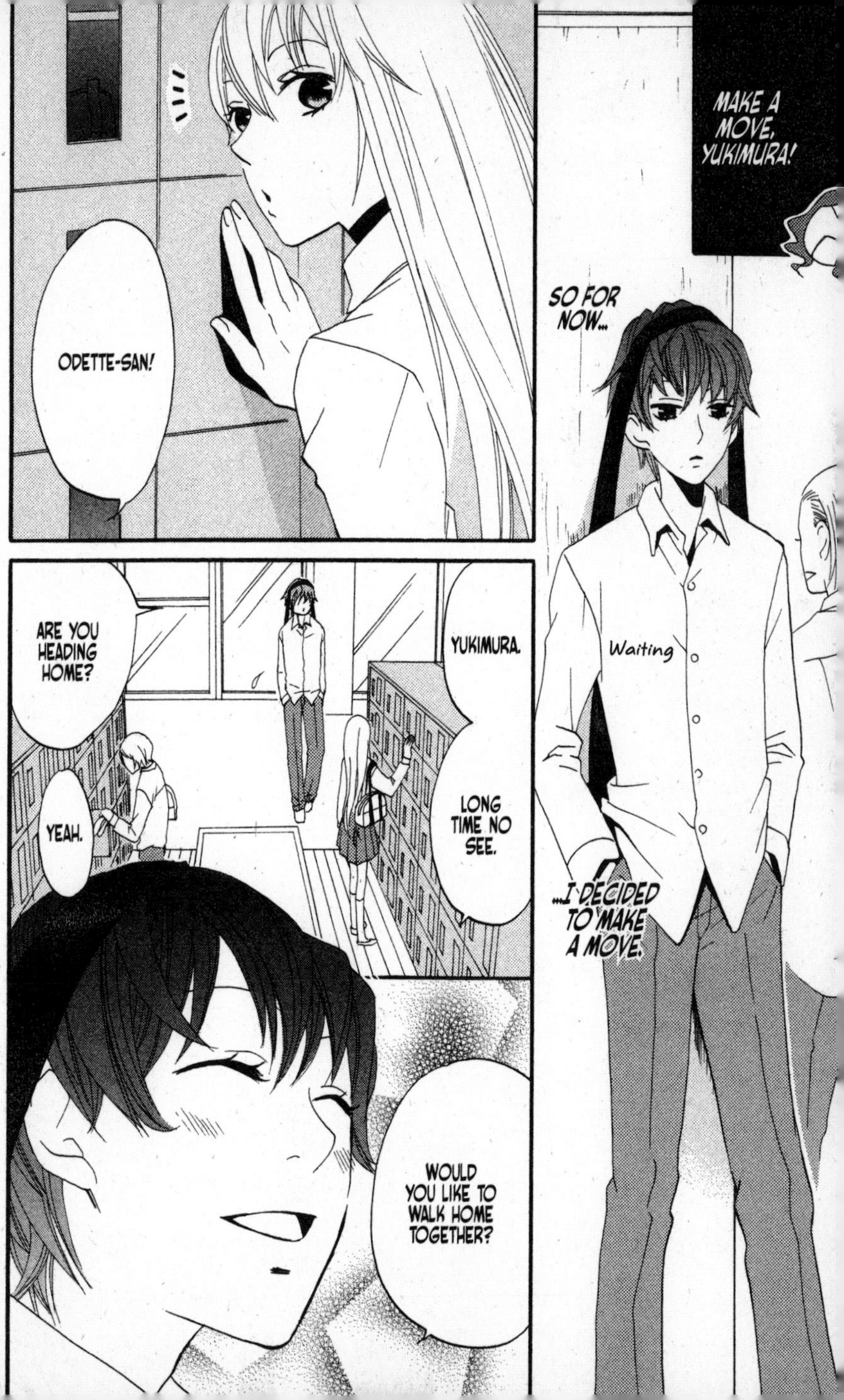
MAKE A MOVE, YUKIMURA!
SO FOR NOW...
Waiting
...I DECIDED TO MAKE A MOVE.
ODETTE-SAN!
YUKIMURA.
LONG TIME NO SEE.
ARE YOU HEADING HOME?
YEAH.
WOULD YOU LIKE TO WALK HOME TOGETHER?

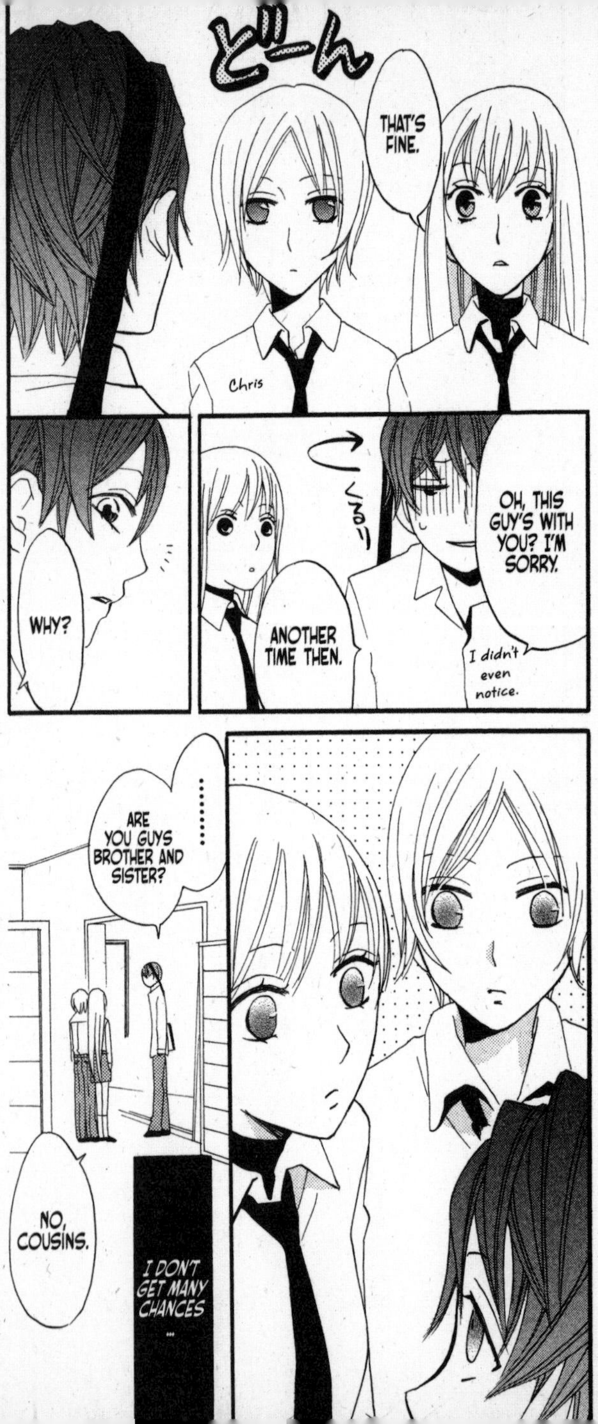
どーん
THAT'S FINE.
Chris
OH, THIS GUY'S WITH YOU? I'M SORRY.
I didn't even notice.
ANOTHER TIME THEN.
WHY?
....
ARE YOU GUYS BROTHER AND SISTER?
NO, COUSINS.
I DON'T GET MANY CHANCES ...

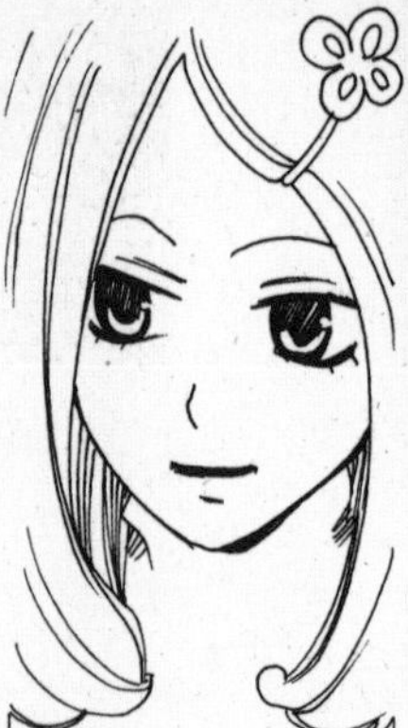

Just the other day I bought my first DVD recorder. (Until then, I was using a TV/VCR combo.) It's just amazing, this DVD recorder! Scheduled recording is easy too, so I'm recording things left and right. Even if I don't ever get around to watching them. What I'm recording now is Agatha Christies' Poirot and Countdown TV, and I use an edited version of that as my BGM as I write my manga. I wish they'd rerun Poirot again! And Holmes too.

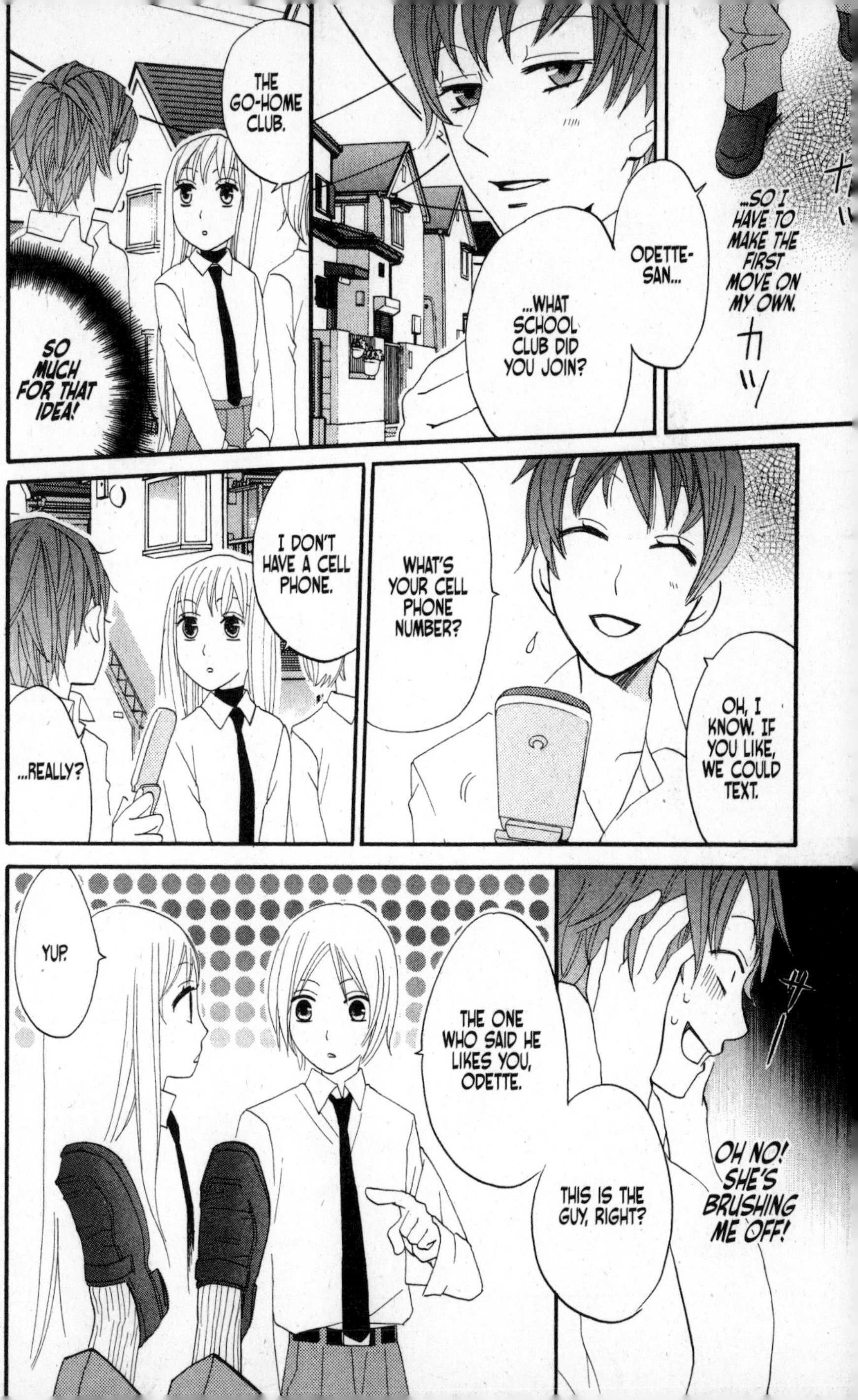
...SO I HAVE TO MAKE THE FIRST MOVE ON MY OWN.
ODETTE-SAN...
...WHAT SCHOOL CLUB DID YOU JOIN?
THE GO-HOME CLUB.
SO MUCH FOR THAT IDEA!
WHAT'S YOUR CELL PHONE NUMBER?
OH, I KNOW. IF YOU LIKE, WE COULD TEXT.
I DON'T HAVE A CELL PHONE.
...REALLY?
OH NO! SHE'S BRUSHING ME OFF!
THE ONE WHO SAID HE LIKES YOU, ODETTE.
THIS IS THE GUY, RIGHT?
YUP.

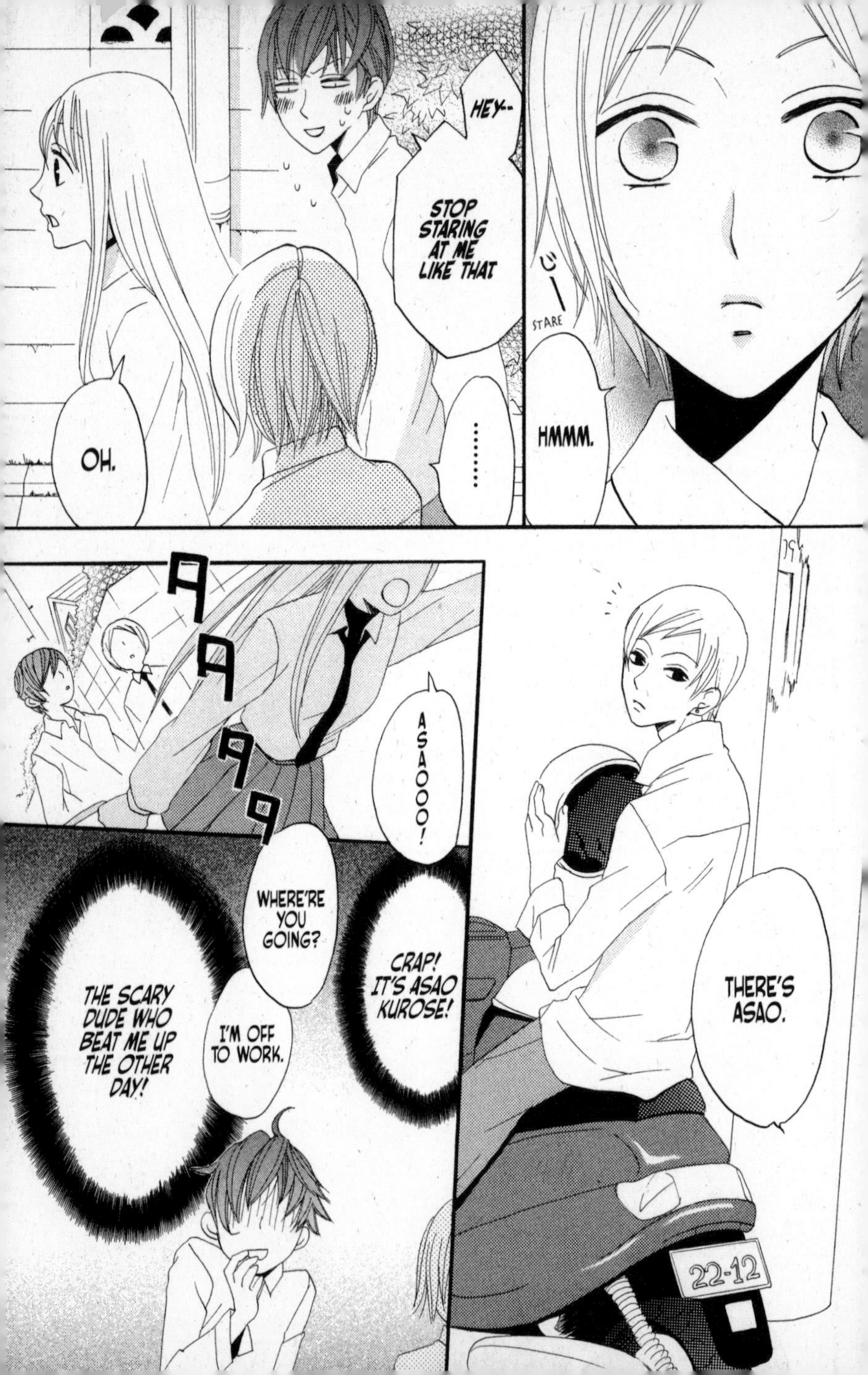

じー
STARE
HMMM.
HEY--
STOP STARING AT ME LIKE THAT.
......
OH.
THERE'S ASAO.
22-12
ASAOOO!
WHERE'RE YOU GOING?
CRAP! IT'S ASAO KUROSE!
I'M OFF TO WORK.
THE SCARY DUDE WHO BEAT ME UP THE OTHER DAY!

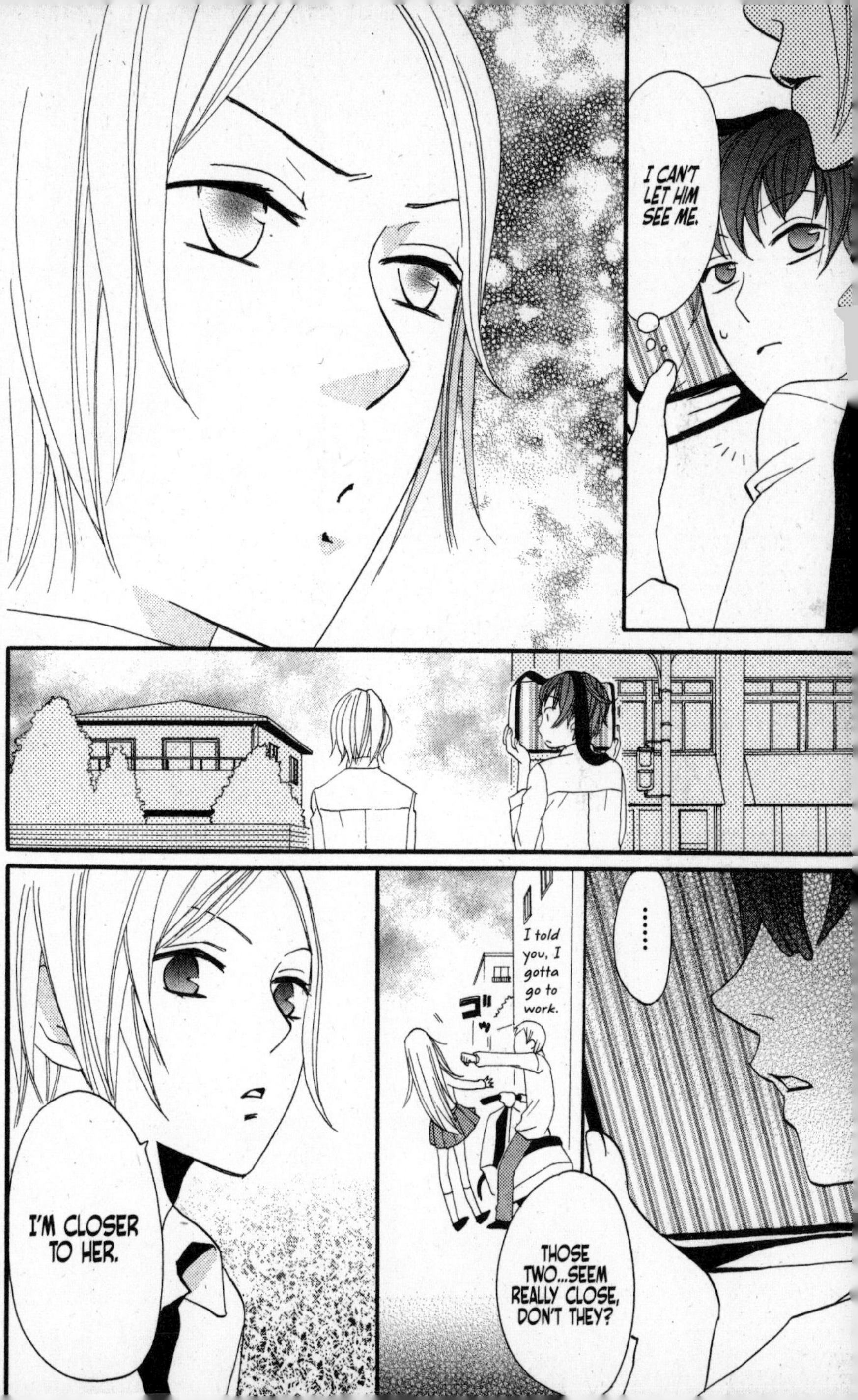
I CAN'T LET HIM SEE ME.
......
THOSE TWO...SEEM REALLY CLOSE, DON'T THEY?
I told you, I gotta go to work.
ゴッ
I'M CLOSER TO HER.

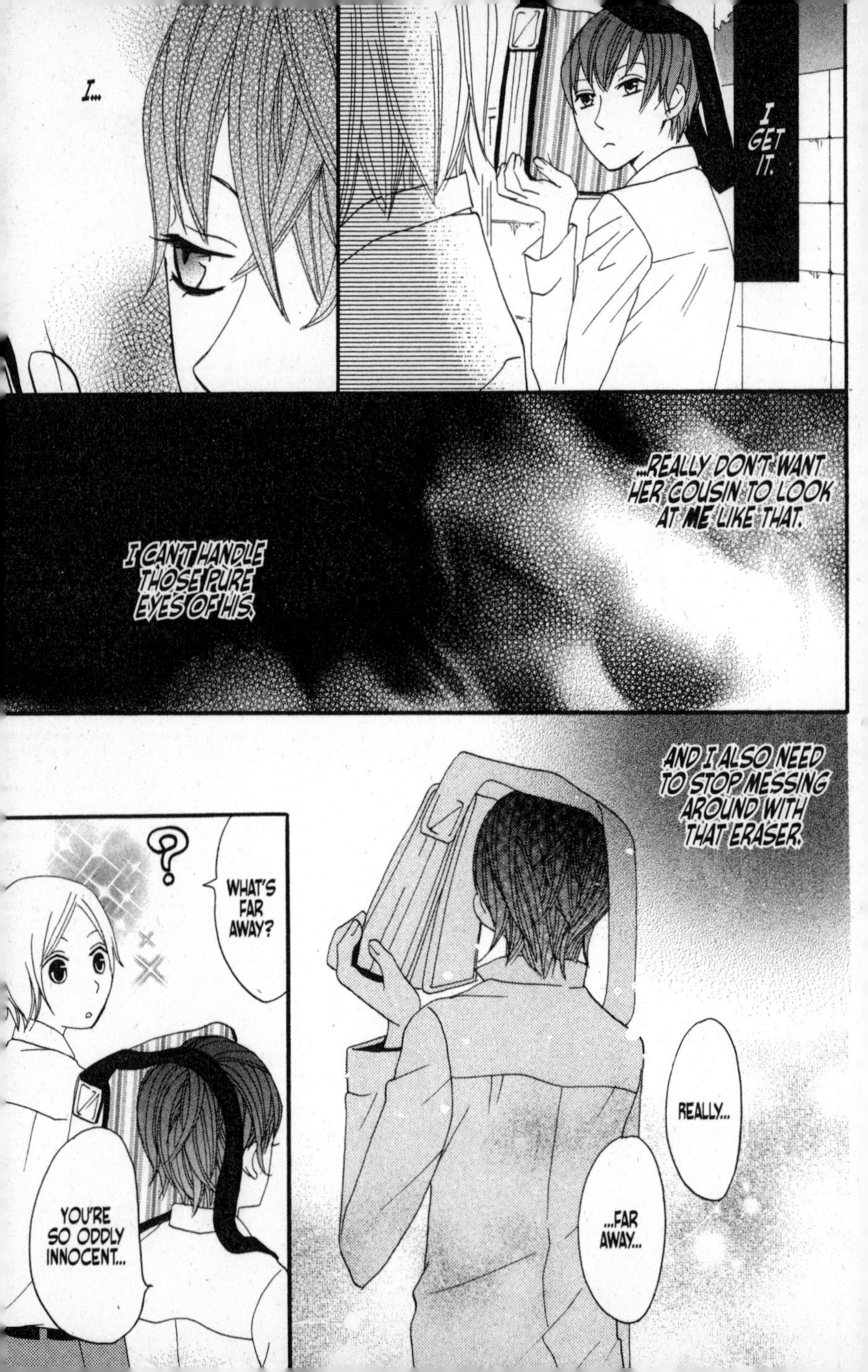
I GET IT.
I...
...REALLY DON'T WANT HER COUSIN TO LOOK AT ME LIKE THAT.
I CAN'T HANDLE THOSE PURE EYES OF HIS.
AND I ALSO NEED TO STOP MESSING AROUND WITH THAT ERASER.
REALLY...
...FAR AWAY...
WHAT'S FAR AWAY?
YOU'RE SO ODDLY INNOCENT...

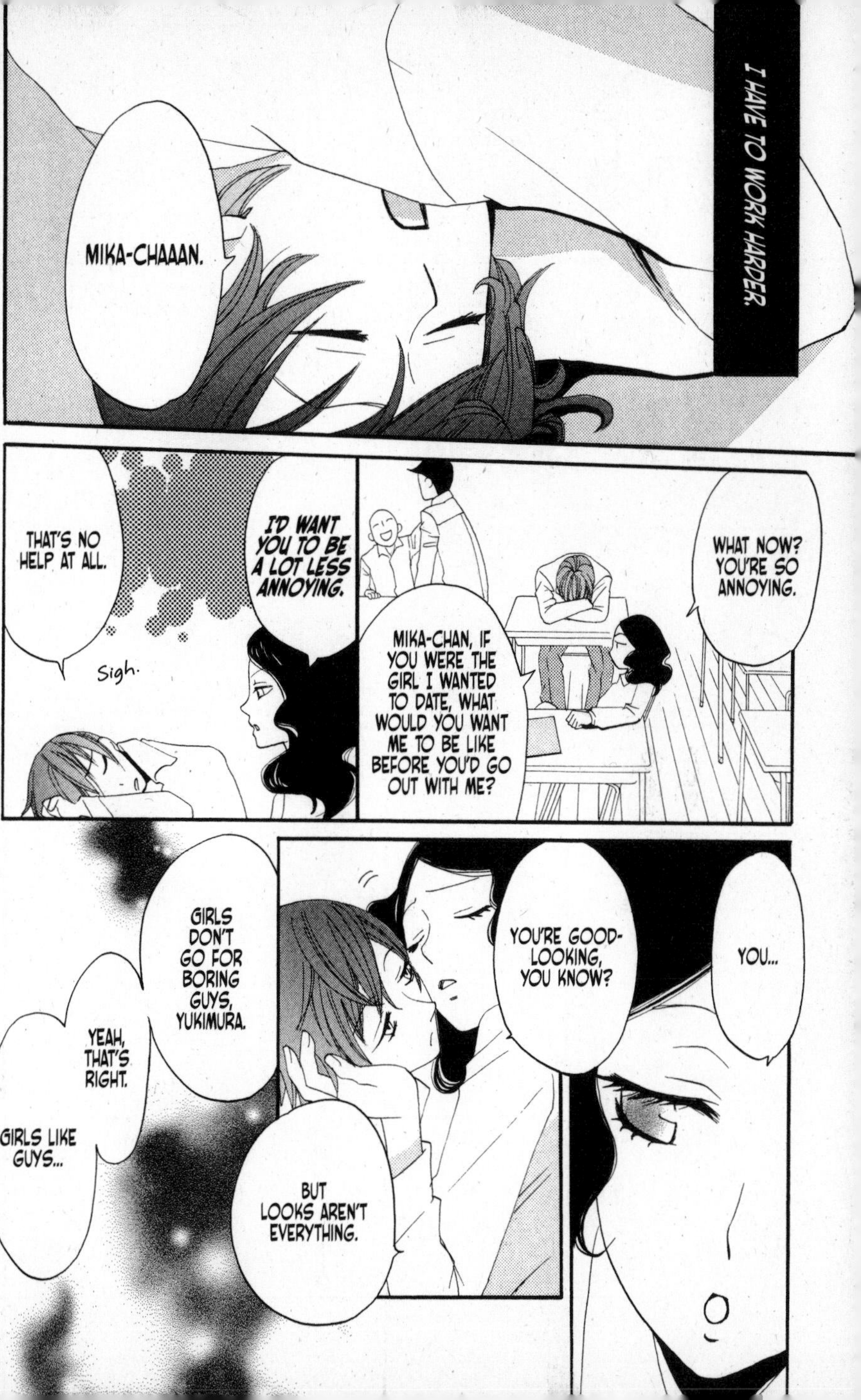
I HAVE TO WORK HARDER.
MIKA-CHAAAN.
WHAT NOW? YOU'RE SO ANNOYING.
MIKA-CHAN, IF YOU WERE THE GIRL I WANTED TO DATE, WHAT WOULD YOU WANT ME TO BE LIKE BEFORE YOU'D GO OUT WITH ME?
I'D WANT YOU TO BE A LOT LESS ANNOYING.
THAT'S NO HELP AT ALL.
Sigh.
YOU...
YOU'RE GOOD-LOOKING, YOU KNOW?
GIRLS DON'T GO FOR BORING GUYS, YUKIMURA.
BUT LOOKS AREN'T EVERYTHING.
YEAH, THAT'S RIGHT.
GIRLS LIKE GUYS...

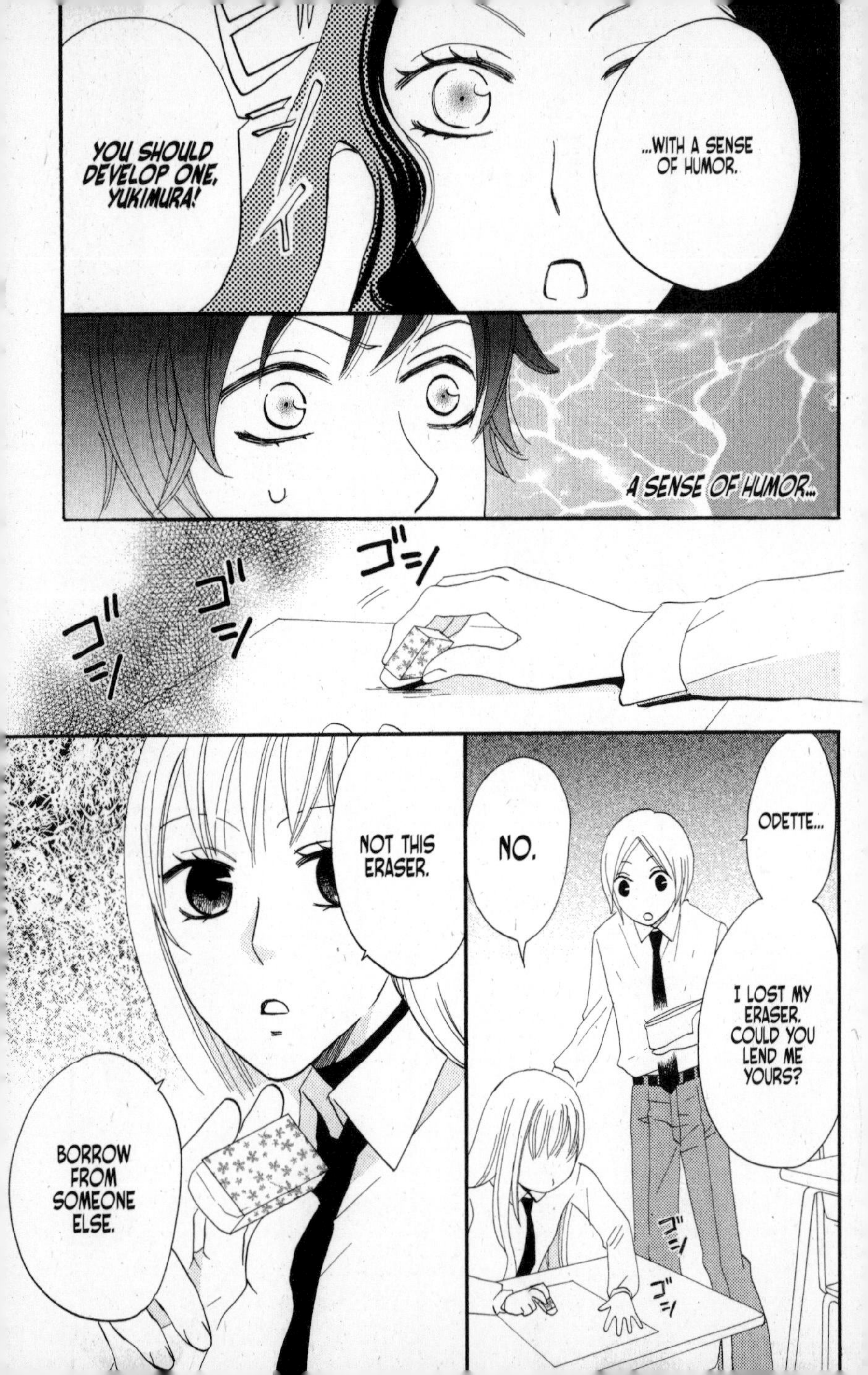
...WITH A SENSE OF HUMOR.
YOU SHOULD DEVELOP ONE, YUKIMURA!
A SENSE OF HUMOR...
ゴシ
ゴシ
ゴシ
ODETTE...
I LOST MY ERASER. COULD YOU LEND ME YOURS?
NO.
ゴシ
ゴシ
NOT THIS ERASER.
BORROW FROM SOMEONE ELSE.

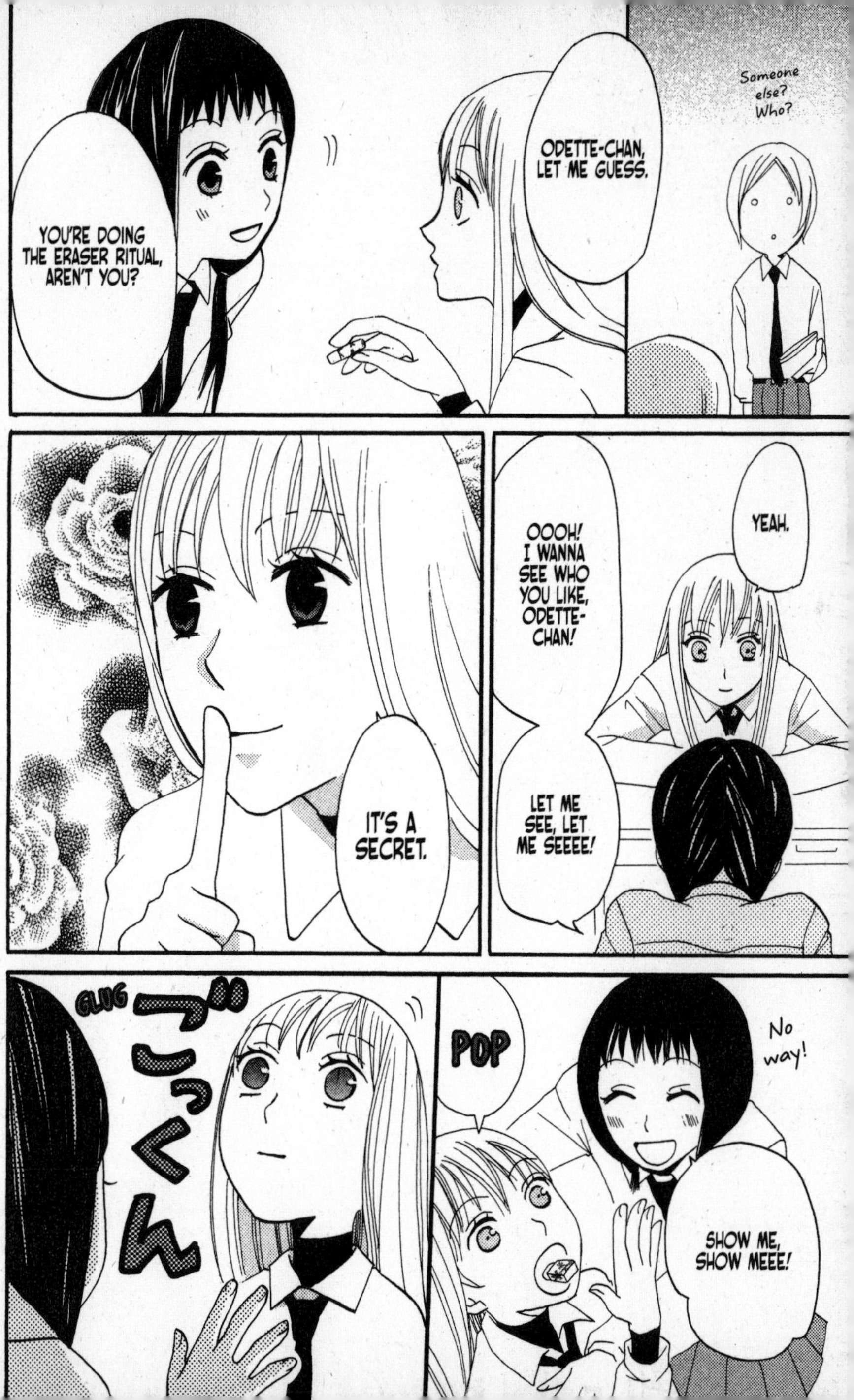
Someone else? Who?
ODETTE-CHAN, LET ME GUESS.
YOU'RE DOING THE ERASER RITUAL, AREN'T YOU?
YEAH.
OOOH! I WANNA SEE WHO YOU LIKE, ODETTE-CHAN!
LET ME SEE, LET ME SEEEE!
IT'S A SECRET.
No way!
POP
SHOW ME, SHOW MEEE!
GLUG
ごっくん

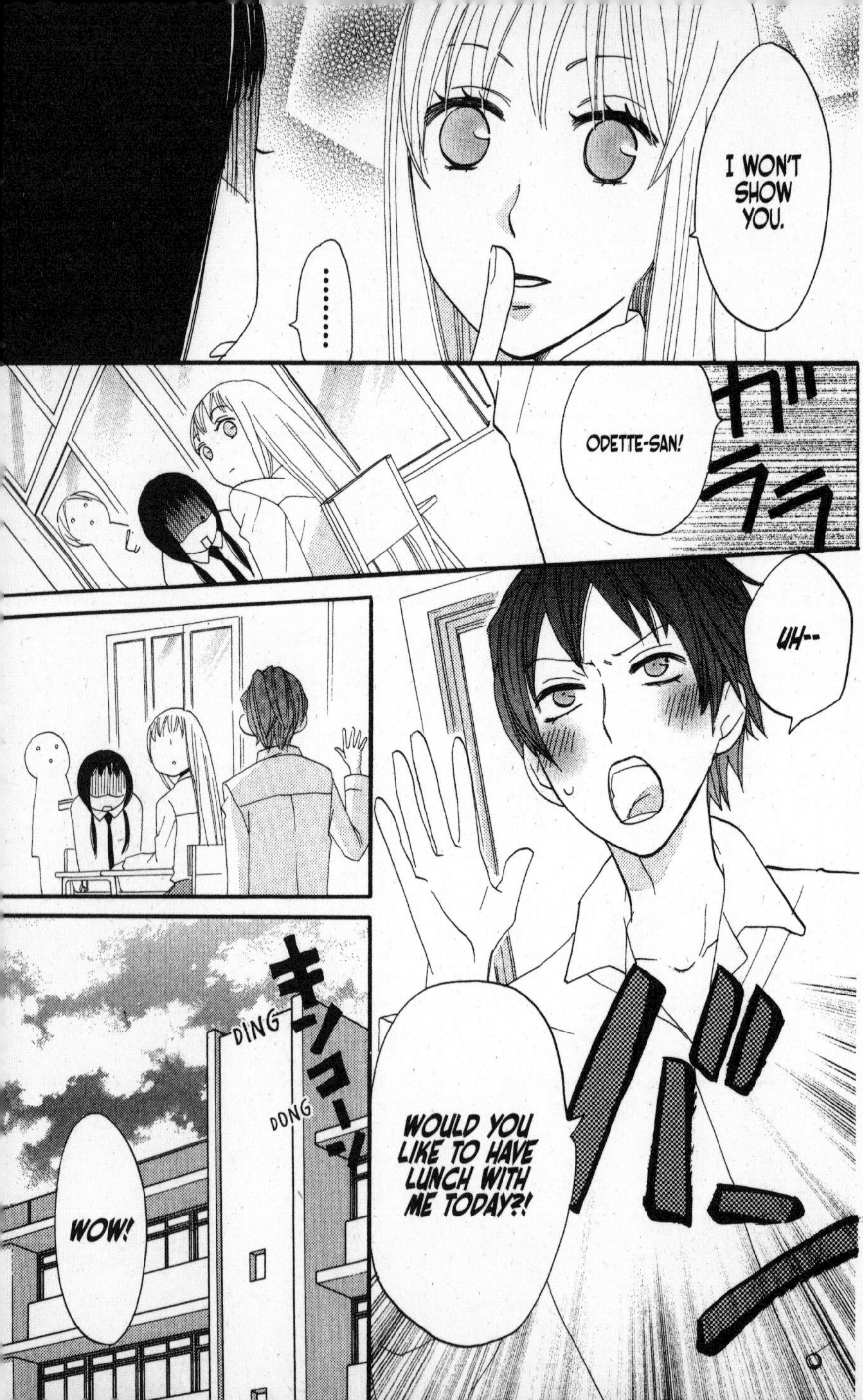
I WON'T SHOW YOU.
......
ガラララ
ODETTE-SAN!
UH--
バーン
WOULD YOU LIKE TO HAVE LUNCH WITH ME TODAY?!
キンコーン
DING
DONG
WOW!

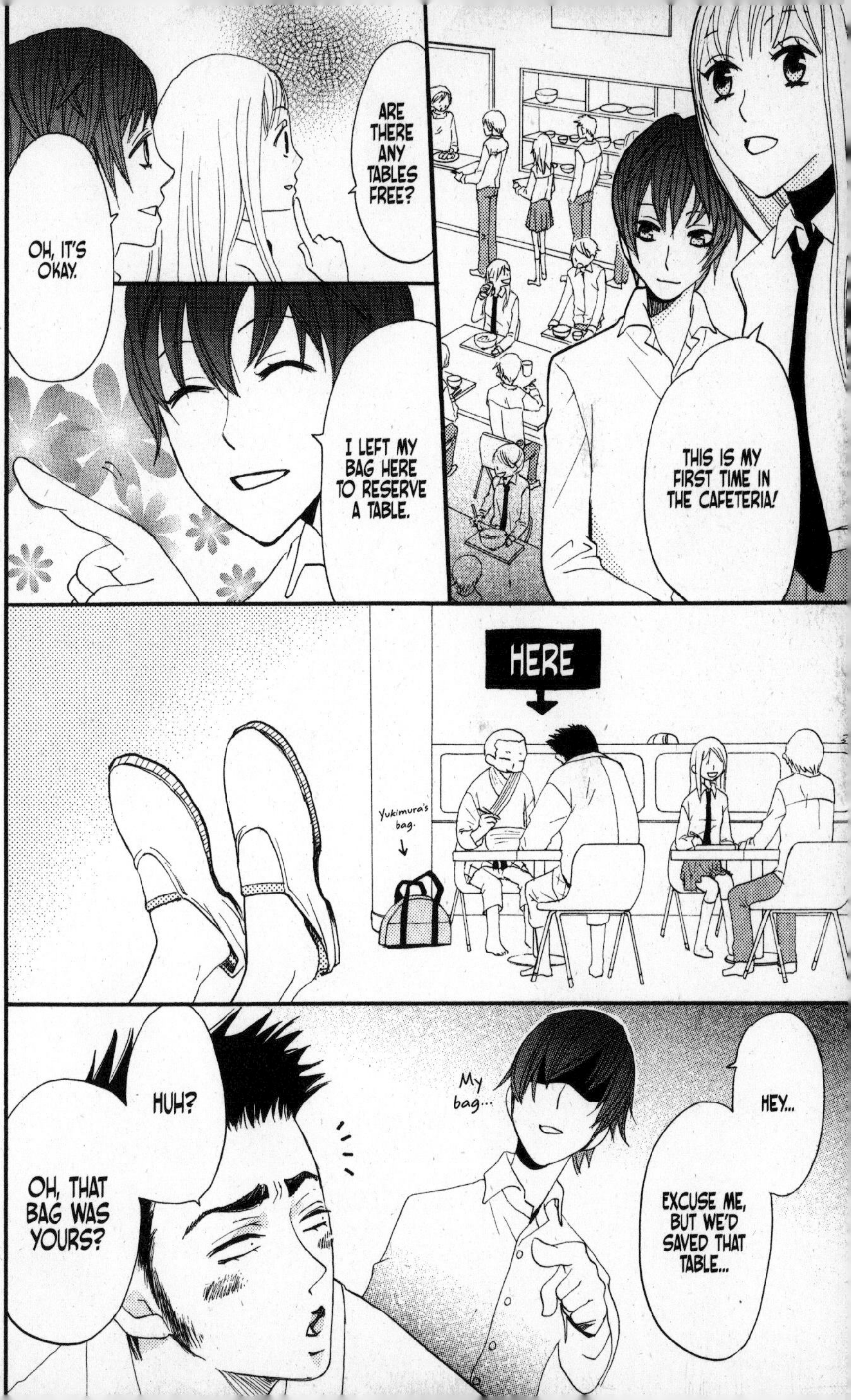
THIS IS MY FIRST TIME IN THE CAFETERIA!
ARE THERE ANY TABLES FREE?
OH, IT'S OKAY.
I LEFT MY BAG HERE TO RESERVE A TABLE.
HERE
Yukimura's bag.
HEY...
EXCUSE ME, BUT WE'D SAVED THAT TABLE...
My bag...
HUH?
OH, THAT BAG WAS YOURS?

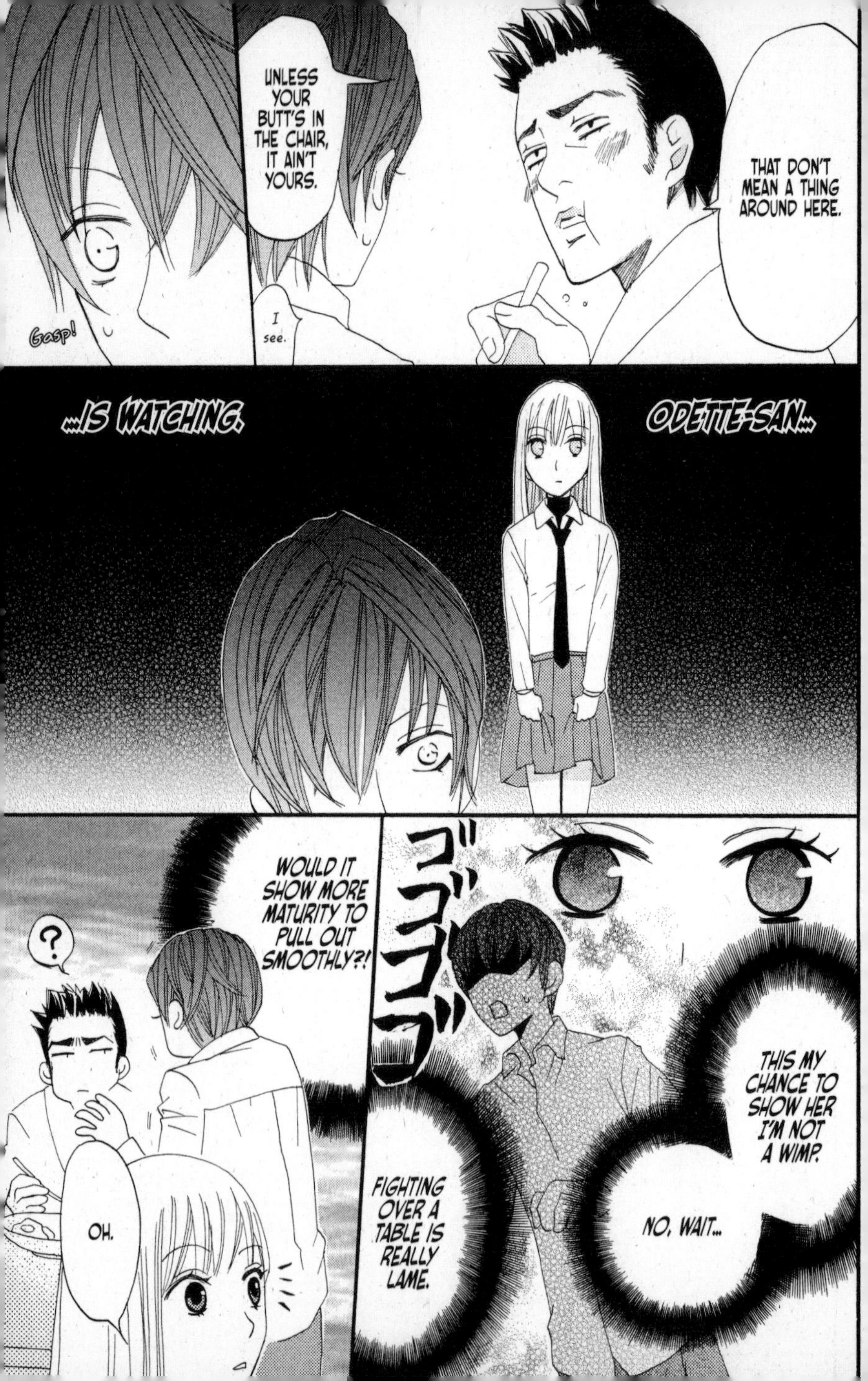
THAT DON'T MEAN A THING AROUND HERE.
UNLESS YOUR BUTT'S IN THE CHAIR, IT AIN'T YOURS.
I see.
Gasp!
ODETTE-SAN...
...IS WATCHING.
THIS MY CHANCE TO SHOW HER I'M NOT A WIMP.
NO, WAIT...
FIGHTING OVER A TABLE IS REALLY LAME.
WOULD IT SHOW MORE MATURITY TO PULL OUT SMOOTHLY?!
ゴゴゴ
?
OH.

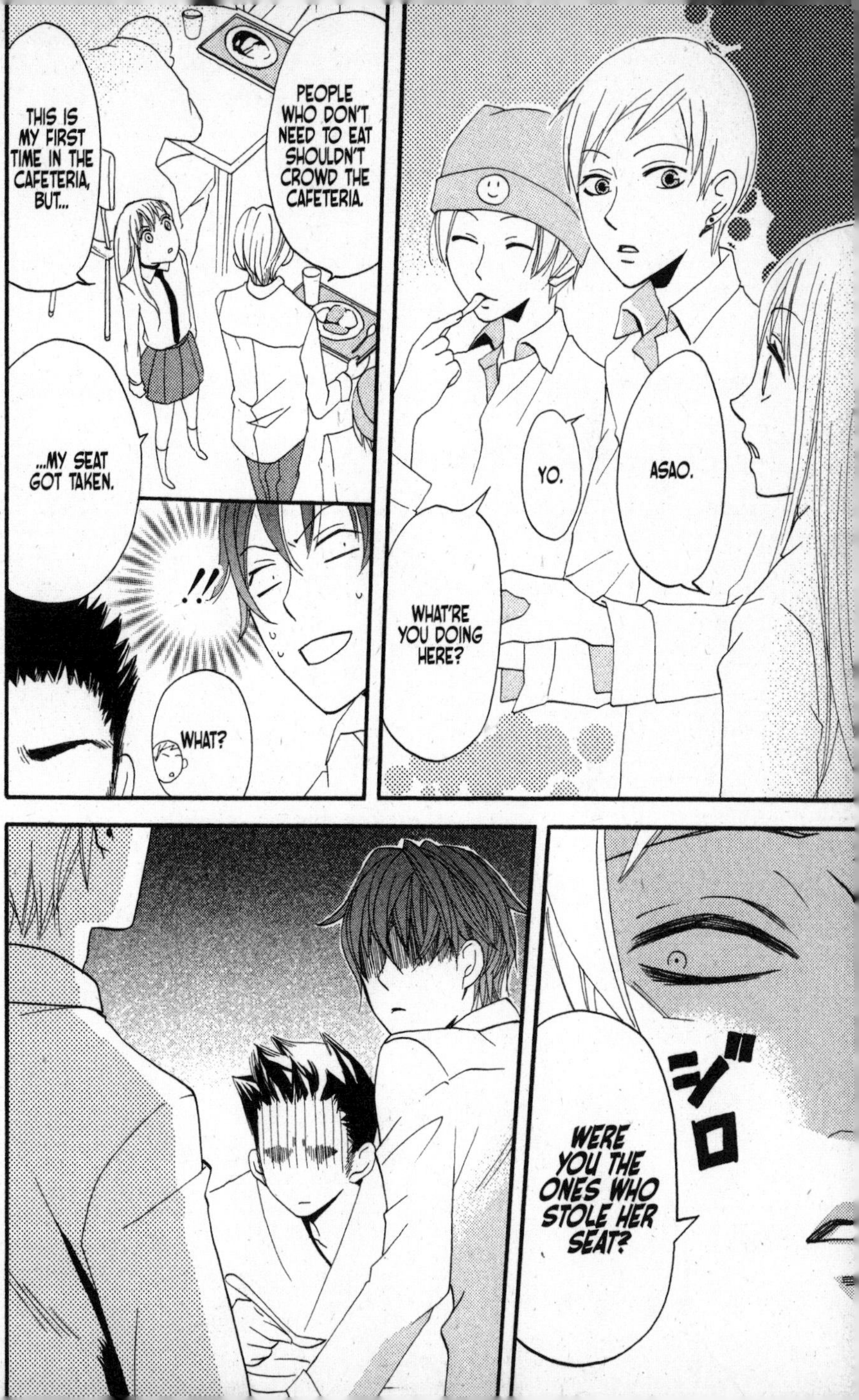
ASAO.
YO.
WHAT'RE YOU DOING HERE?
PEOPLE WHO DON'T NEED TO EAT SHOULDN'T CROWD THE CAFETERIA.
THIS IS MY FIRST TIME IN THE CAFETERIA, BUT...
...MY SEAT GOT TAKEN.
!!
WHAT?
ジロ
WERE YOU THE ONES WHO STOLE HER SEAT?

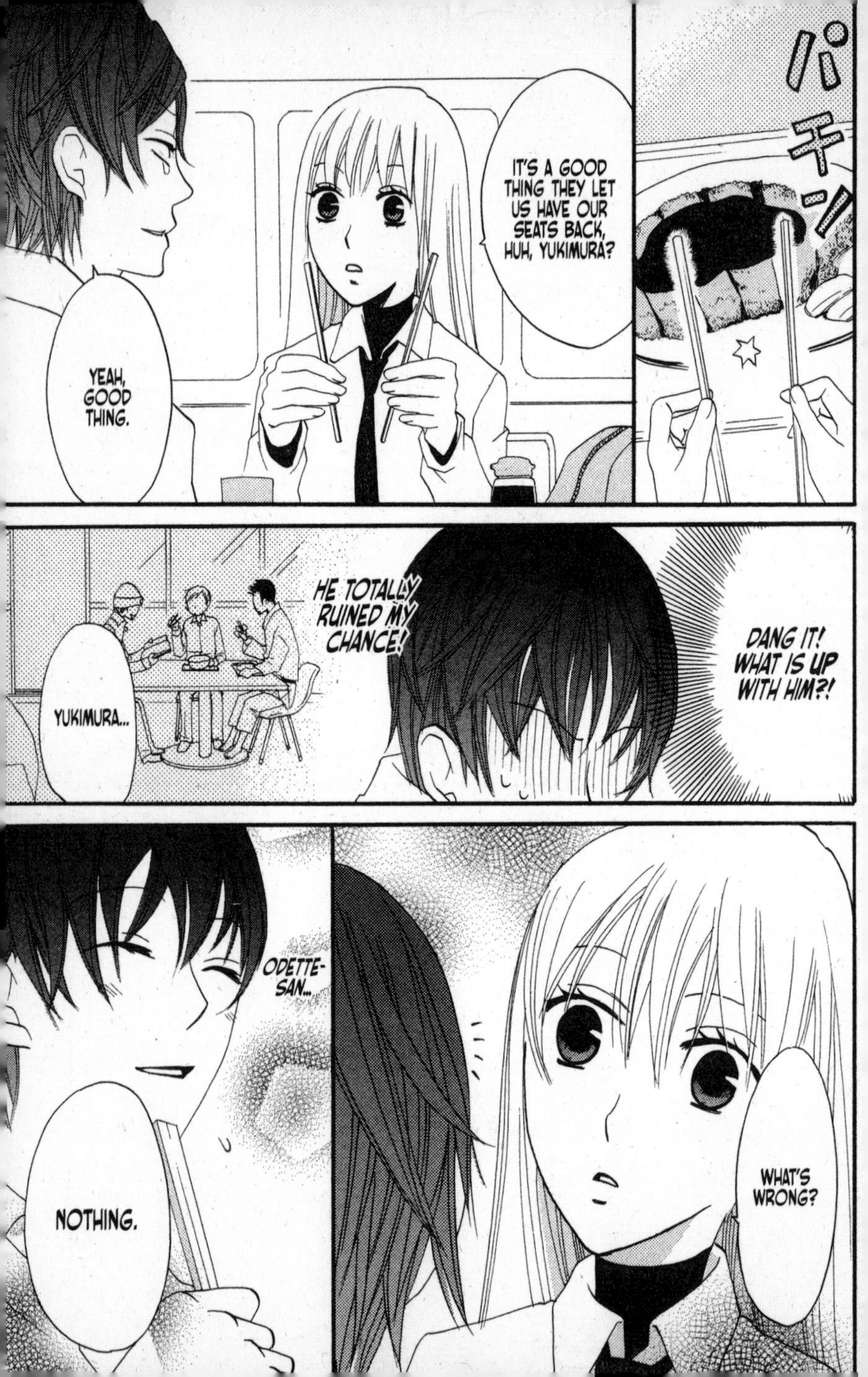
パチッ
IT'S A GOOD THING THEY LET US HAVE OUR SEATS BACK, HUH, YUKIMURA?
YEAH, GOOD THING.
DANG IT! WHAT IS UP WITH HIM?!
HE TOTALLY RUINED MY CHANCE!
YUKIMURA...
WHAT'S WRONG?
ODETTE-SAN...
NOTHING.

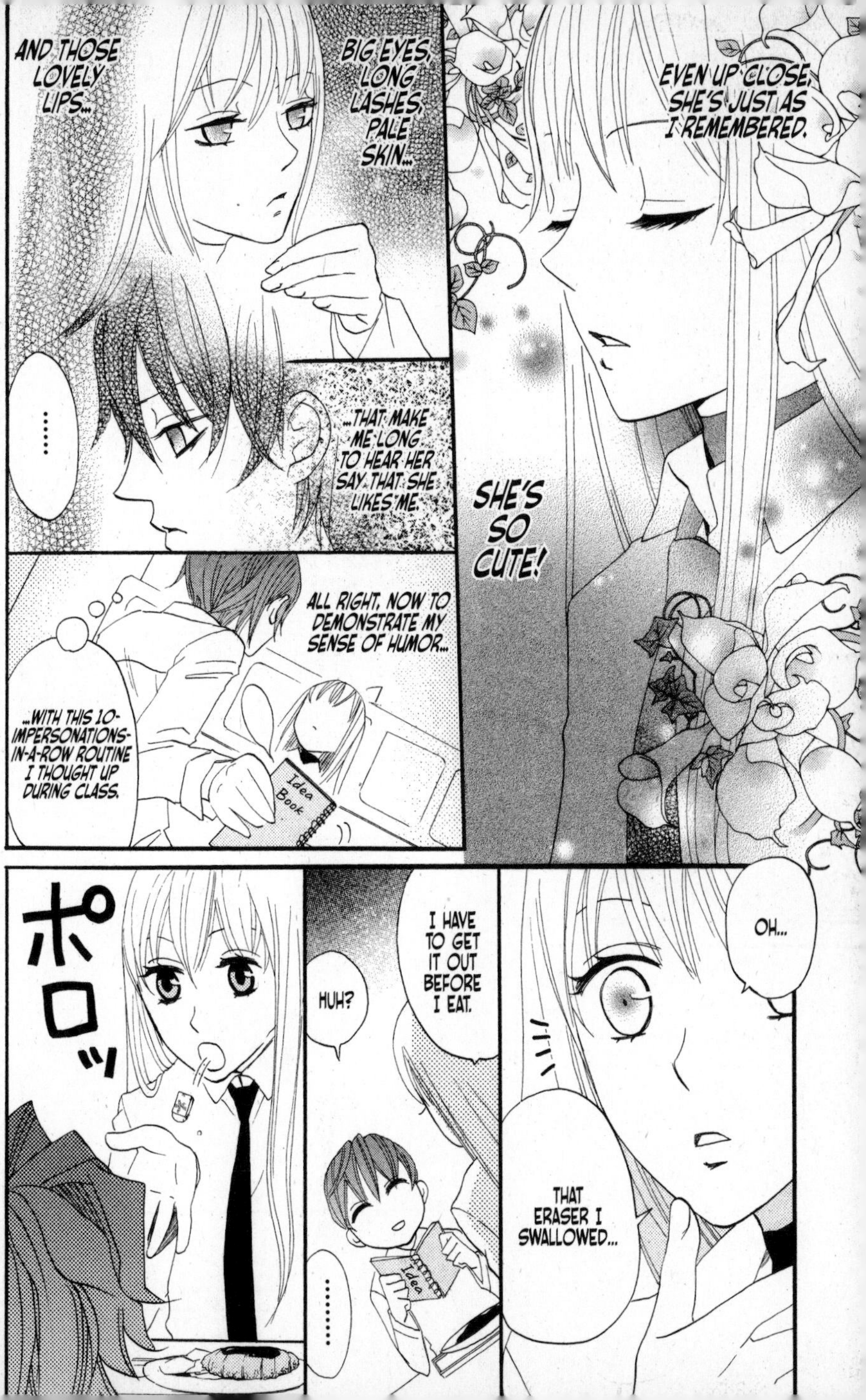
EVEN UP CLOSE, SHE'S JUST AS I REMEMBERED.
SHE'S SO CUTE!
BIG EYES, LONG LASHES, PALE SKIN...
AND THOSE LOVELY LIPS...
...THAT MAKE ME LONG TO HEAR HER SAY THAT SHE LIKES ME.
......
ALL RIGHT. NOW TO DEMONSTRATE MY SENSE OF HUMOR...
...WITH THIS 10-IMPERSONATIONS-IN-A-ROW ROUTINE I THOUGHT UP DURING CLASS.
Idea Book
OH...
THAT ERASER I SWALLOWED...
I HAVE TO GET IT OUT BEFORE I EAT.
HUH?
Idea
......
ポロッ

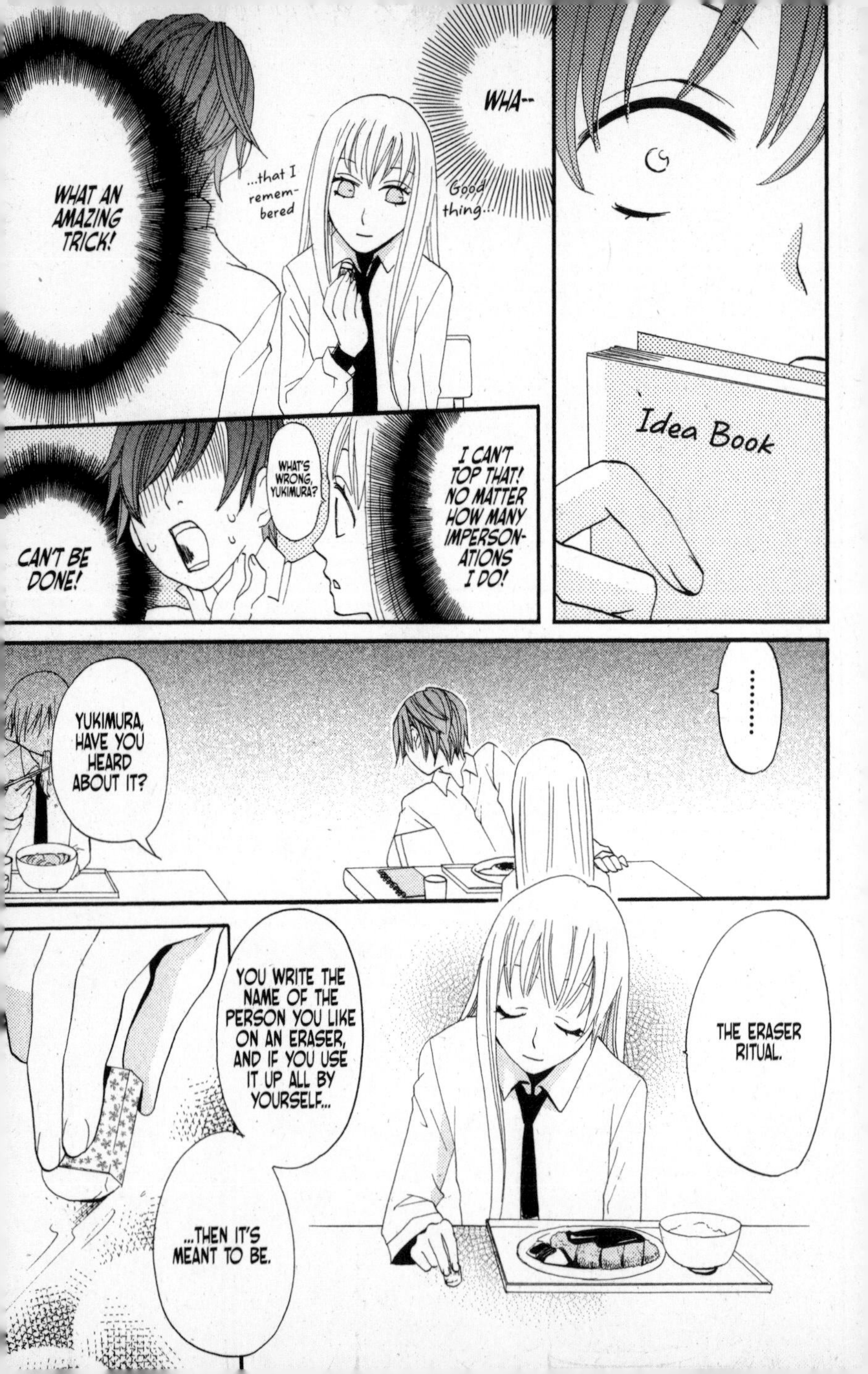
Idea Book
WHA--
Good thing...
...that I remembered
WHAT AN AMAZING TRICK!
I CAN'T TOP THAT! NO MATTER HOW MANY IMPERSONATIONS I DO!
WHAT'S WRONG, YUKIMURA?
CAN'T BE DONE!
....
YUKIMURA, HAVE YOU HEARD ABOUT IT?
THE ERASER RITUAL.
YOU WRITE THE NAME OF THE PERSON YOU LIKE ON AN ERASER, AND IF YOU USE IT UP ALL BY YOURSELF...
...THEN IT'S MEANT TO BE.

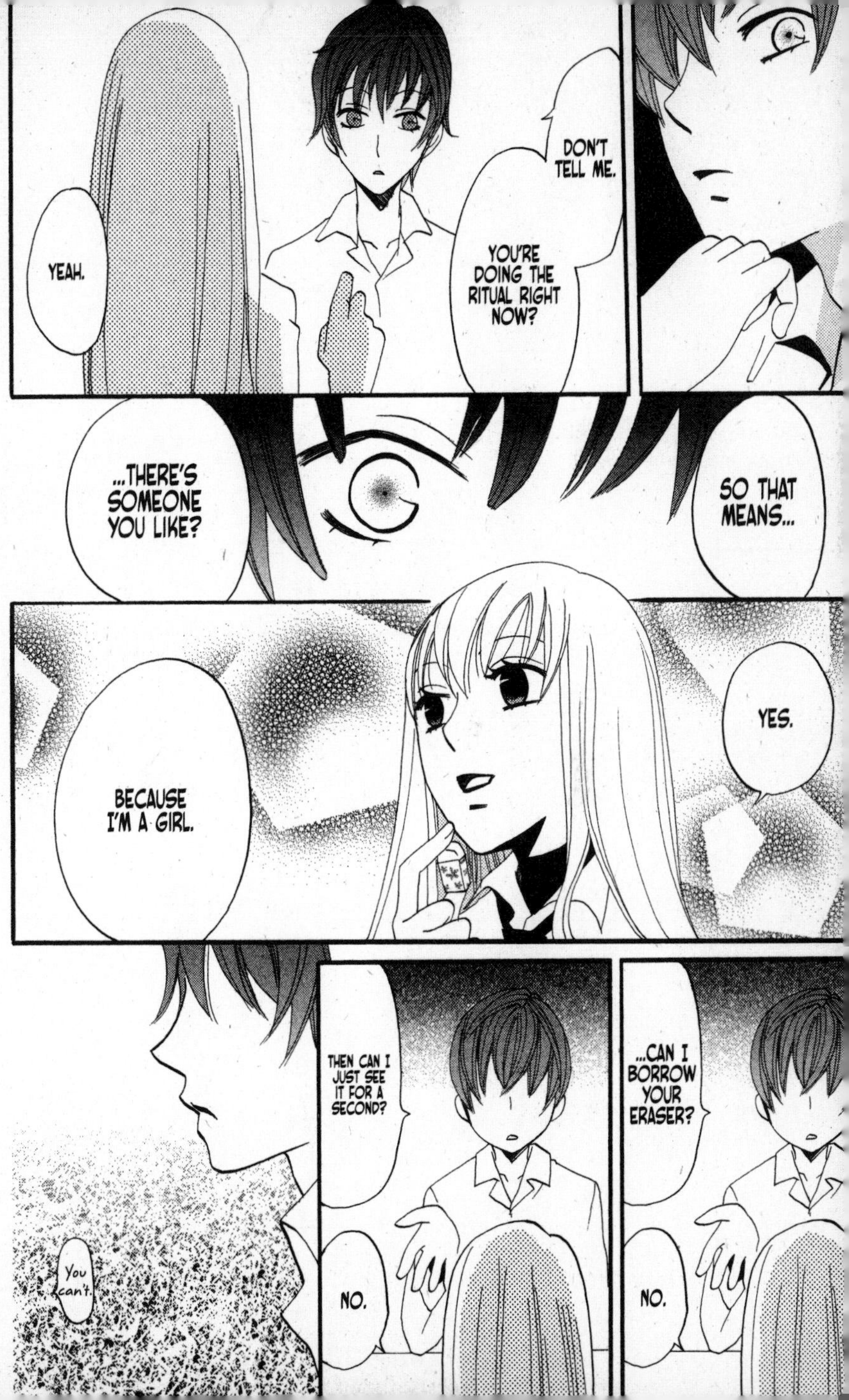
DON'T TELL ME.
YOU'RE DOING THE RITUAL RIGHT NOW?
YEAH.
SO THAT MEANS...
...THERE'S SOMEONE YOU LIKE?
YES.
BECAUSE I'M A GIRL.
...CAN I BORROW YOUR ERASER?
NO.
THEN CAN I JUST SEE IT FOR A SECOND?
NO.
You can't.

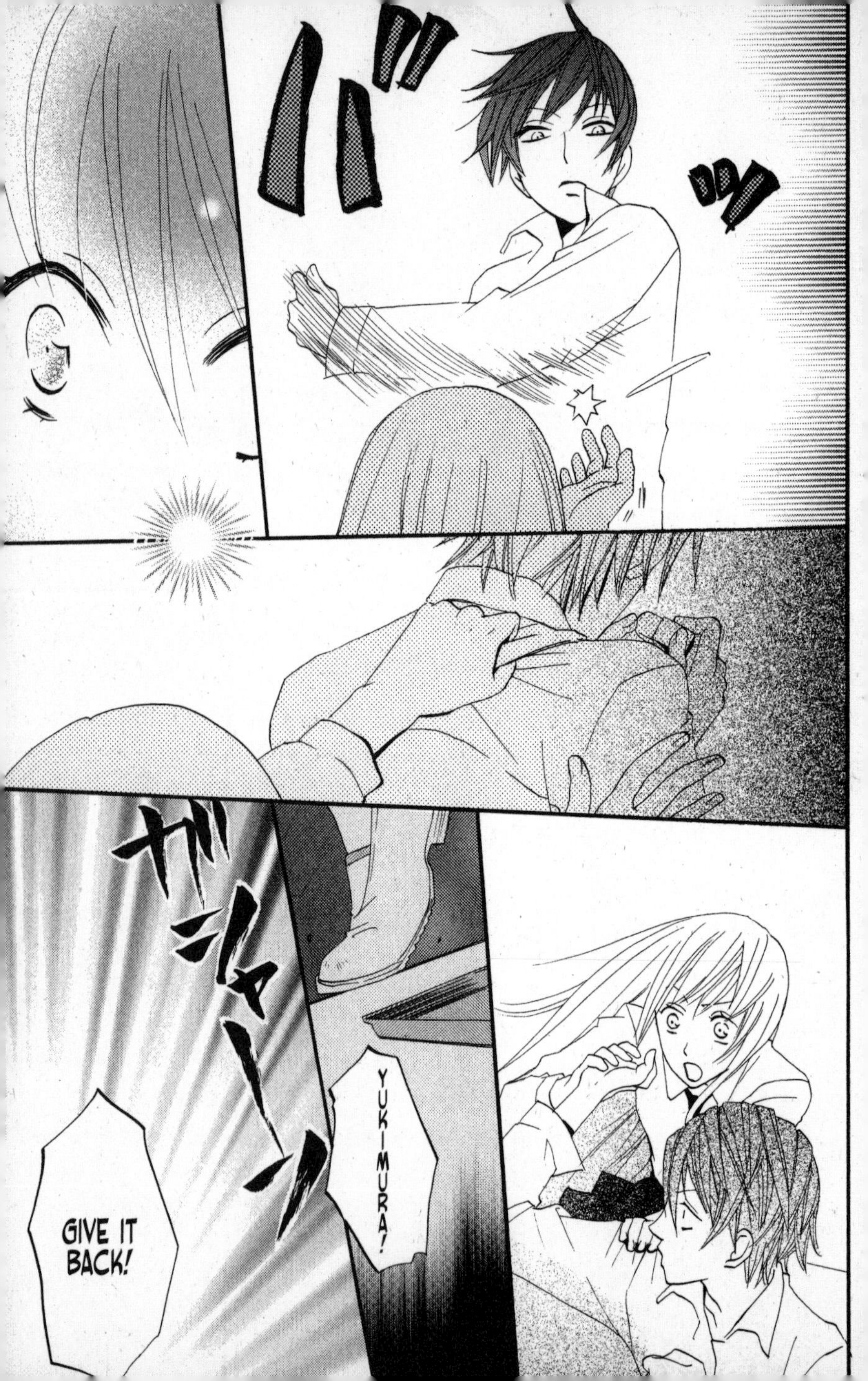
バッ
YUKIMURA!
ガシャーン
GIVE IT BACK!

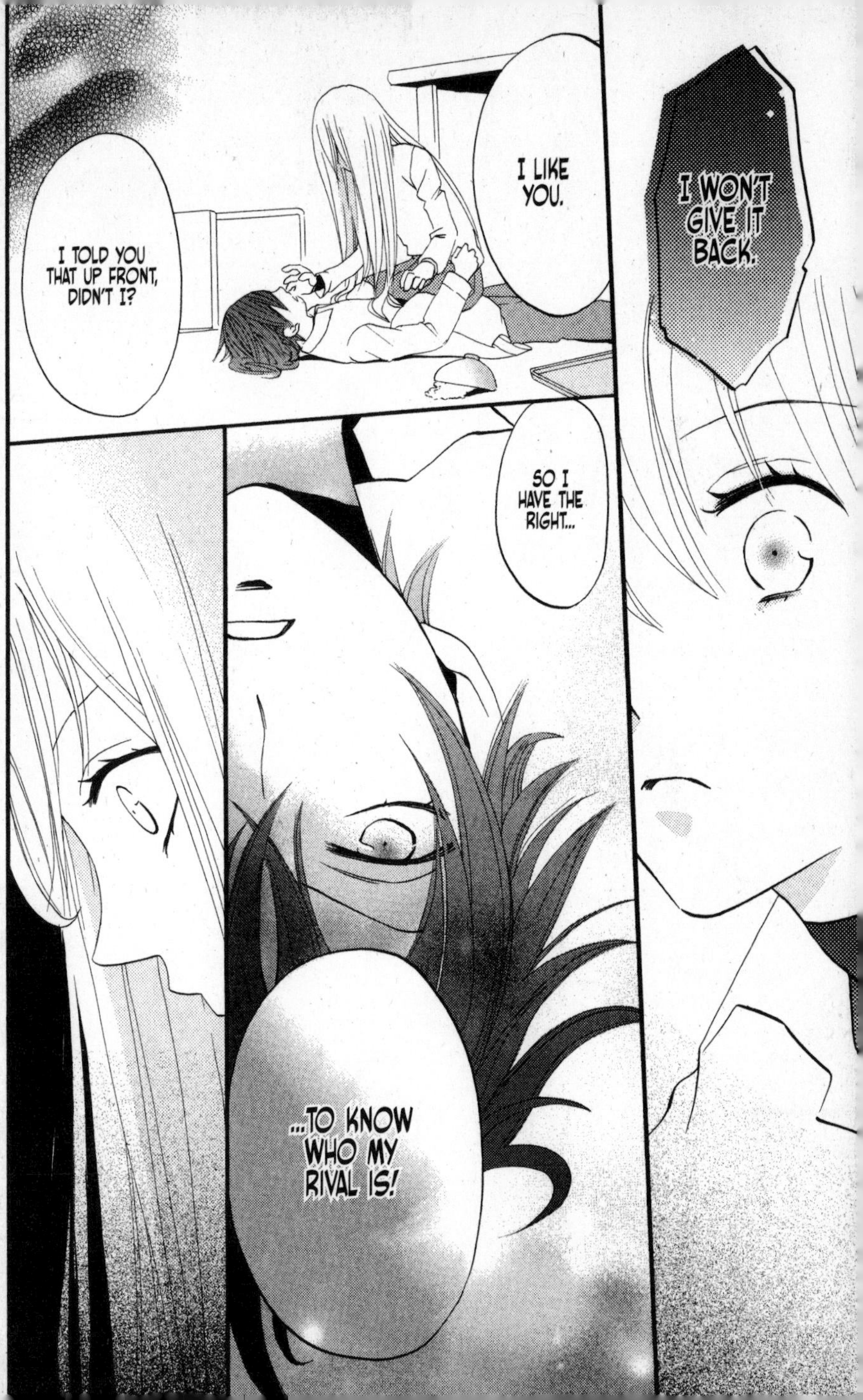
I WON'T GIVE IT BACK.
I LIKE YOU.
I TOLD YOU THAT UP FRONT, DIDN'T I?
SO I HAVE THE RIGHT...
...TO KNOW WHO MY RIVAL IS!

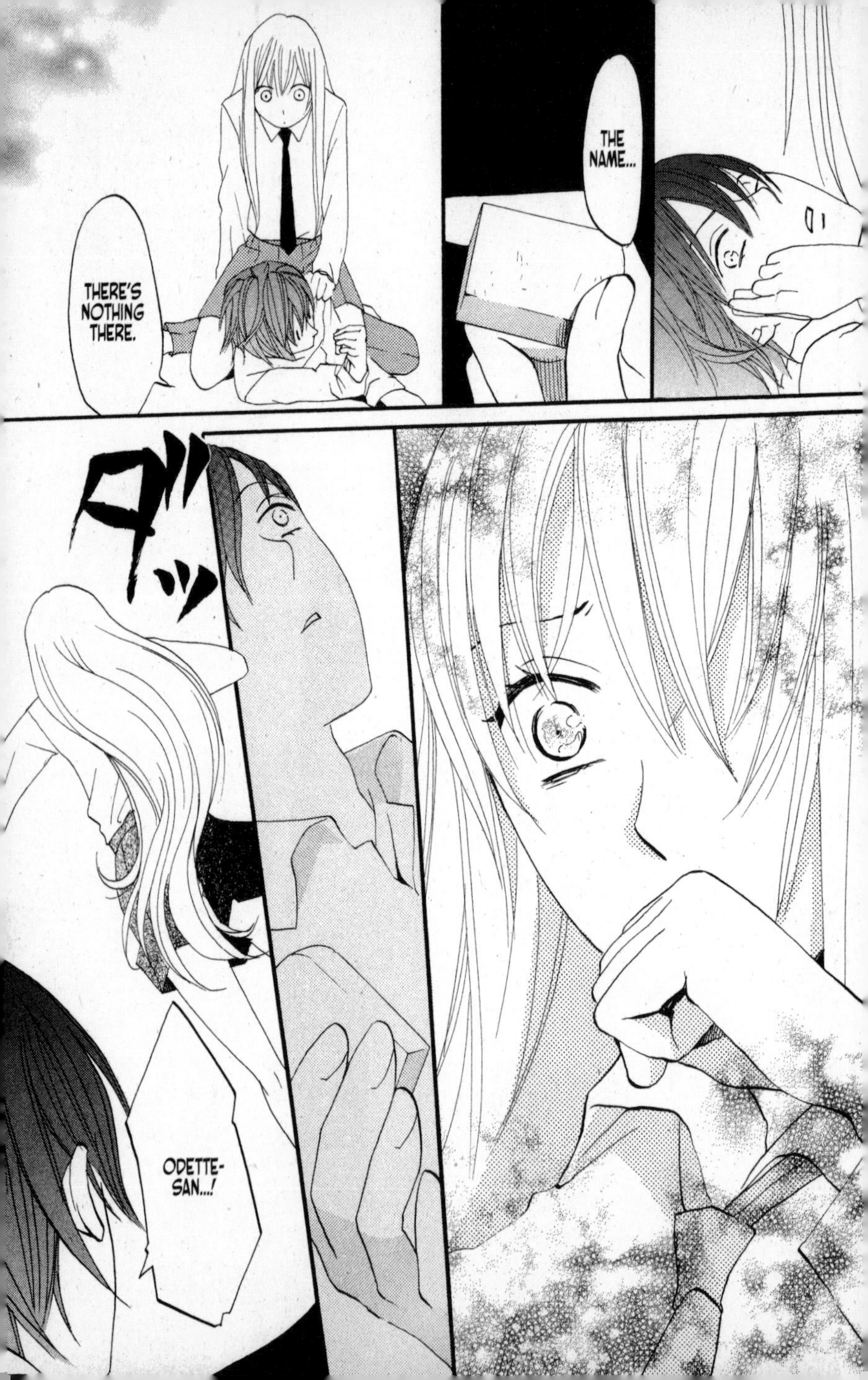
THE NAME...
THERE'S NOTHING THERE.
タッ
ODETTE-SAN...!

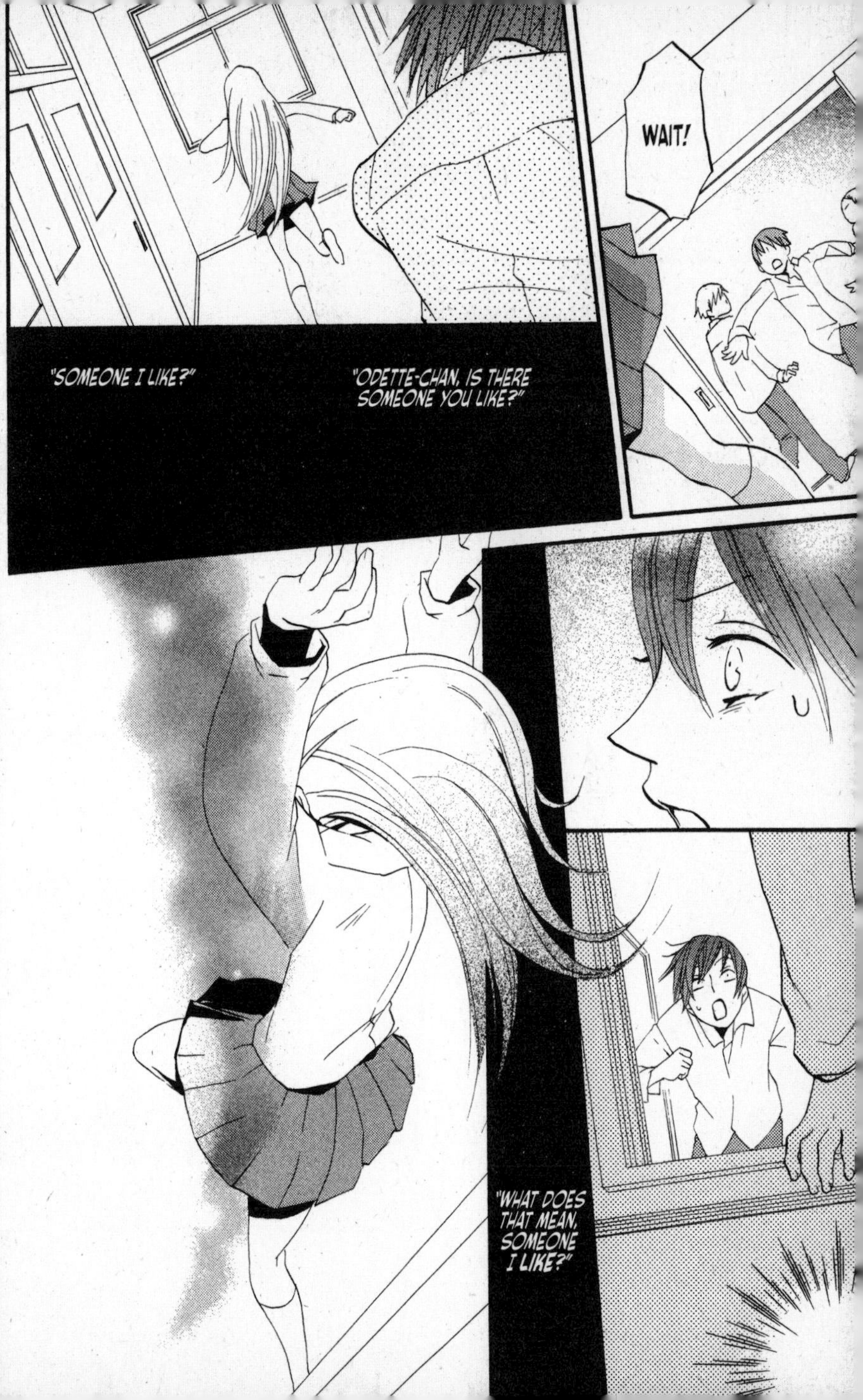
WAIT!
"ODETTE-CHAN, IS THERE SOMEONE YOU LIKE?"
"SOMEONE I LIKE?"
"WHAT DOES THAT MEAN, SOMEONE I LIKE?"

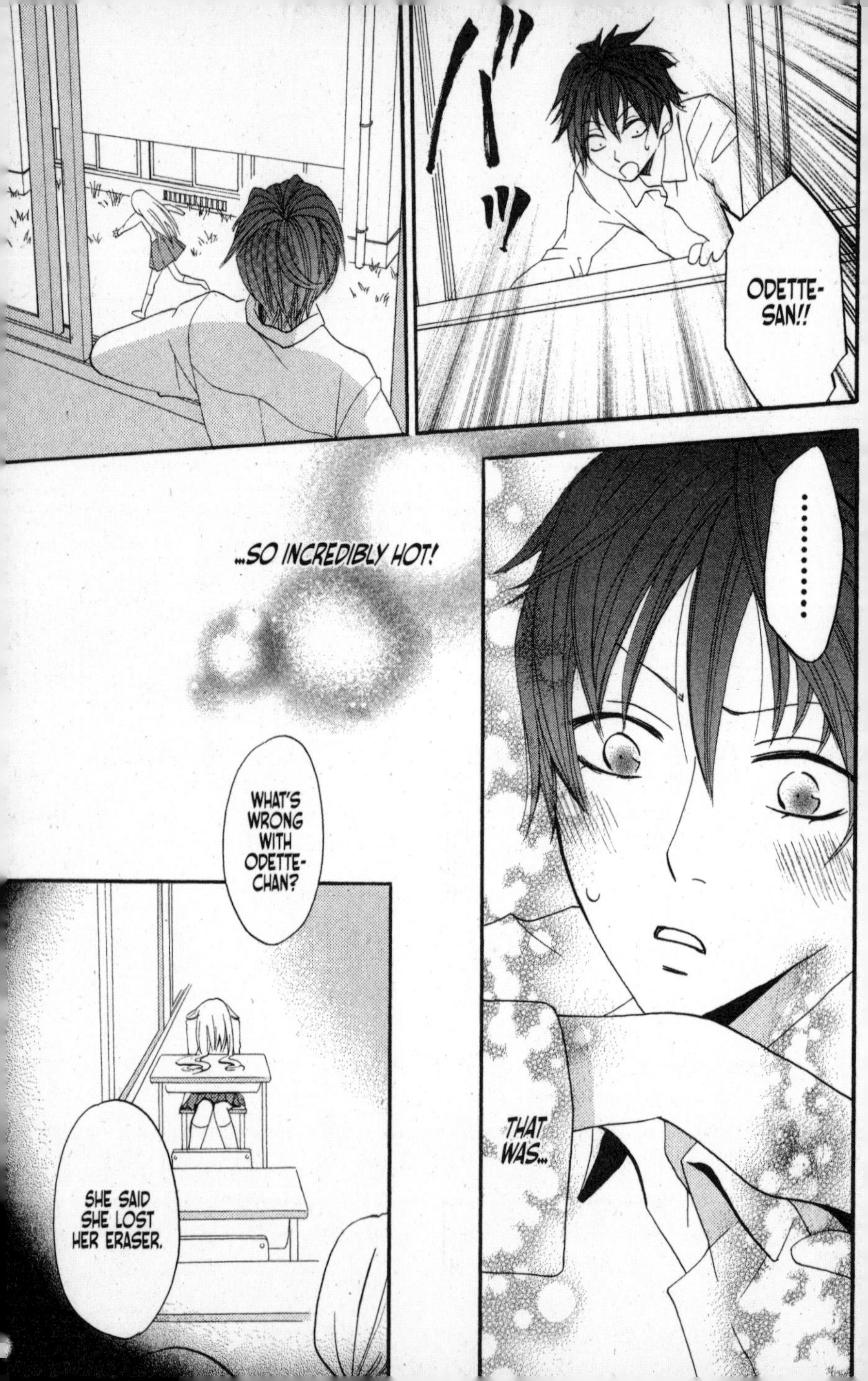
バッ
ODETTE-SAN!!
......
THAT WAS...
...SO INCREDIBLY HOT!
WHAT'S WRONG WITH ODETTE-CHAN?
SHE SAID SHE LOST HER ERASER.

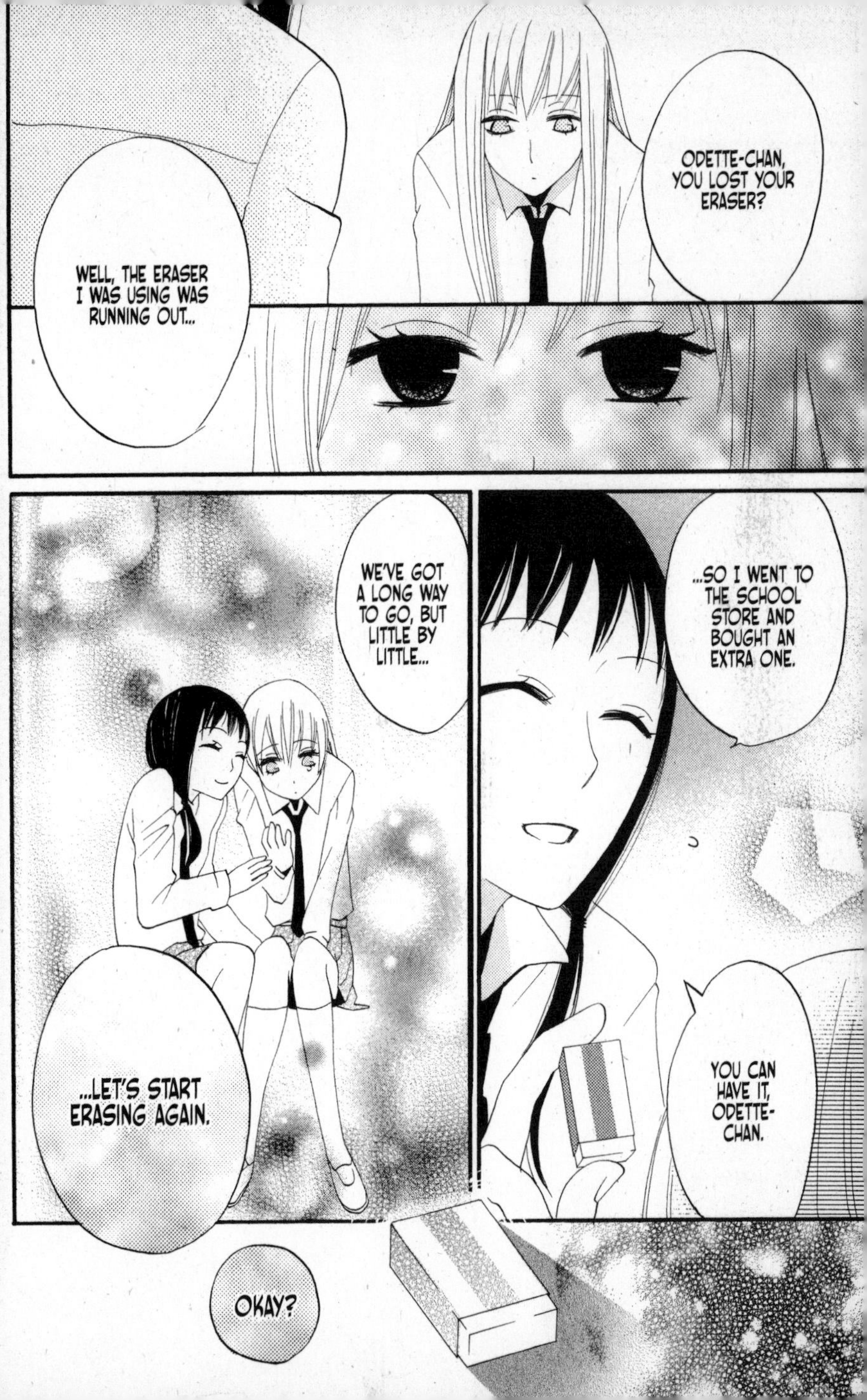
ODETTE-CHAN, YOU LOST YOUR ERASER?
WELL, THE ERASER I WAS USING WAS RUNNING OUT...
...SO I WENT TO THE SCHOOL STORE AND BOUGHT AN EXTRA ONE.
YOU CAN HAVE IT, ODETTE-CHAN.
WE'VE GOT A LONG WAY TO GO, BUT LITTLE BY LITTLE...
...LET'S START ERASING AGAIN.
OKAY?

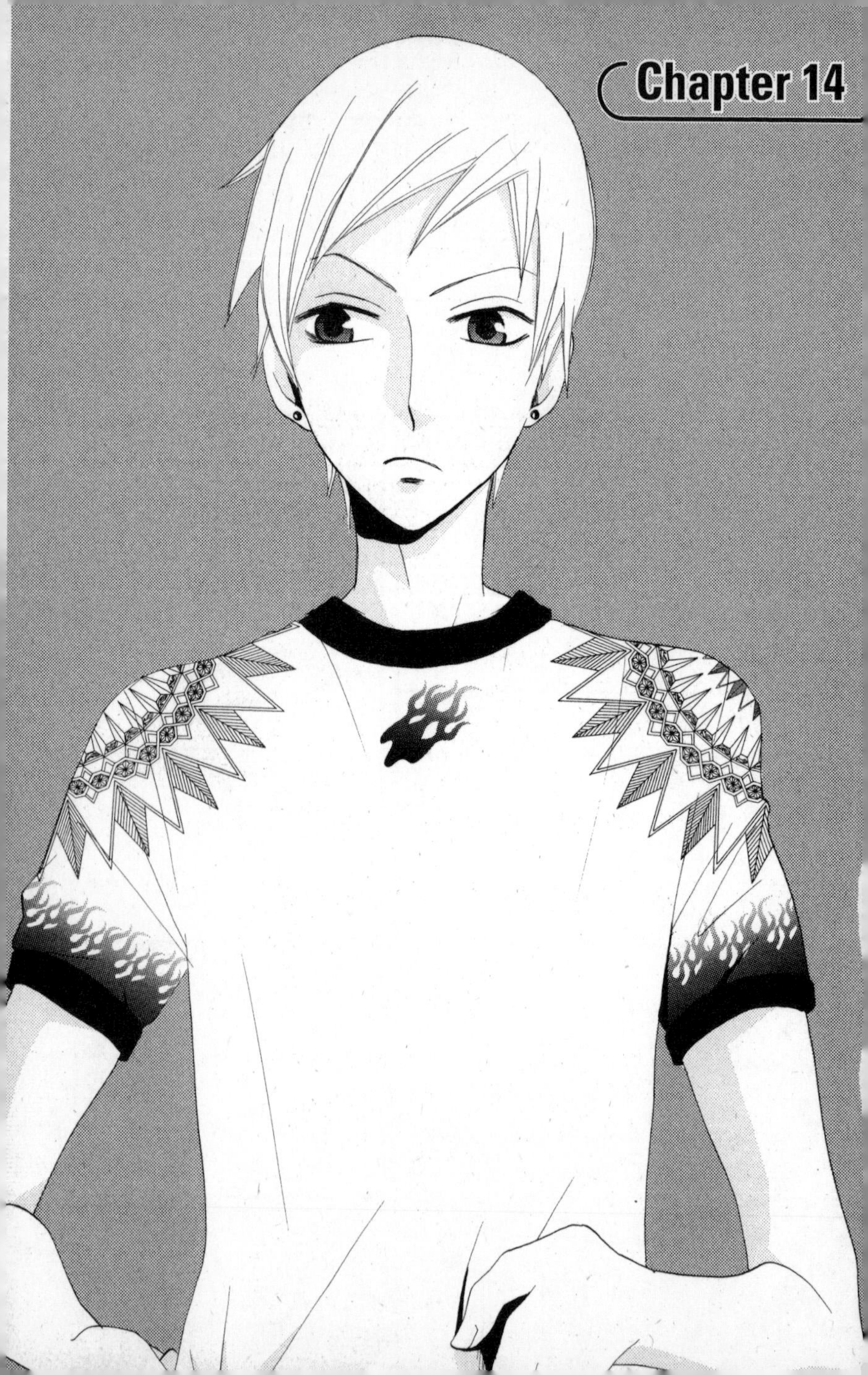
Chapter 14

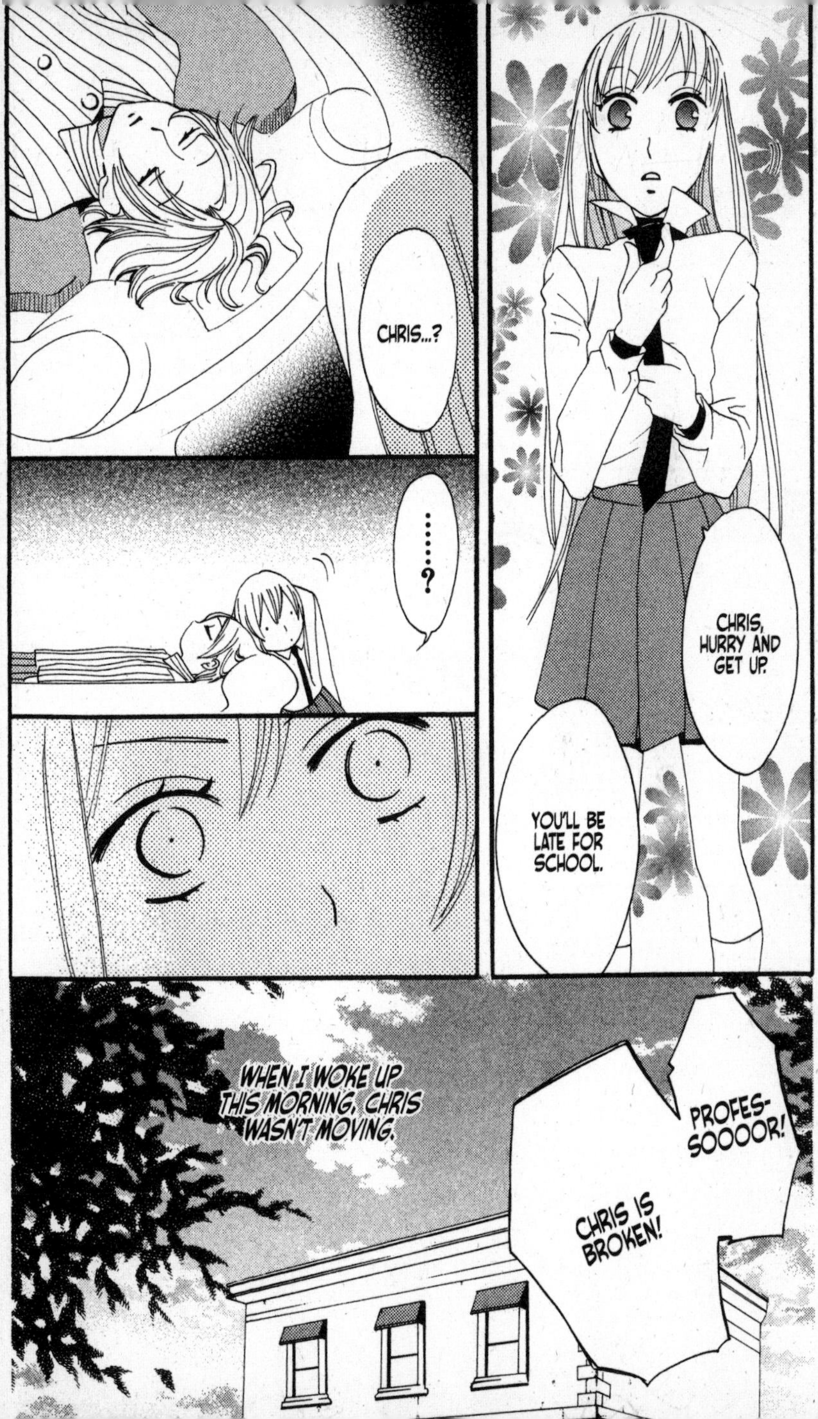
CHRIS, HURRY AND GET UP.
YOU'LL BE LATE FOR SCHOOL.
CHRIS...?
......?
WHEN I WOKE UP THIS MORNING, CHRIS WASN'T MOVING.
PROFES-SOOOOR!
CHRIS IS BROKEN!

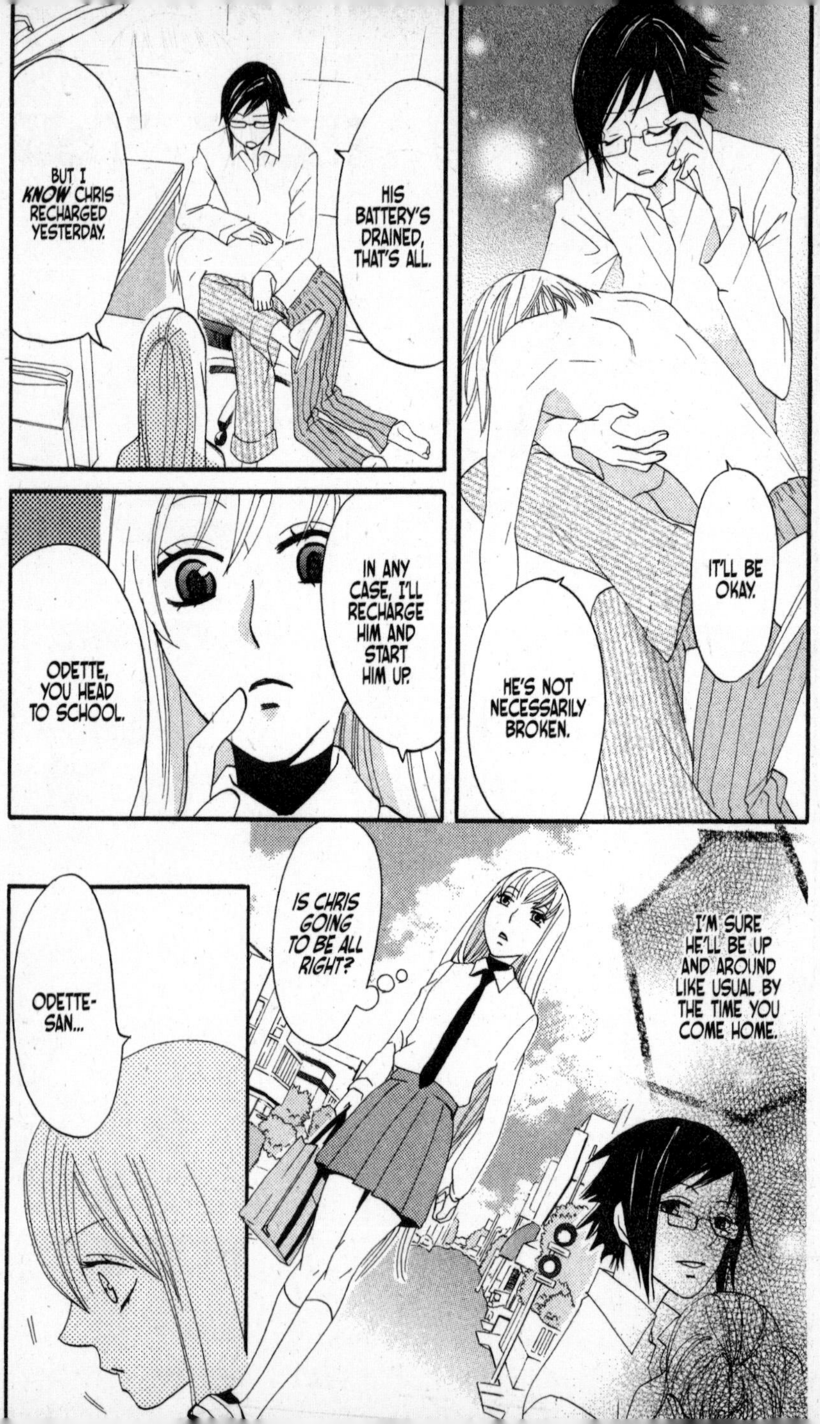
IT'LL BE OKAY.
HE'S NOT NECESSARILY BROKEN.
HIS BATTERY'S DRAINED, THAT'S ALL.
BUT I *KNOW* CHRIS RECHARGED YESTERDAY.
IN ANY CASE, I'LL RECHARGE HIM AND START HIM UP.
ODETTE, YOU HEAD TO SCHOOL.
I'M SURE HE'LL BE UP AND AROUND LIKE USUAL BY THE TIME YOU COME HOME.
IS CHRIS GOING TO BE ALL RIGHT?
ODETTE-SAN...

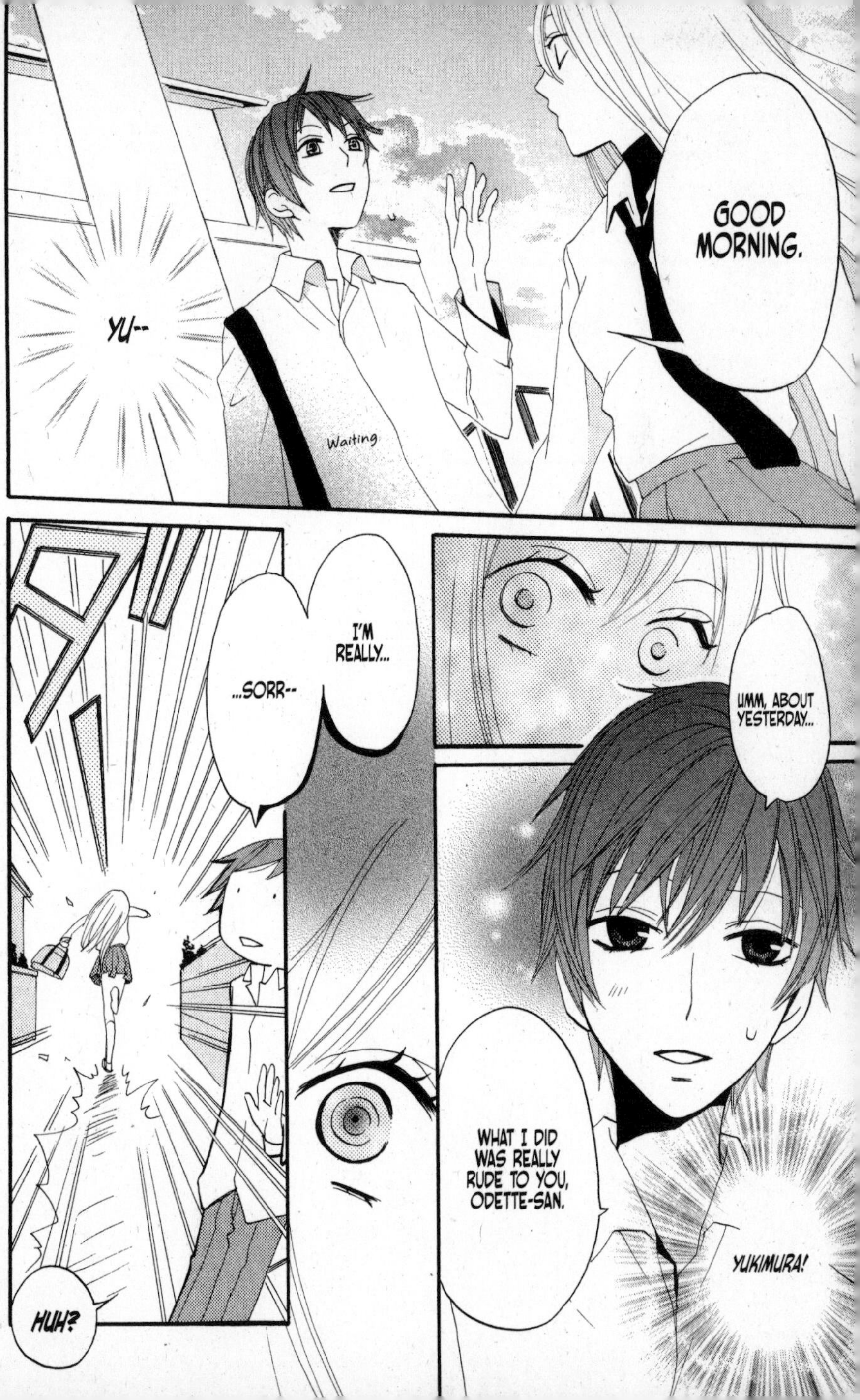
GOOD MORNING.
YU--
Waiting
UMM, ABOUT YESTERDAY...
WHAT I DID WAS REALLY RUDE TO YOU, ODETTE-SAN.
YUKIMURA!
I'M REALLY...
...SORR--
HUH?

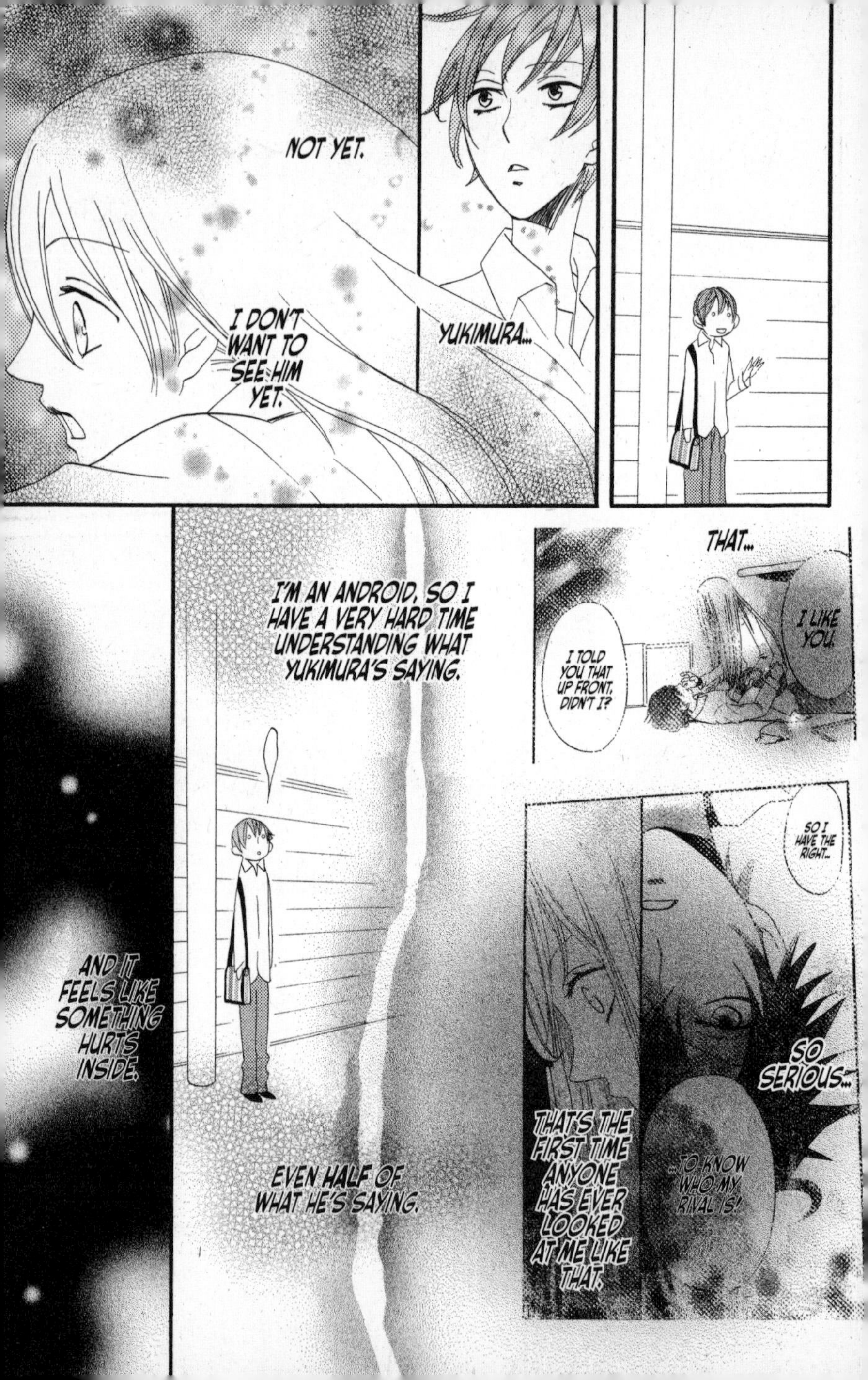

YUKIMURA...
NOT YET.
I DON'T WANT TO SEE HIM YET.
THAT...
I LIKE YOU.
I TOLD YOU THAT UP FRONT, DIDN'T I?
SO I HAVE THE RIGHT...
...TO KNOW WHO MY RIVAL IS!
SO SERIOUS...
THAT'S THE FIRST TIME ANYONE HAS EVER LOOKED AT ME LIKE THAT.
I'M AN ANDROID, SO I HAVE A VERY HARD TIME UNDERSTANDING WHAT YUKIMURA'S SAYING.
EVEN HALF OF WHAT HE'S SAYING.
AND IT FEELS LIKE SOMETHING HURTS INSIDE.

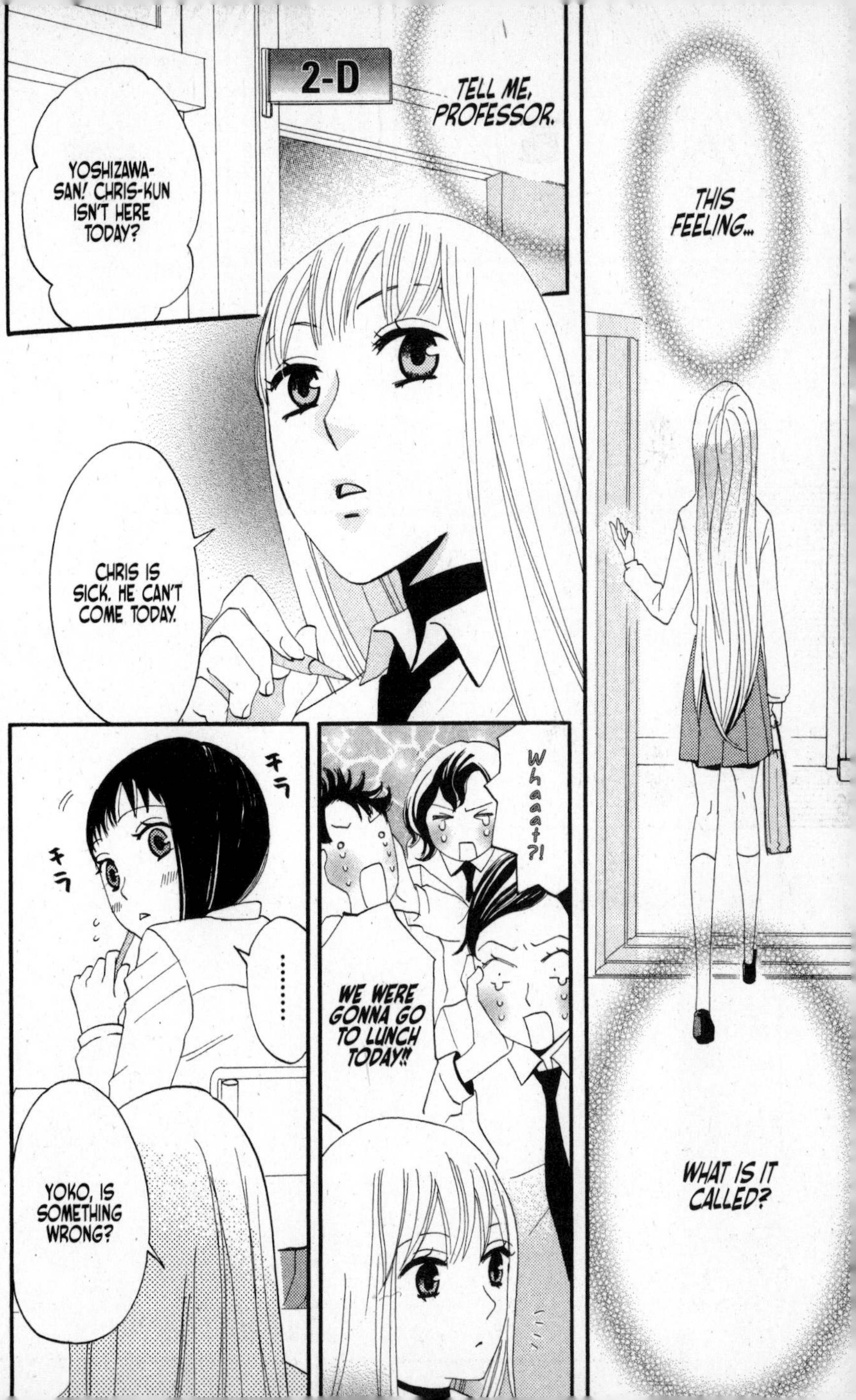
THIS FEELING...
WHAT IS IT CALLED?
TELL ME, PROFESSOR.
2-D
YOSHIZAWA-SAN! CHRIS-KUN ISN'T HERE TODAY?
CHRIS IS SICK. HE CAN'T COME TODAY.
Whaaat?!
WE WERE GONNA GO TO LUNCH TODAY!!
チラ
チラ
....
YOKO, IS SOMETHING WRONG?

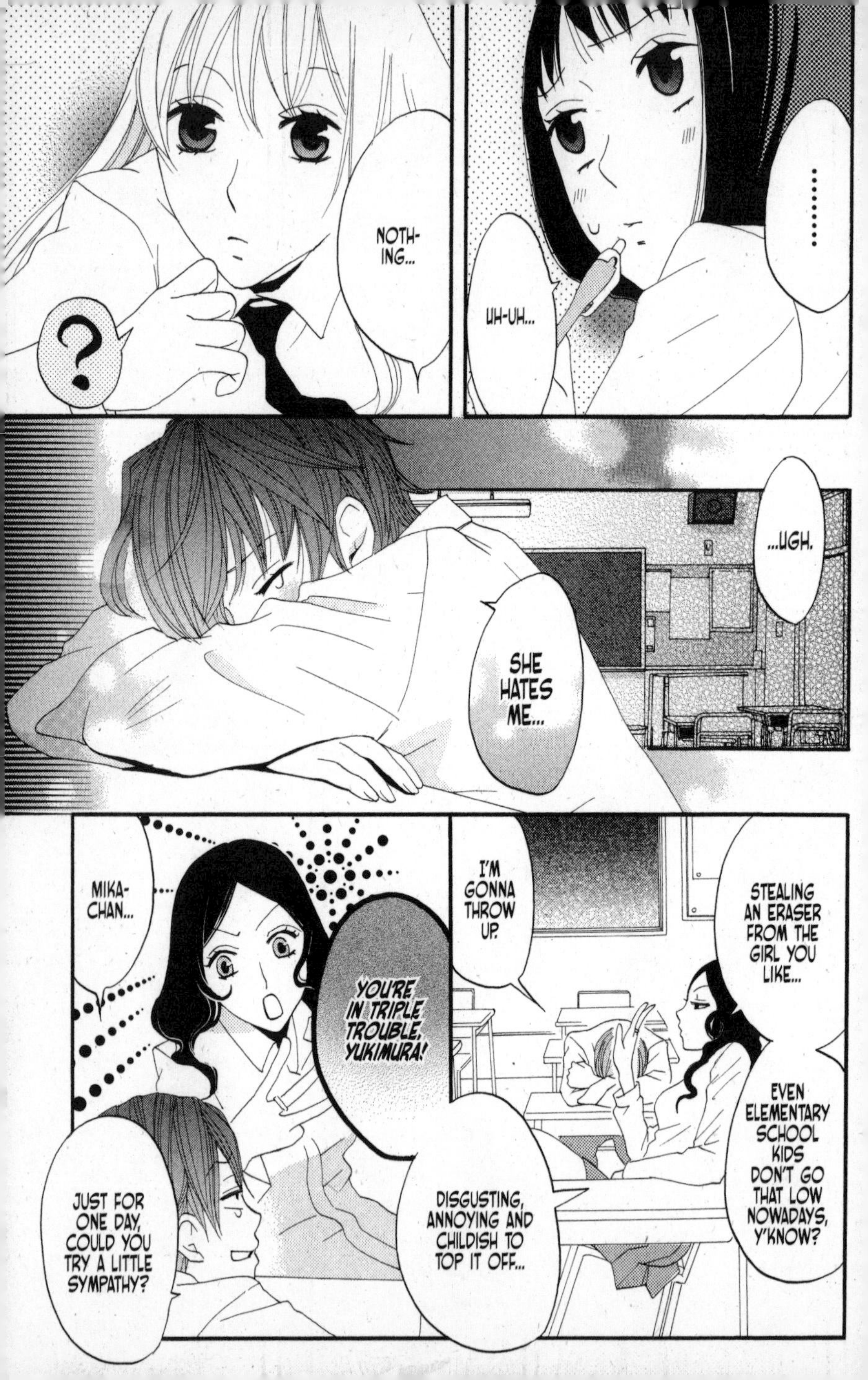
......
UH-UH...
NOTH-ING...
?
...UGH.
SHE HATES ME...
STEALING AN ERASER FROM THE GIRL YOU LIKE...
EVEN ELEMENTARY SCHOOL KIDS DON'T GO THAT LOW NOWADAYS, Y'KNOW?
I'M GONNA THROW UP.
DISGUSTING, ANNOYING AND CHILDISH TO TOP IT OFF...
YOU'RE IN TRIPLE TROUBLE, YUKIMURA!
MIKA-CHAN...
JUST FOR ONE DAY, COULD YOU TRY A LITTLE SYMPATHY?

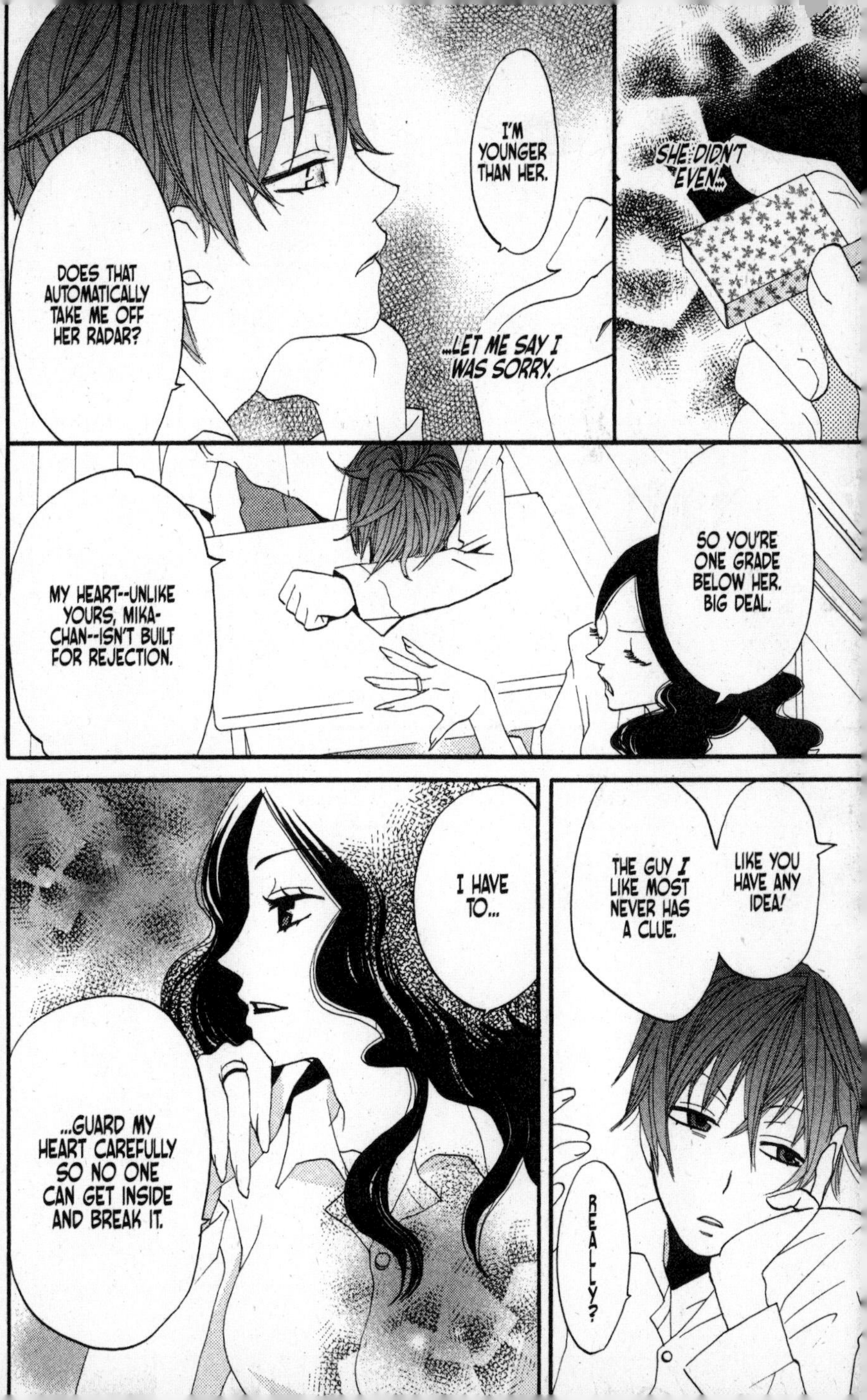
SHE DIDN'T EVEN...
...LET ME SAY I WAS SORRY.
I'M YOUNGER THAN HER.
DOES THAT AUTOMATICALLY TAKE ME OFF HER RADAR?
SO YOU'RE ONE GRADE BELOW HER. BIG DEAL.
MY HEART--UNLIKE YOURS, MIKA-CHAN--ISN'T BUILT FOR REJECTION.
LIKE YOU HAVE ANY IDEA!
THE GUY *I* LIKE MOST NEVER HAS A CLUE.
REALLY?
I HAVE TO...
...GUARD MY HEART CAREFULLY SO NO ONE CAN GET INSIDE AND BREAK IT.

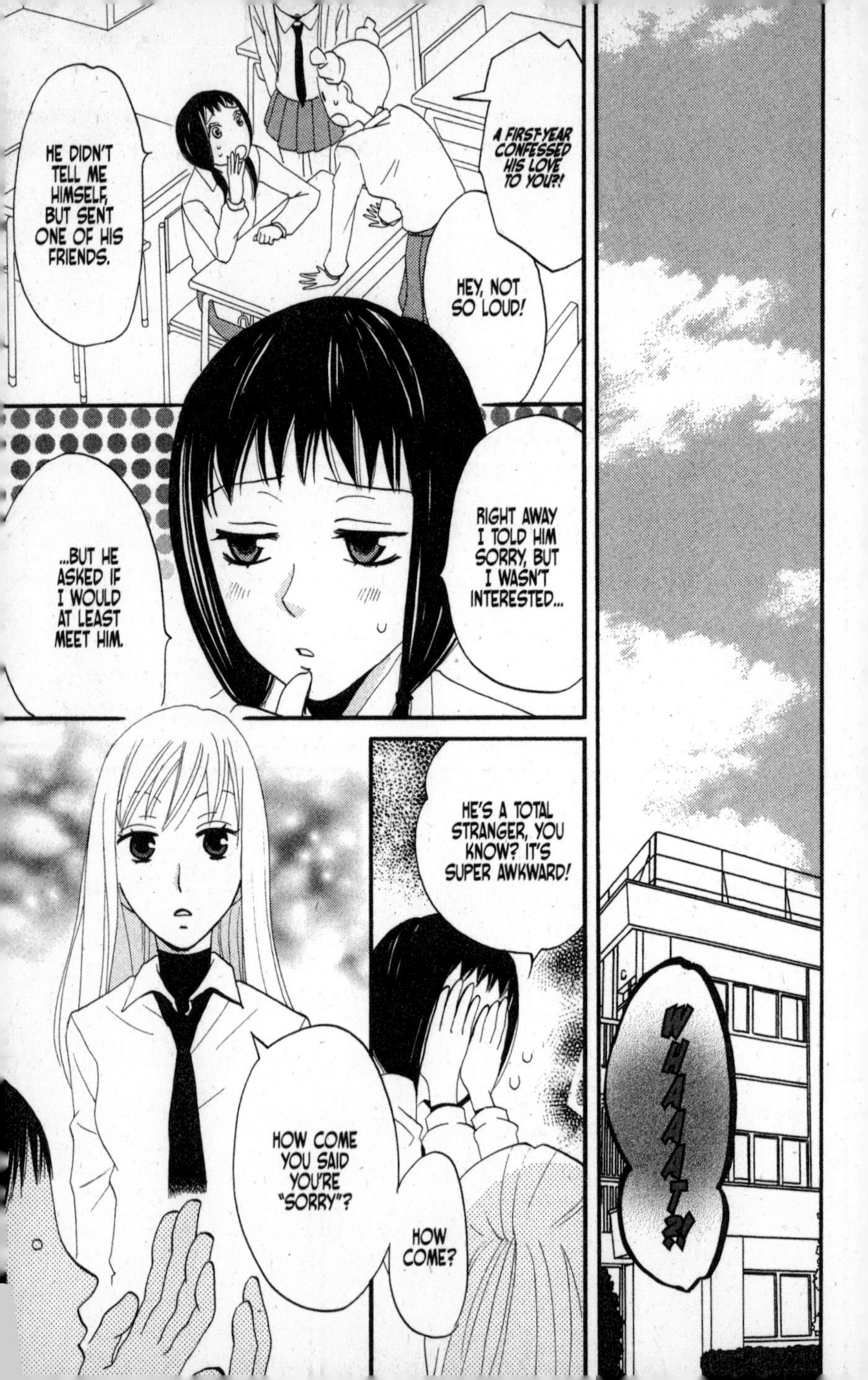
WHAAAT?!
A FIRST-YEAR CONFESSED HIS LOVE TO YOU?!
HEY, NOT SO LOUD!
HE DIDN'T TELL ME HIMSELF, BUT SENT ONE OF HIS FRIENDS.
RIGHT AWAY I TOLD HIM SORRY, BUT I WASN'T INTERESTED...
...BUT HE ASKED IF I WOULD AT LEAST MEET HIM.
HE'S A TOTAL STRANGER, YOU KNOW? IT'S SUPER AWKWARD!
HOW COME?
HOW COME YOU SAID YOU'RE "SORRY"?

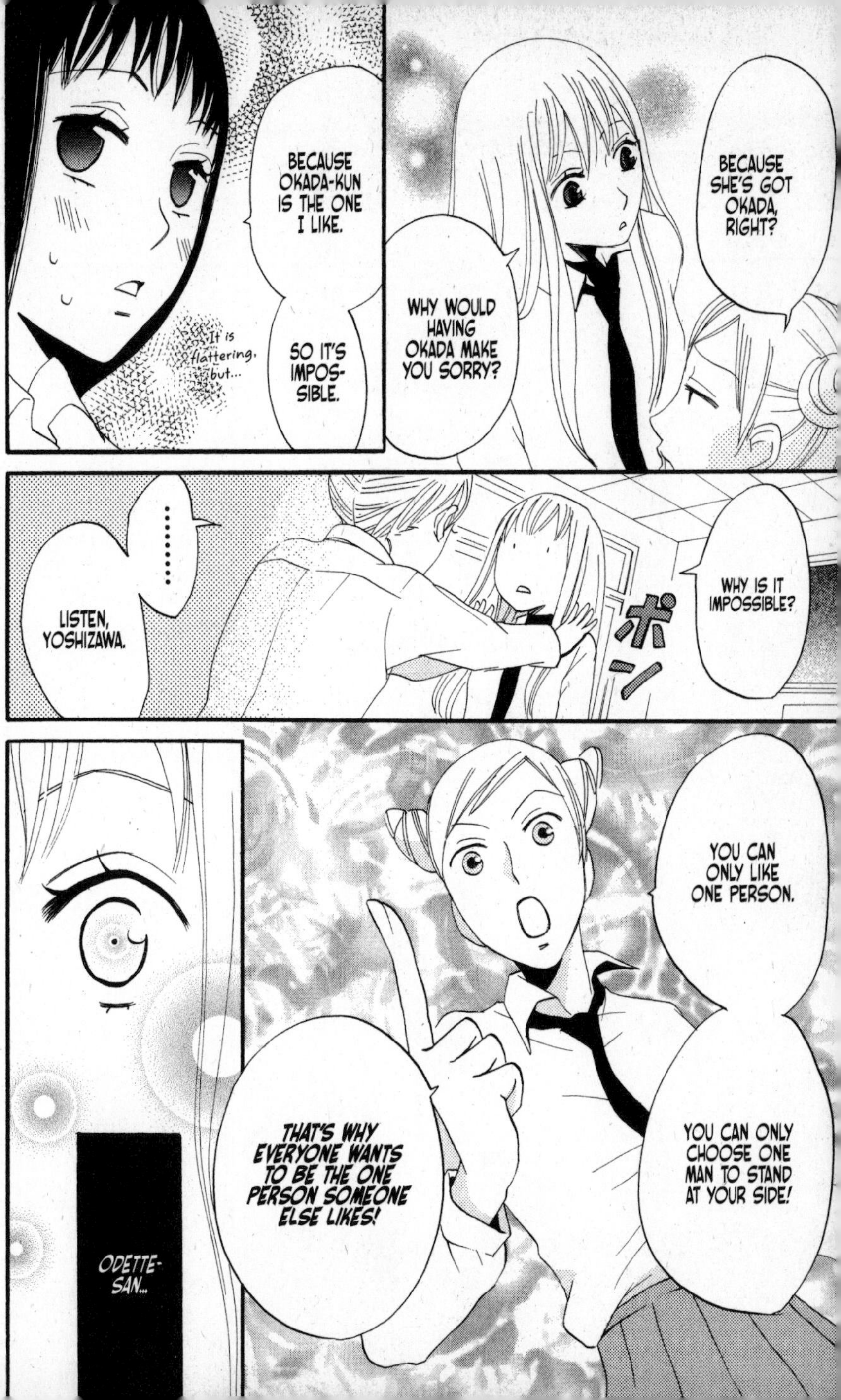
BECAUSE SHE'S GOT OKADA, RIGHT?
WHY WOULD HAVING OKADA MAKE YOU SORRY?
BECAUSE OKADA-KUN IS THE ONE I LIKE.
SO IT'S IMPOSSIBLE.
It is flattering, but...
WHY IS IT IMPOSSIBLE?
ポン
......
LISTEN, YOSHIZAWA.
YOU CAN ONLY LIKE ONE PERSON.
YOU CAN ONLY CHOOSE ONE MAN TO STAND AT YOUR SIDE!
THAT'S WHY EVERYONE WANTS TO BE THE ONE PERSON SOMEONE ELSE LIKES!
ODETTE-SAN...

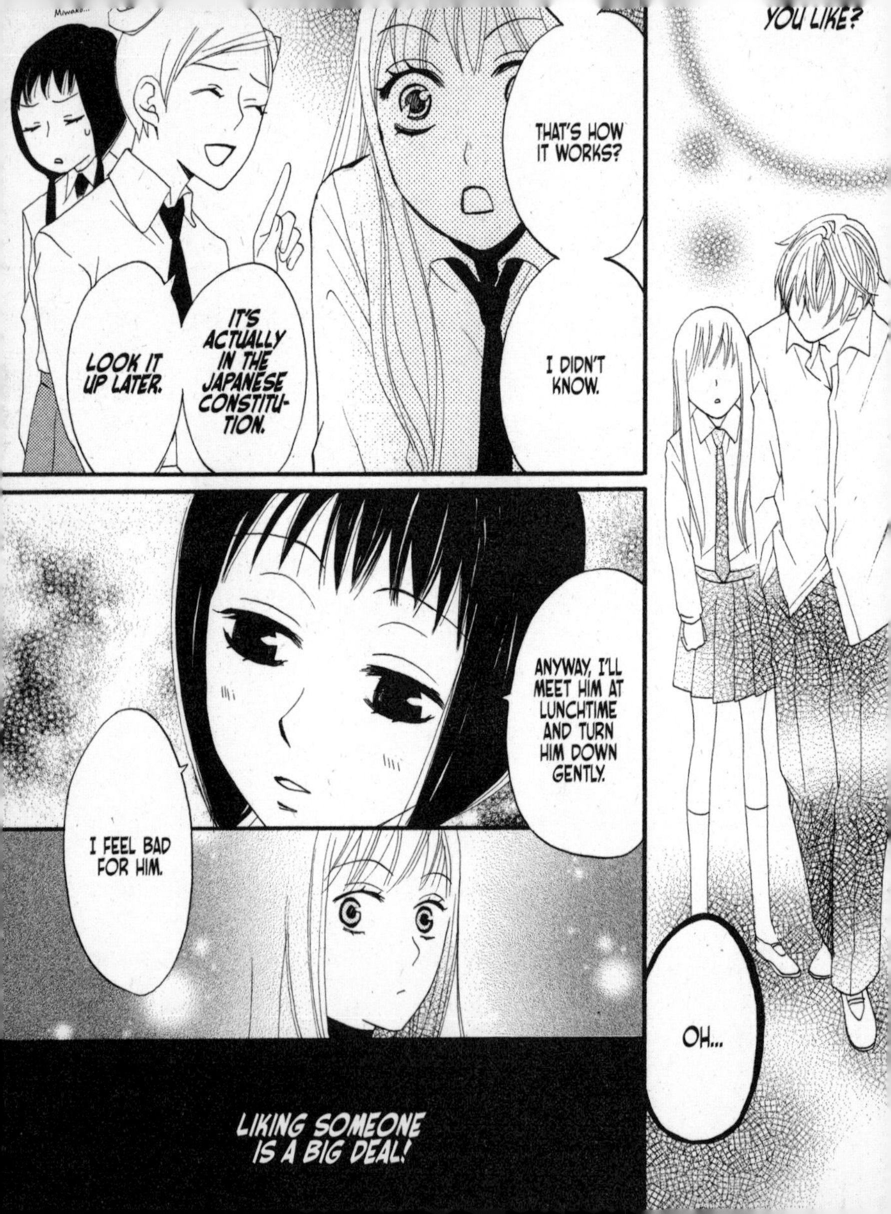
YOU LIKE?
OH...
THAT'S HOW IT WORKS?
I DIDN'T KNOW.
Miwako...
IT'S ACTUALLY IN THE JAPANESE CONSTITUTION.
LOOK IT UP LATER.
ANYWAY, I'LL MEET HIM AT LUNCHTIME AND TURN HIM DOWN GENTLY.
I FEEL BAD FOR HIM.
LIKING SOMEONE IS A BIG DEAL!

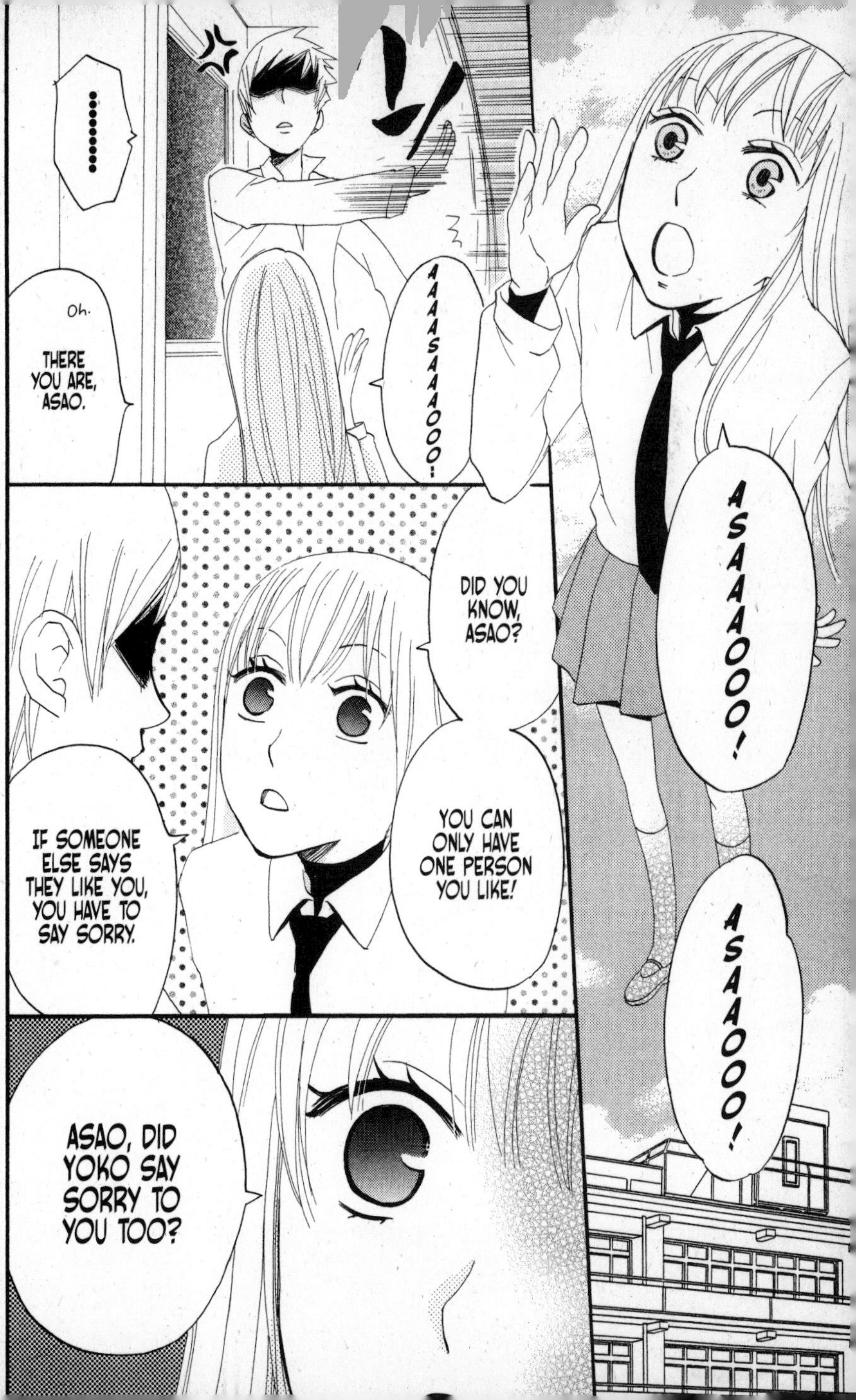
ASAAAAOOO!
ASAAAOOO!
AAAASAAAAOOO!
....
Oh.
THERE YOU ARE, ASAO.
DID YOU KNOW, ASAO?
YOU CAN ONLY HAVE ONE PERSON YOU LIKE!
IF SOMEONE ELSE SAYS THEY LIKE YOU, YOU HAVE TO SAY SORRY.
ASAO, DID YOKO SAY SORRY TO YOU TOO?

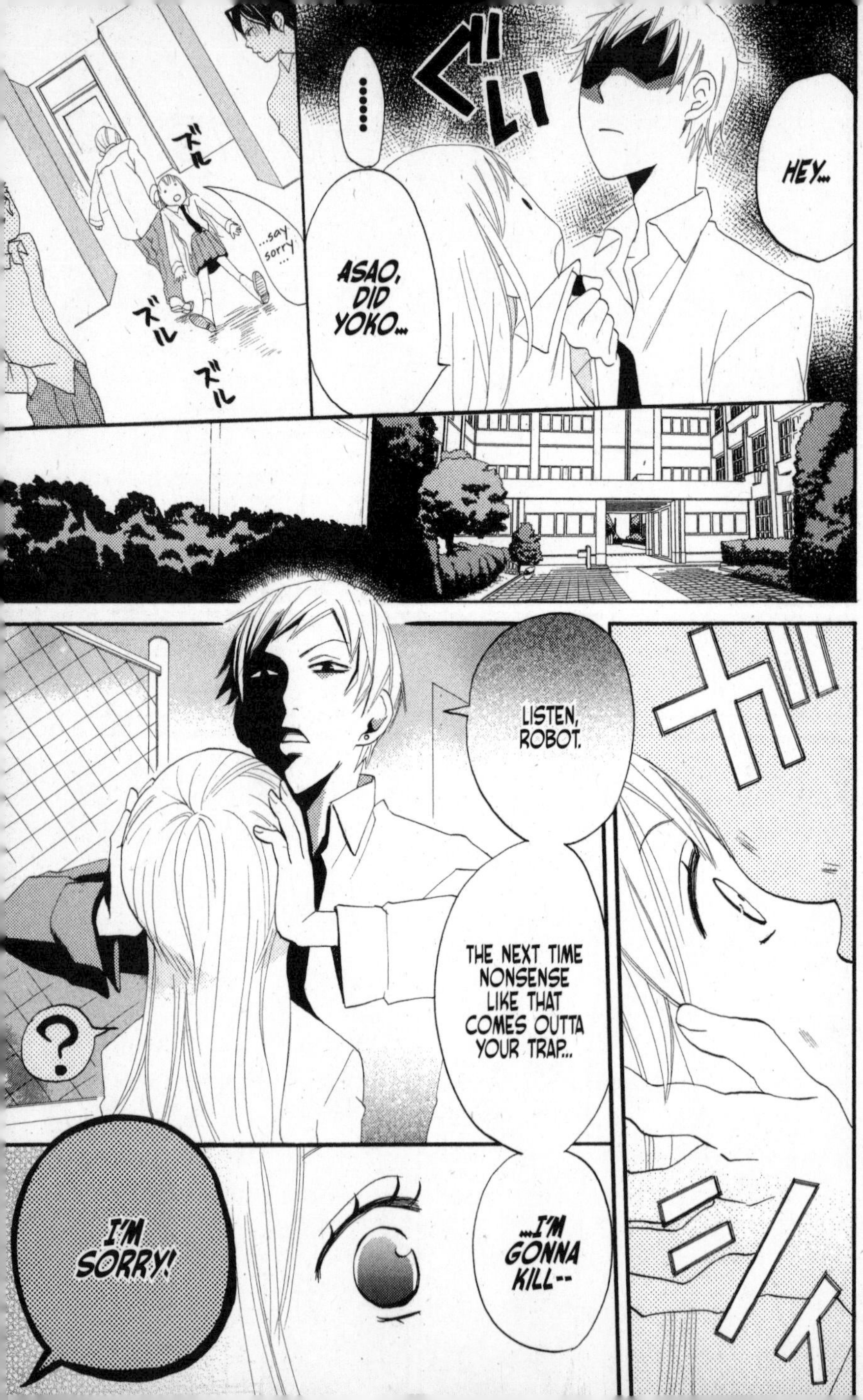
HEY...
ぐい
......
ASAO, DID YOKO...
ズル
...say sorry ...
ズル
ズル
ガッ
LISTEN, ROBOT.
THE NEXT TIME NONSENSE LIKE THAT COMES OUTTA YOUR TRAP...
...I'M GONNA KILL--
?
ミシィ
I'M SORRY!

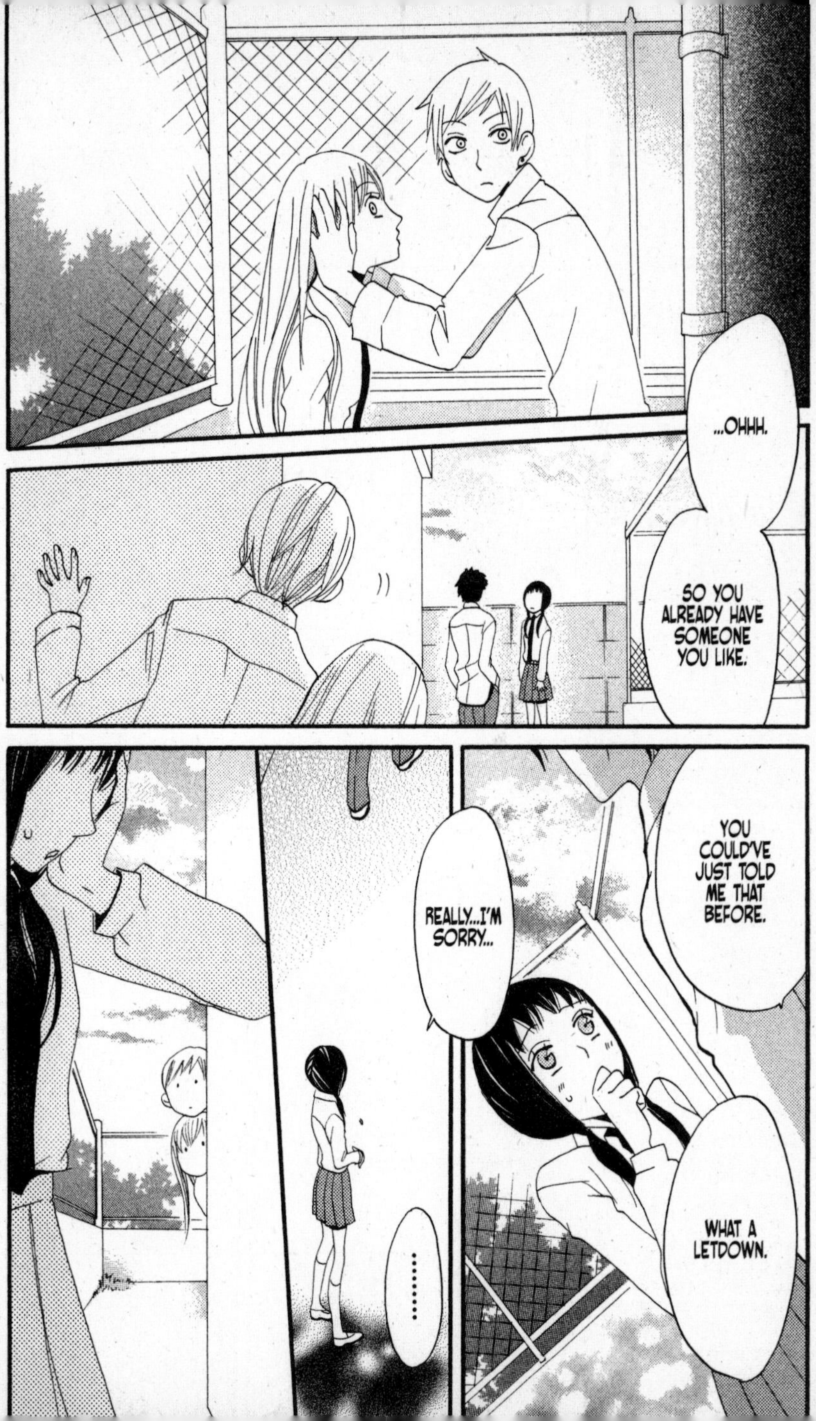
...OHHH.
SO YOU ALREADY HAVE SOMEONE YOU LIKE.
YOU COULD'VE JUST TOLD ME THAT BEFORE.
WHAT A LETDOWN.
REALLY...I'M SORRY...
....

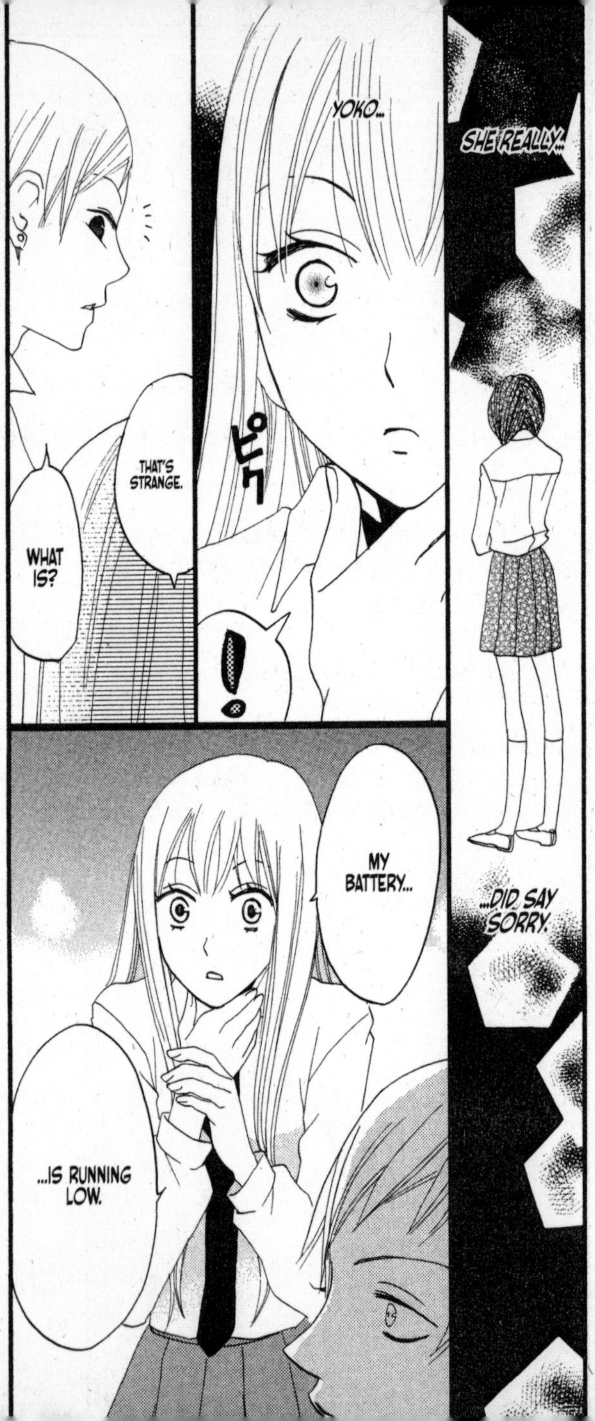
SHE REALLY...
...DID SAY SORRY.
YOKO...
ピク
!
THAT'S STRANGE.
WHAT IS?
MY BATTERY...
...IS RUNNING LOW.

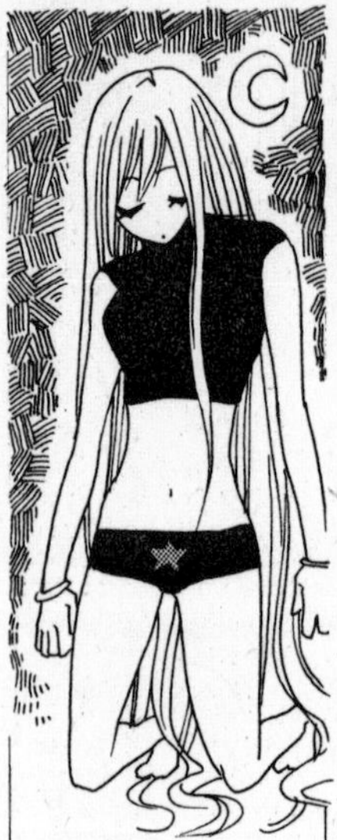

Recently, I've started shopping online more often. Like for cat food or DVDs or books. And I've ordered some art supplies online for the first time--I'm waiting for them to arrive. Wow, I'm excited! I wanted a lightbox...

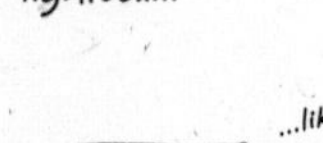
...like this...

...but they didn't have the large size in stock, so I couldn't buy it.

If you use a lightbox for long periods of time, your face gets tan, which is a hassle! But I want one!

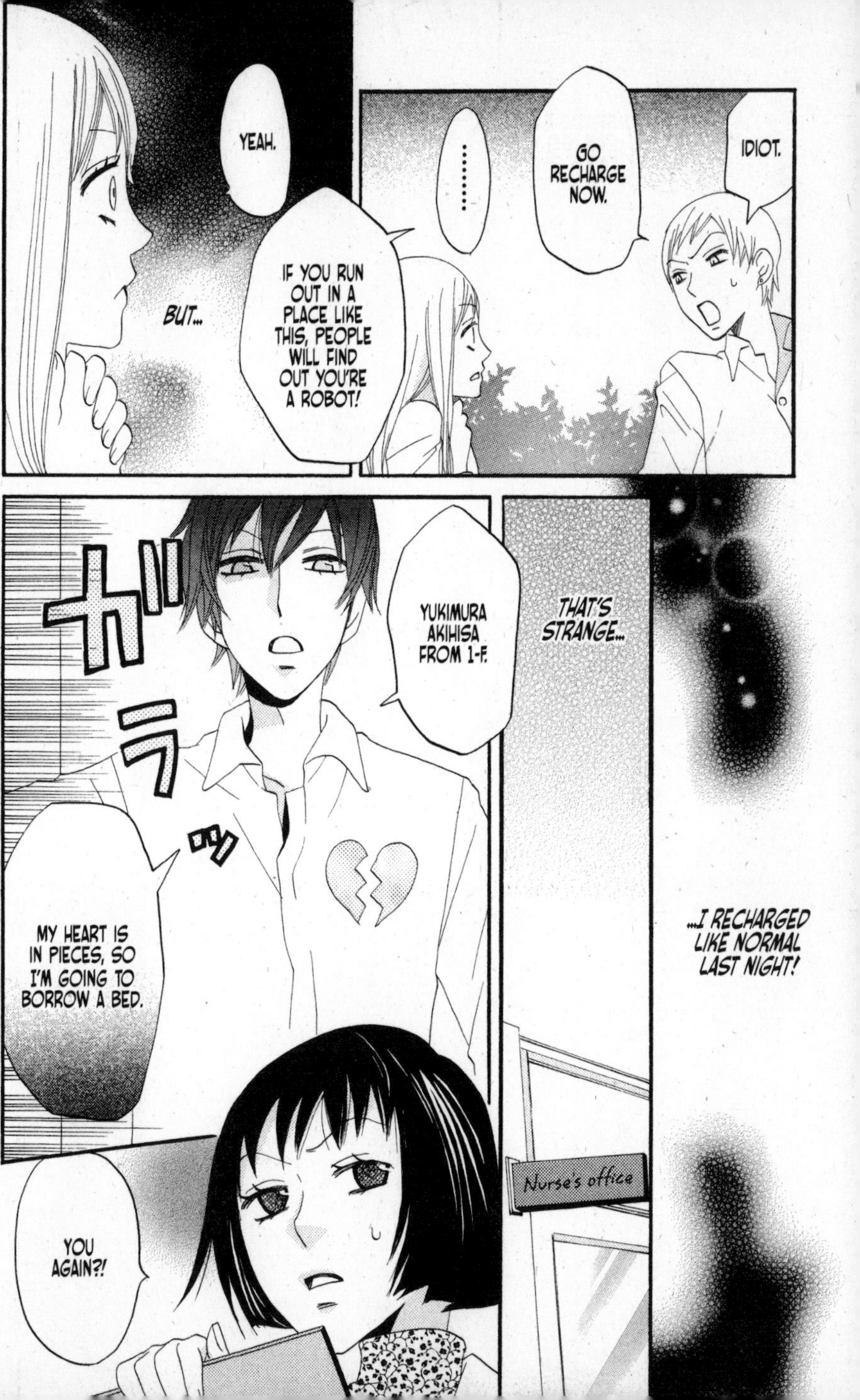
IDIOT.
GO RECHARGE NOW.
....
IF YOU RUN OUT IN A PLACE LIKE THIS, PEOPLE WILL FIND OUT YOU'RE A ROBOT!
YEAH.
BUT...
THAT'S STRANGE...
...I RECHARGED LIKE NORMAL LAST NIGHT!
ガラッ
YUKIMURA AKIHISA FROM 1-F.
MY HEART IS IN PIECES, SO I'M GOING TO BORROW A BED.
Nurse's office
YOU AGAIN?!

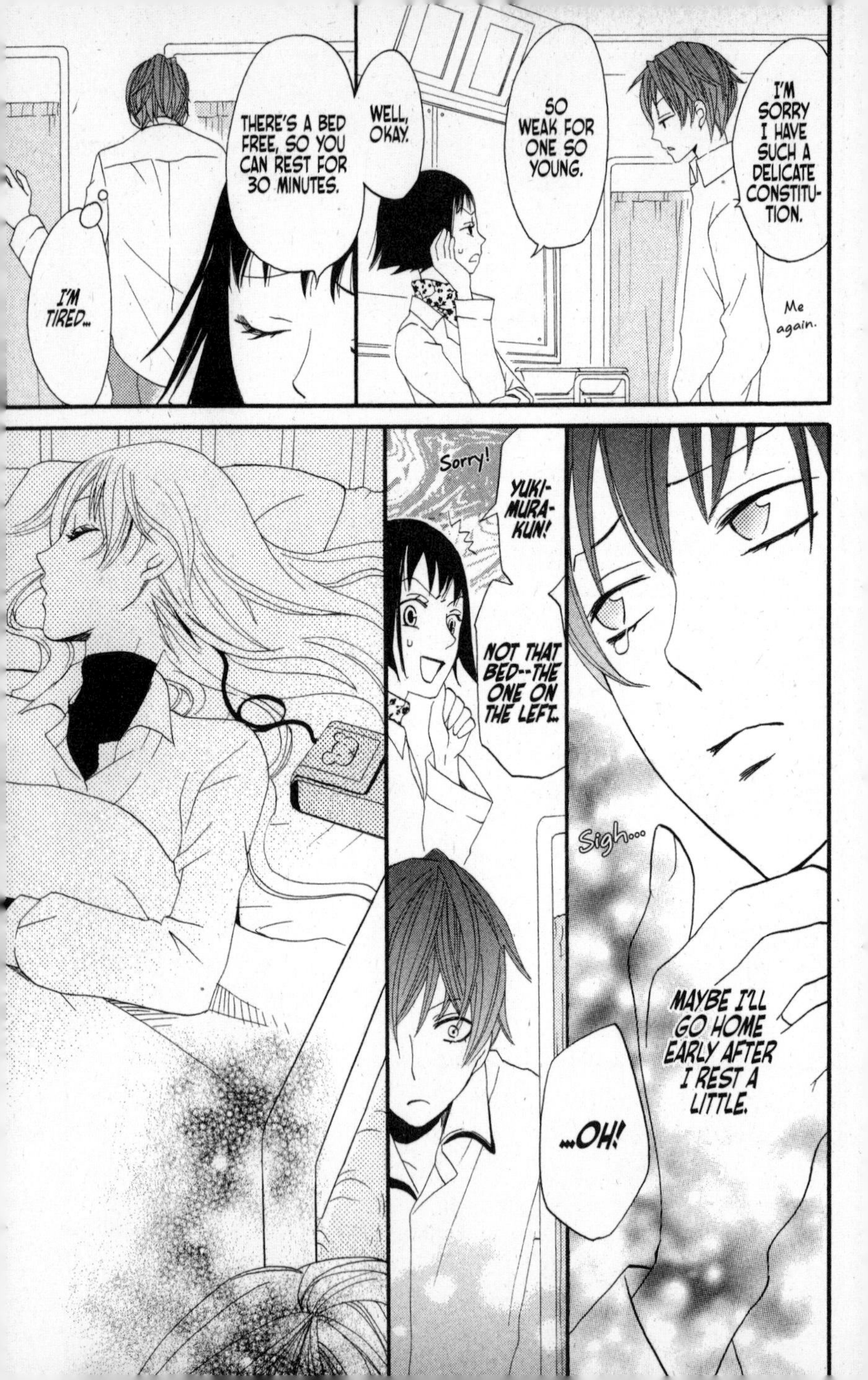
I'M SORRY I HAVE SUCH A DELICATE CONSTITUTION.
Me again.
SO WEAK FOR ONE SO YOUNG.
WELL, OKAY.
THERE'S A BED FREE, SO YOU CAN REST FOR 30 MINUTES.
I'M TIRED...
Sigh...
MAYBE I'LL GO HOME EARLY AFTER I REST A LITTLE.
YUKI-MURA-KUN!
Sorry!
NOT THAT BED--THE ONE ON THE LEFT..
...OH!

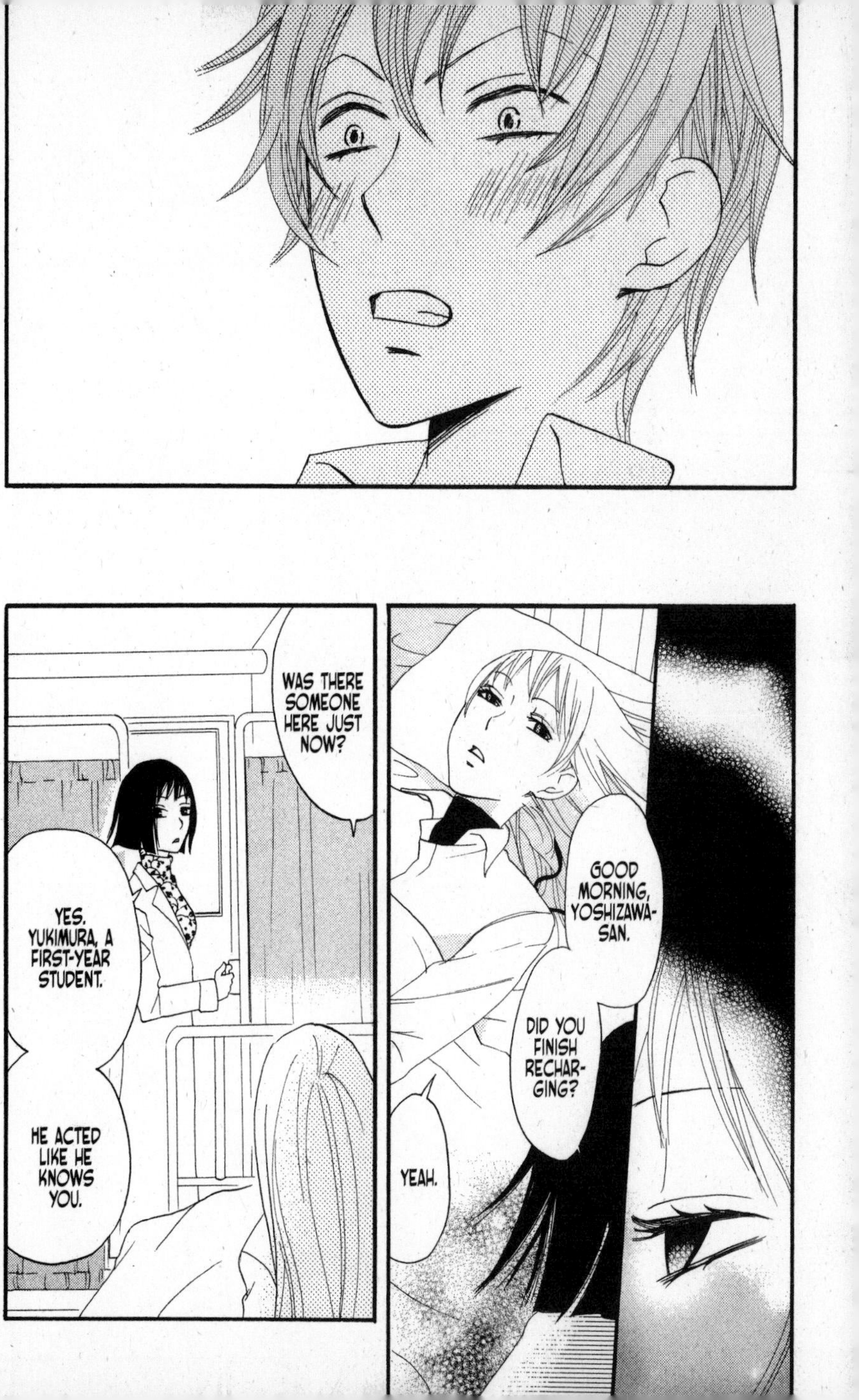
GOOD MORNING, YOSHIZAWA-SAN.
DID YOU FINISH RECHAR-GING?
YEAH.
WAS THERE SOMEONE HERE JUST NOW?
YES. YUKIMURA, A FIRST-YEAR STUDENT.
HE ACTED LIKE HE KNOWS YOU.

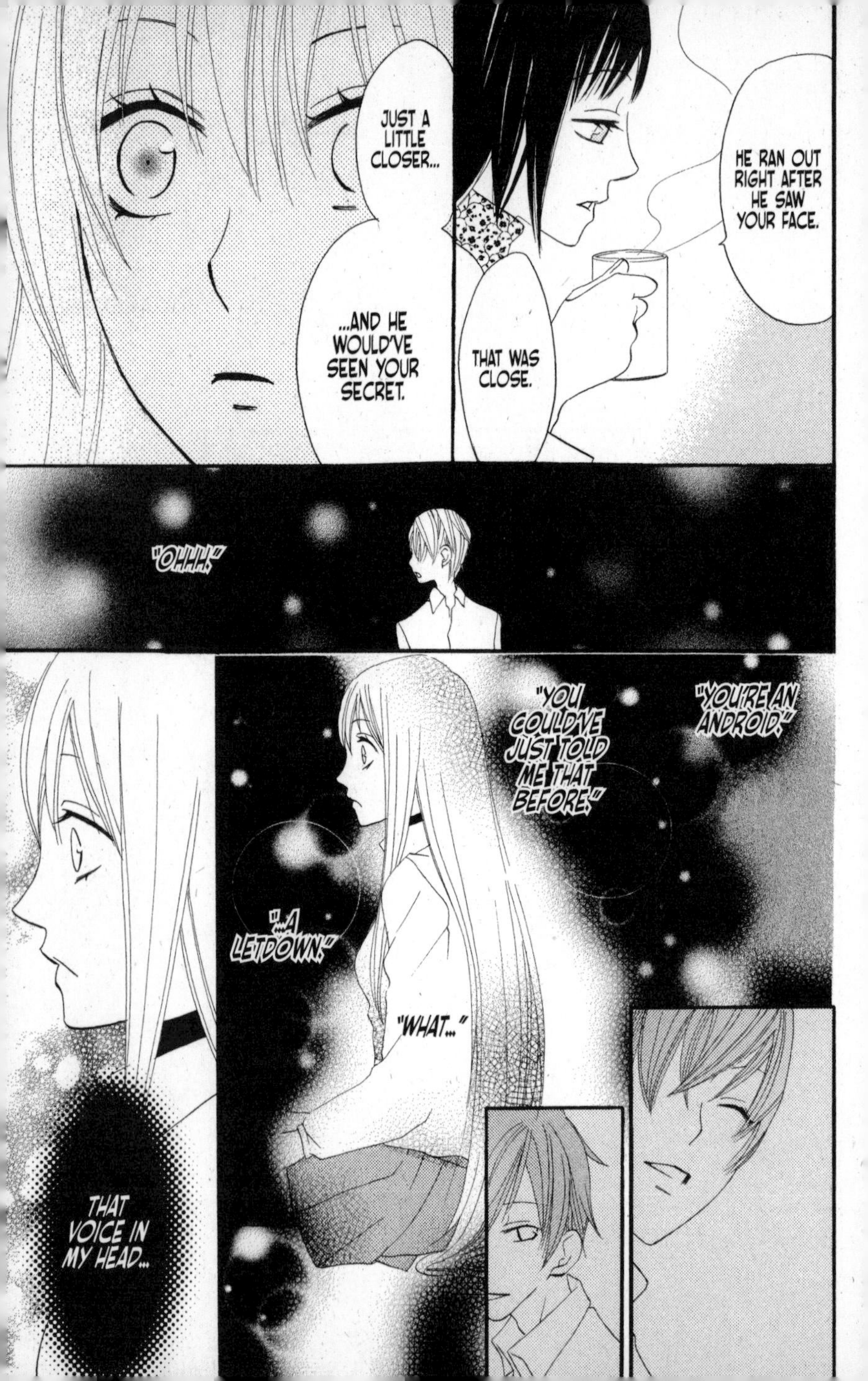
HE RAN OUT RIGHT AFTER HE SAW YOUR FACE.
THAT WAS CLOSE.
JUST A LITTLE CLOSER...
...AND HE WOULD'VE SEEN YOUR SECRET.
"OHHH."
"YOU'RE AN ANDROID."
"YOU COULD'VE JUST TOLD ME THAT BEFORE."
"...A LETDOWN."
"WHAT..."
THAT VOICE IN MY HEAD...

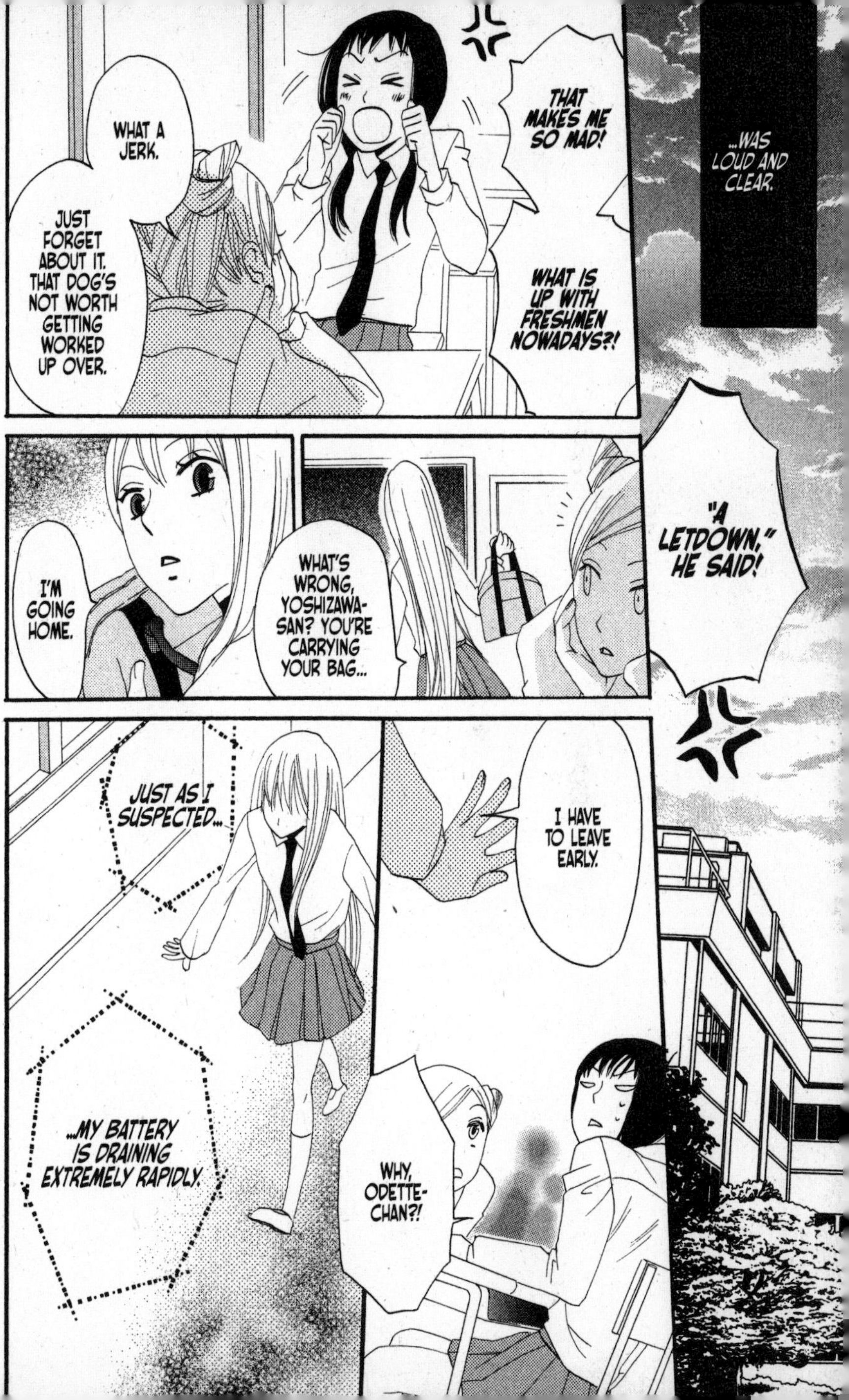
...WAS LOUD AND CLEAR.
"A LETDOWN," HE SAID!
THAT MAKES ME SO MAD!
WHAT IS UP WITH FRESHMEN NOWADAYS?!
WHAT A JERK.
JUST FORGET ABOUT IT. THAT DOG'S NOT WORTH GETTING WORKED UP OVER.
WHAT'S WRONG, YOSHIZAWA-SAN? YOU'RE CARRYING YOUR BAG...
I'M GOING HOME.
I HAVE TO LEAVE EARLY.
WHY, ODETTE-CHAN?!
JUST AS I SUSPECTED...
...MY BATTERY IS DRAINING EXTREMELY RAPIDLY.

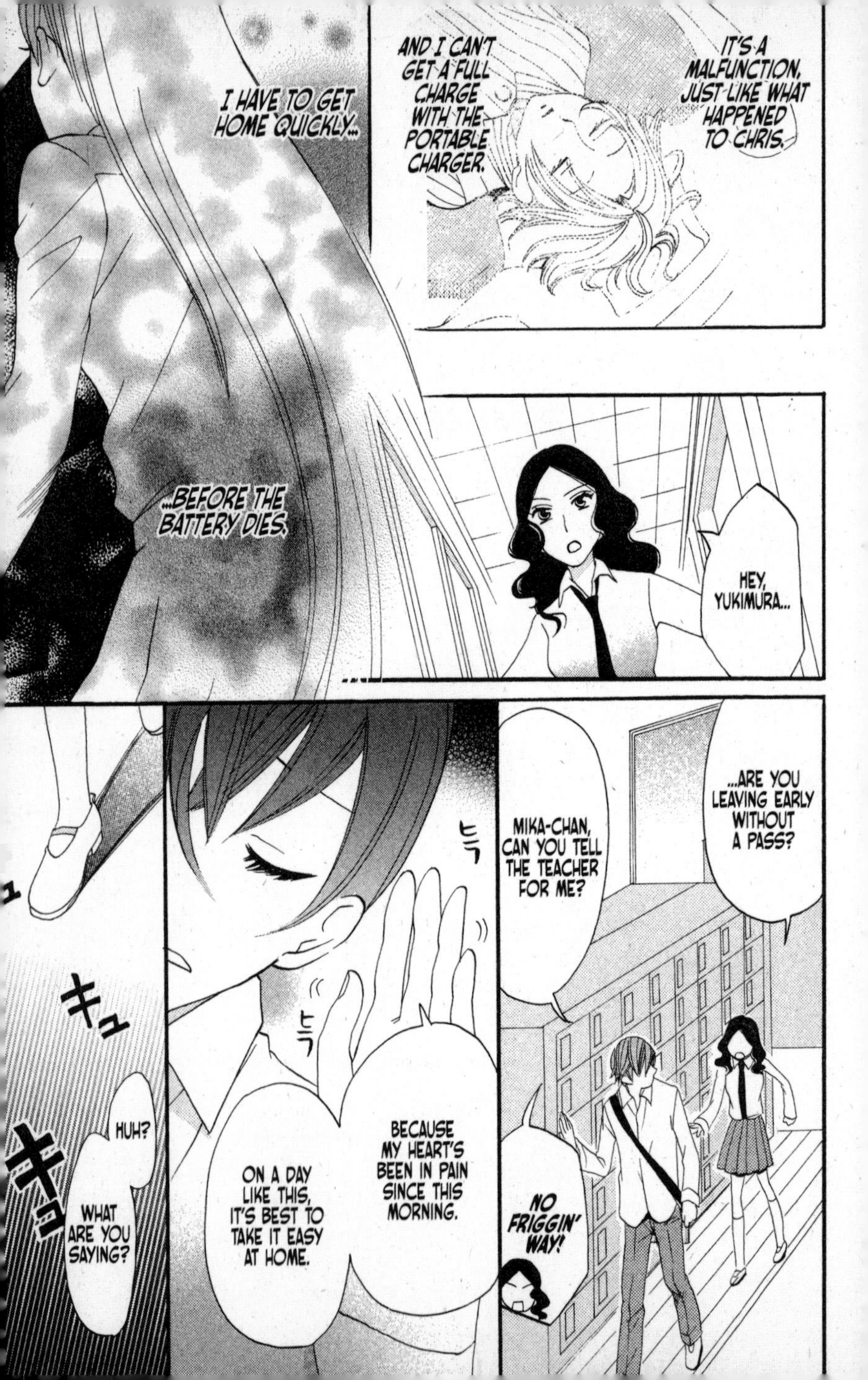
IT'S A MALFUNCTION, JUST LIKE WHAT HAPPENED TO CHRIS.
AND I CAN'T GET A FULL CHARGE WITH THE PORTABLE CHARGER.
HEY, YUKIMURA...
I HAVE TO GET HOME QUICKLY...
...BEFORE THE BATTERY DIES.
...ARE YOU LEAVING EARLY WITHOUT A PASS?
MIKA-CHAN, CAN YOU TELL THE TEACHER FOR ME?
NO FRIGGIN' WAY!
ヒラ
ヒラ
BECAUSE MY HEART'S BEEN IN PAIN SINCE THIS MORNING.
ON A DAY LIKE THIS, IT'S BEST TO TAKE IT EASY AT HOME.
キュ
キュ
HUH?
WHAT ARE YOU SAYING?

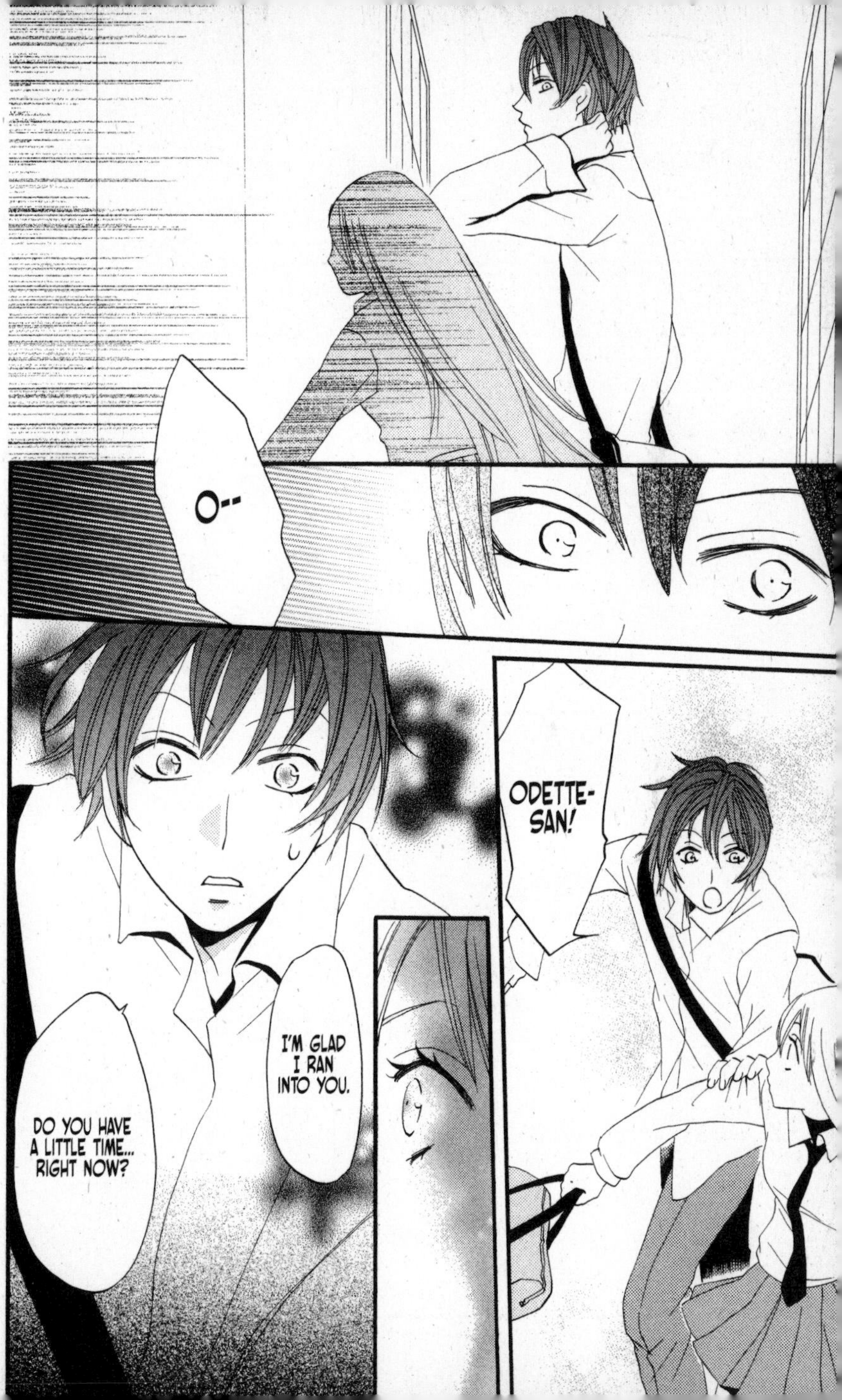
O--
ODETTE-SAN!
I'M GLAD I RAN INTO YOU.
DO YOU HAVE A LITTLE TIME... RIGHT NOW?

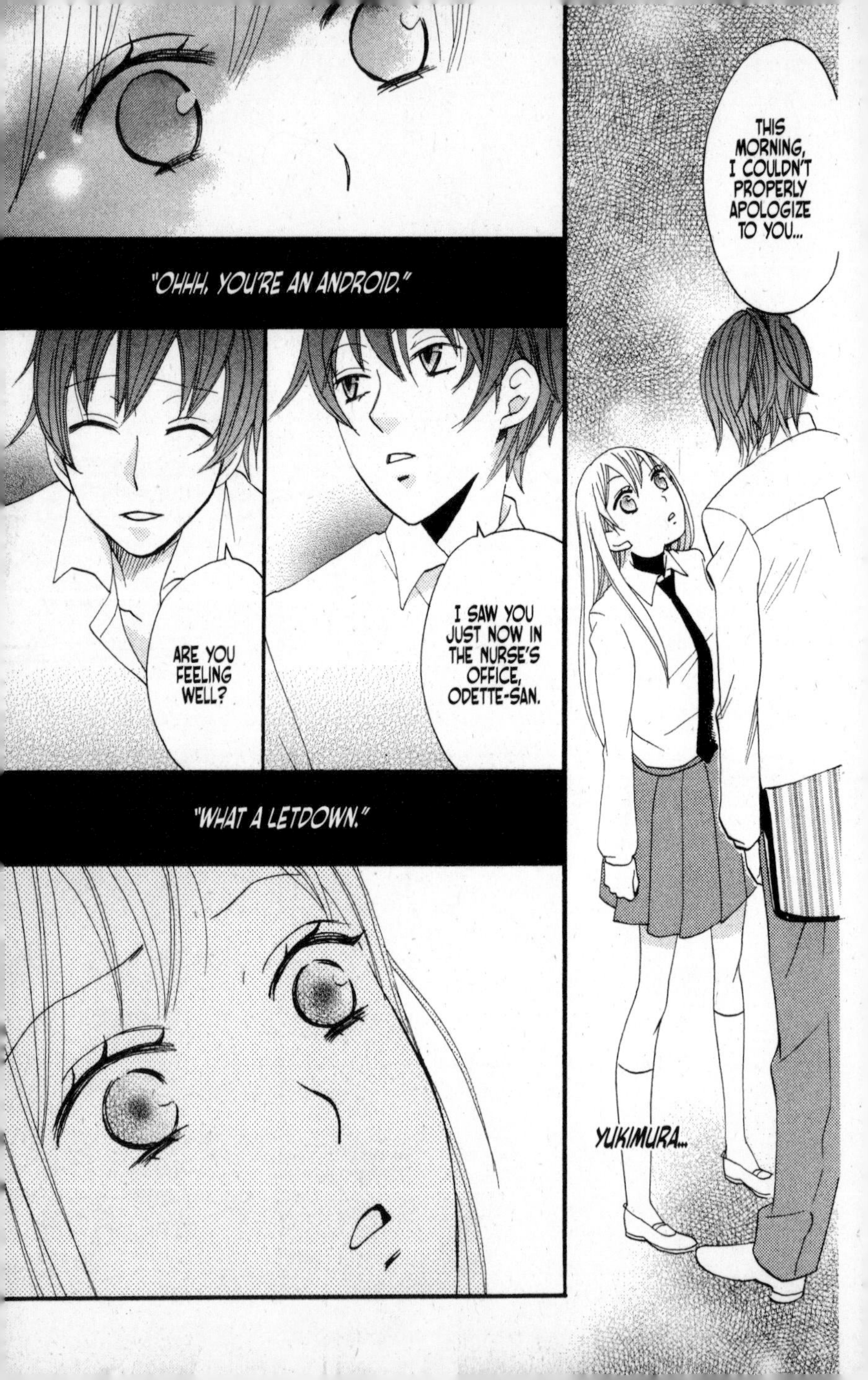
THIS MORNING, I COULDN'T PROPERLY APOLOGIZE TO YOU...
YUKIMURA...
"OHHH, YOU'RE AN ANDROID."
I SAW YOU JUST NOW IN THE NURSE'S OFFICE, ODETTE-SAN.
ARE YOU FEELING WELL?
"WHAT A LETDOWN."

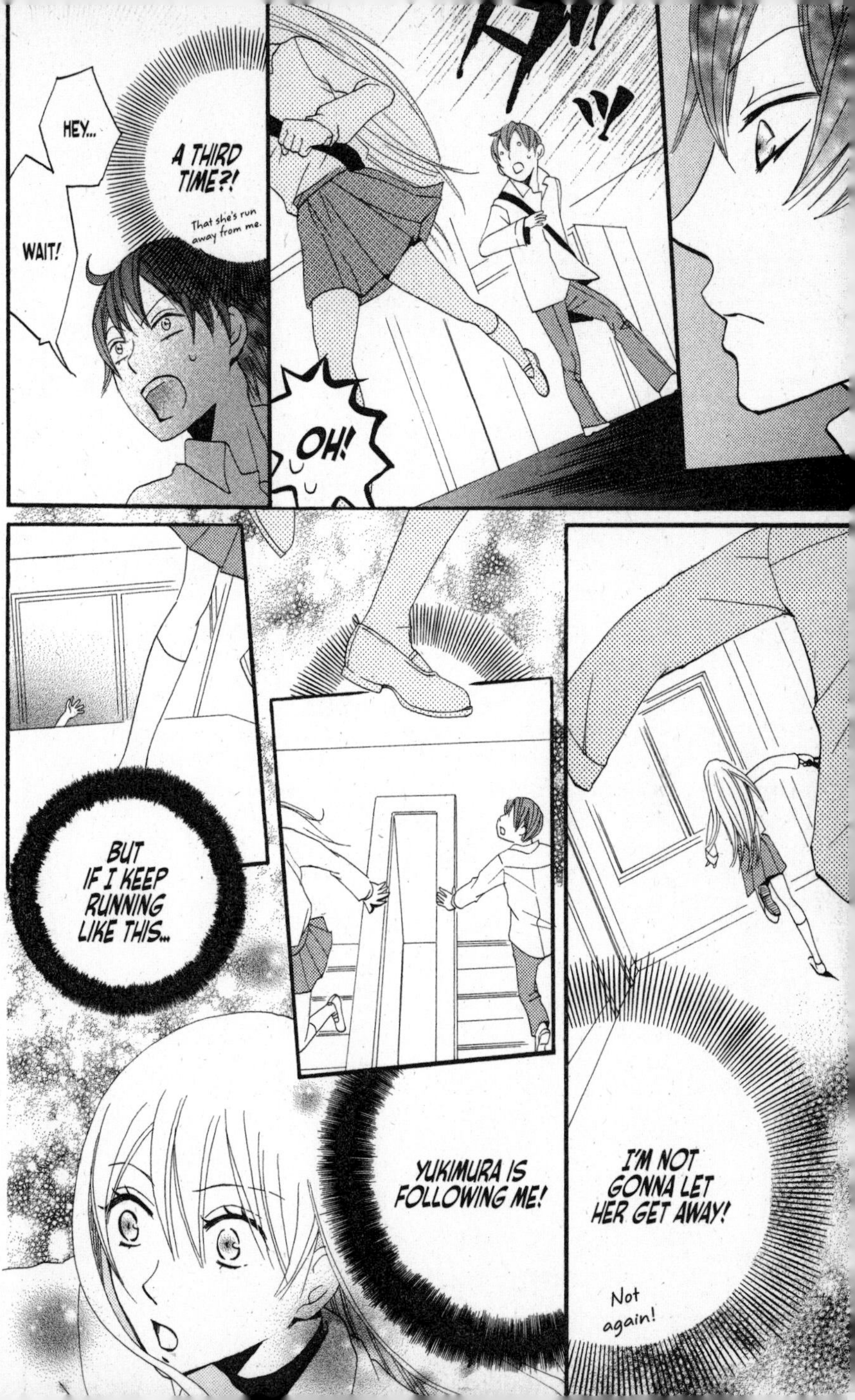
OH!
A THIRD TIME?!
That she's run away from me.
HEY...
WAIT!
I'M NOT GONNA LET HER GET AWAY!
Not again!
BUT IF I KEEP RUNNING LIKE THIS...
YUKIMURA IS FOLLOWING ME!

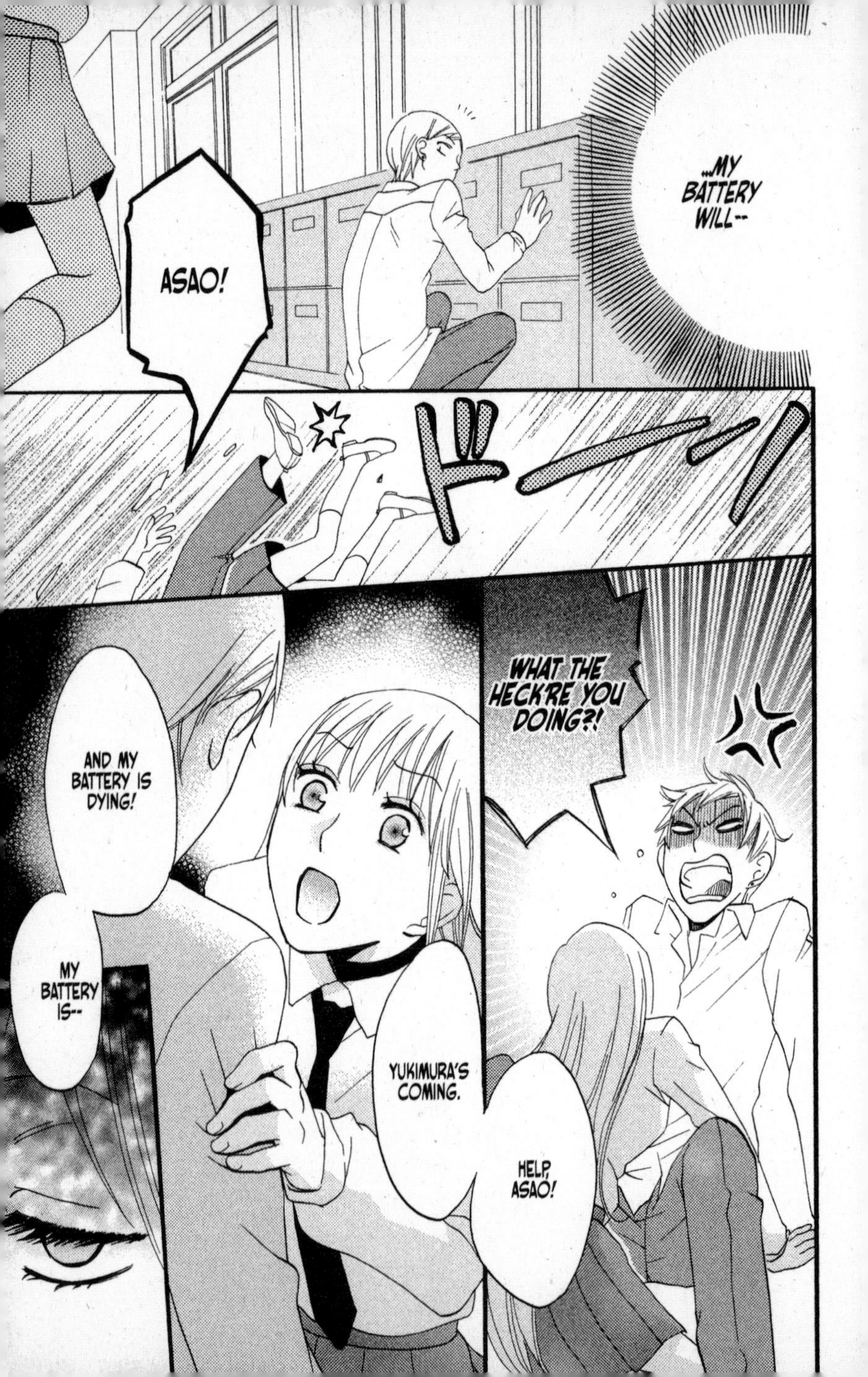
...MY BATTERY WILL--
ASAO!
ドーッ
WHAT THE HECK'RE YOU DOING?!
HELP, ASAO!
YUKIMURA'S COMING.
AND MY BATTERY IS DYING!
MY BATTERY IS--

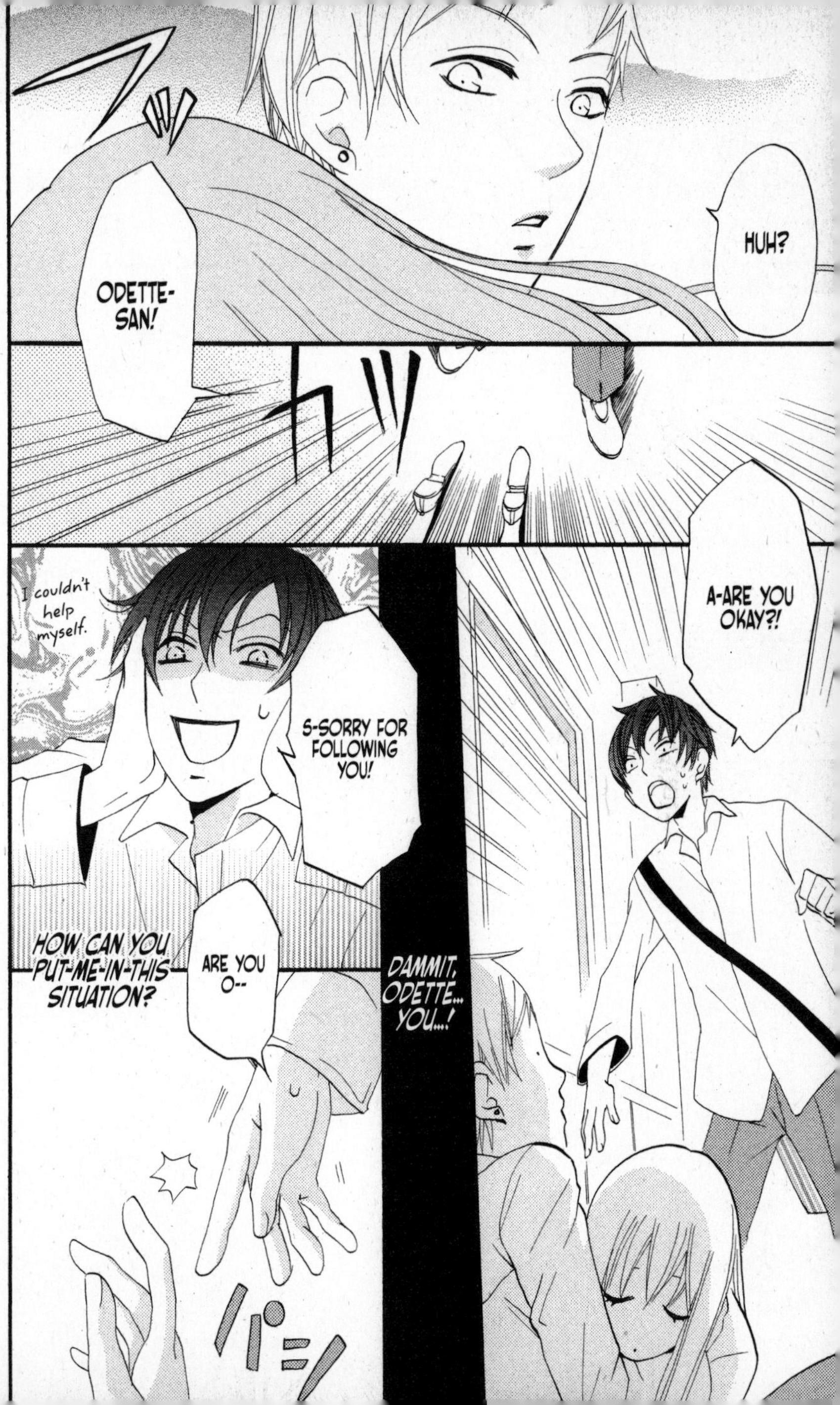
HUH?
ODETTE-SAN!
A-ARE YOU OKAY?!
S-SORRY FOR FOLLOWING YOU!
I couldn't help myself.
DAMMIT, ODETTE... YOU...!
ARE YOU O--
HOW CAN YOU PUT-ME-IN-THIS SITUATION?

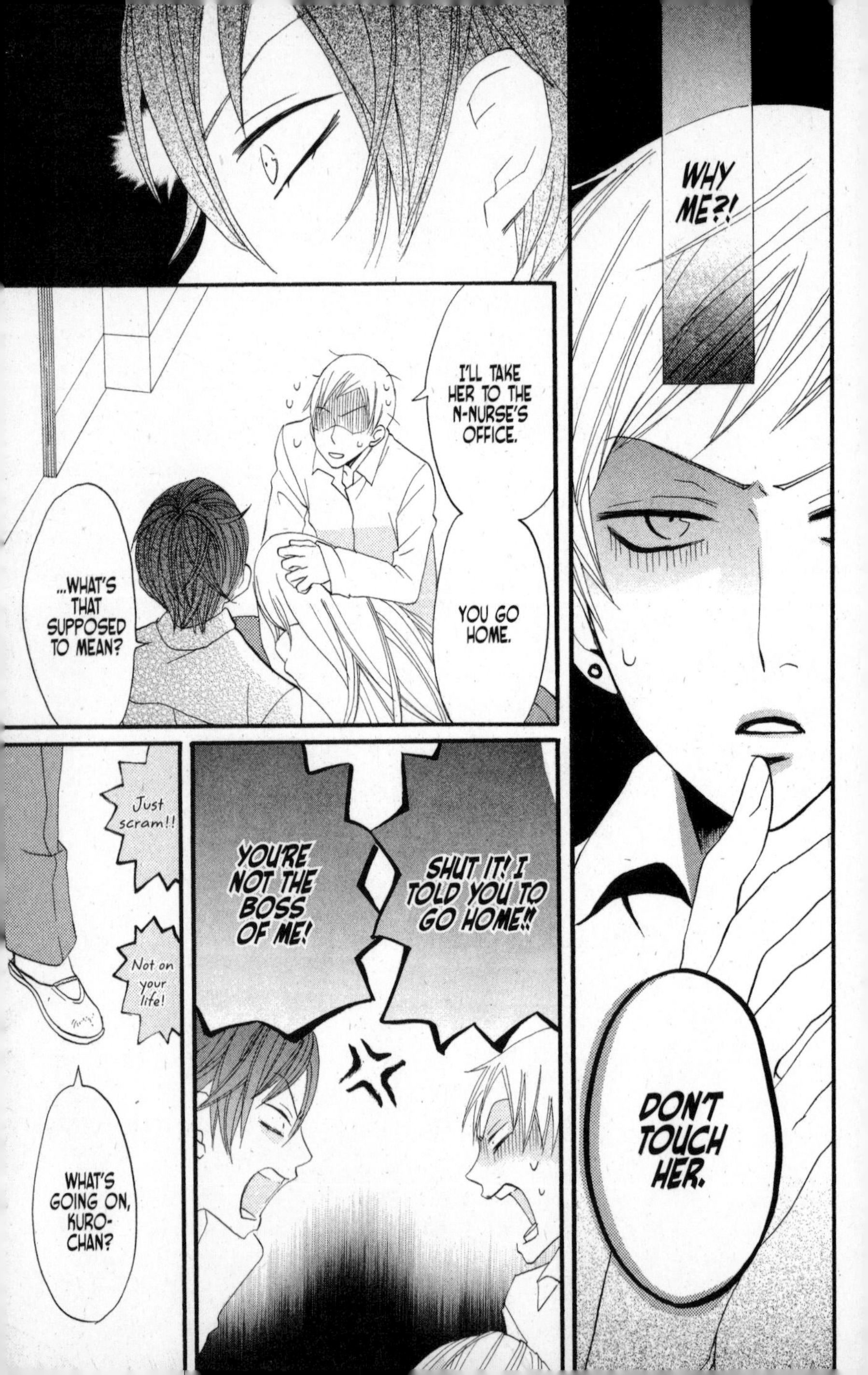
WHY ME?!
DON'T TOUCH HER.
I'LL TAKE HER TO THE N-NURSE'S OFFICE.
YOU GO HOME.
...WHAT'S THAT SUPPOSED TO MEAN?
SHUT IT! I TOLD YOU TO GO HOME!!
YOU'RE NOT THE BOSS OF ME!
Just scram!!
Not on your life!
WHAT'S GOING ON, KURO-CHAN?

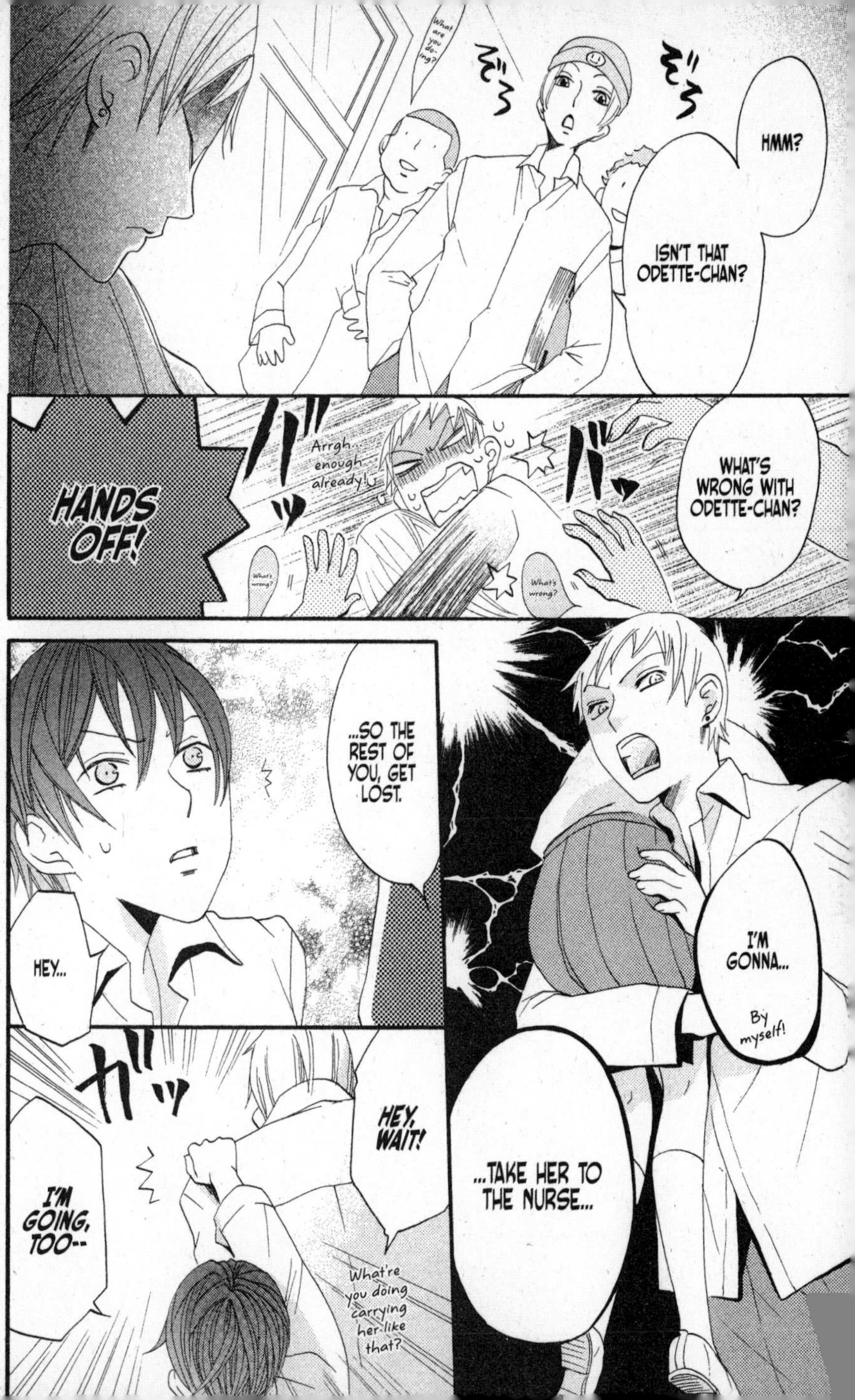
ぞろ
HMM?
ISN'T THAT ODETTE-CHAN?
ぞろ
What are you doing?
WHAT'S WRONG WITH ODETTE-CHAN?
バッ
What's wrong?
What's wrong?
Arrgh... enough already!
バッ
HANDS OFF!
I'M GONNA...
By myself!
...TAKE HER TO THE NURSE...
...SO THE REST OF YOU, GET LOST.
HEY...
HEY, WAIT!
What're you doing carrying her like that?
ガッ
I'M GOING, TOO--

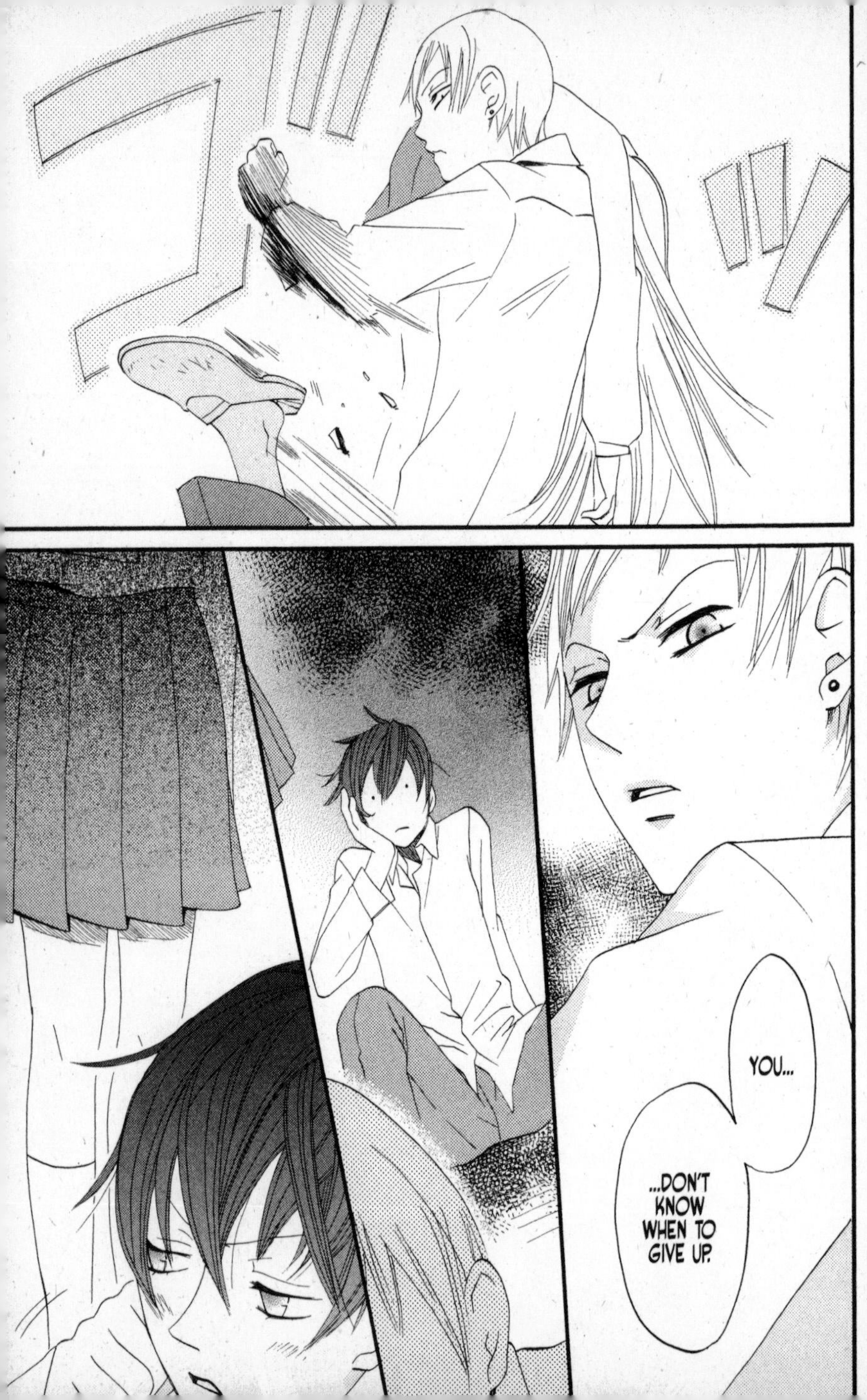
YOU...
...DON'T KNOW WHEN TO GIVE UP.

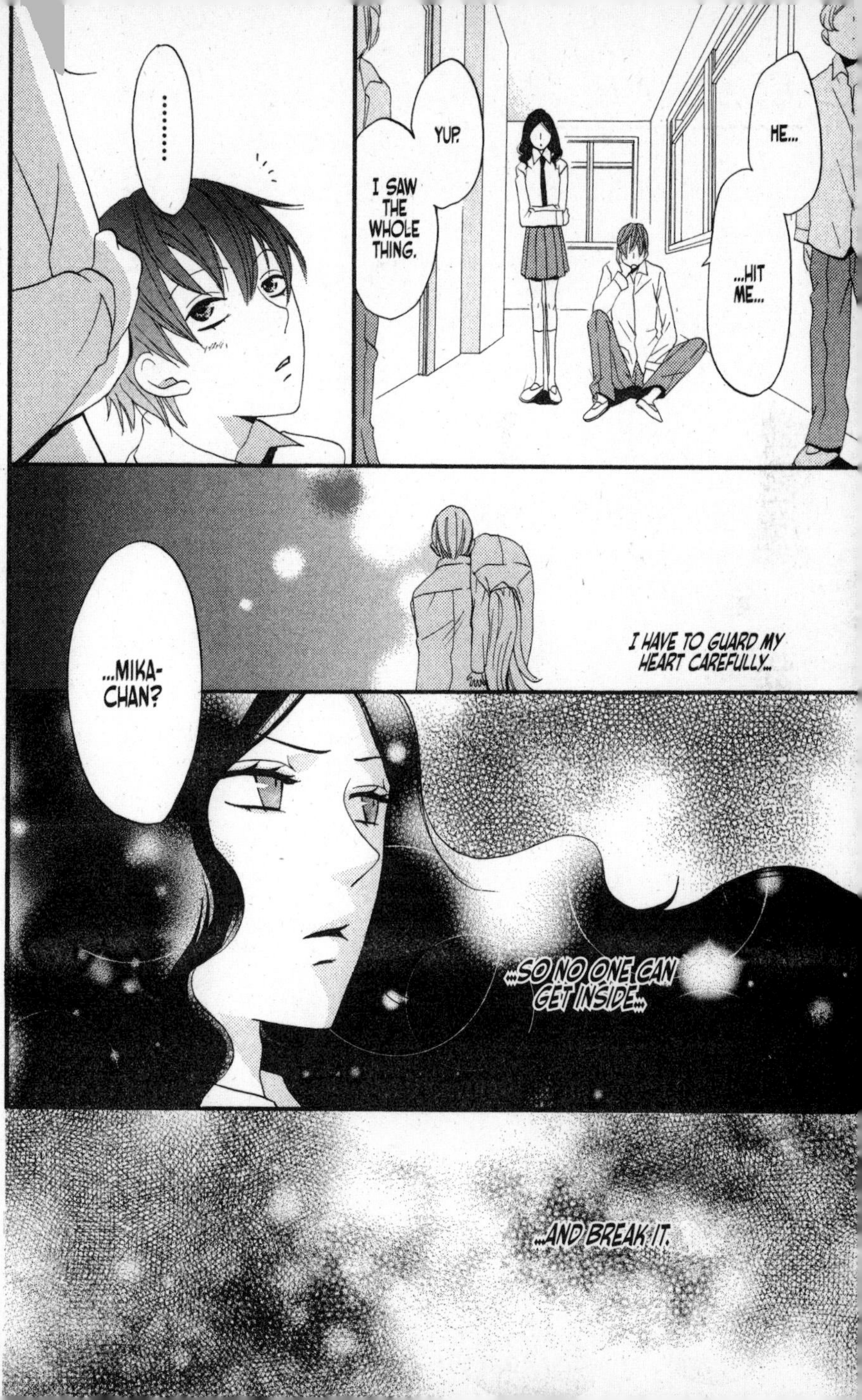
HE...
...HIT ME...
YUP.
I SAW THE WHOLE THING.
....
I HAVE TO GUARD MY HEART CAREFULLY...
...MIKA-CHAN?
...SO NO ONE CAN GET INSIDE...
...AND BREAK IT.

Chapter 15

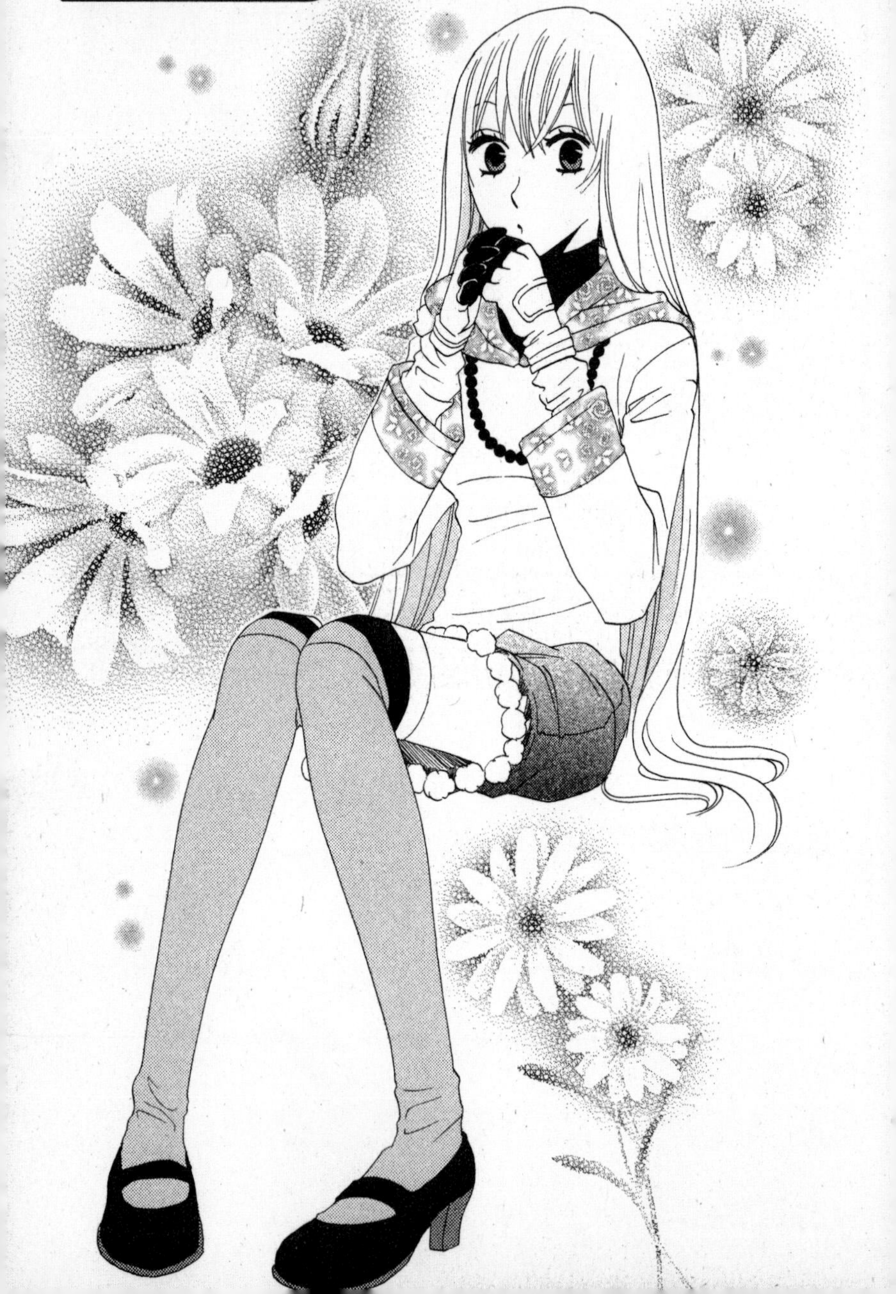

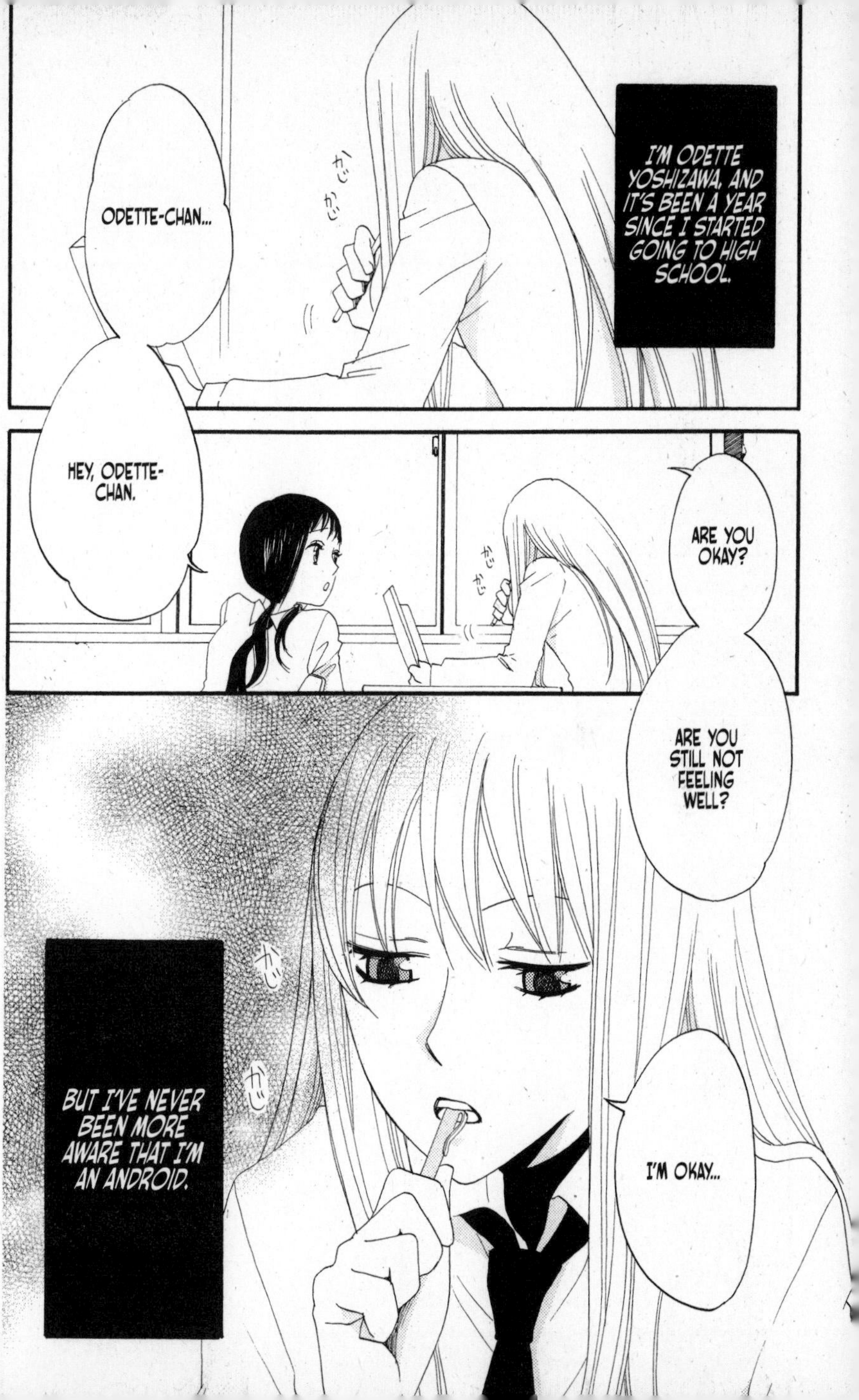
I'M ODETTE YOSHIZAWA, AND IT'S BEEN A YEAR SINCE I STARTED GOING TO HIGH SCHOOL.
かじかじ
ODETTE-CHAN...
HEY, ODETTE-CHAN.
かじかじ
ARE YOU OKAY?
ARE YOU STILL NOT FEELING WELL?
I'M OKAY...
かじかじ
BUT I'VE NEVER BEEN MORE AWARE THAT I'M AN ANDROID.

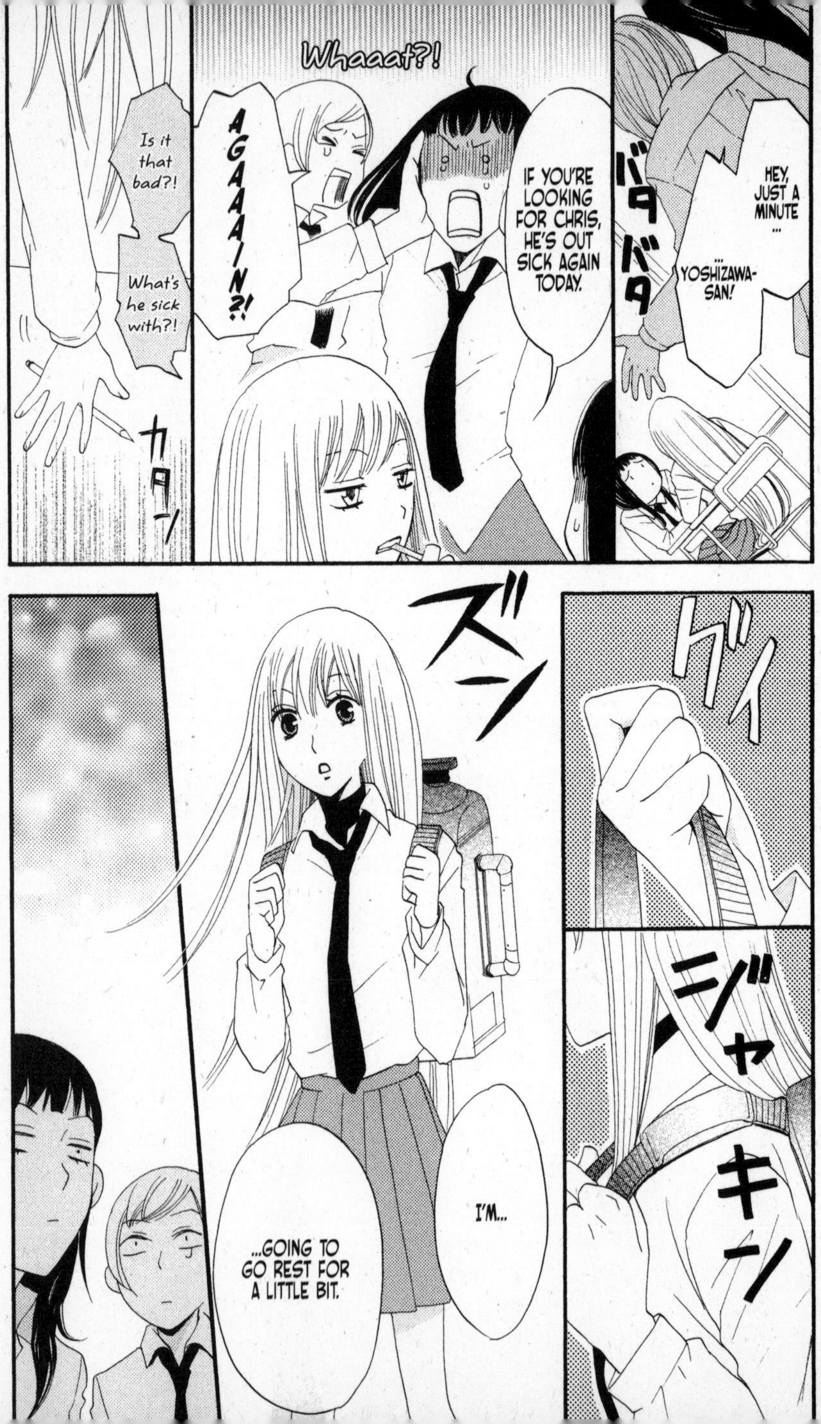
HEY, JUST A MINUTE ...
...YOSHIZAWA-SAN!
バタバタ
IF YOU'RE LOOKING FOR CHRIS, HE'S OUT SICK AGAIN TODAY.
Whaaat?!
AGAAAAIN?!
Is it that bad?!
What's he sick with?!
カタン
グイ
ジャキーン
ズーン
I'M...
...GOING TO GO REST FOR A LITTLE BIT.

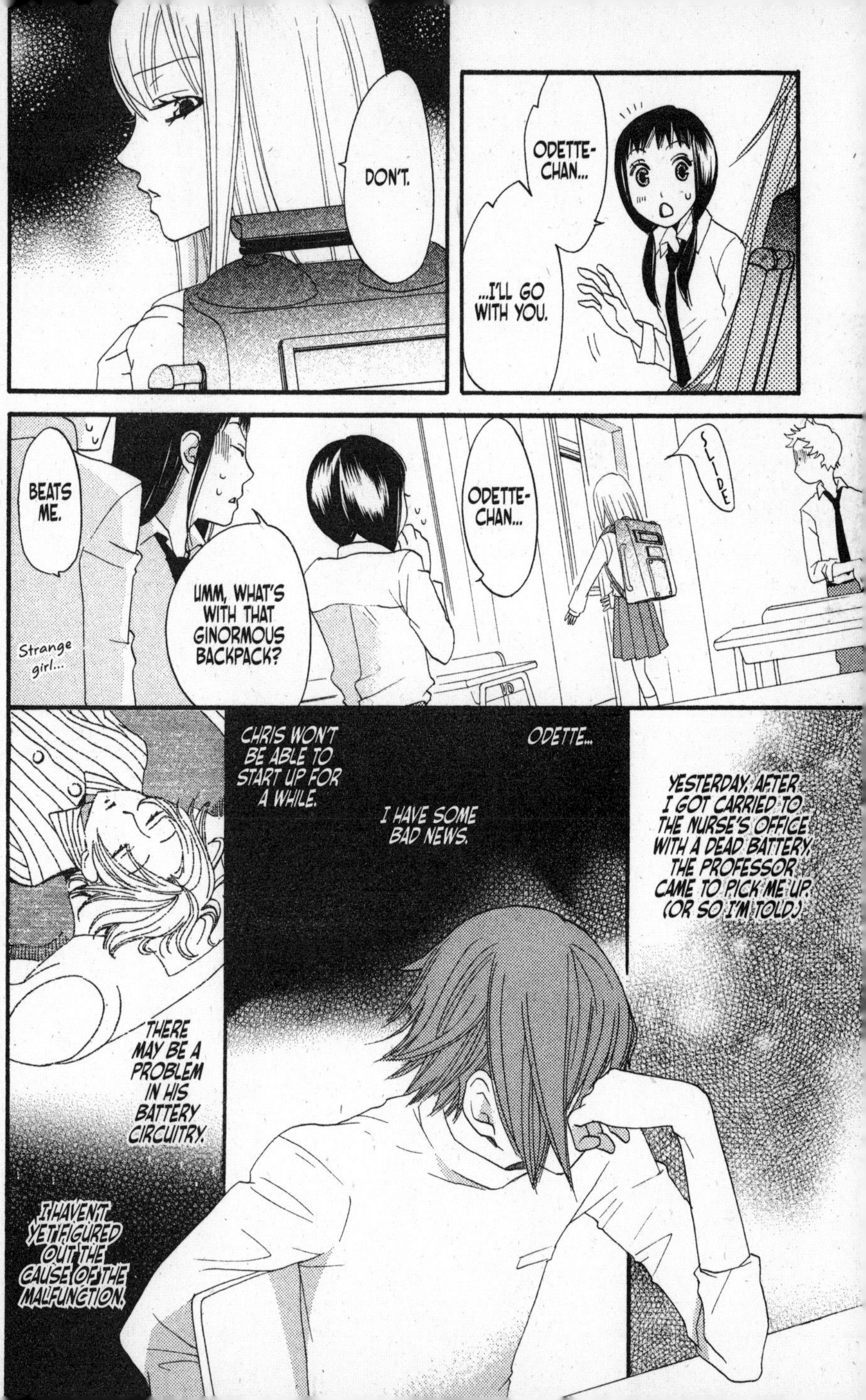
ODETTE-CHAN...
...I'LL GO WITH YOU.
DON'T.
SLIDE
ODETTE-CHAN...
UMM, WHAT'S WITH THAT GINORMOUS BACKPACK?
BEATS ME.
Strange girl...
YESTERDAY, AFTER I GOT CARRIED TO THE NURSE'S OFFICE WITH A DEAD BATTERY, THE PROFESSOR CAME TO PICK ME UP. (OR SO I'M TOLD.)
ODETTE...
I HAVE SOME BAD NEWS.
CHRIS WON'T BE ABLE TO START UP FOR A WHILE.
THERE MAY BE A PROBLEM IN HIS BATTERY CIRCUITRY.
I HAVEN'T YET FIGURED OUT THE CAUSE OF THE MALFUNCTION.

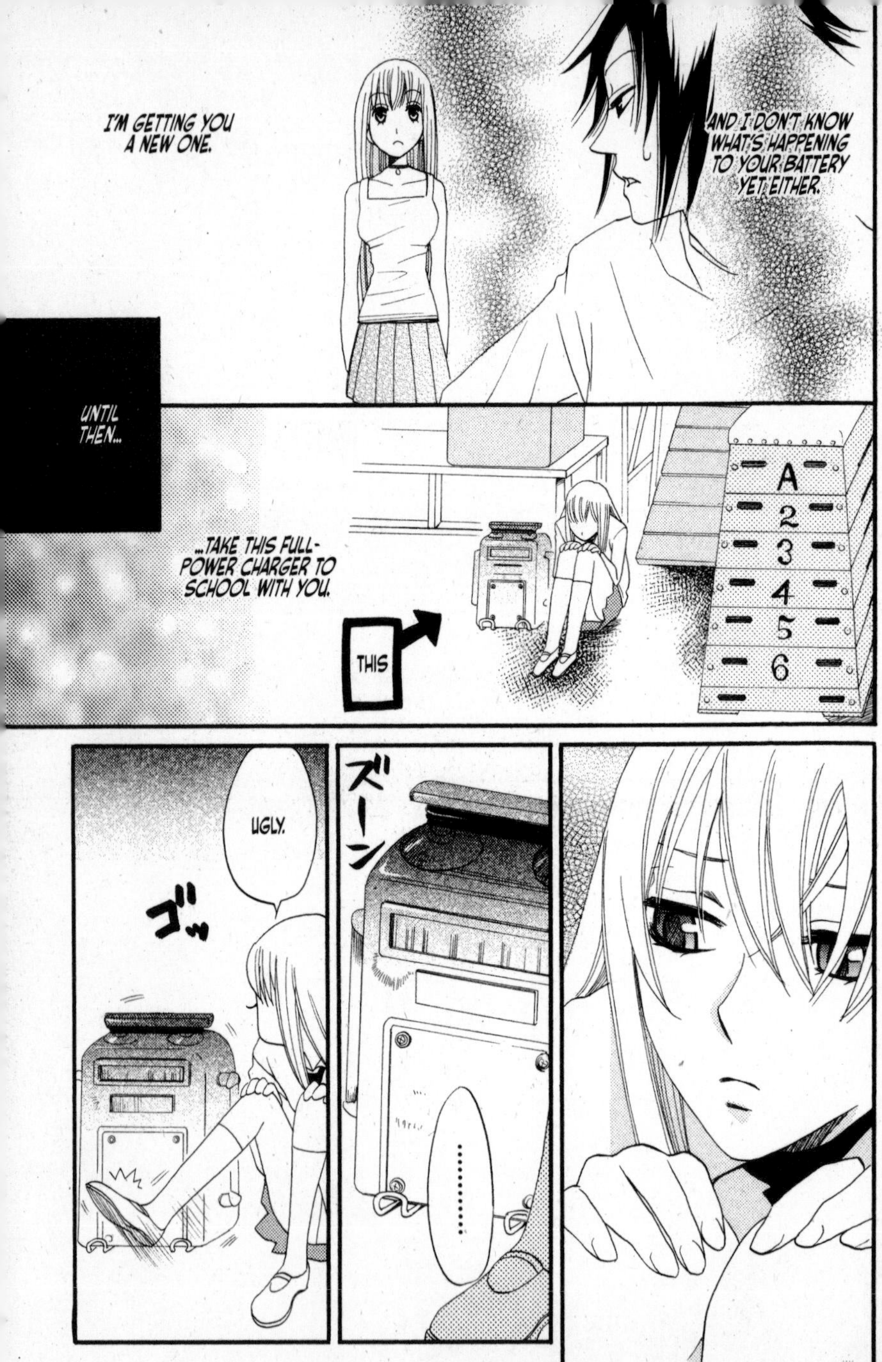
AND I DON'T KNOW WHAT'S HAPPENING TO YOUR BATTERY YET EITHER.
I'M GETTING YOU A NEW ONE.
UNTIL THEN...
...TAKE THIS FULL-POWER CHARGER TO SCHOOL WITH YOU.
THIS
A
2
3
4
5
6
ズーン
......
UGLY.
ゴッ

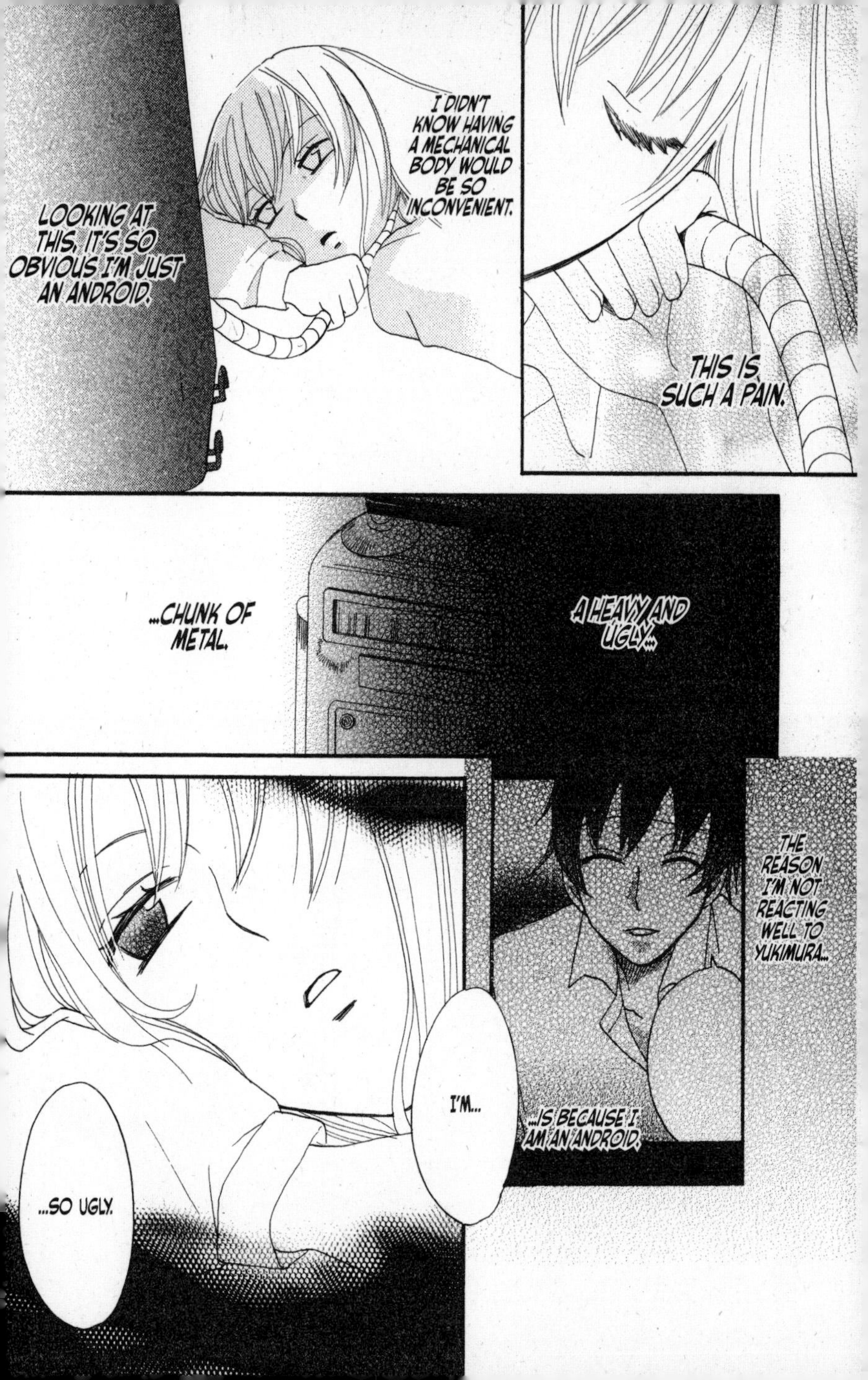
THIS IS SUCH A PAIN.
I DIDN'T KNOW HAVING A MECHANICAL BODY WOULD BE SO INCONVENIENT.
LOOKING AT THIS, IT'S SO OBVIOUS I'M JUST AN ANDROID.
A HEAVY AND UGLY...
...CHUNK OF METAL.
THE REASON I'M NOT REACTING WELL TO YUKIMURA...
...IS BECAUSE I AM AN ANDROID.
I'M...
...SO UGLY.

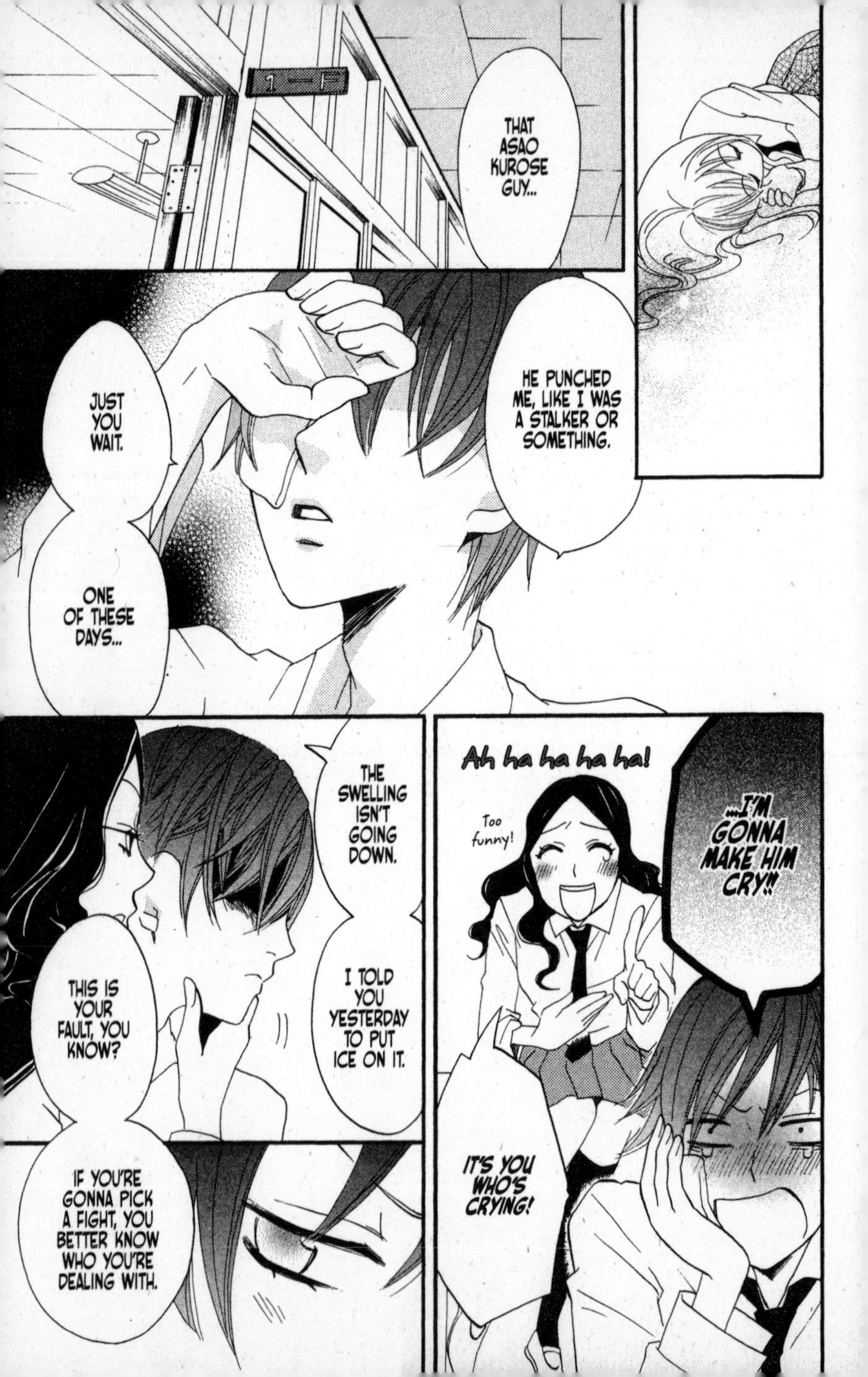
THAT ASAO KUROSE GUY...
HE PUNCHED ME, LIKE I WAS A STALKER OR SOMETHING.
JUST YOU WAIT.
ONE OF THESE DAYS...
...I'M GONNA MAKE HIM CRY!!
Ah ha ha ha ha!
Too funny!
IT'S YOU WHO'S CRYING!
THE SWELLING ISN'T GOING DOWN.
I TOLD YOU YESTERDAY TO PUT ICE ON IT.
THIS IS YOUR FAULT, YOU KNOW?
IF YOU'RE GONNA PICK A FIGHT, YOU BETTER KNOW WHO YOU'RE DEALING WITH.

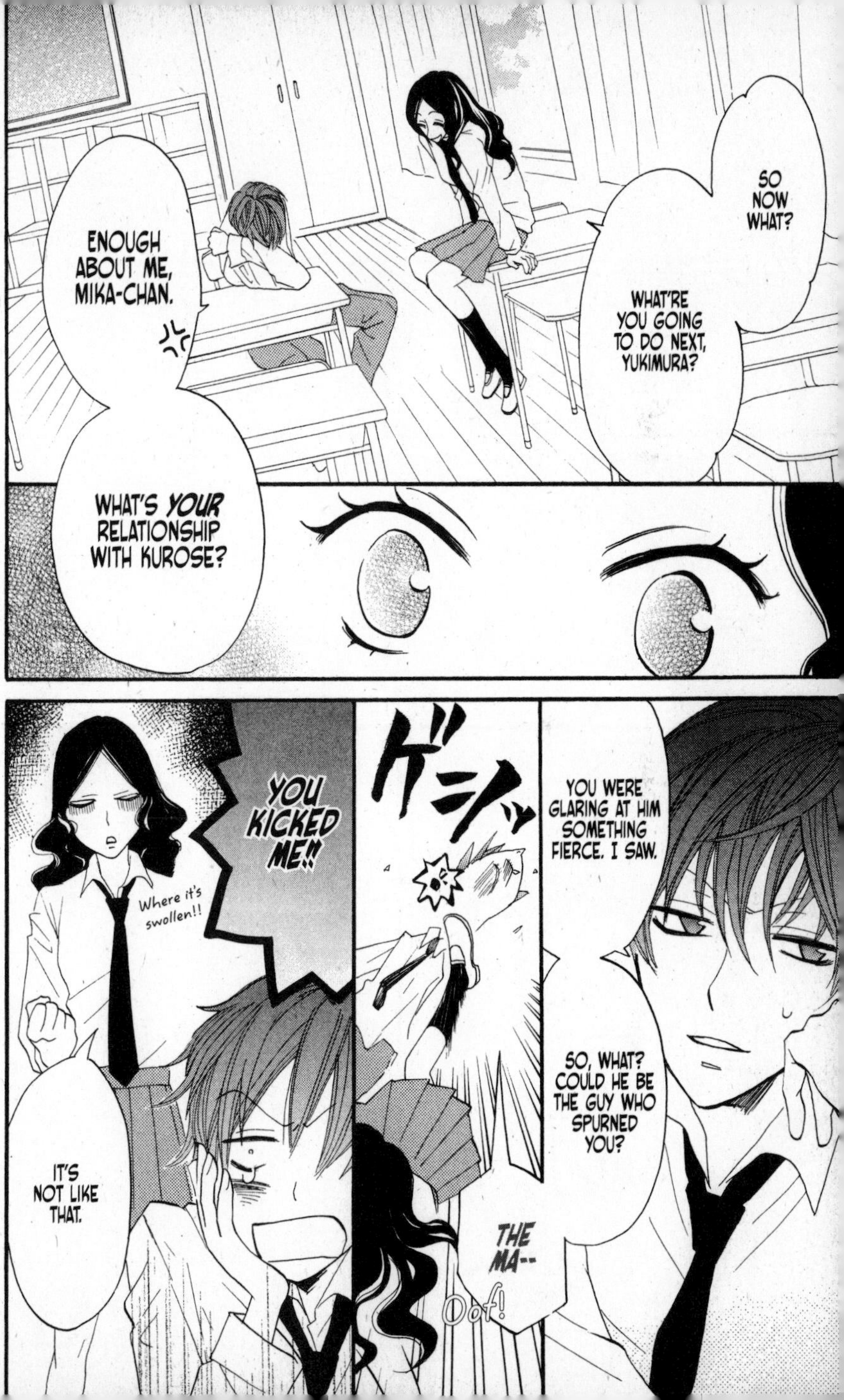
SO NOW WHAT?
WHAT'RE YOU GOING TO DO NEXT, YUKIMURA?
ENOUGH ABOUT ME, MIKA-CHAN.
WHAT'S *YOUR* RELATIONSHIP WITH KUROSE?
YOU WERE GLARING AT HIM SOMETHING FIERCE. I SAW.
SO, WHAT? COULD HE BE THE GUY WHO SPURNED YOU?
ゲシッ
THE MA--
Oof!
YOU KICKED ME!!
Where it's swollen!!
IT'S NOT LIKE THAT.

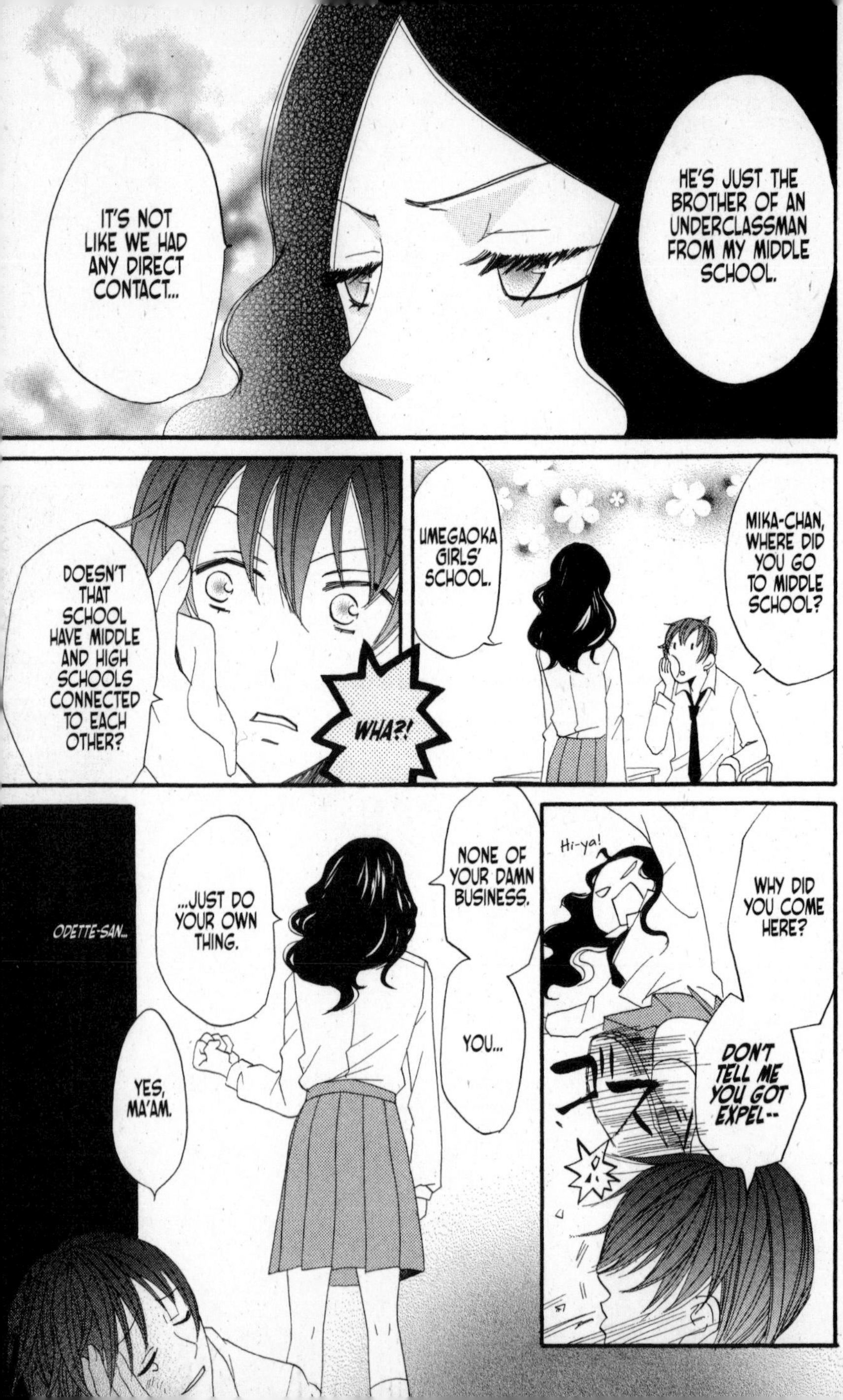

HE'S JUST THE BROTHER OF AN UNDERCLASSMAN FROM MY MIDDLE SCHOOL.
IT'S NOT LIKE WE HAD ANY DIRECT CONTACT...
MIKA-CHAN, WHERE DID YOU GO TO MIDDLE SCHOOL?
UMEGAOKA GIRLS' SCHOOL.
WHA?!
DOESN'T THAT SCHOOL HAVE MIDDLE AND HIGH SCHOOLS CONNECTED TO EACH OTHER?
WHY DID YOU COME HERE?
Hi-ya!
DON'T TELL ME YOU GOT EXPEL--
NONE OF YOUR DAMN BUSINESS.
...JUST DO YOUR OWN THING.
YOU...
YES, MA'AM.
ODETTE-SAN...

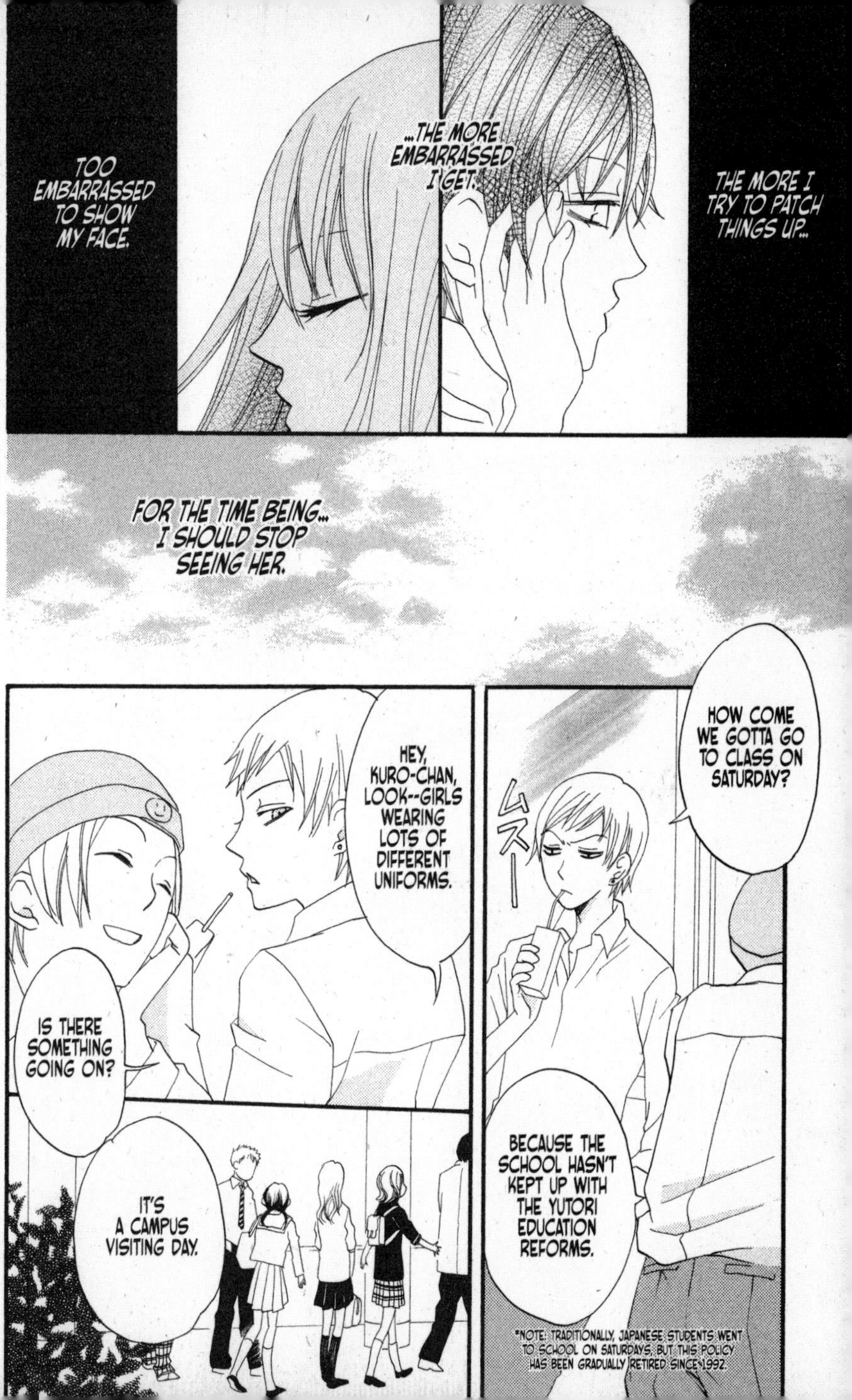
THE MORE I TRY TO PATCH THINGS UP...
...THE MORE EMBARRASSED I GET.
TOO EMBARRASSED TO SHOW MY FACE.
FOR THE TIME BEING... I SHOULD STOP SEEING HER.
HOW COME WE GOTTA GO TO CLASS ON SATURDAY?
ムスー
BECAUSE THE SCHOOL HASN'T KEPT UP WITH THE YUTORI EDUCATION REFORMS.
*NOTE: TRADITIONALLY, JAPANESE STUDENTS WENT TO SCHOOL ON SATURDAYS, BUT THIS POLICY HAS BEEN GRADUALLY RETIRED SINCE 1992.
HEY, KURO-CHAN, LOOK--GIRLS WEARING LOTS OF DIFFERENT UNIFORMS.
IS THERE SOMETHING GOING ON?
IT'S A CAMPUS VISITING DAY.

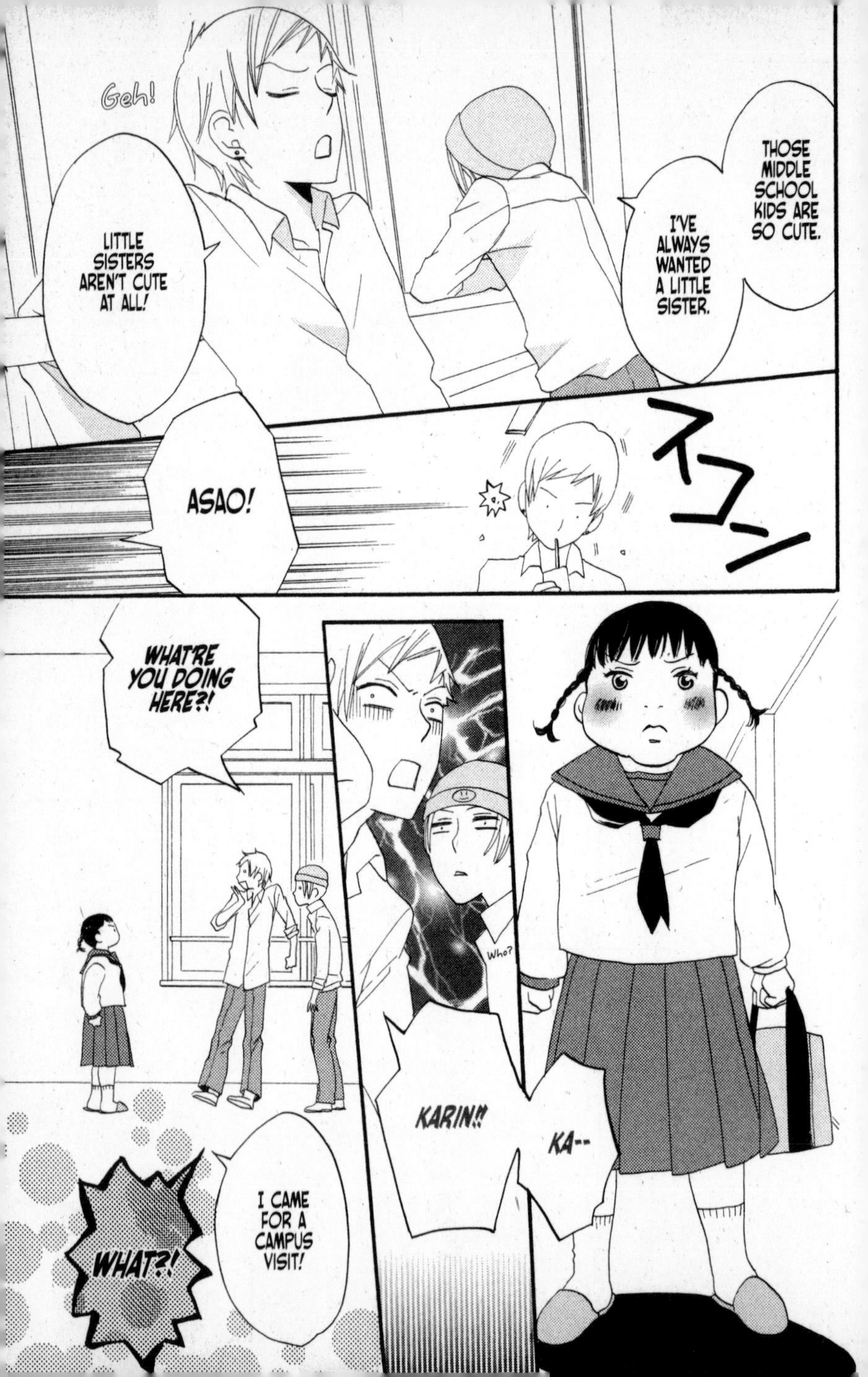
THOSE MIDDLE SCHOOL KIDS ARE SO CUTE.
I'VE ALWAYS WANTED A LITTLE SISTER.
Geh!
LITTLE SISTERS AREN'T CUTE AT ALL!
ASAO!
Who?
KA--
KARIN!!
WHAT'RE YOU DOING HERE?!
I CAME FOR A CAMPUS VISIT!
WHAT?!

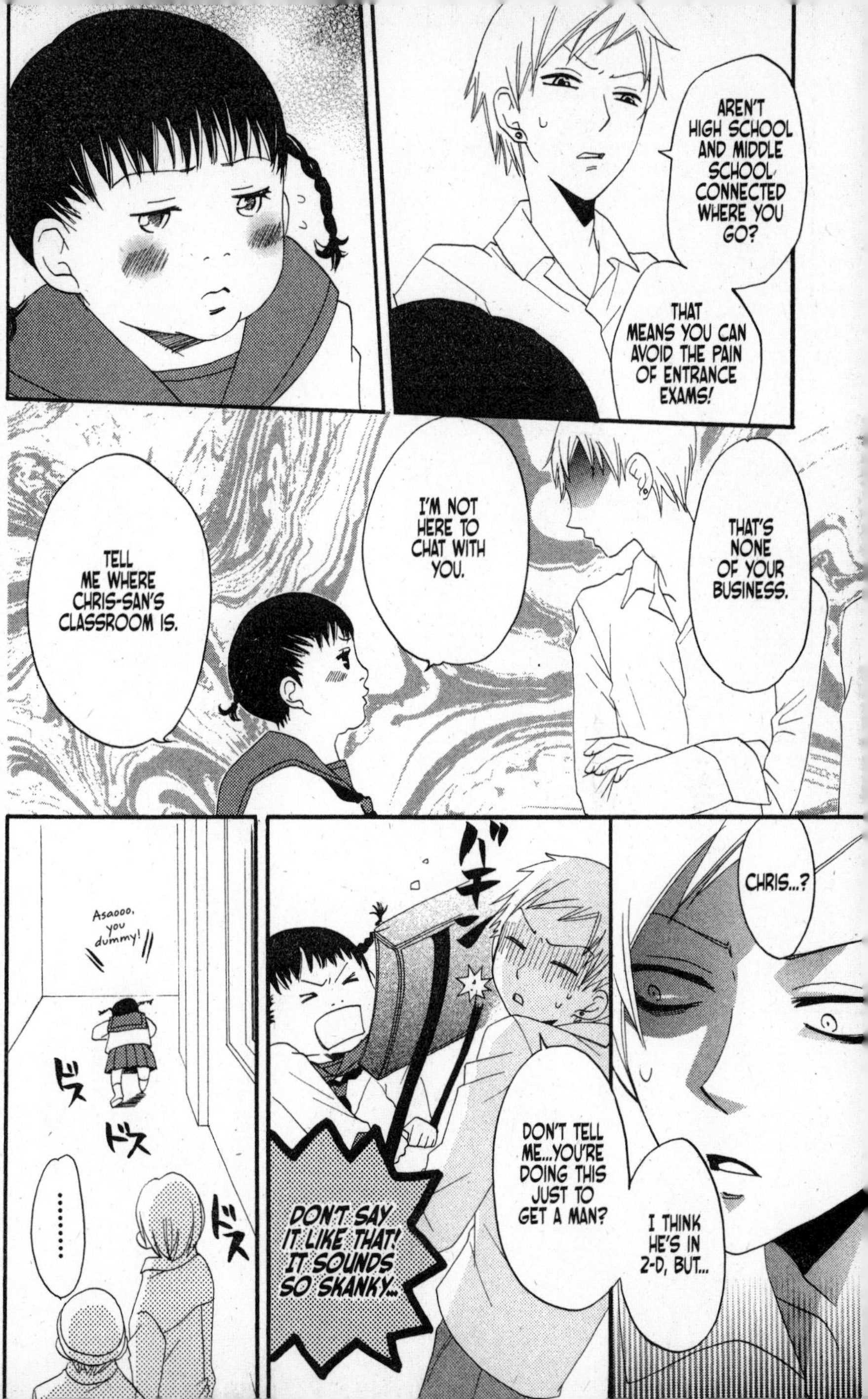
AREN'T HIGH SCHOOL AND MIDDLE SCHOOL CONNECTED WHERE YOU GO?
THAT MEANS YOU CAN AVOID THE PAIN OF ENTRANCE EXAMS!
THAT'S NONE OF YOUR BUSINESS.
I'M NOT HERE TO CHAT WITH YOU.
TELL ME WHERE CHRIS-SAN'S CLASSROOM IS.
CHRIS...?
I THINK HE'S IN 2-D, BUT...
DON'T TELL ME...YOU'RE DOING THIS JUST TO GET A MAN?
バキン
DON'T SAY IT LIKE THAT! IT SOUNDS SO SKANKY...
Asaooo, you dummy!
ドス
ドス
ドス
....

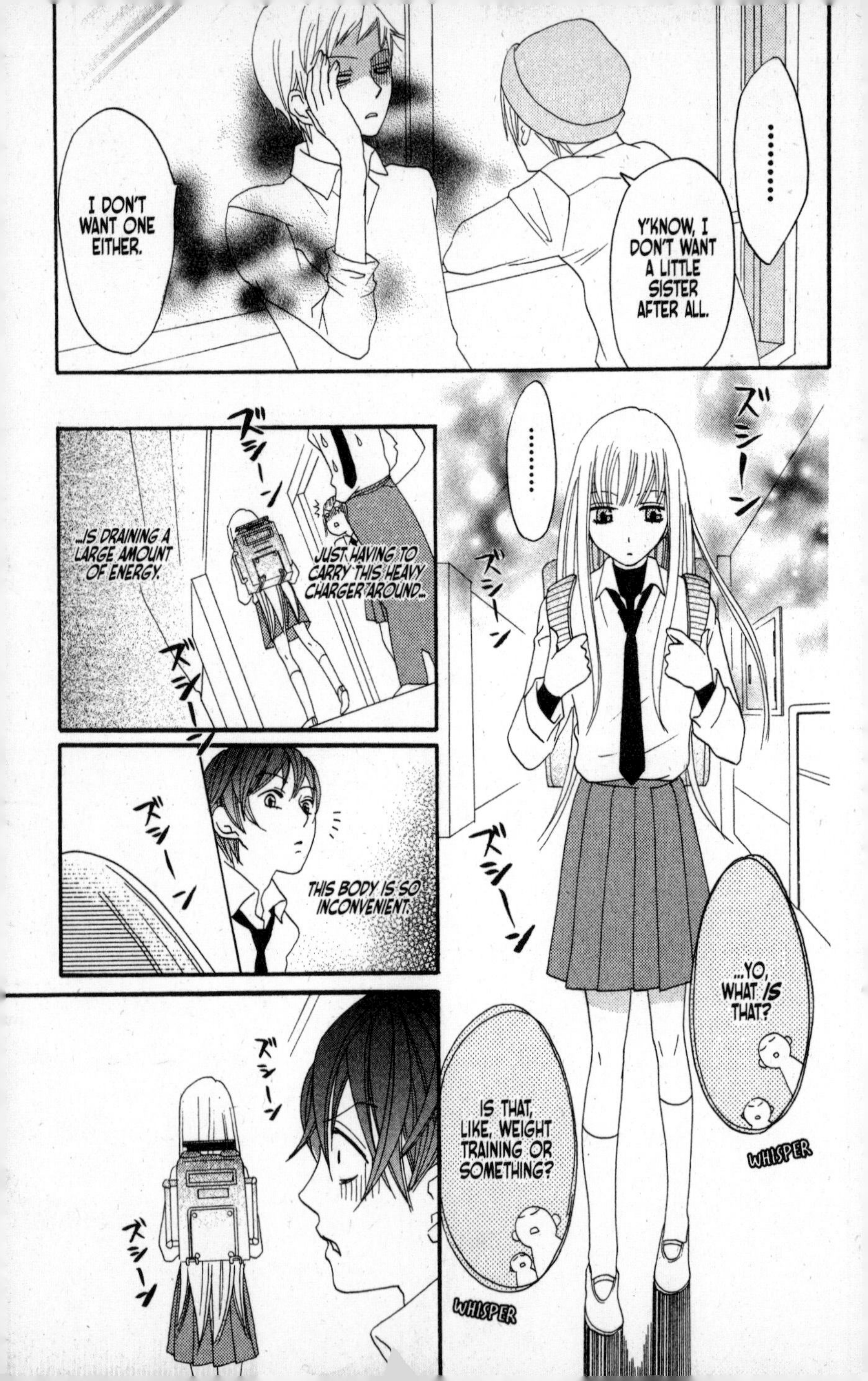

......
Y'KNOW, I DON'T WANT A LITTLE SISTER AFTER ALL.
I DON'T WANT ONE EITHER.
ズシーン
......
ズシーン
ズシーン
...YO, WHAT IS THAT?
WHISPER
IS THAT, LIKE, WEIGHT TRAINING OR SOMETHING?
WHISPER
ズシーン
JUST HAVING TO CARRY THIS HEAVY CHARGER AROUND...
...IS DRAINING A LARGE AMOUNT OF ENERGY.
ズシーン
ズシーン
THIS BODY IS SO INCONVENIENT.
ズシーン
ズシーン

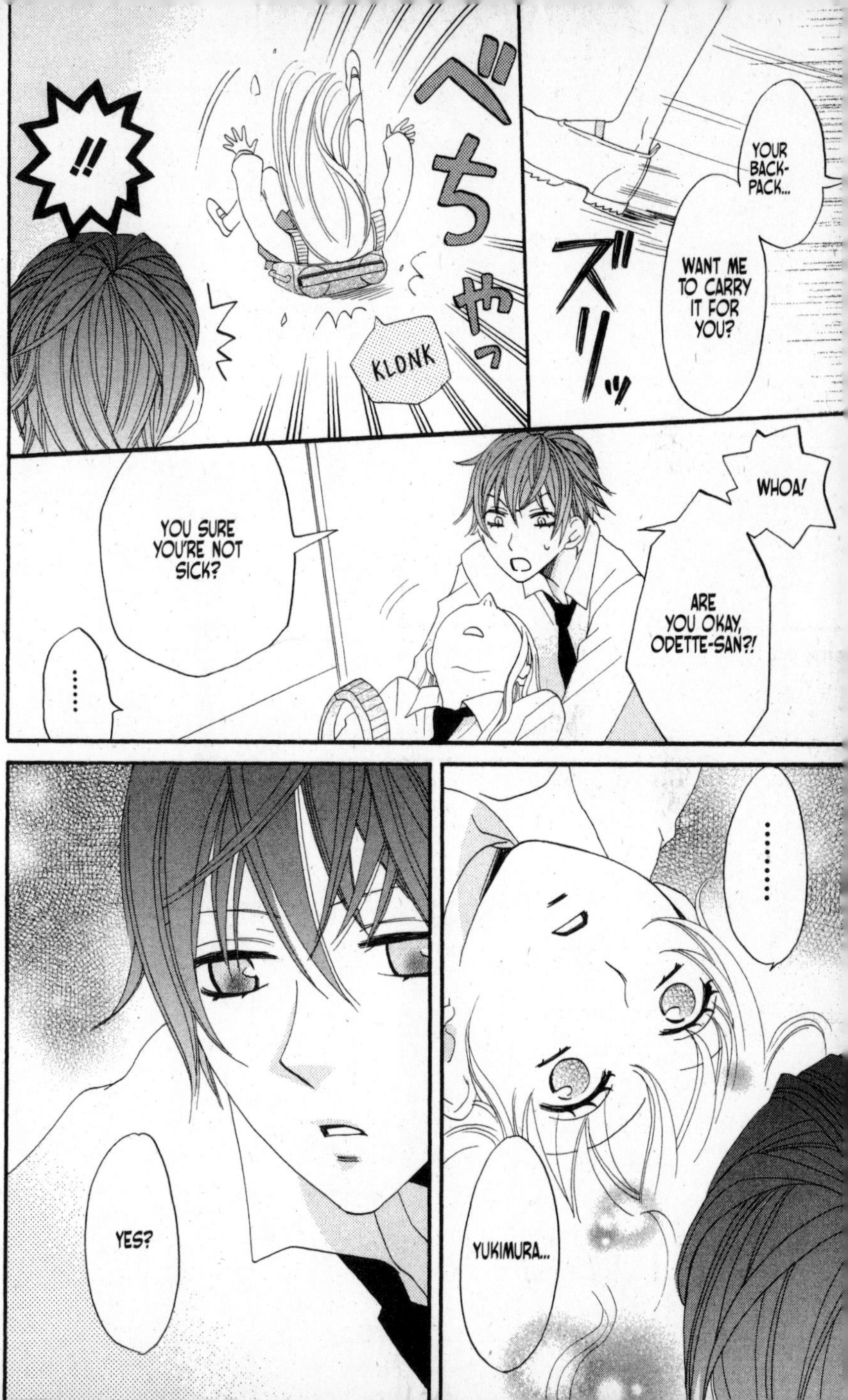
YOUR BACK-PACK...
WANT ME TO CARRY IT FOR YOU?
ズリッ
!!
べちゃっ
KLONK
WHOA!
ARE YOU OKAY, ODETTE-SAN?!
YOU SURE YOU'RE NOT SICK?
......
....
YUKIMURA...
YES?

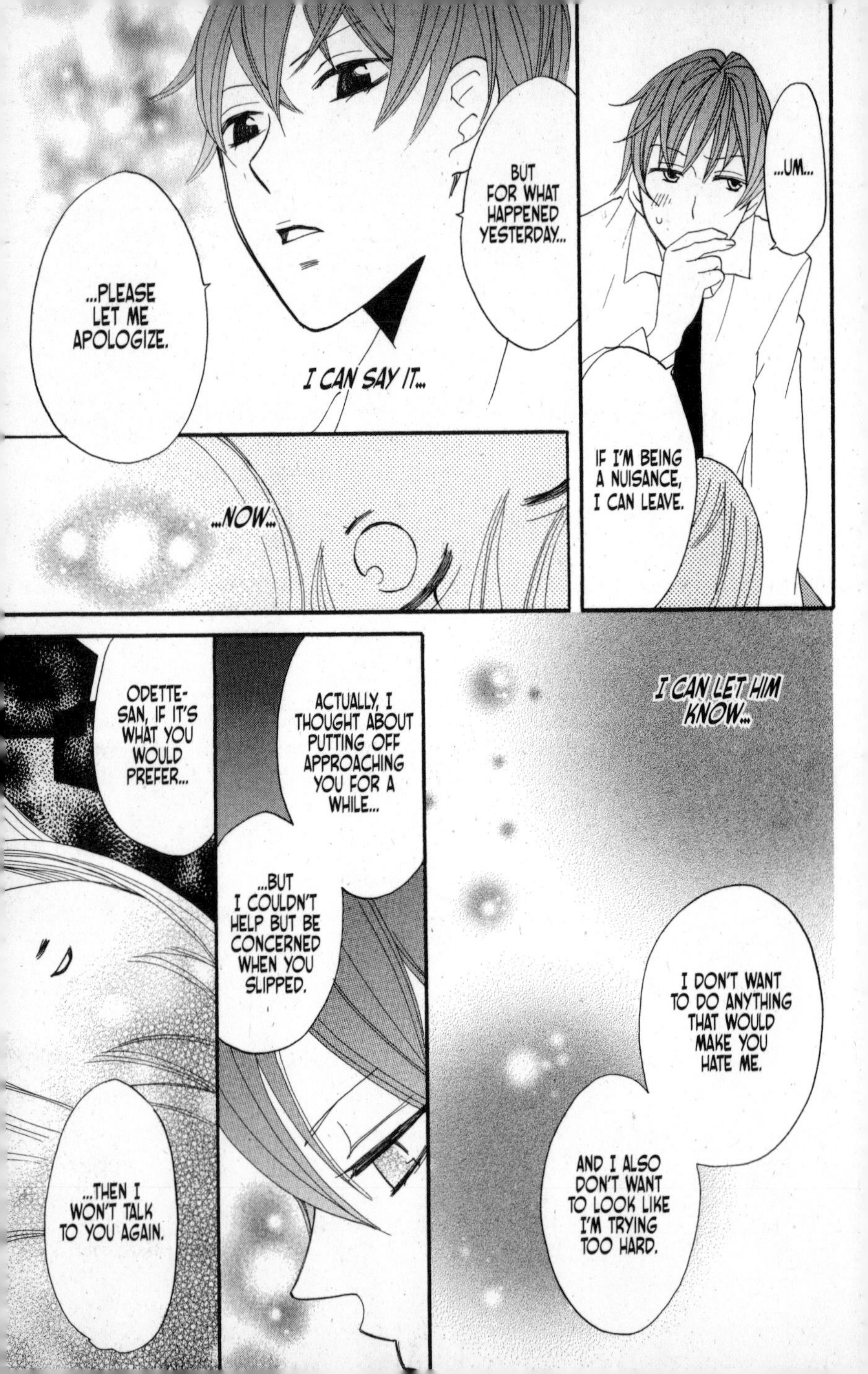
...UM...
IF I'M BEING A NUISANCE, I CAN LEAVE.
BUT FOR WHAT HAPPENED YESTERDAY...
...PLEASE LET ME APOLOGIZE.
I CAN SAY IT...
...NOW...
I CAN LET HIM KNOW...
I DON'T WANT TO DO ANYTHING THAT WOULD MAKE YOU HATE ME.
AND I ALSO DON'T WANT TO LOOK LIKE I'M TRYING TOO HARD.
ACTUALLY, I THOUGHT ABOUT PUTTING OFF APPROACHING YOU FOR A WHILE...
...BUT I COULDN'T HELP BUT BE CONCERNED WHEN YOU SLIPPED.
ODETTE-SAN, IF IT'S WHAT YOU WOULD PREFER...
...THEN I WON'T TALK TO YOU AGAIN.

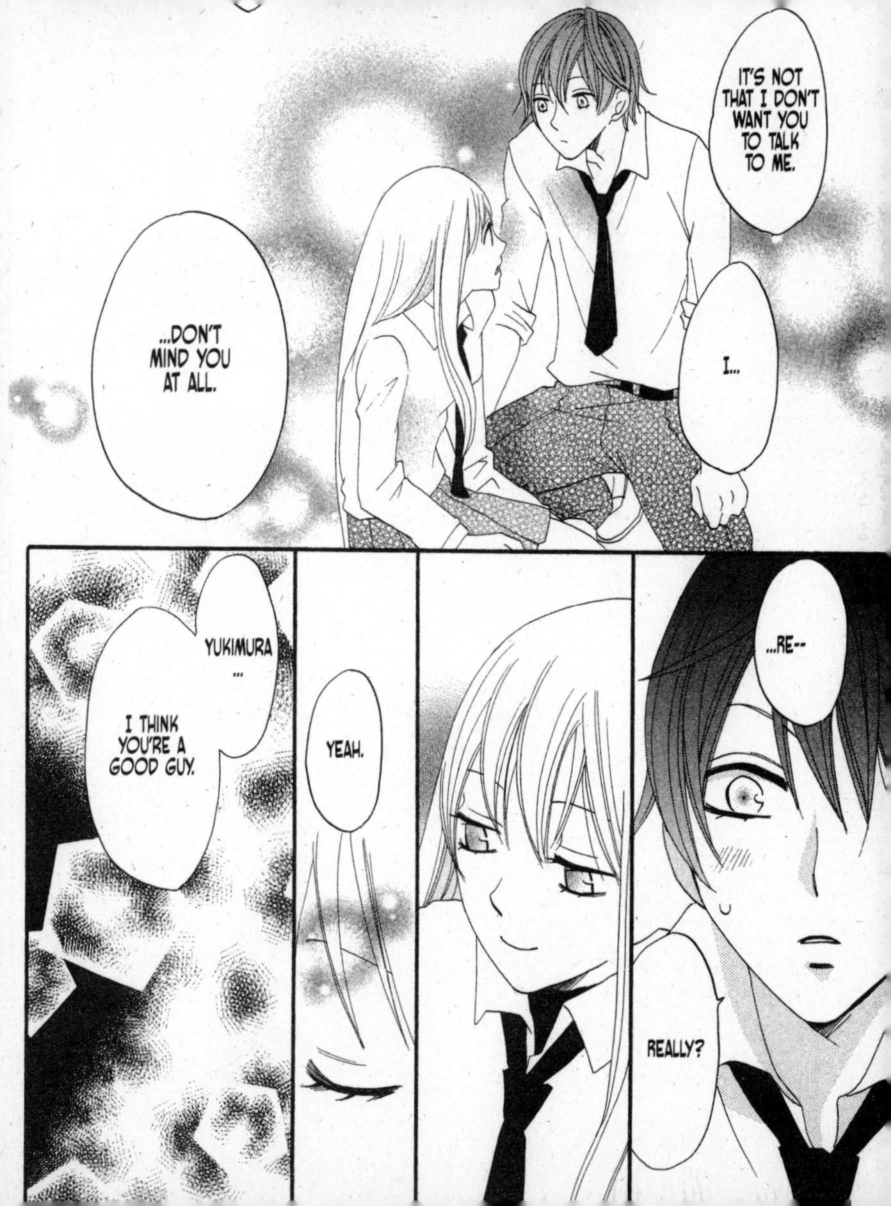
IT'S NOT THAT I DON'T WANT YOU TO TALK TO ME.
I...
...DON'T MIND YOU AT ALL.
...RE--
REALLY?
YEAH.
YUKIMURA ...
I THINK YOU'RE A GOOD GUY.

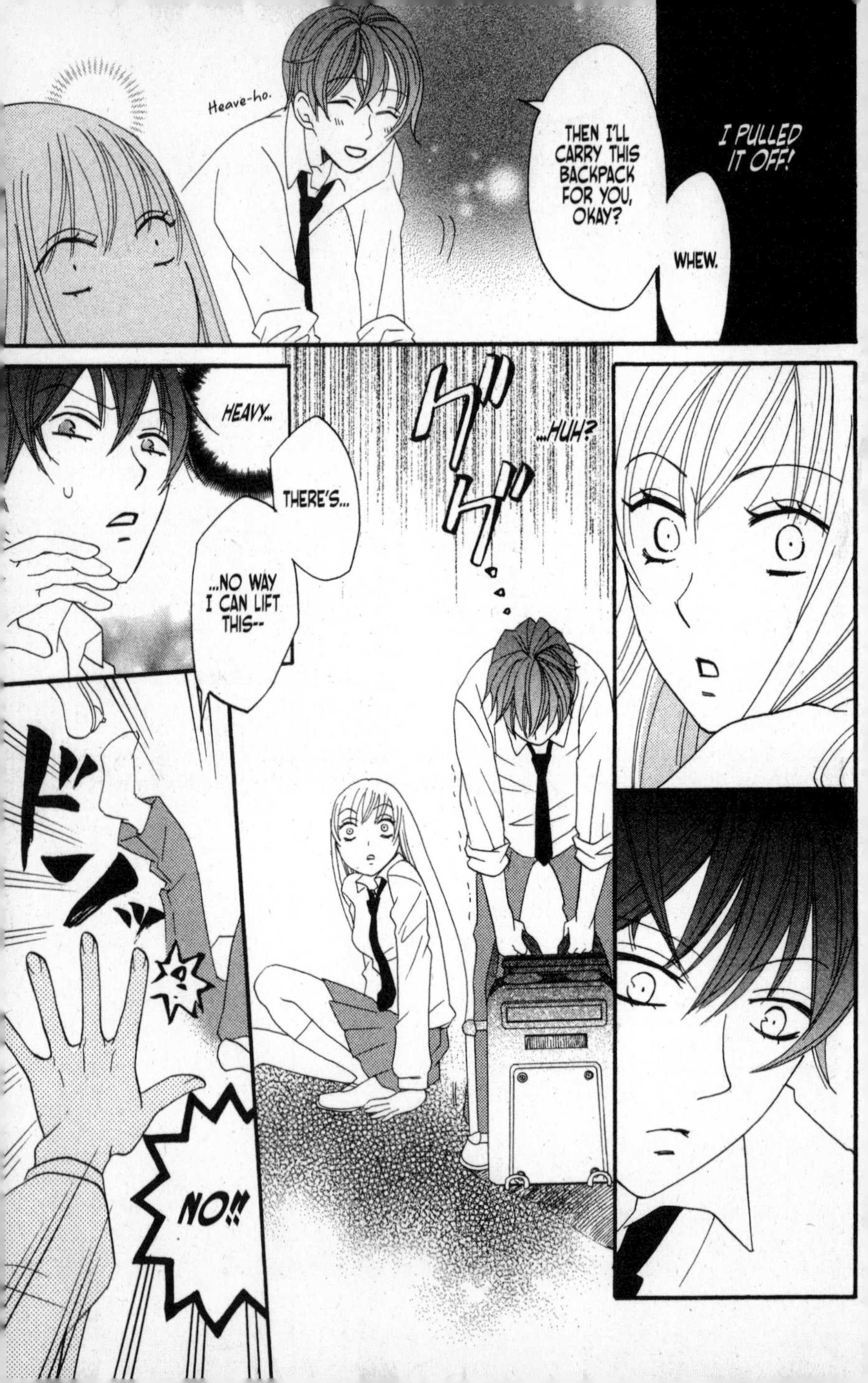
I PULLED IT OFF!
WHEW.
THEN I'LL CARRY THIS BACKPACK FOR YOU, OKAY?
Heave-ho.
...HUH?
HEAVY...
THERE'S...
...NO WAY I CAN LIFT THIS--
NO!!

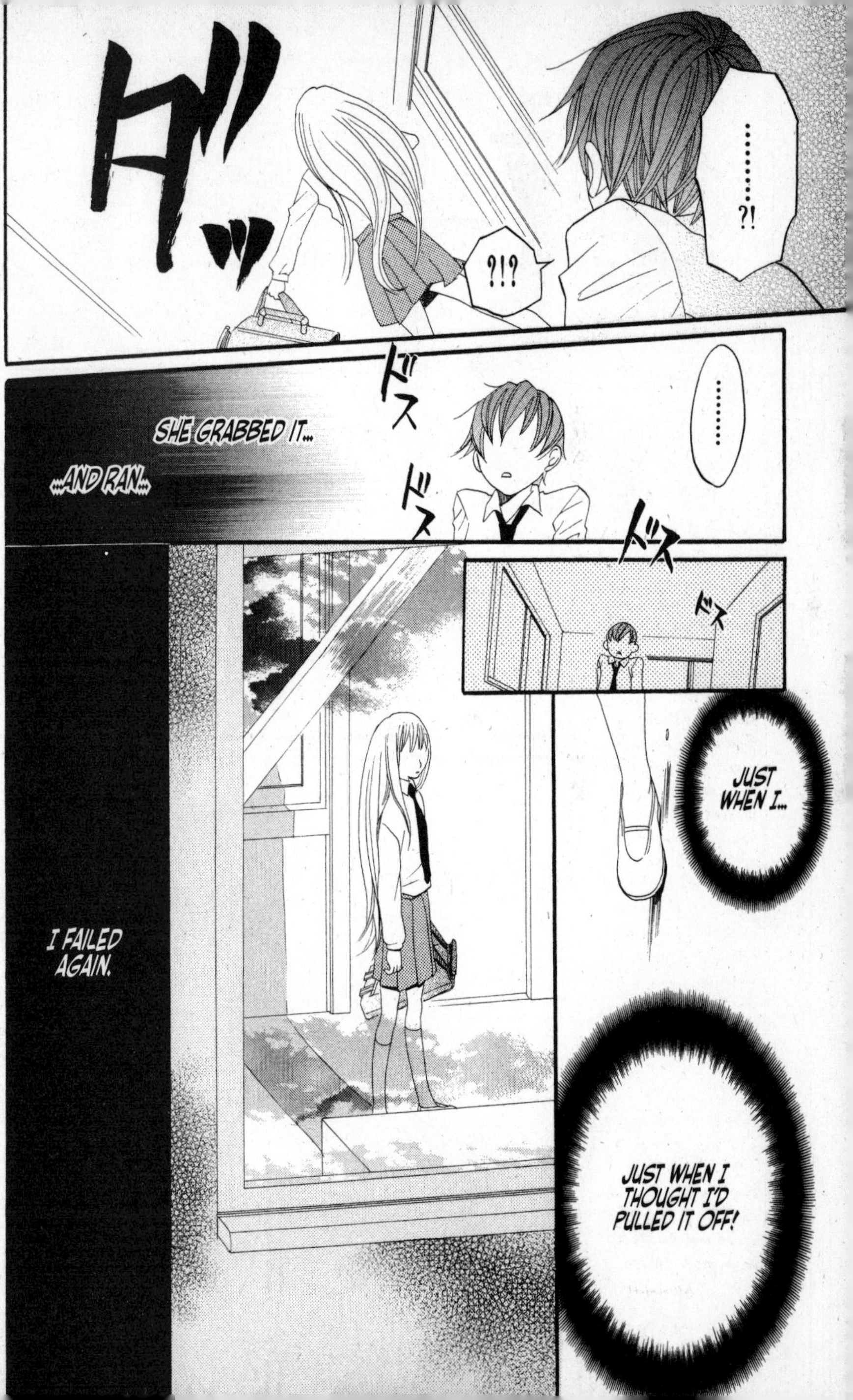
......?!
?!?
ダッ
......
ドス
ドス
SHE GRABBED IT...
...AND RAN...
ドス
ドス
JUST WHEN I...
JUST WHEN I THOUGHT I'D PULLED IT OFF!
I FAILED AGAIN.

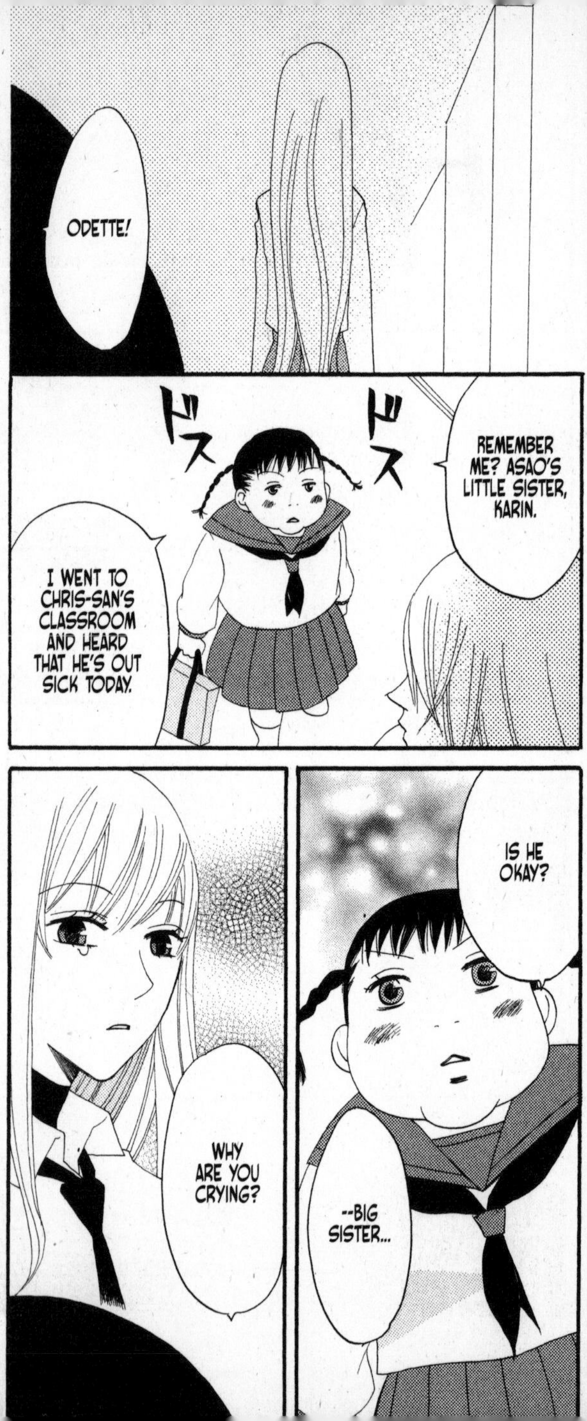
ODETTE!
ドス
REMEMBER ME? ASAO'S LITTLE SISTER, KARIN.
ドス
I WENT TO CHRIS-SAN'S CLASSROOM AND HEARD THAT HE'S OUT SICK TODAY.
IS HE OKAY?
--BIG SISTER...
WHY ARE YOU CRYING?

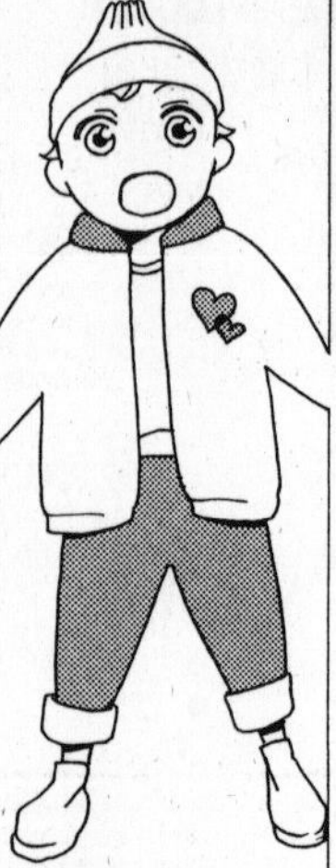

I was going to write something about the manga, but I can't think of anything so I'm just wasting sidebar space.
The other day, I went to a spiritual (?) psychic who claims to be able to see your past life. The result...she couldn't see anything! Well, I guess if she can't see into my present, then there's no way she can see my past...I'm so disappointed. ♪
Not to mention it was expensive. I only went there for fun, so that's okay--but in any case, there are lots of liars (?) out there, so everyone please be careful. I'm going to be more careful from now on too.

All right!

I wrote some confusing stuff. Sorry.

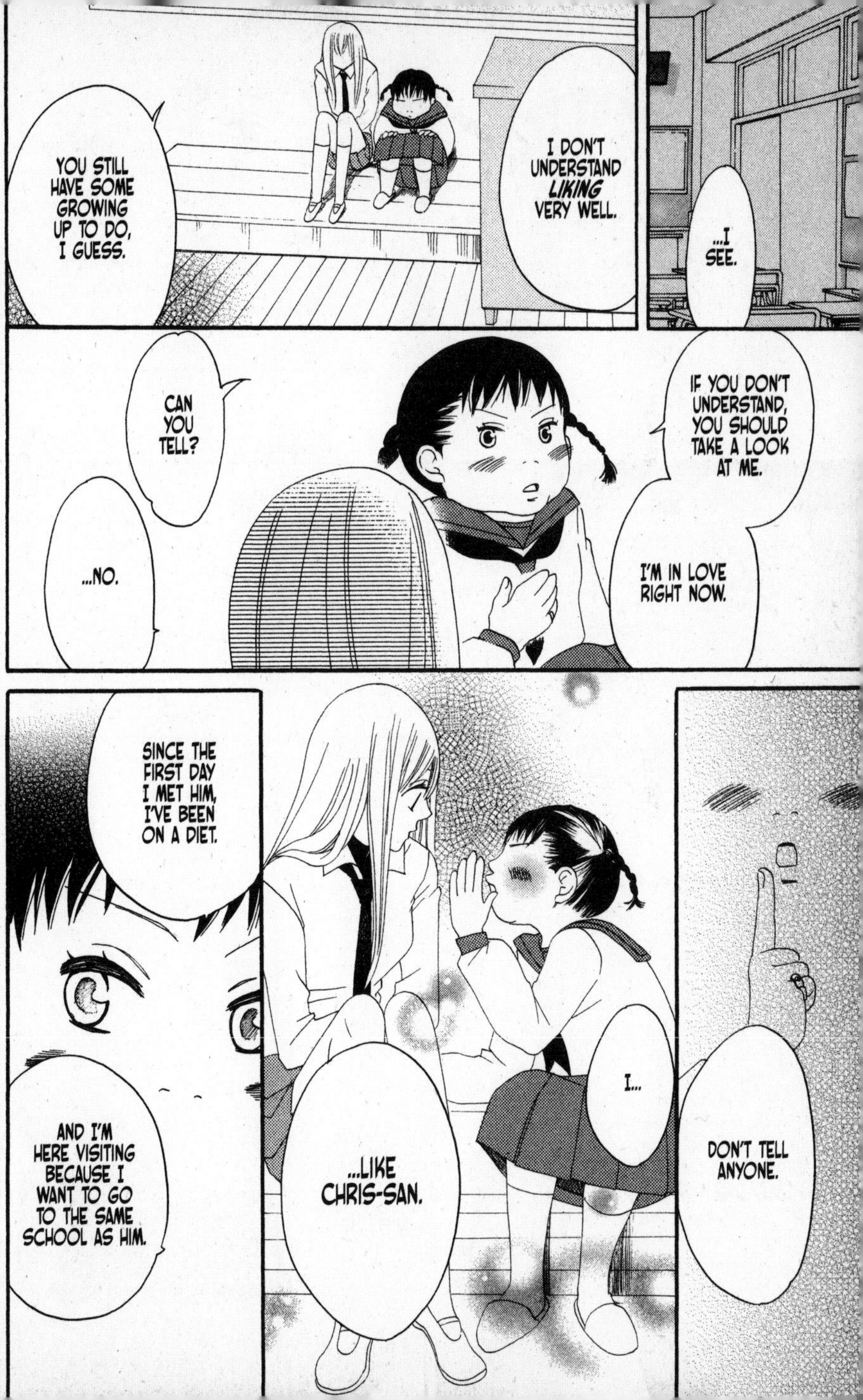
...I SEE.
I DON'T UNDERSTAND *LIKING* VERY WELL.
YOU STILL HAVE SOME GROWING UP TO DO, I GUESS.
IF YOU DON'T UNDERSTAND, YOU SHOULD TAKE A LOOK AT ME.
I'M IN LOVE RIGHT NOW.
CAN YOU TELL?
...NO.
DON'T TELL ANYONE.
I...
...LIKE CHRIS-SAN.
SINCE THE FIRST DAY I MET HIM, I'VE BEEN ON A DIET.
AND I'M HERE VISITING BECAUSE I WANT TO GO TO THE SAME SCHOOL AS HIM.

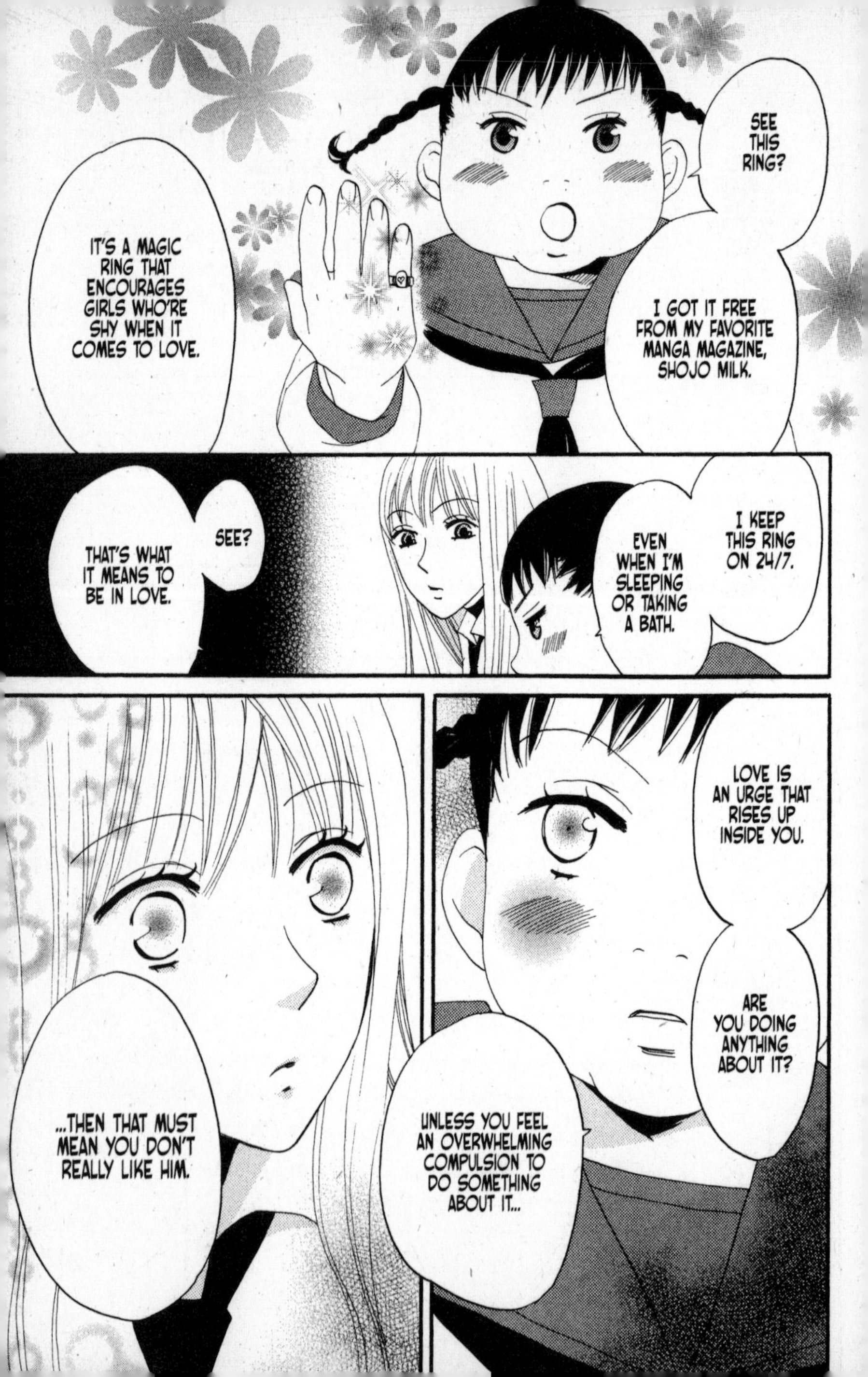
SEE THIS RING?
I GOT IT FREE FROM MY FAVORITE MANGA MAGAZINE, SHOJO MILK.
IT'S A MAGIC RING THAT ENCOURAGES GIRLS WHO'RE SHY WHEN IT COMES TO LOVE.
I KEEP THIS RING ON 24/7.
EVEN WHEN I'M SLEEPING OR TAKING A BATH.
SEE?
THAT'S WHAT IT MEANS TO BE IN LOVE.
LOVE IS AN URGE THAT RISES UP INSIDE YOU.
ARE YOU DOING ANYTHING ABOUT IT?
UNLESS YOU FEEL AN OVERWHELMING COMPULSION TO DO SOMETHING ABOUT IT...
...THEN THAT MUST MEAN YOU DON'T REALLY LIKE HIM.

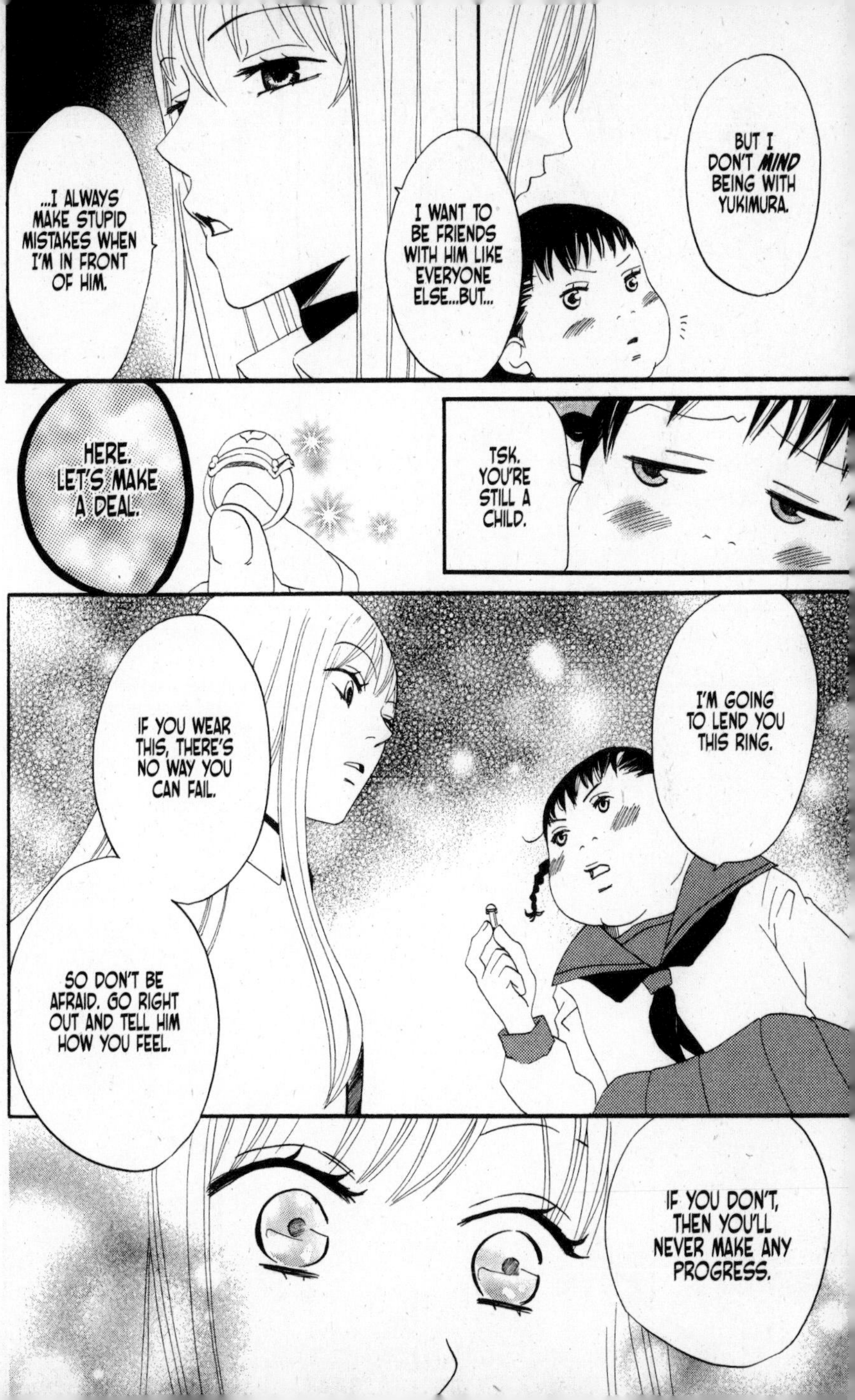
BUT I DON'T *MIND* BEING WITH YUKIMURA.
I WANT TO BE FRIENDS WITH HIM LIKE EVERYONE ELSE...BUT...
...I ALWAYS MAKE STUPID MISTAKES WHEN I'M IN FRONT OF HIM.
TSK. YOU'RE STILL A CHILD.
HERE. LET'S MAKE A DEAL.
I'M GOING TO LEND YOU THIS RING.
IF YOU WEAR THIS, THERE'S NO WAY YOU CAN FAIL.
SO DON'T BE AFRAID. GO RIGHT OUT AND TELL HIM HOW YOU FEEL.
IF YOU DON'T, THEN YOU'LL NEVER MAKE ANY PROGRESS.

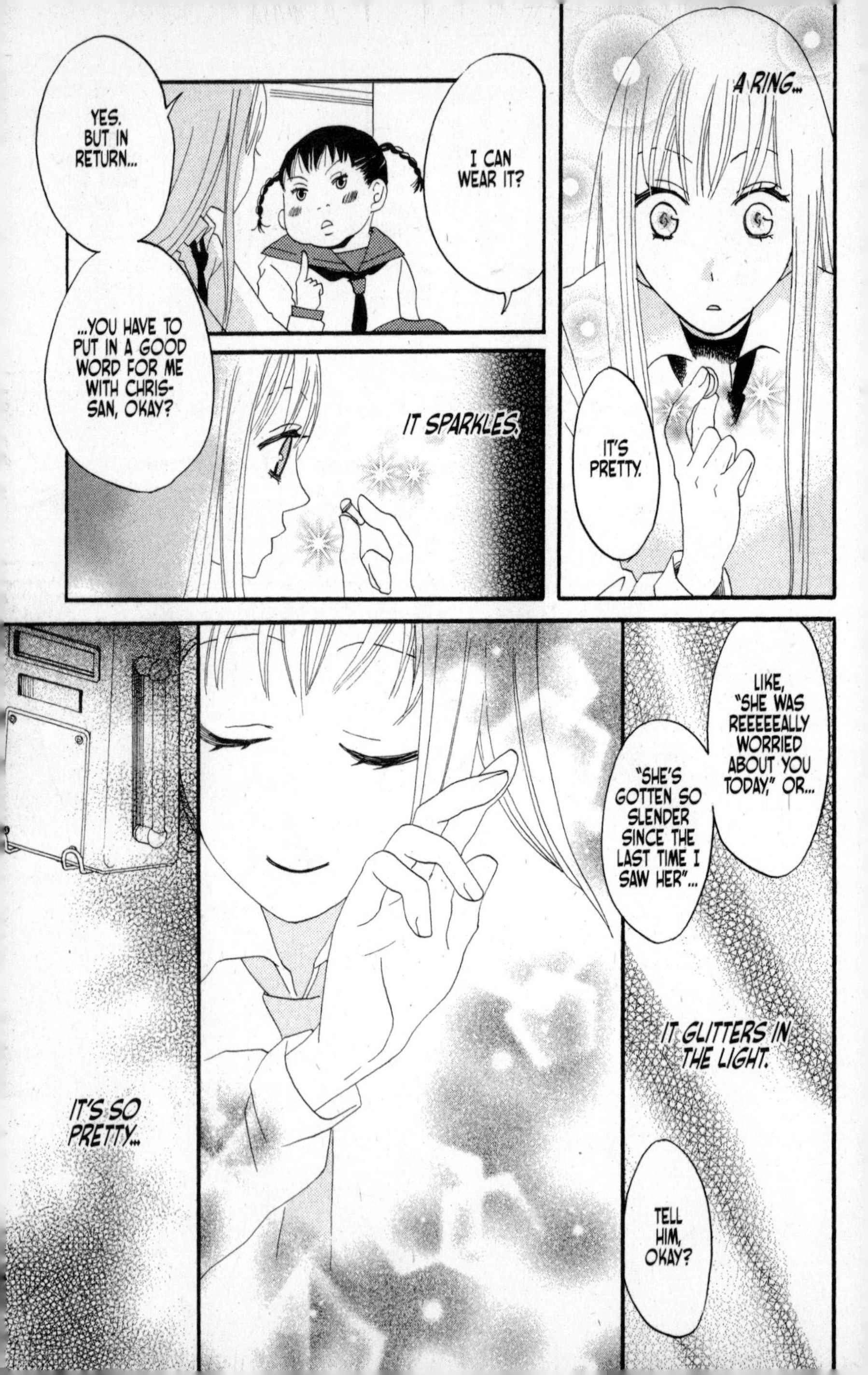
A RING...
IT'S PRETTY.
I CAN WEAR IT?
YES. BUT IN RETURN...
...YOU HAVE TO PUT IN A GOOD WORD FOR ME WITH CHRIS-SAN, OKAY?
IT SPARKLES.
LIKE, "SHE WAS REEEEEALLY WORRIED ABOUT YOU TODAY," OR...
"SHE'S GOTTEN SO SLENDER SINCE THE LAST TIME I SAW HER"...
IT GLITTERS IN THE LIGHT.
TELL HIM, OKAY?
IT'S SO PRETTY...

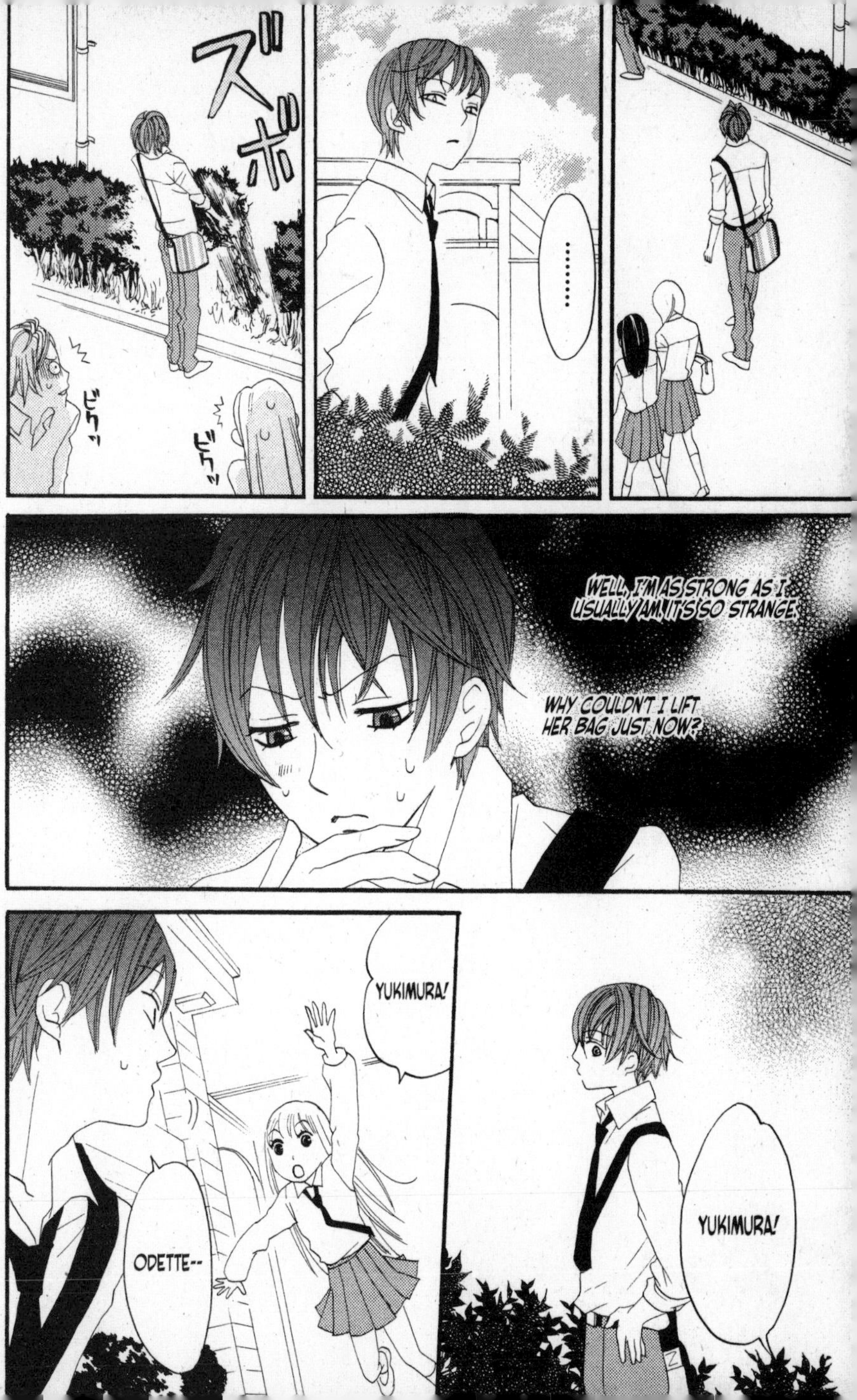
......
ズボ
ビクッ
ビクッ
WELL, I'M AS STRONG AS I USUALLY AM. IT'S SO STRANGE.
WHY COULDN'T I LIFT HER BAG JUST NOW?
YUKIMURA!
YUKIMURA!
ODETTE--

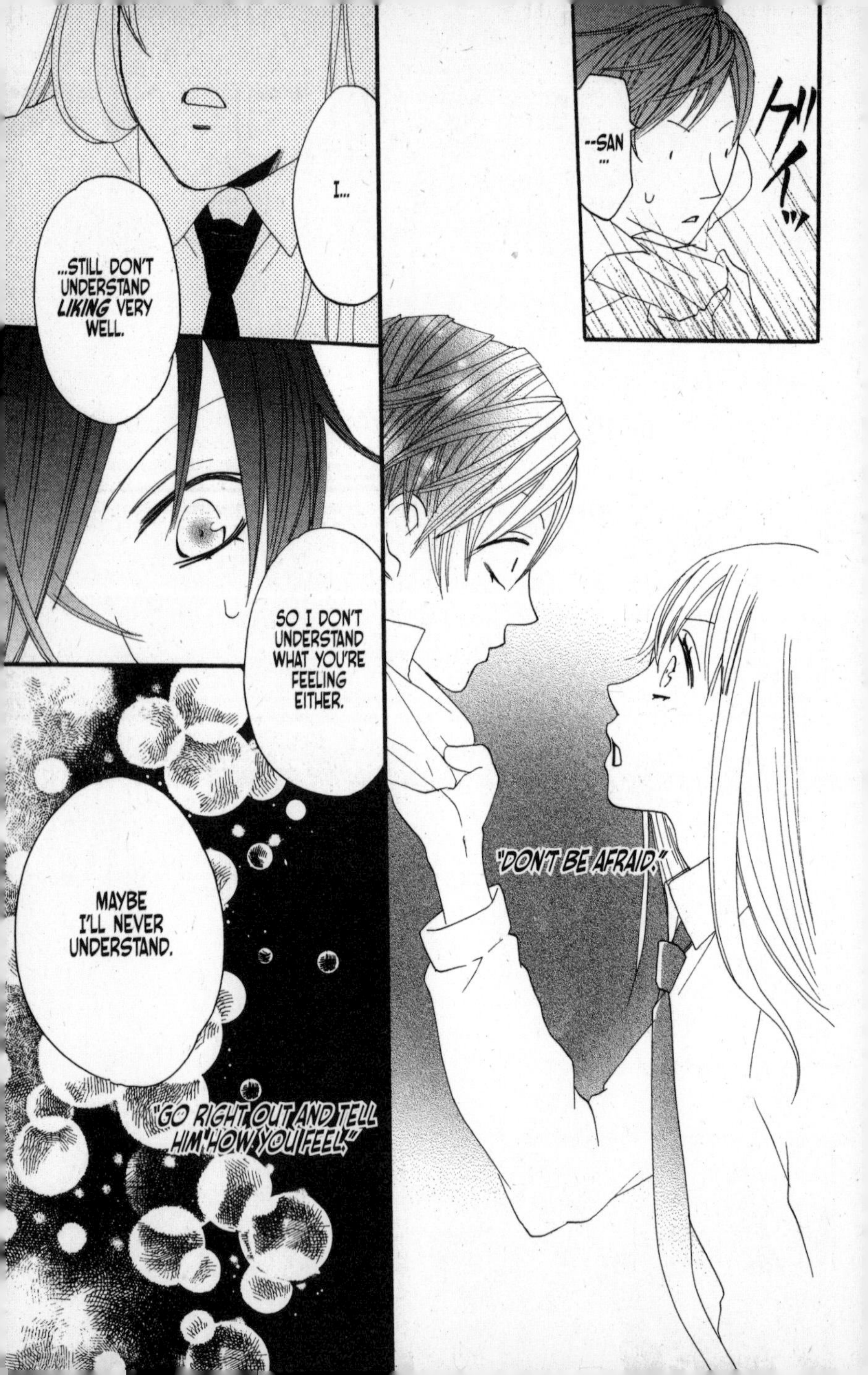
--SAN ...
ギクッ
"DON'T BE AFRAID."
I...
...STILL DON'T UNDERSTAND *LIKING* VERY WELL.
SO I DON'T UNDERSTAND WHAT YOU'RE FEELING EITHER.
MAYBE I'LL NEVER UNDERSTAND.
"GO RIGHT OUT AND TELL HIM HOW YOU FEEL."

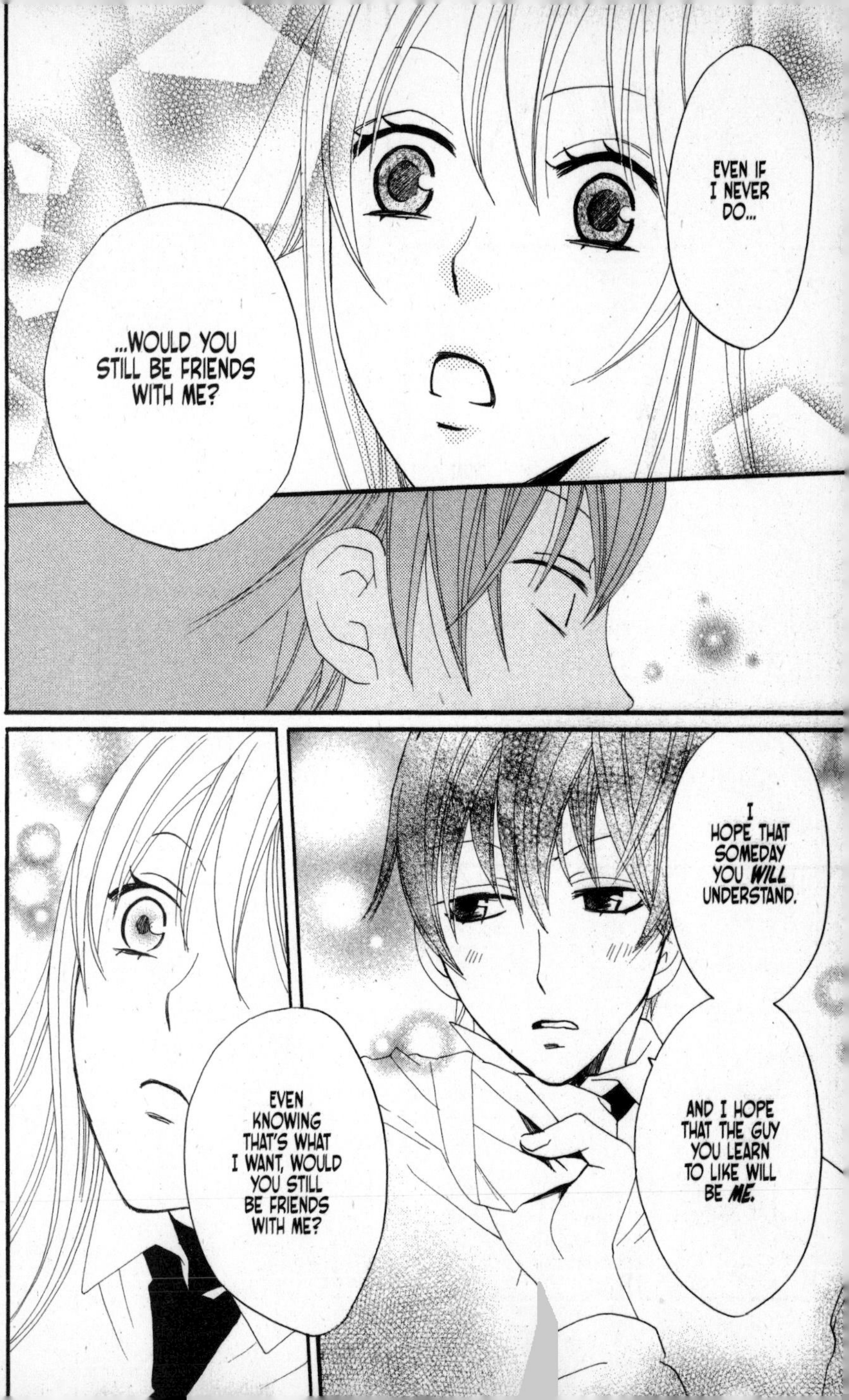
EVEN IF I NEVER DO...
...WOULD YOU STILL BE FRIENDS WITH ME?
I HOPE THAT SOMEDAY YOU *WILL* UNDERSTAND.
AND I HOPE THAT THE GUY YOU LEARN TO LIKE WILL BE *ME.*
EVEN KNOWING THAT'S WHAT I WANT, WOULD YOU STILL BE FRIENDS WITH ME?

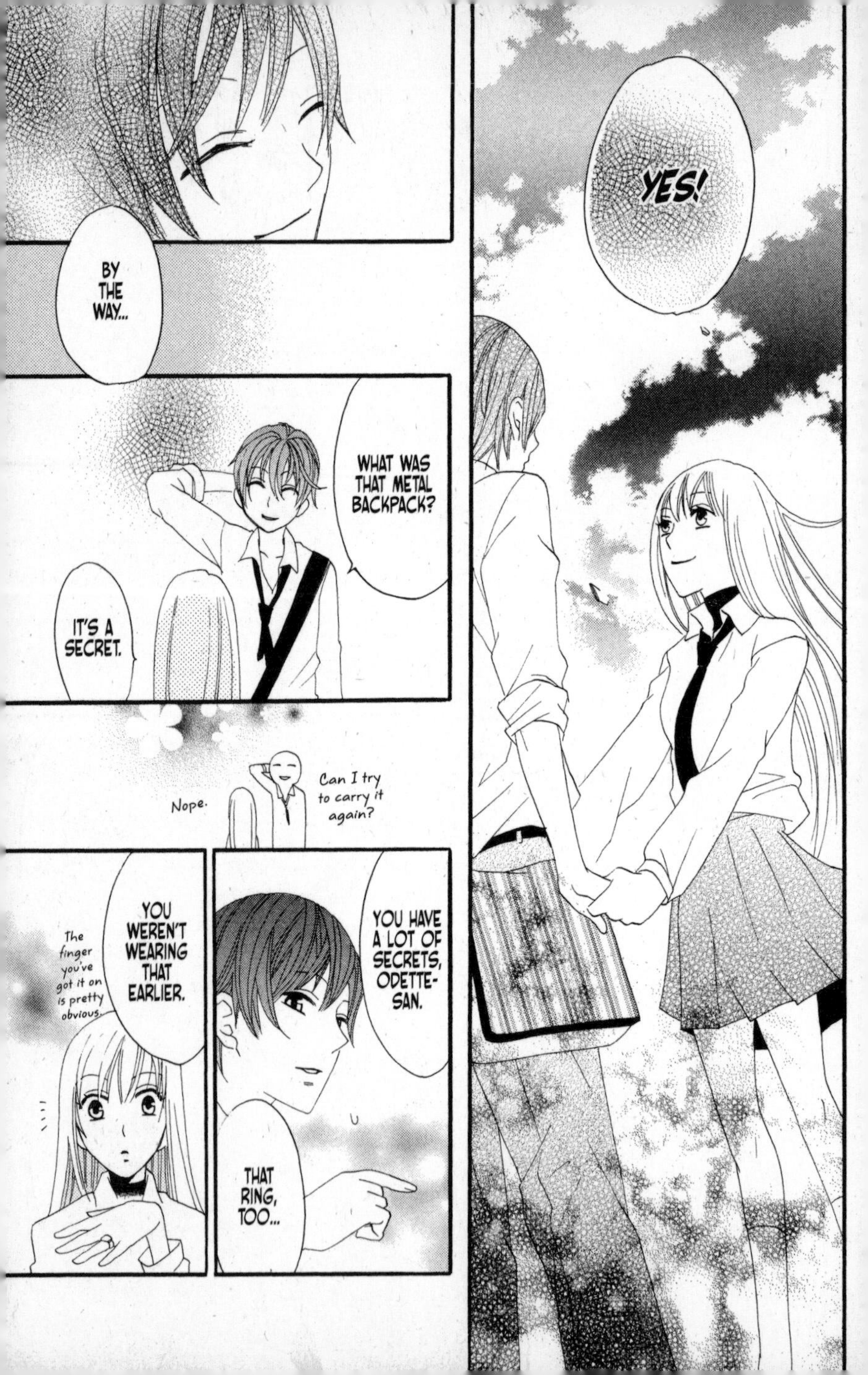
YES!
BY THE WAY...
WHAT WAS THAT METAL BACKPACK?
IT'S A SECRET.
Can I try to carry it again?
Nope.
YOU HAVE A LOT OF SECRETS, ODETTE-SAN.
THAT RING, TOO...
YOU WEREN'T WEARING THAT EARLIER.
The finger you've got it on is pretty obvious.

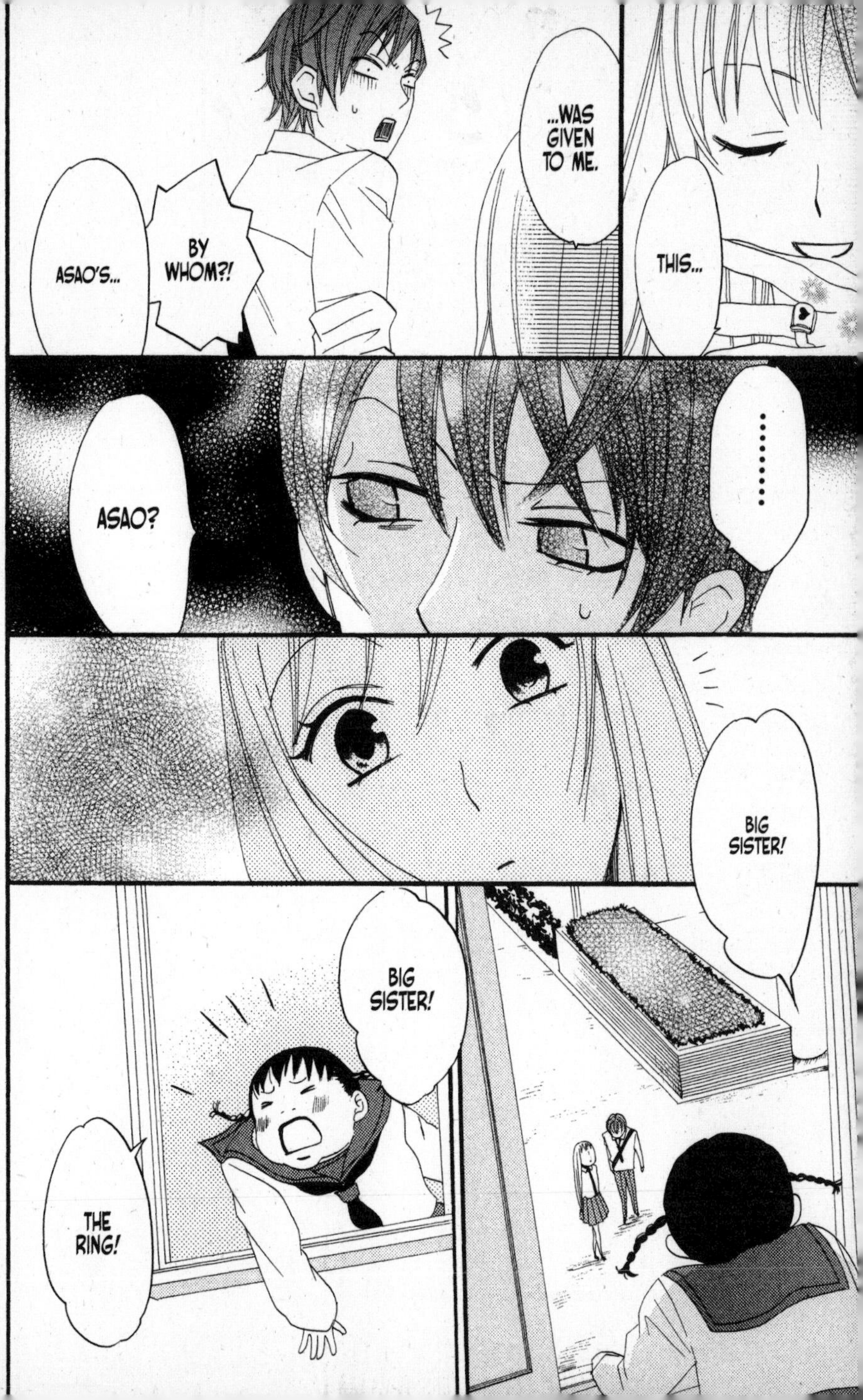
THIS...
...WAS GIVEN TO ME.
BY WHOM?!
ASAO'S...
......
ASAO?
BIG SISTER!
BIG SISTER!
THE RING!

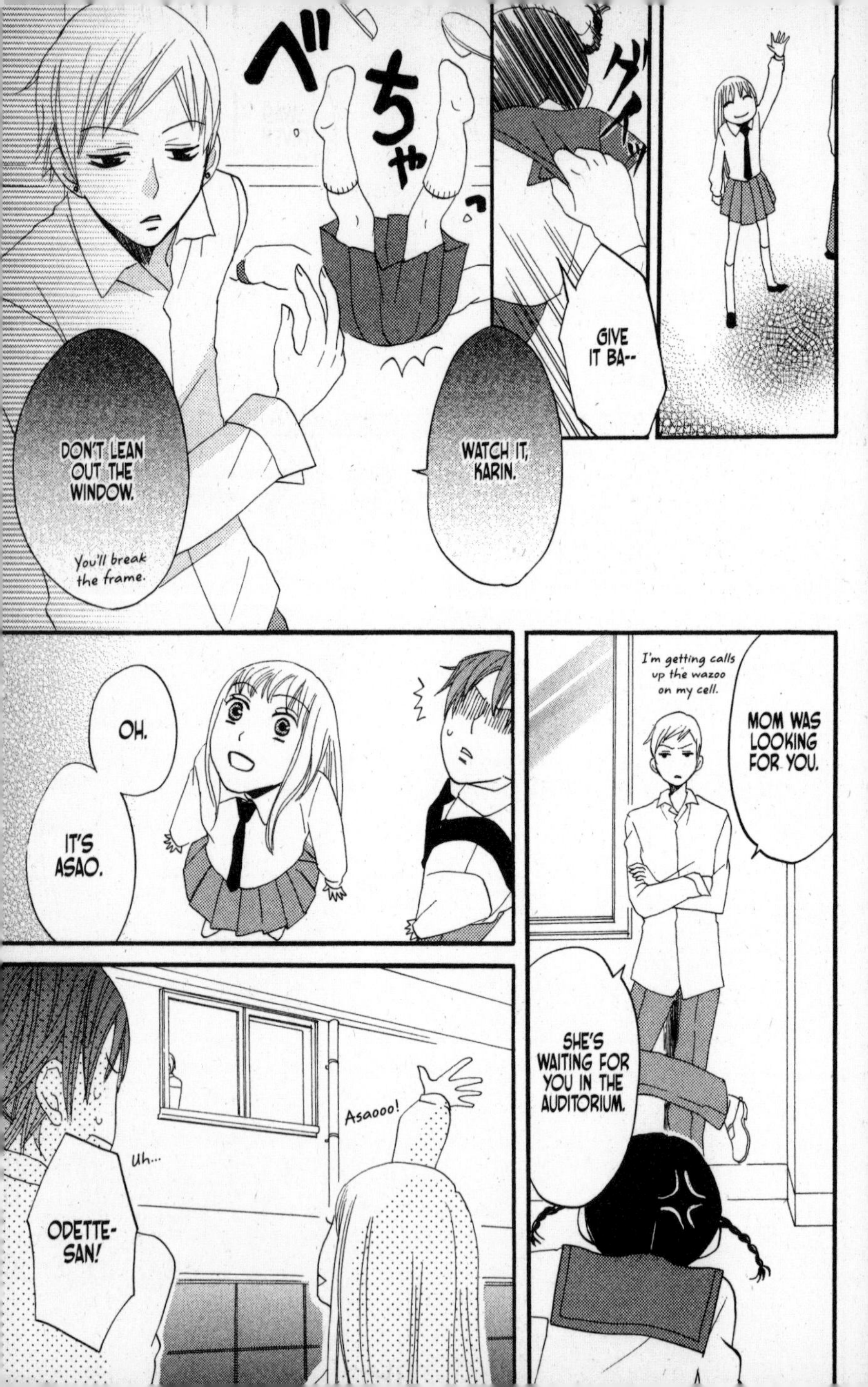
ダイッ
GIVE IT BA--
べちゃ
WATCH IT, KARIN.
DON'T LEAN OUT THE WINDOW.
You'll break the frame.
MOM WAS LOOKING FOR YOU.
I'm getting calls up the wazoo on my cell.
SHE'S WAITING FOR YOU IN THE AUDITORIUM.
OH.
IT'S ASAO.
Asaooo!
Uh...
ODETTE-SAN!

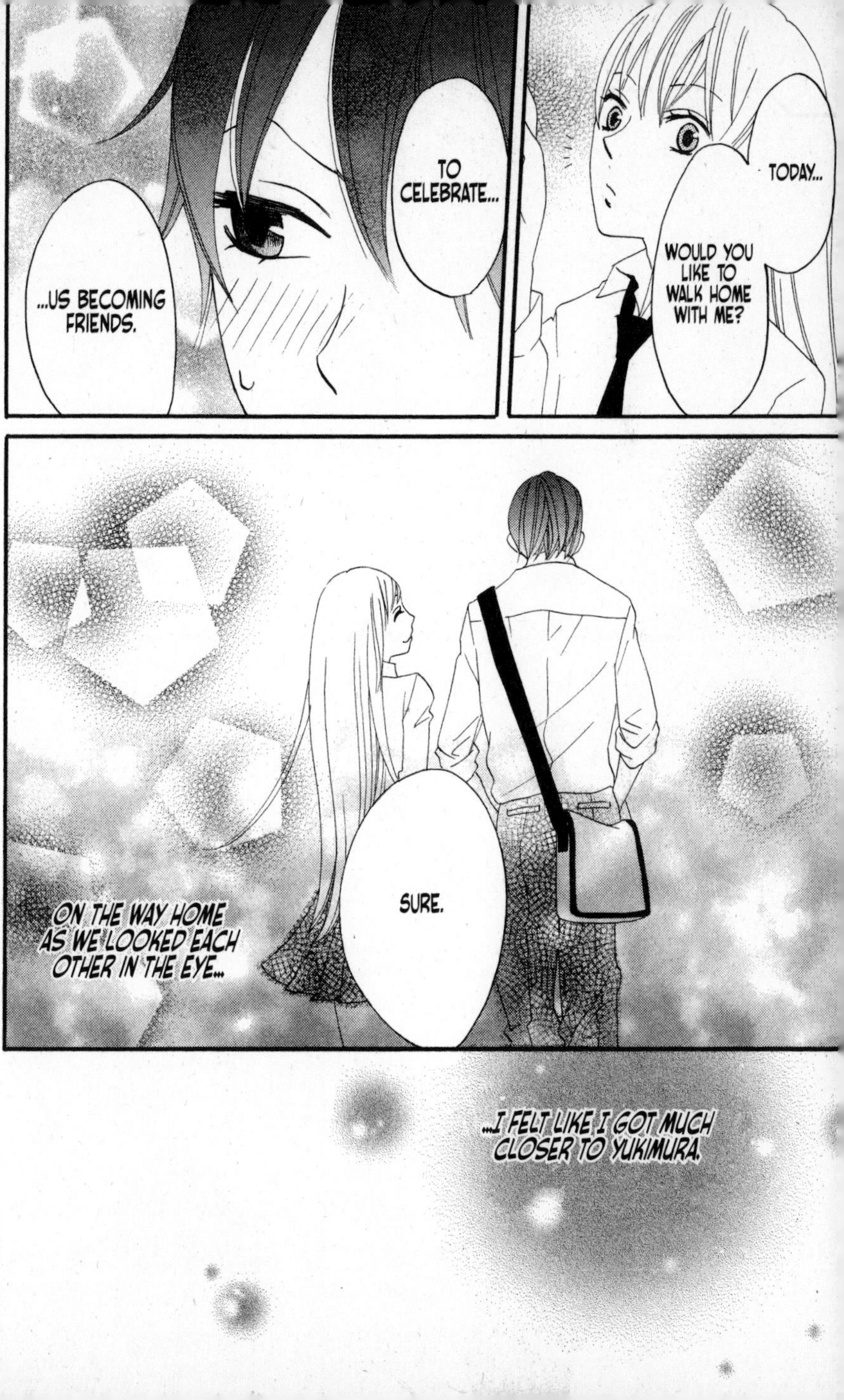
TODAY...
WOULD YOU LIKE TO WALK HOME WITH ME?
TO CELEBRATE...
...US BECOMING FRIENDS.
SURE.
ON THE WAY HOME AS WE LOOKED EACH OTHER IN THE EYE...
...I FELT LIKE I GOT MUCH CLOSER TO YUKIMURA.

Chapter 16

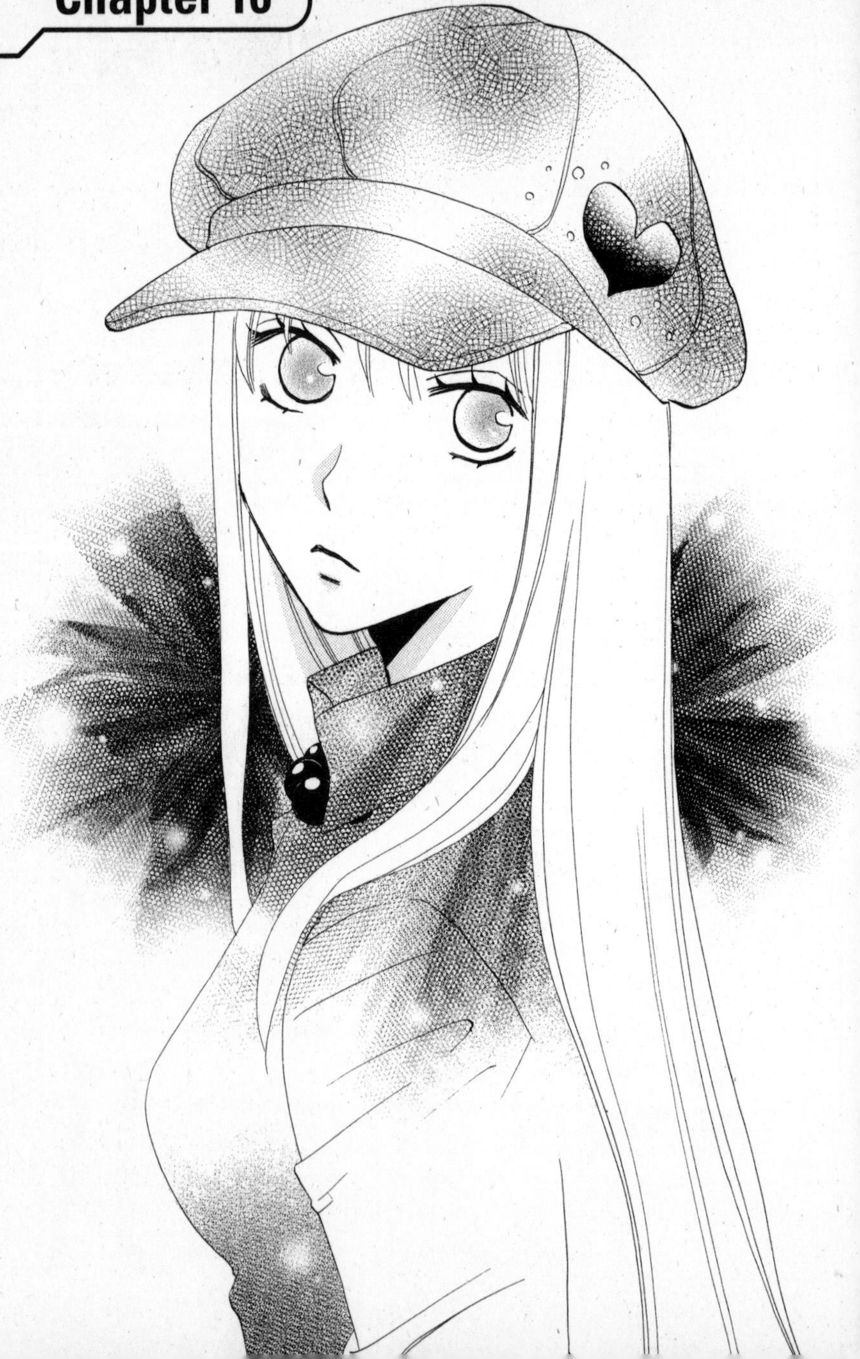

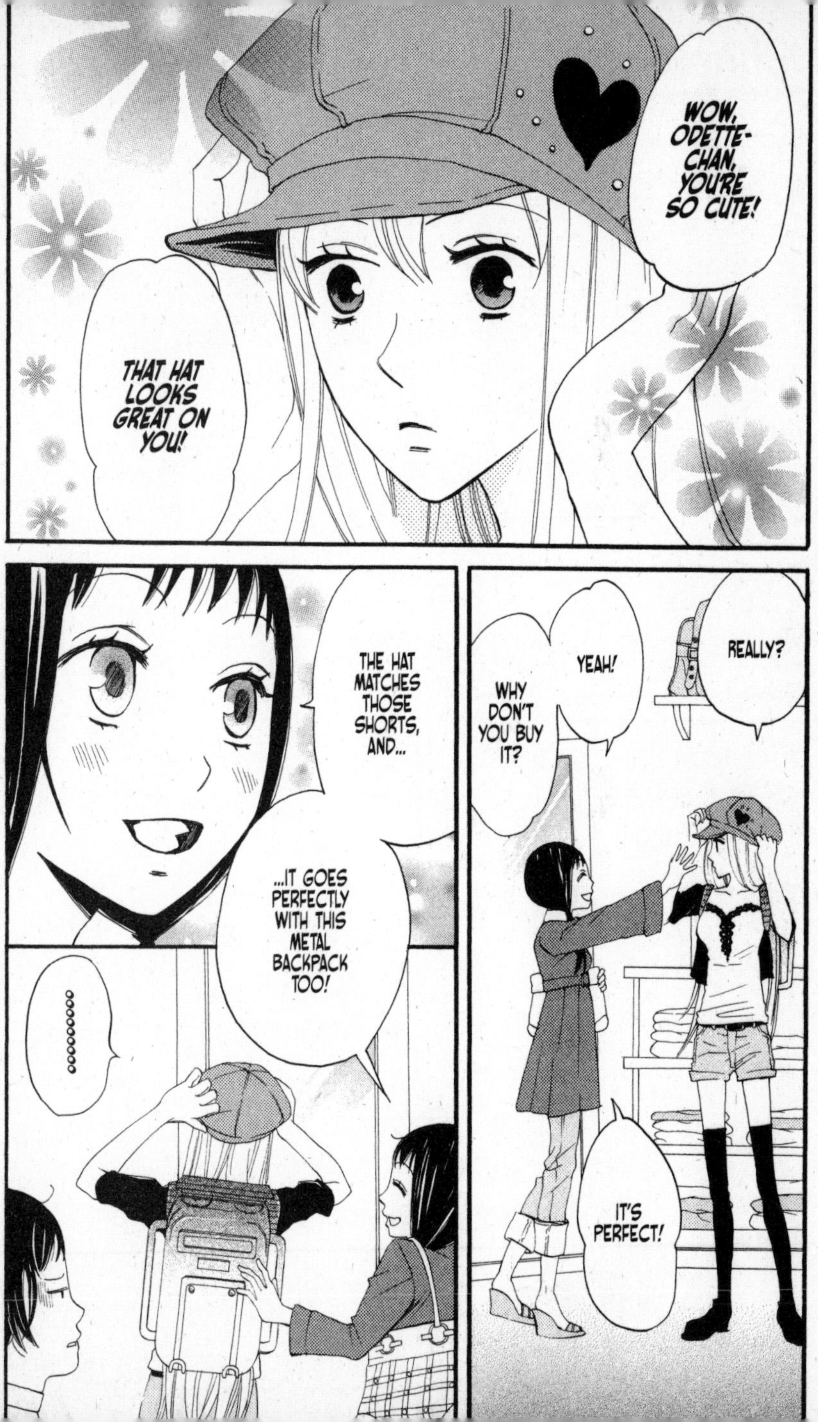
WOW, ODETTE-CHAN, YOU'RE SO CUTE!
THAT HAT LOOKS GREAT ON YOU!
REALLY?
YEAH!
WHY DON'T YOU BUY IT?
IT'S PERFECT!
THE HAT MATCHES THOSE SHORTS, AND...
...IT GOES PERFECTLY WITH THIS METAL BACKPACK TOO!
....

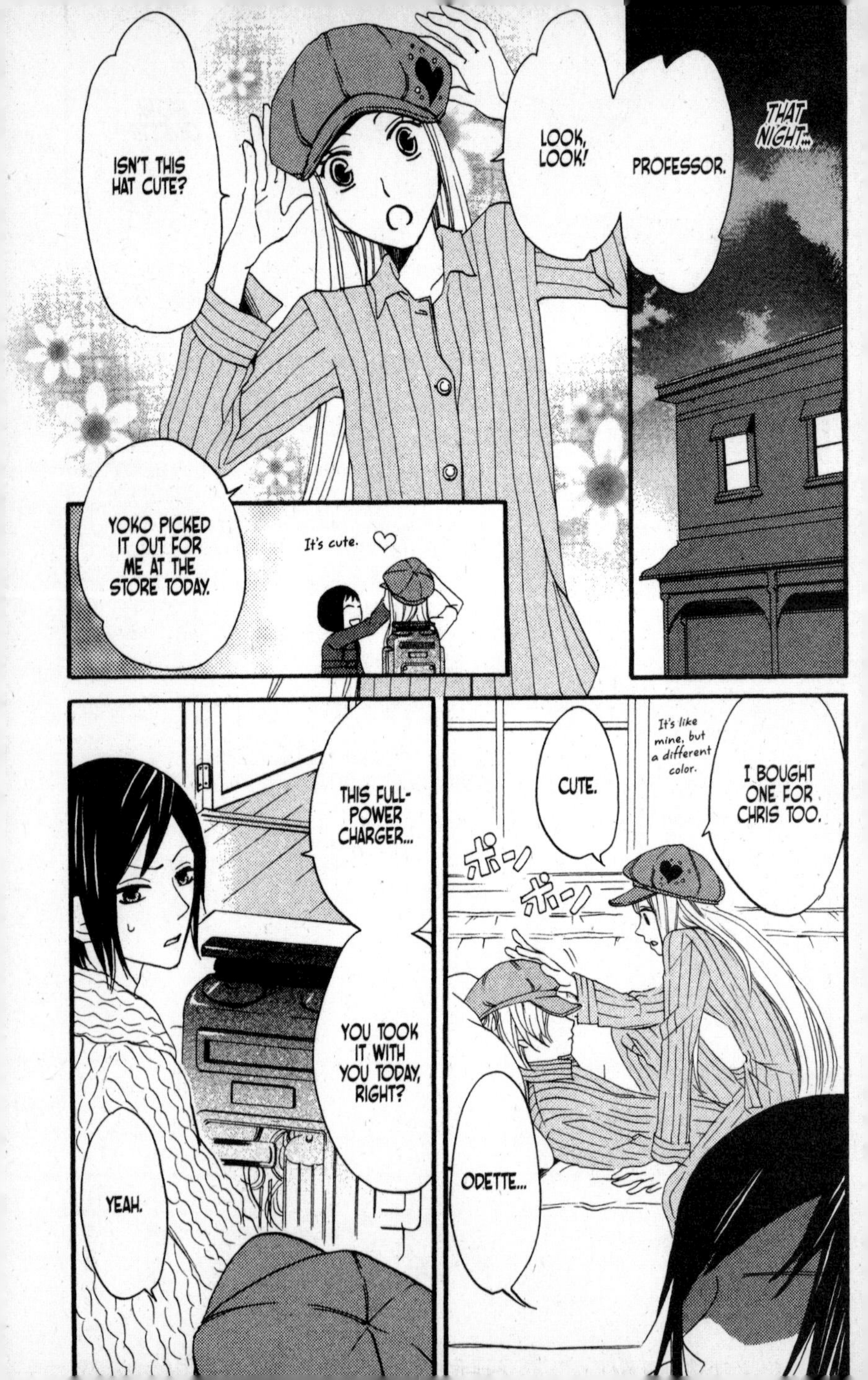
THAT NIGHT...
PROFESSOR.
LOOK, LOOK!
ISN'T THIS HAT CUTE?
YOKO PICKED IT OUT FOR ME AT THE STORE TODAY.
It's cute.
I BOUGHT ONE FOR CHRIS TOO.
It's like mine, but a different color.
CUTE.
ポーン
ポーン
ODETTE...
THIS FULL-POWER CHARGER...
YOU TOOK IT WITH YOU TODAY, RIGHT?
YEAH.

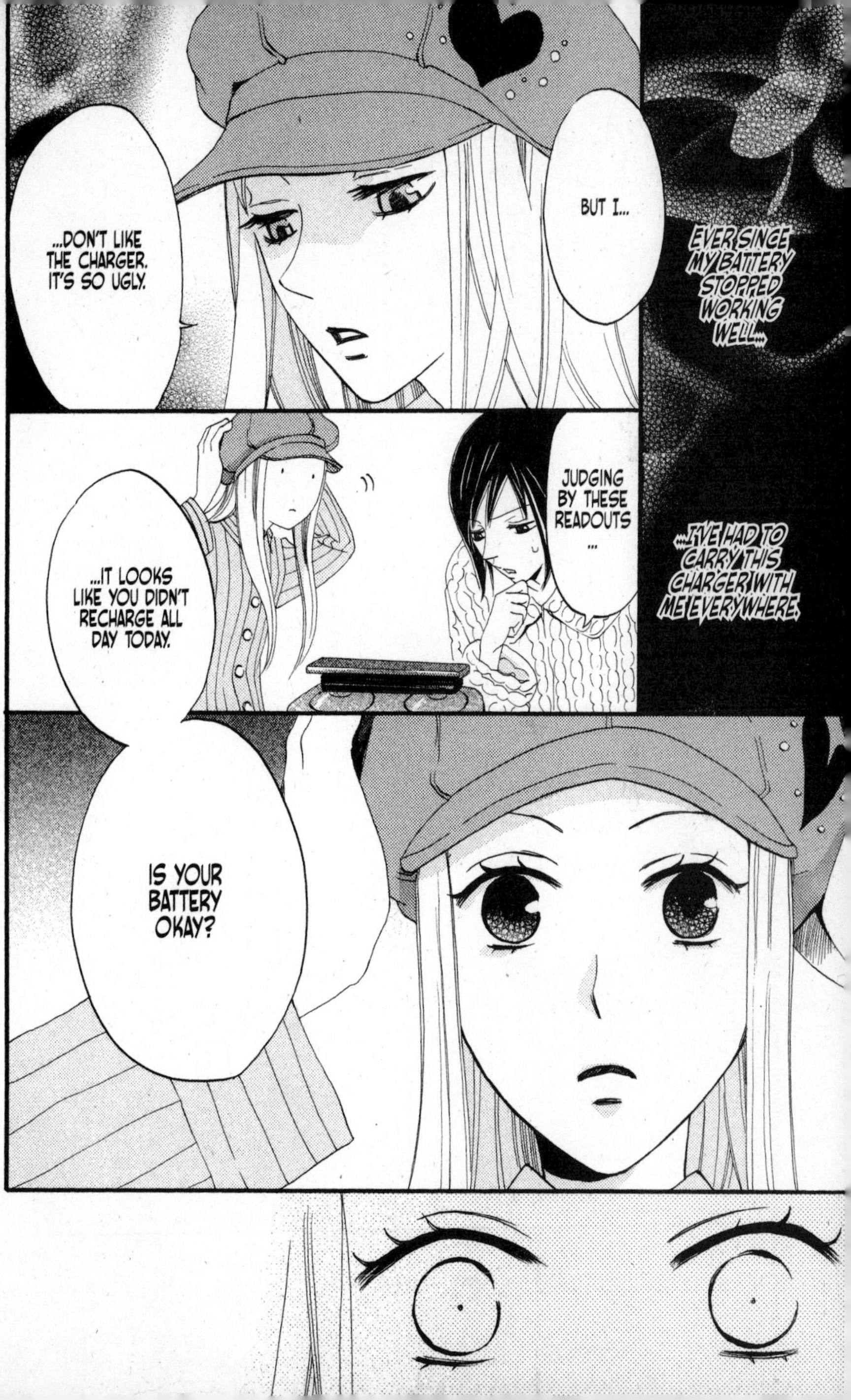

EVER SINCE MY BATTERY STOPPED WORKING WELL...
...I'VE HAD TO CARRY THIS CHARGER WITH ME EVERYWHERE.
BUT I...
...DON'T LIKE THE CHARGER. IT'S SO UGLY.
JUDGING BY THESE READOUTS...
...IT LOOKS LIKE YOU DIDN'T RECHARGE ALL DAY TODAY.
IS YOUR BATTERY OKAY?

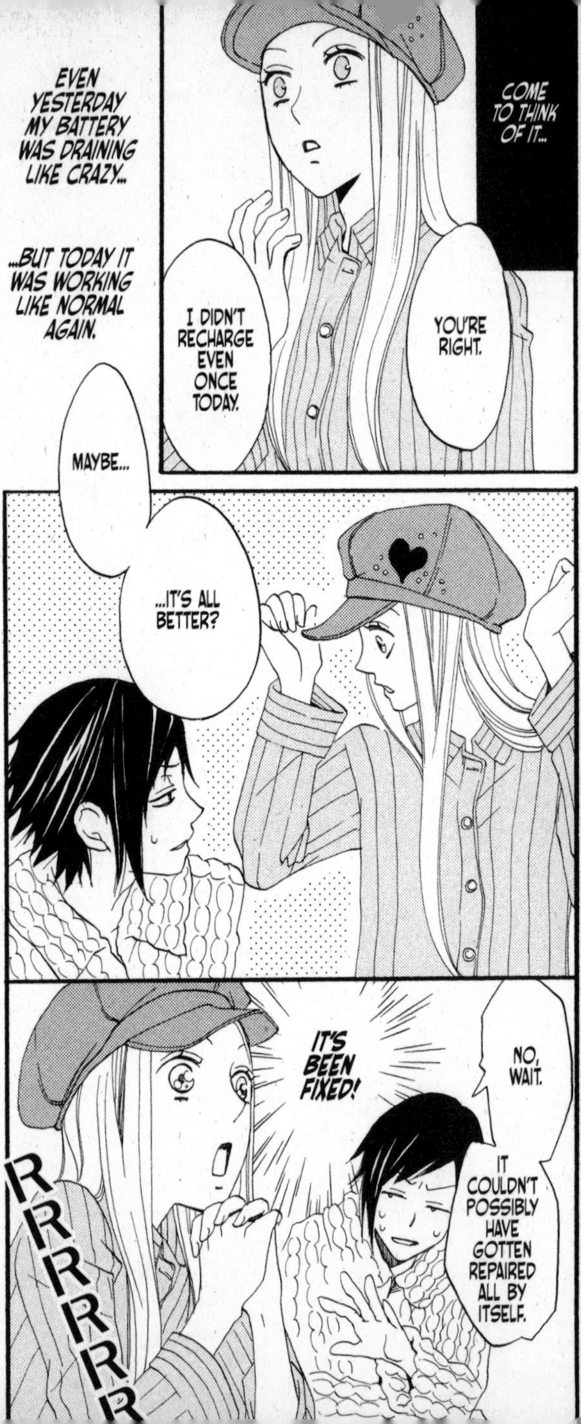
COME TO THINK OF IT...
YOU'RE RIGHT.
I DIDN'T RECHARGE EVEN ONCE TODAY.
EVEN YESTERDAY MY BATTERY WAS DRAINING LIKE CRAZY...
...BUT TODAY IT WAS WORKING LIKE NORMAL AGAIN.
MAYBE...
...IT'S ALL BETTER?
IT'S BEEN FIXED!
NO, WAIT.
IT COULDN'T POSSIBLY HAVE GOTTEN REPAIRED ALL BY ITSELF.
RRRRRR

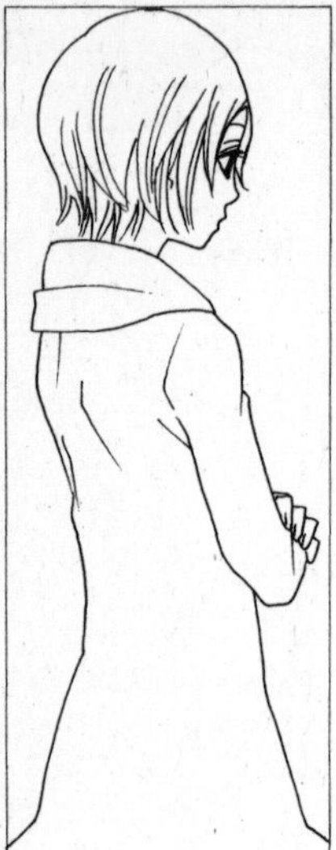

In the next sidebar, Ryoko Fukuyama drew a picture for me! Fukuyama-san, thank you so much❀ Fukuyama-san's Odette and Asao are so cute. I love it!❀

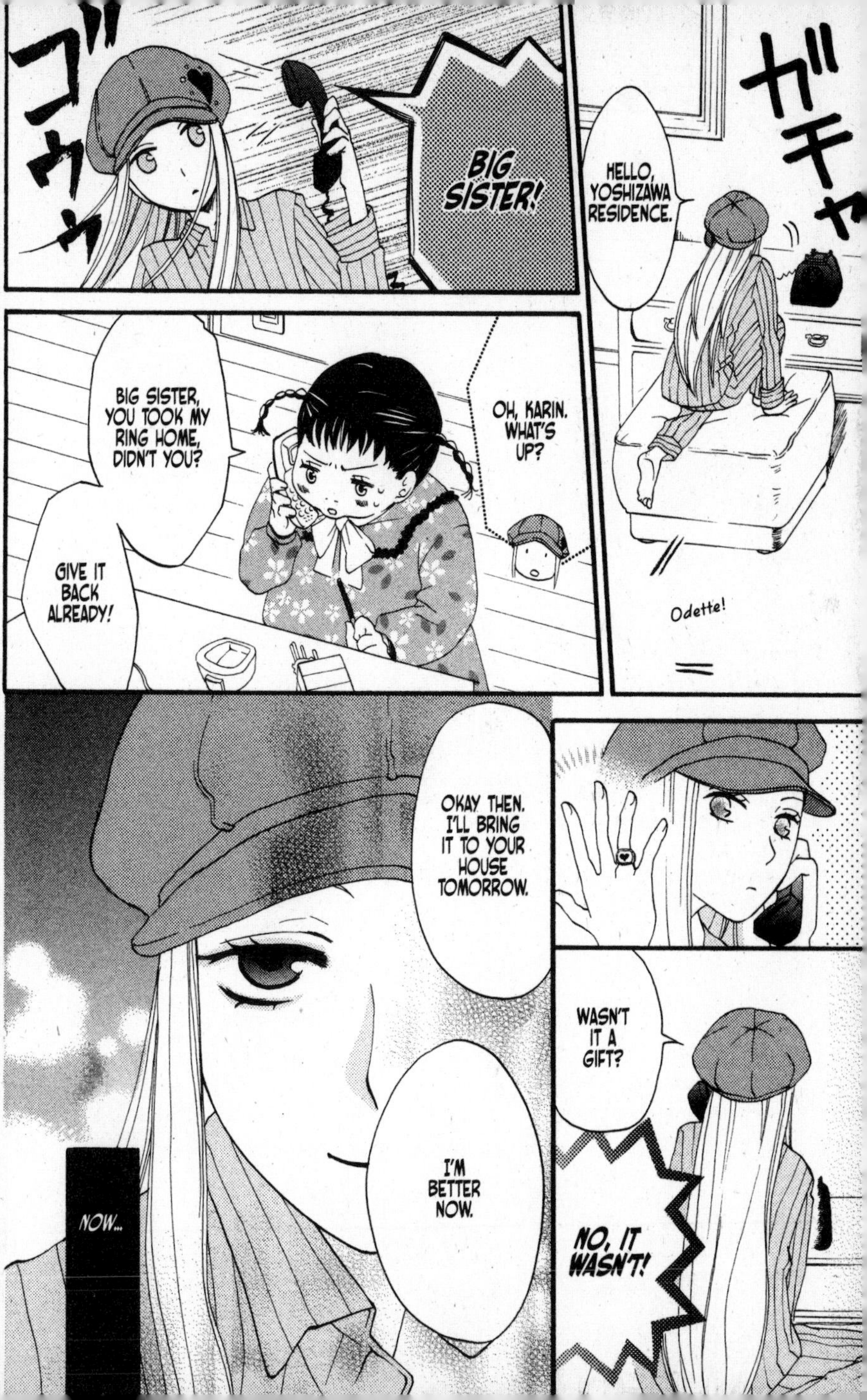
ガチャ
HELLO, YOSHIZAWA RESIDENCE.
Odette!
ゴウゥ
BIG SISTER!
OH, KARIN. WHAT'S UP?
BIG SISTER, YOU TOOK MY RING HOME, DIDN'T YOU?
GIVE IT BACK ALREADY!
WASN'T IT A GIFT?
NO, IT WASN'T!
OKAY THEN. I'LL BRING IT TO YOUR HOUSE TOMORROW.
I'M BETTER NOW.
NOW...

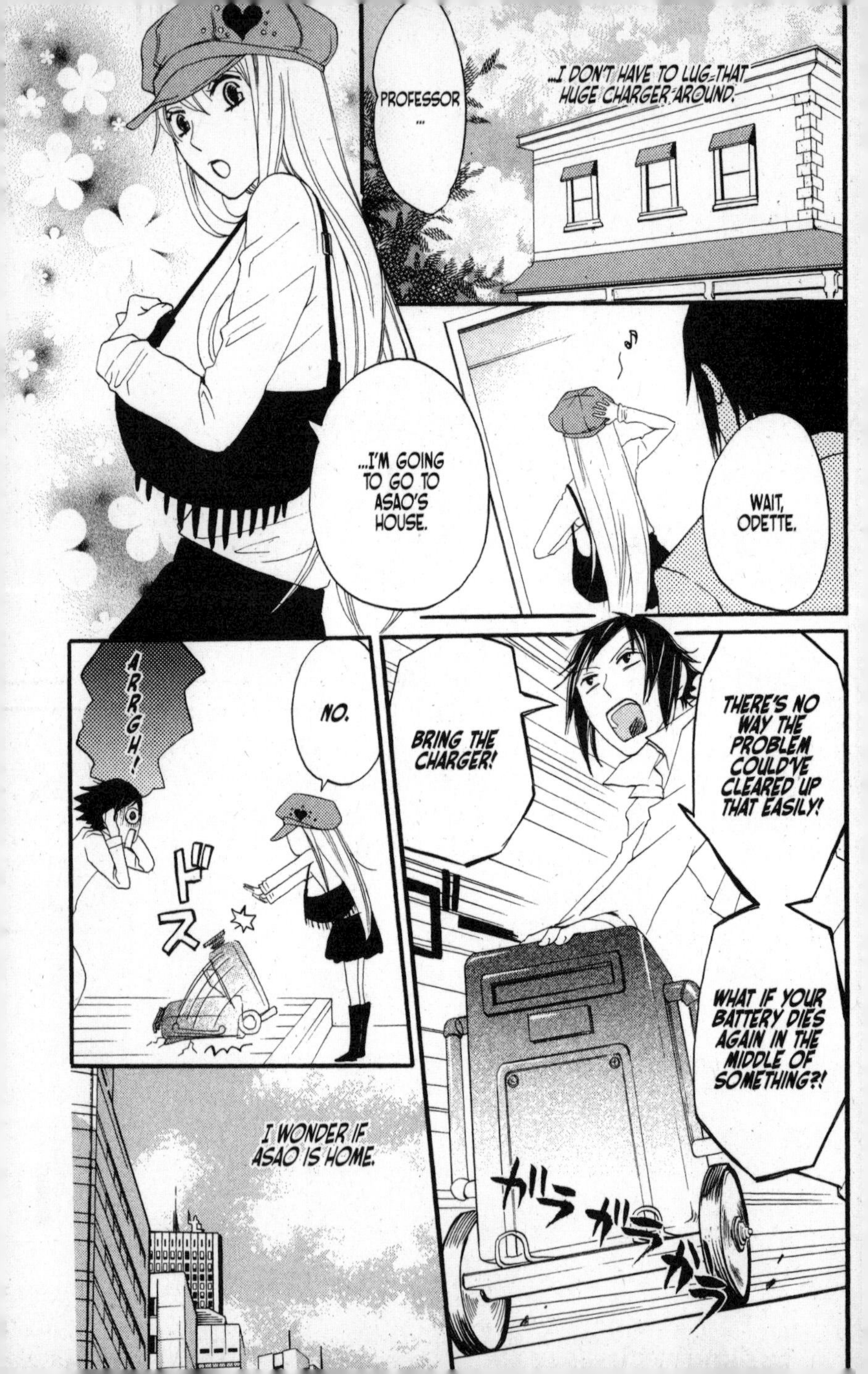

...I DON'T HAVE TO LUG THAT HUGE CHARGER AROUND.
PROFESSOR ...
...I'M GOING TO GO TO ASAO'S HOUSE.
WAIT, ODETTE.
THERE'S NO WAY THE PROBLEM COULD'VE CLEARED UP THAT EASILY!
WHAT IF YOUR BATTERY DIES AGAIN IN THE MIDDLE OF SOMETHING?!
BRING THE CHARGER!
ガラ ガラ ガラ
NO.
ARRGH!
ドス
I WONDER IF ASAO IS HOME.

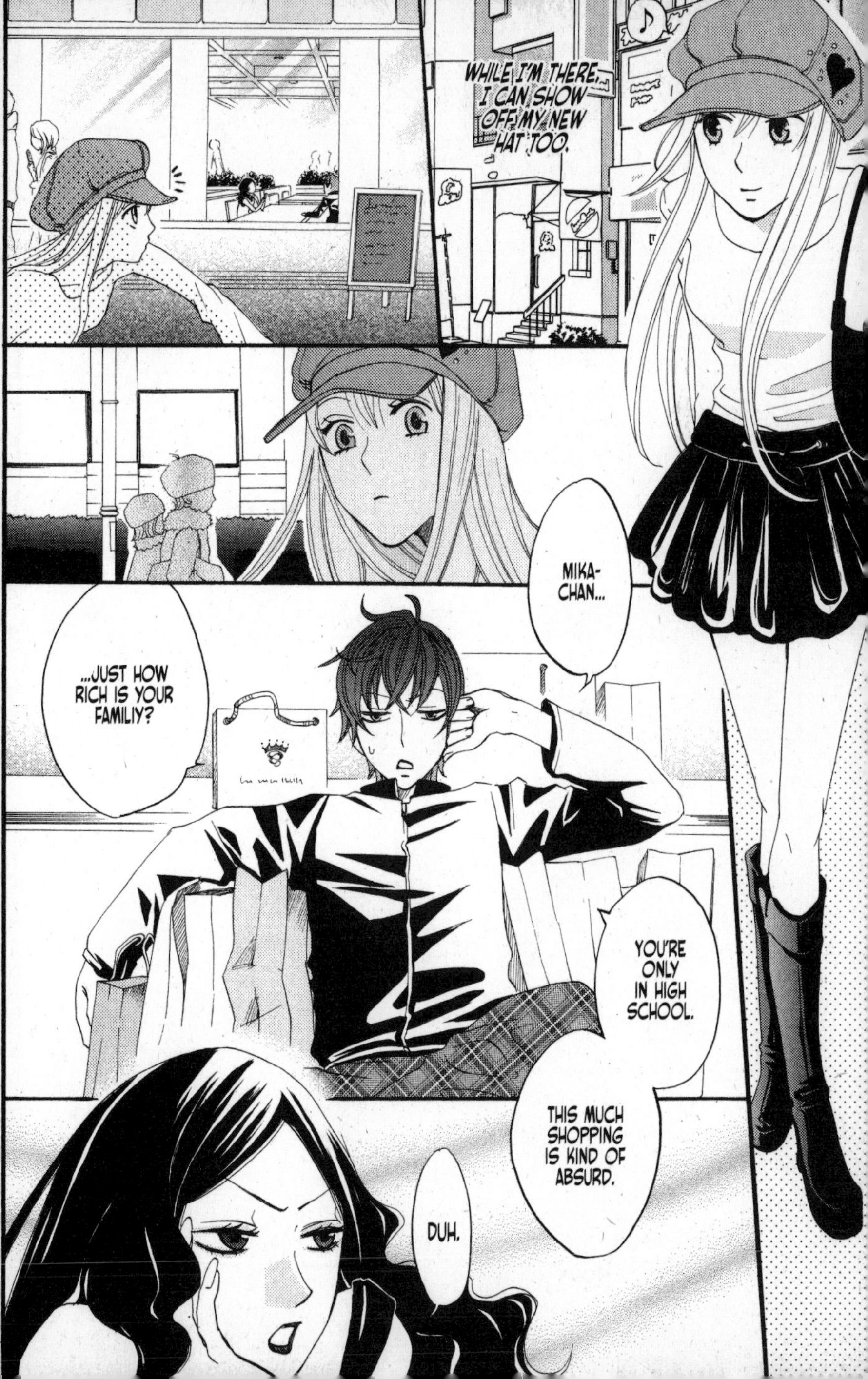
WHILE I'M THERE, I CAN SHOW OFF MY NEW HAT TOO.
MIKA-CHAN...
...JUST HOW RICH IS YOUR FAMILIY?
YOU'RE ONLY IN HIGH SCHOOL.
THIS MUCH SHOPPING IS KIND OF ABSURD.
DUH.

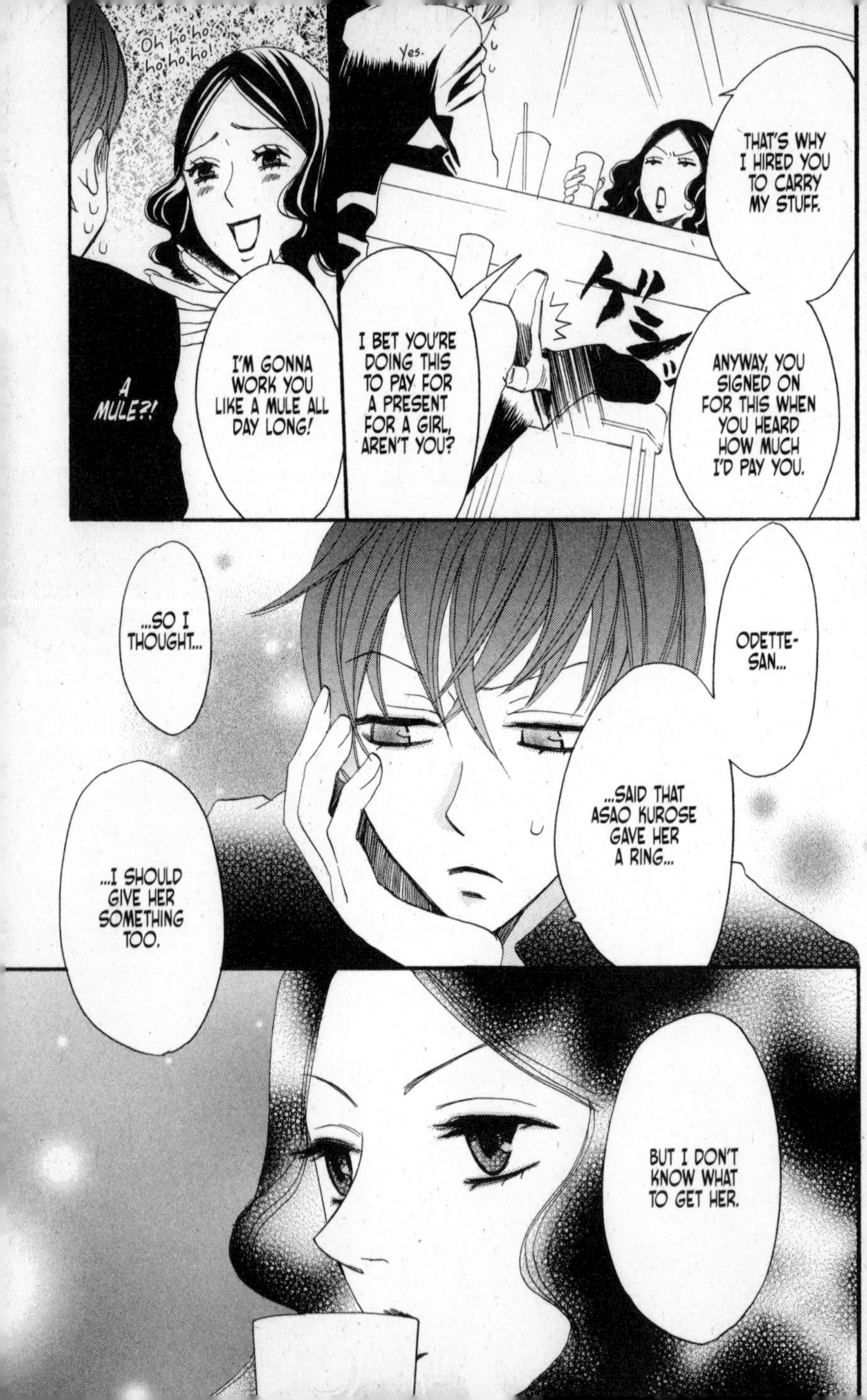
THAT'S WHY I HIRED YOU TO CARRY MY STUFF.
Yes.
ゲシッ
ANYWAY, YOU SIGNED ON FOR THIS WHEN YOU HEARD HOW MUCH I'D PAY YOU.
I BET YOU'RE DOING THIS TO PAY FOR A PRESENT FOR A GIRL, AREN'T YOU?
Oh ho ho ho ho ho!
I'M GONNA WORK YOU LIKE A MULE ALL DAY LONG!
A MULE?!
ODETTE-SAN...
...SAID THAT ASAO KUROSE GAVE HER A RING...
...SO I THOUGHT...
...I SHOULD GIVE HER SOMETHING TOO.
BUT I DON'T KNOW WHAT TO GET HER.

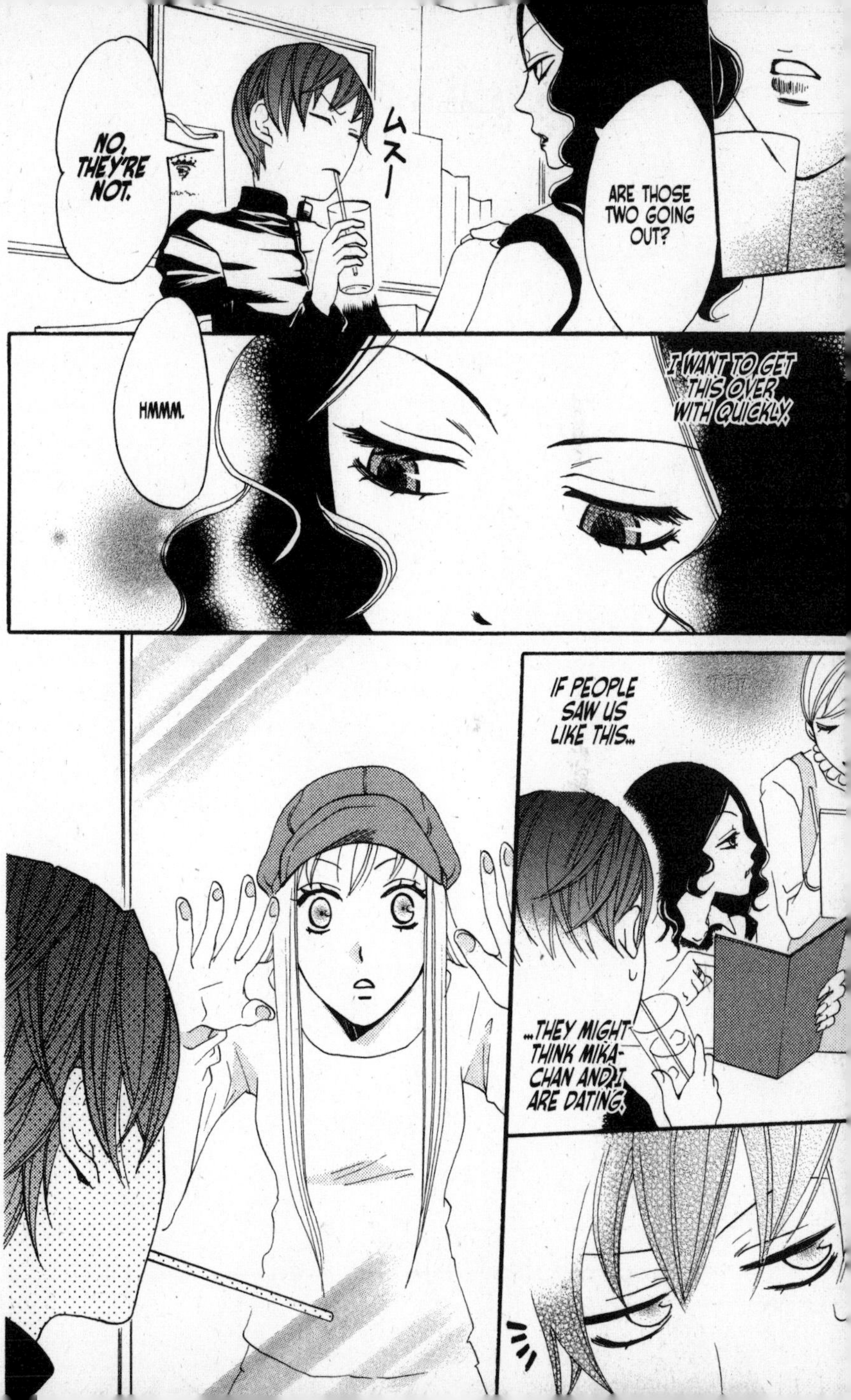
ARE THOSE TWO GOING OUT?
ムスー
NO, THEY'RE NOT.
I WANT TO GET THIS OVER WITH QUICKLY.
HMMM.
IF PEOPLE SAW US LIKE THIS...
...THEY MIGHT THINK MIKA-CHAN AND I ARE DATING.

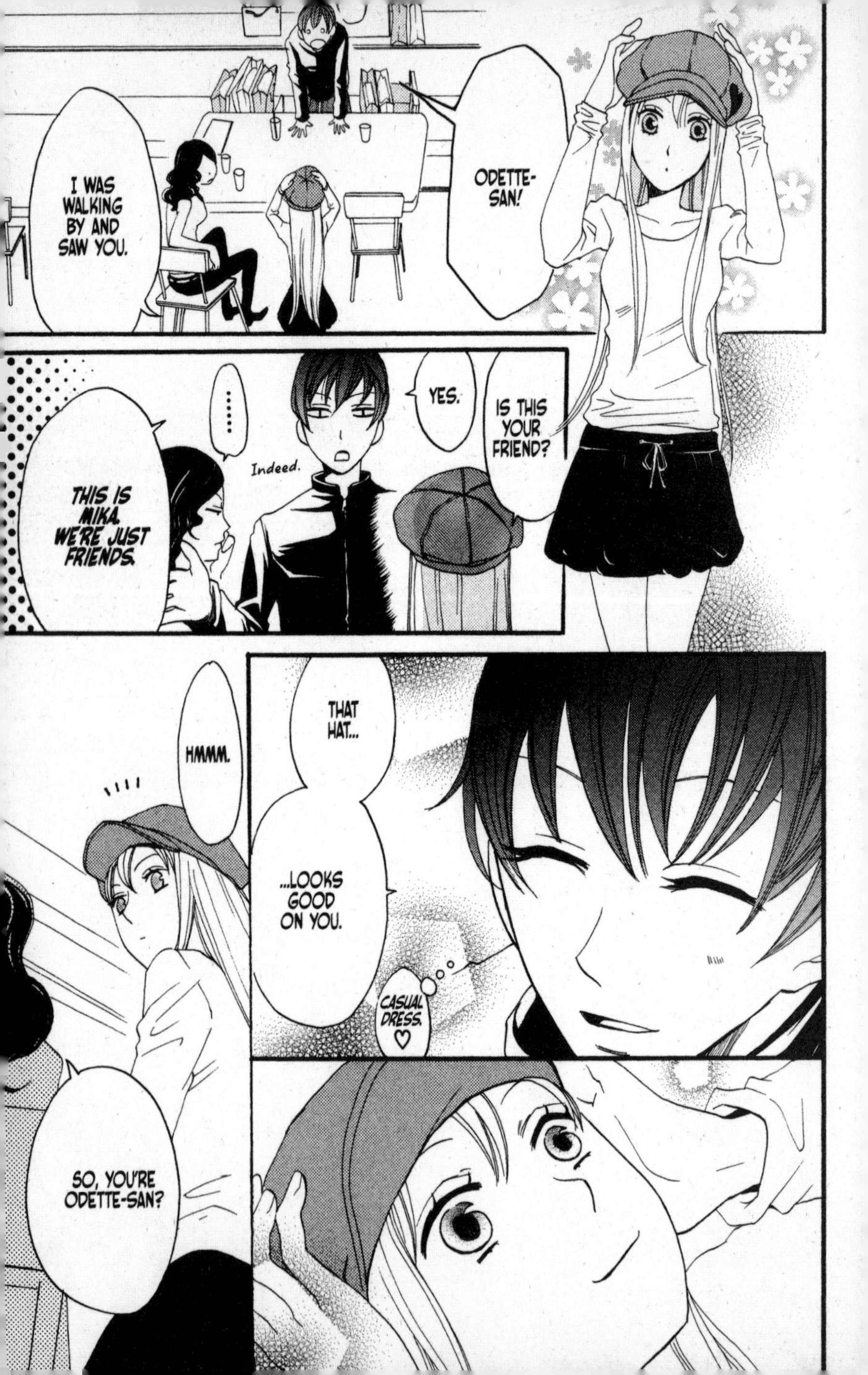
ODETTE-SAN!
I WAS WALKING BY AND SAW YOU.
IS THIS YOUR FRIEND?
YES.
Indeed.
......
THIS IS MIKA. WE'RE JUST FRIENDS.
THAT HAT...
...LOOKS GOOD ON YOU.
CASUAL DRESS. ♡
HMMM.
SO, YOU'RE ODETTE-SAN?

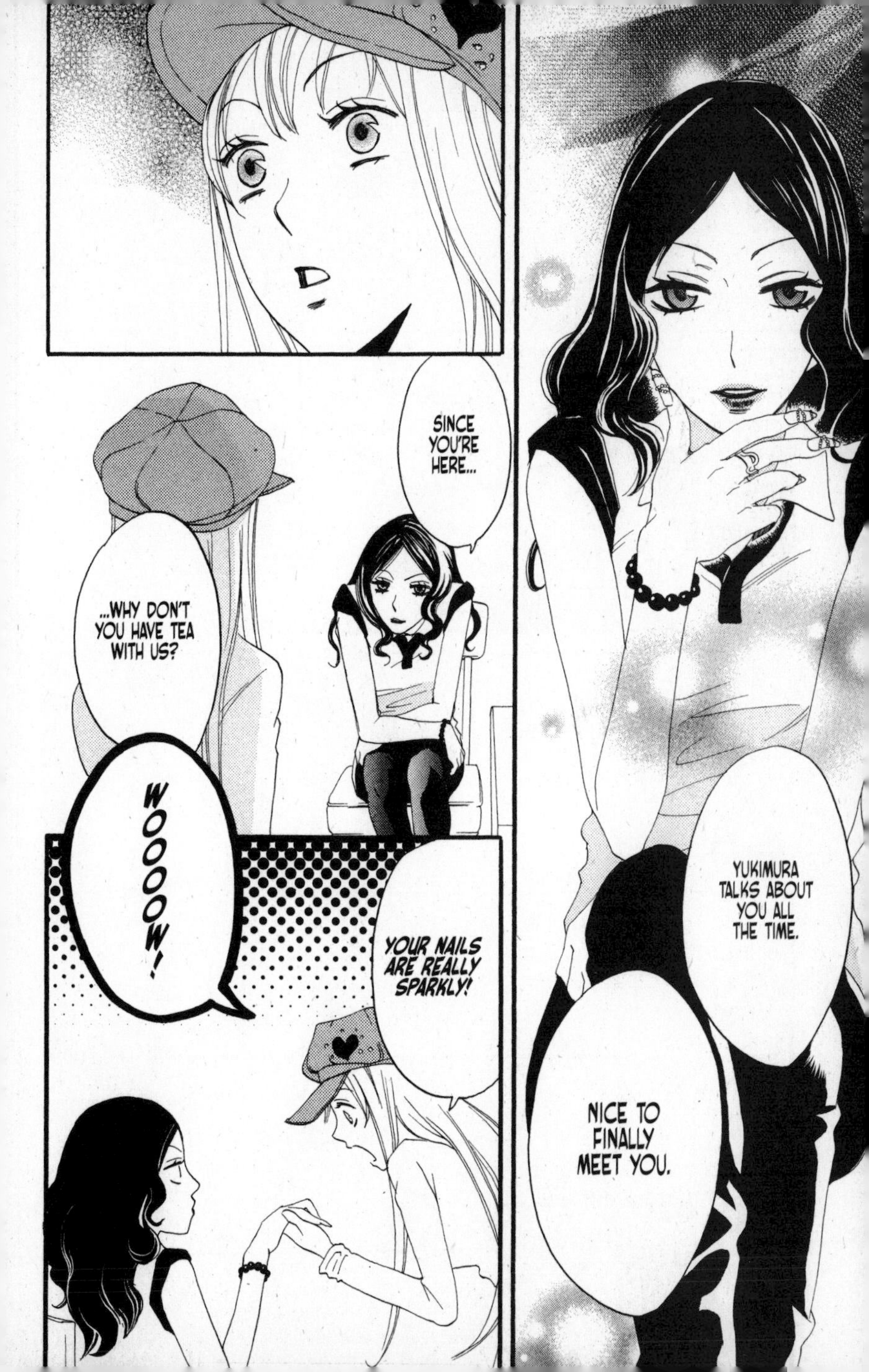
YUKIMURA TALKS ABOUT YOU ALL THE TIME.
NICE TO FINALLY MEET YOU.
SINCE YOU'RE HERE...
...WHY DON'T YOU HAVE TEA WITH US?
WOOOOOW!
YOUR NAILS ARE REALLY SPARKLY!

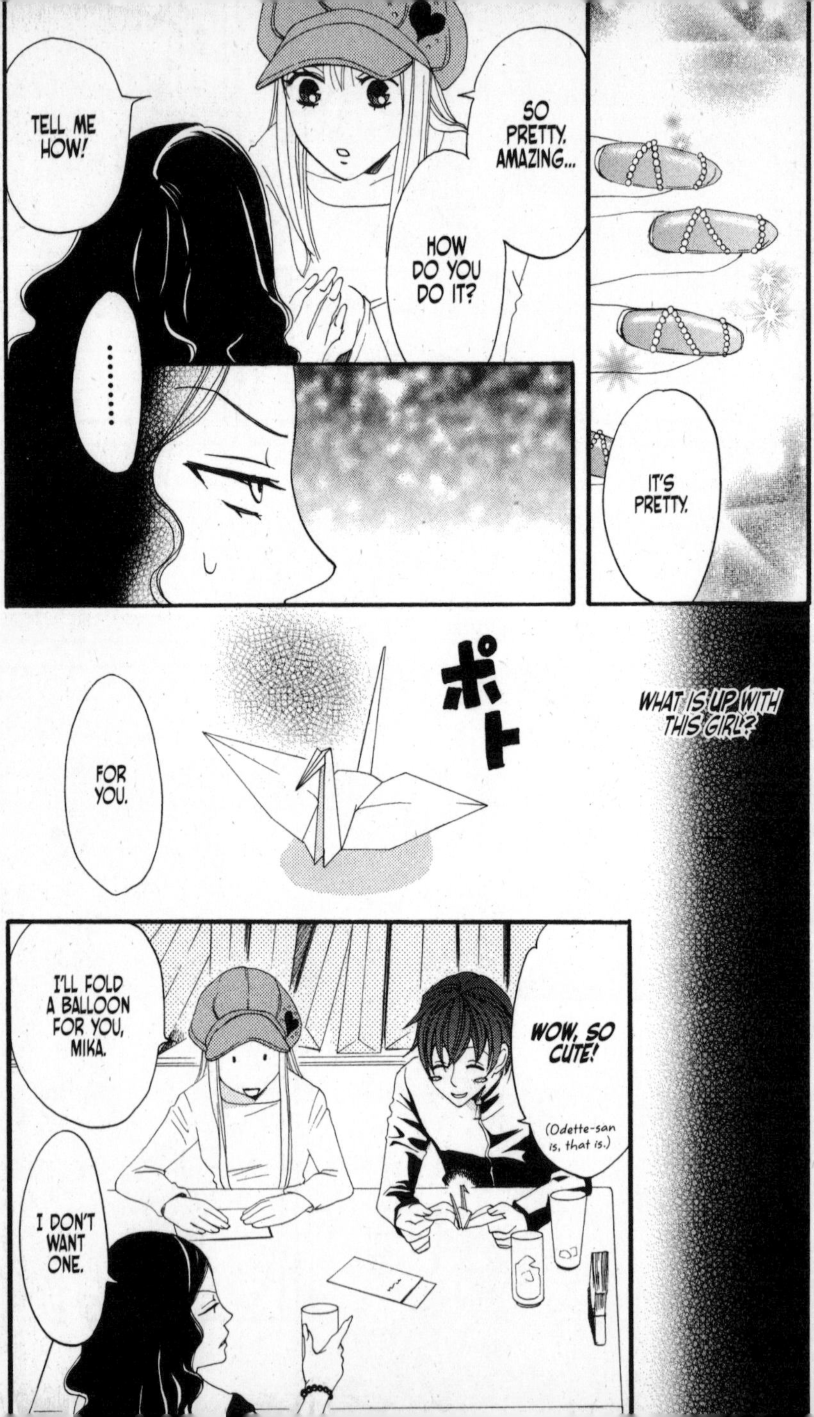
IT'S PRETTY.
SO PRETTY. AMAZING...
HOW DO YOU DO IT?
TELL ME HOW!
....
WHAT IS UP WITH THIS GIRL?
ポト
FOR YOU.
WOW, SO CUTE!
(Odette-san is, that is.)
I'LL FOLD A BALLOON FOR YOU, MIKA.
I DON'T WANT ONE.

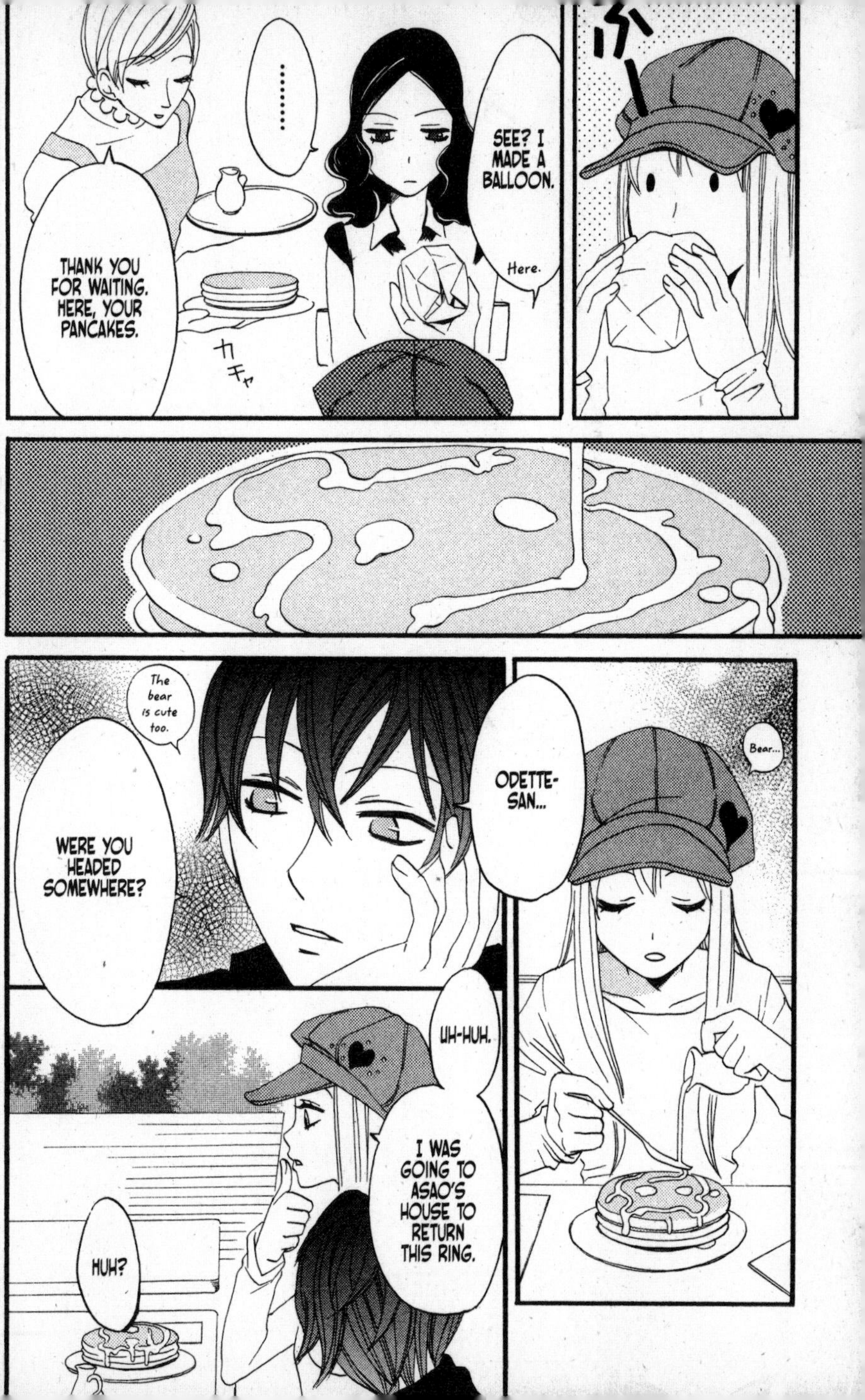
ぷー
SEE? I MADE A BALLOON.
Here.
......
THANK YOU FOR WAITING. HERE, YOUR PANCAKES.
カチャ
Bear...
ODETTE-SAN...
The bear is cute too.
WERE YOU HEADED SOMEWHERE?
UH-HUH.
I WAS GOING TO ASAO'S HOUSE TO RETURN THIS RING.
HUH?

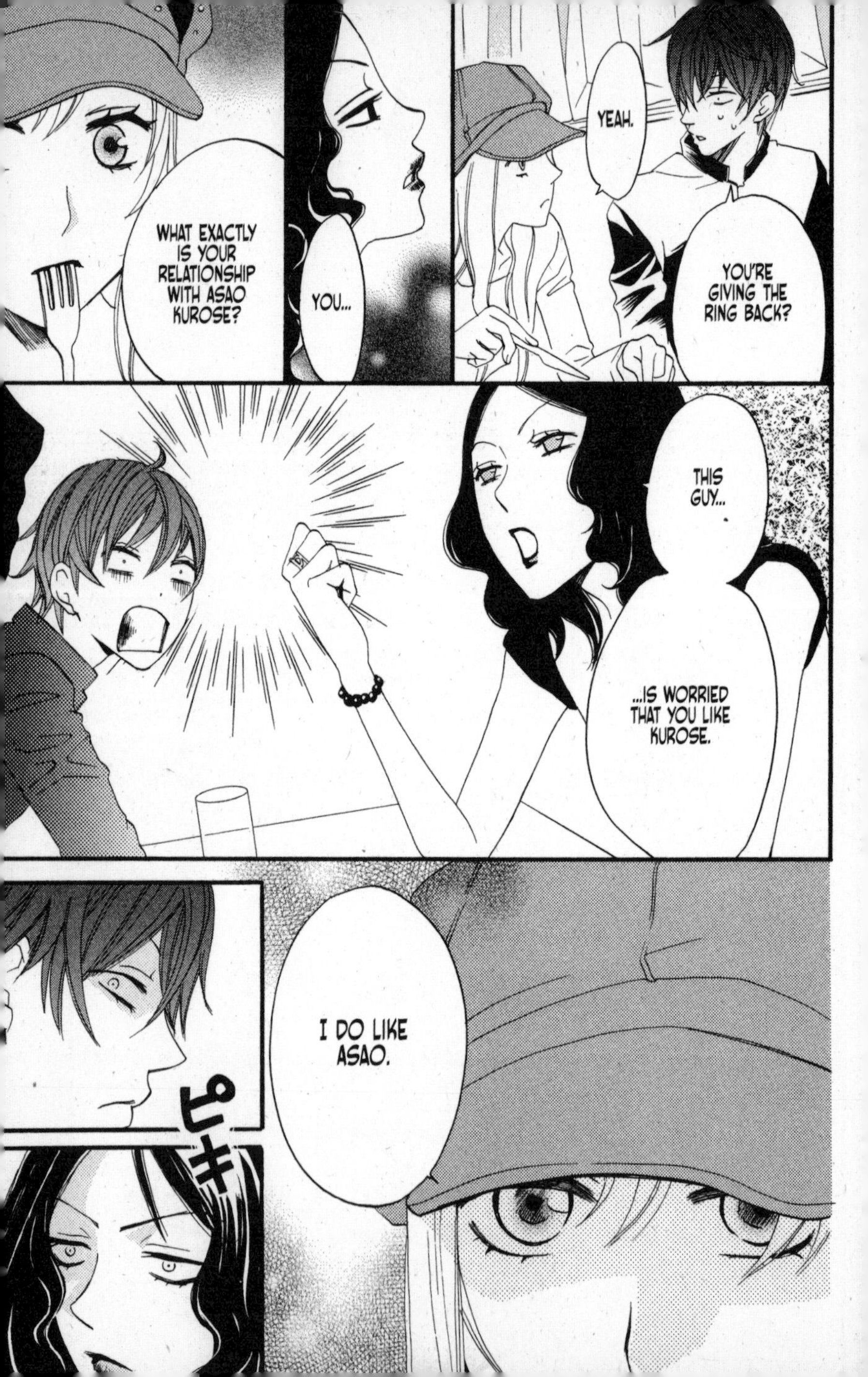
YOU'RE GIVING THE RING BACK?
YEAH.
YOU...
WHAT EXACTLY IS YOUR RELATIONSHIP WITH ASAO KUROSE?
THIS GUY...
...IS WORRIED THAT YOU LIKE KUROSE.
I DO LIKE ASAO.
ピキ

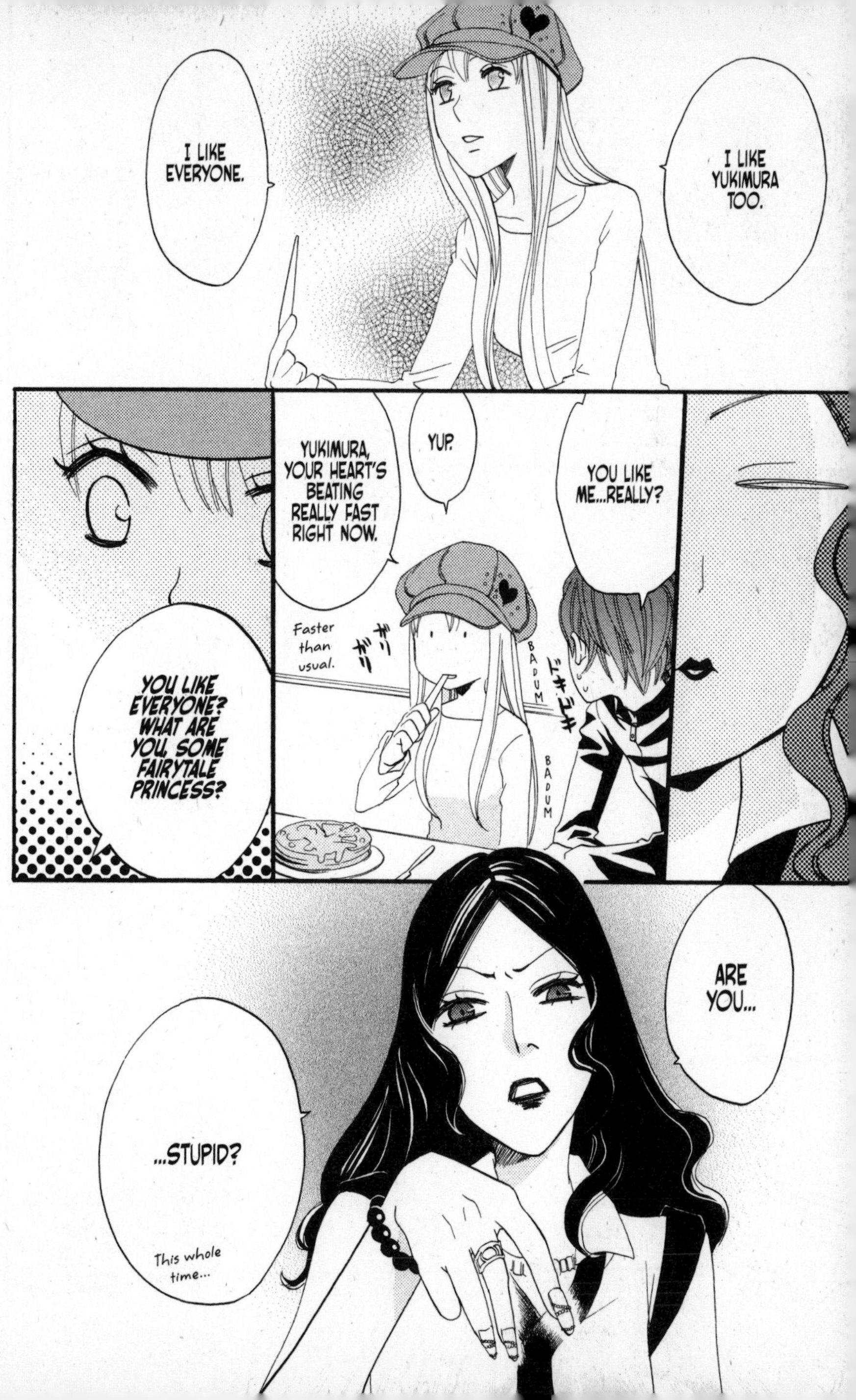
I LIKE YUKIMURA TOO.
I LIKE EVERYONE.
YOU LIKE ME...REALLY?
YUP.
YUKIMURA, YOUR HEART'S BEATING REALLY FAST RIGHT NOW.
BADUM
BADUM
Faster than usual.
YOU LIKE EVERYONE? WHAT ARE YOU, SOME FAIRYTALE PRINCESS?
ARE YOU...
...STUPID?
This whole time...

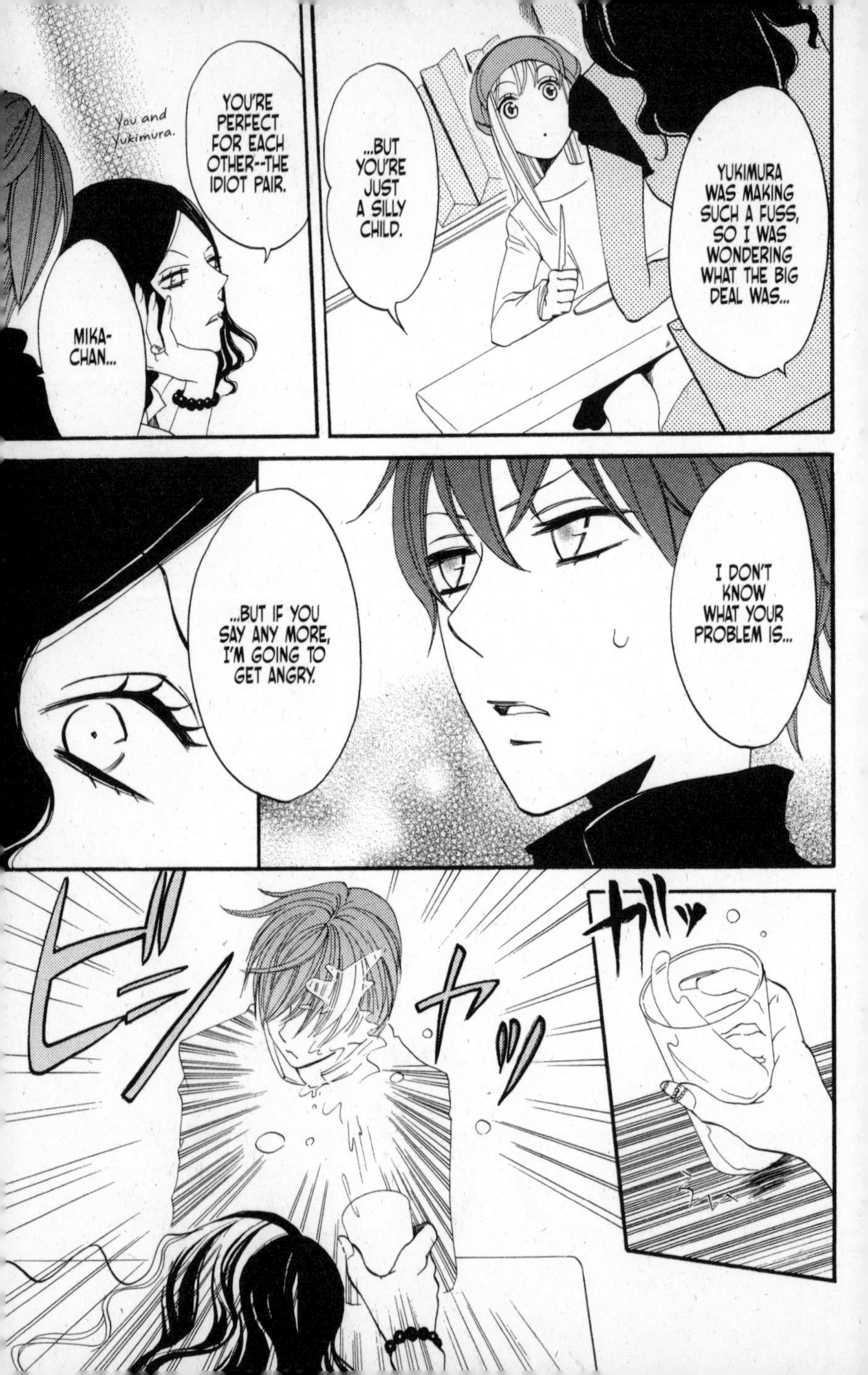
YUKIMURA WAS MAKING SUCH A FUSS, SO I WAS WONDERING WHAT THE BIG DEAL WAS...
...BUT YOU'RE JUST A SILLY CHILD.
YOU'RE PERFECT FOR EACH OTHER--THE IDIOT PAIR.
You and Yukimura.
MIKA-CHAN...
I DON'T KNOW WHAT YOUR PROBLEM IS...
...BUT IF YOU SAY ANY MORE, I'M GOING TO GET ANGRY.

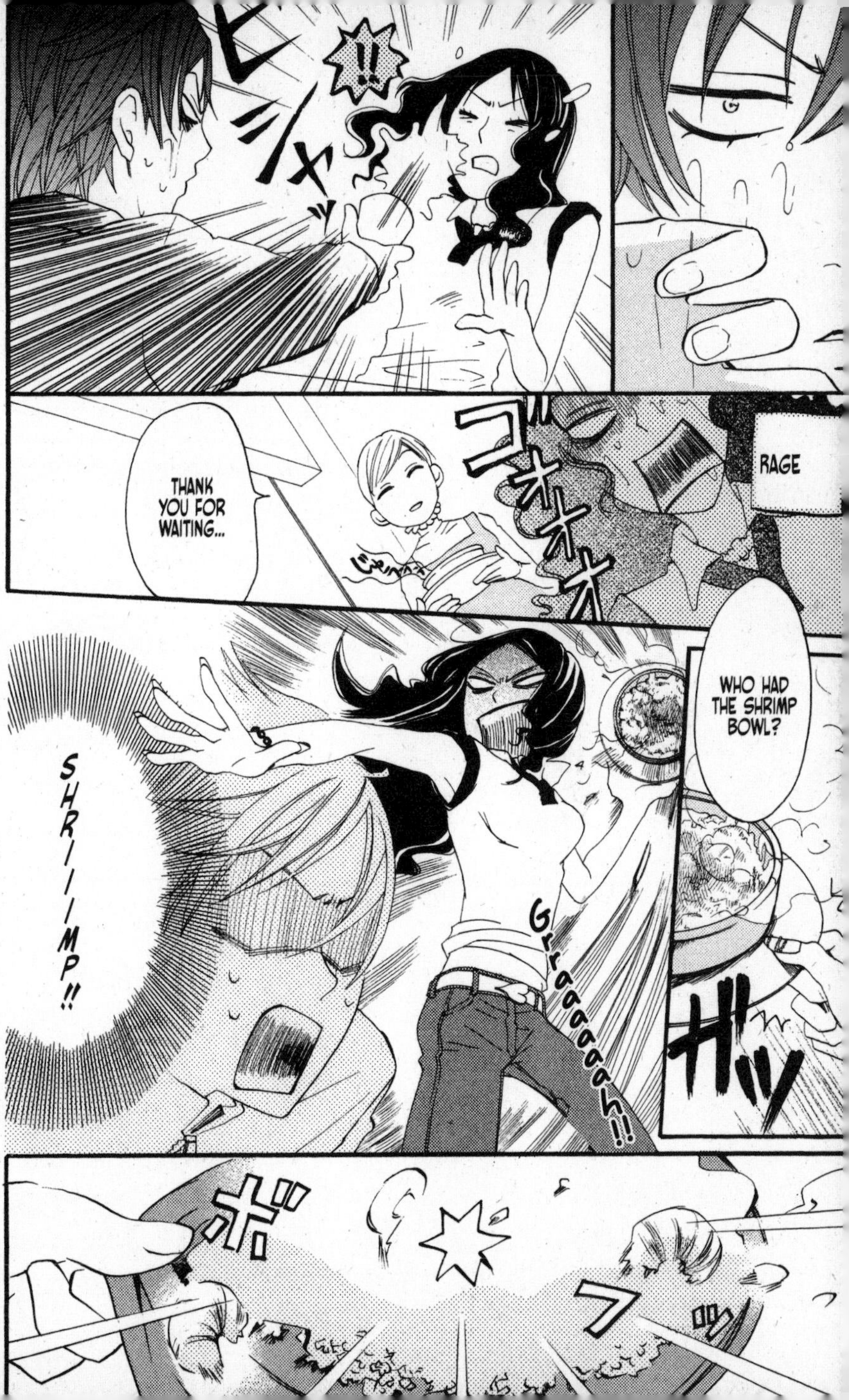

ビシャッ
!!
RAGE
ゴオオオ
THANK YOU FOR WAITING...
WHO HAD THE SHRIMP BOWL?
ガッ
Graaaaaah!!
SHRIIIIMP!!
フッ
ボ

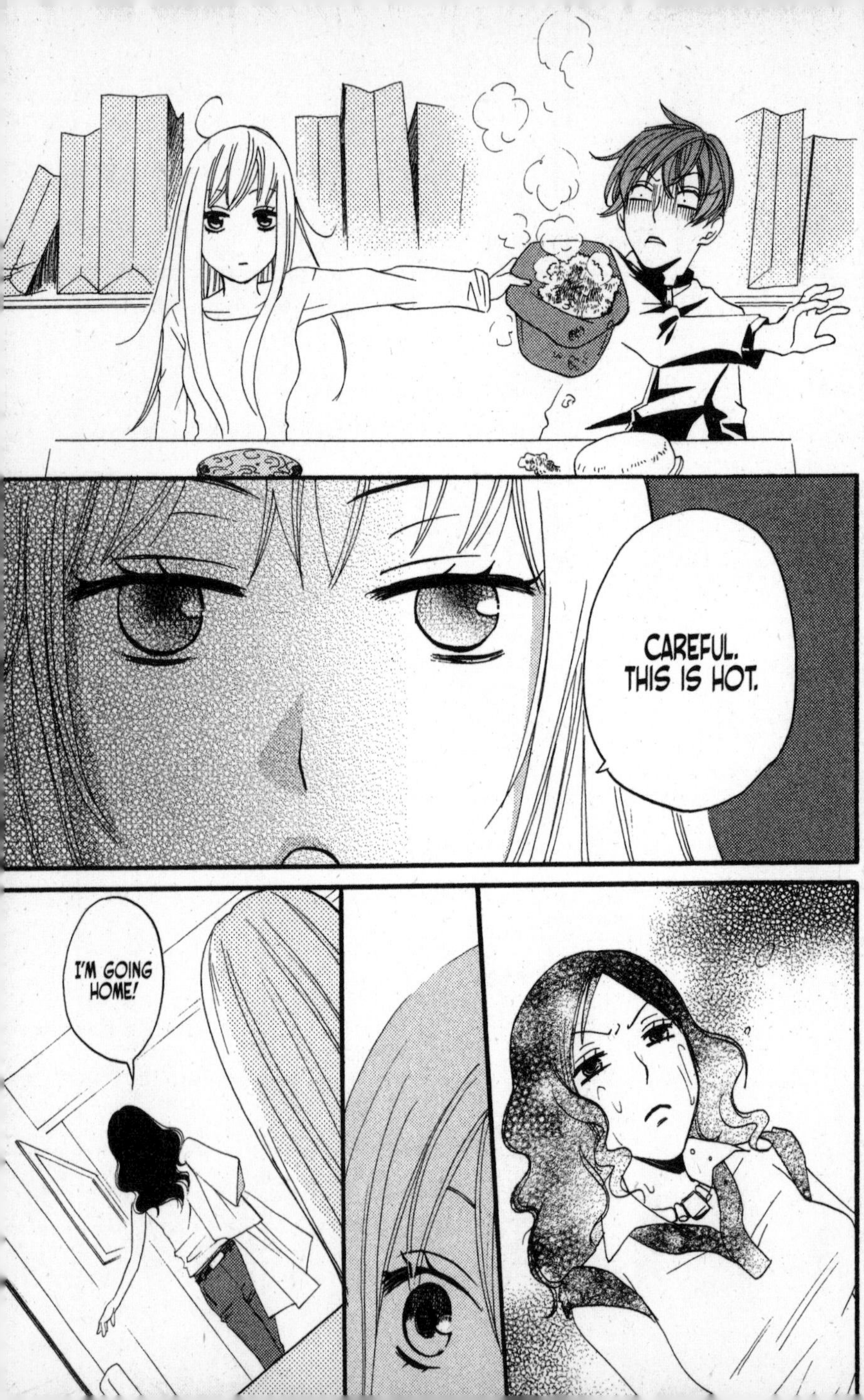
CAREFUL. THIS IS HOT.
I'M GOING HOME!

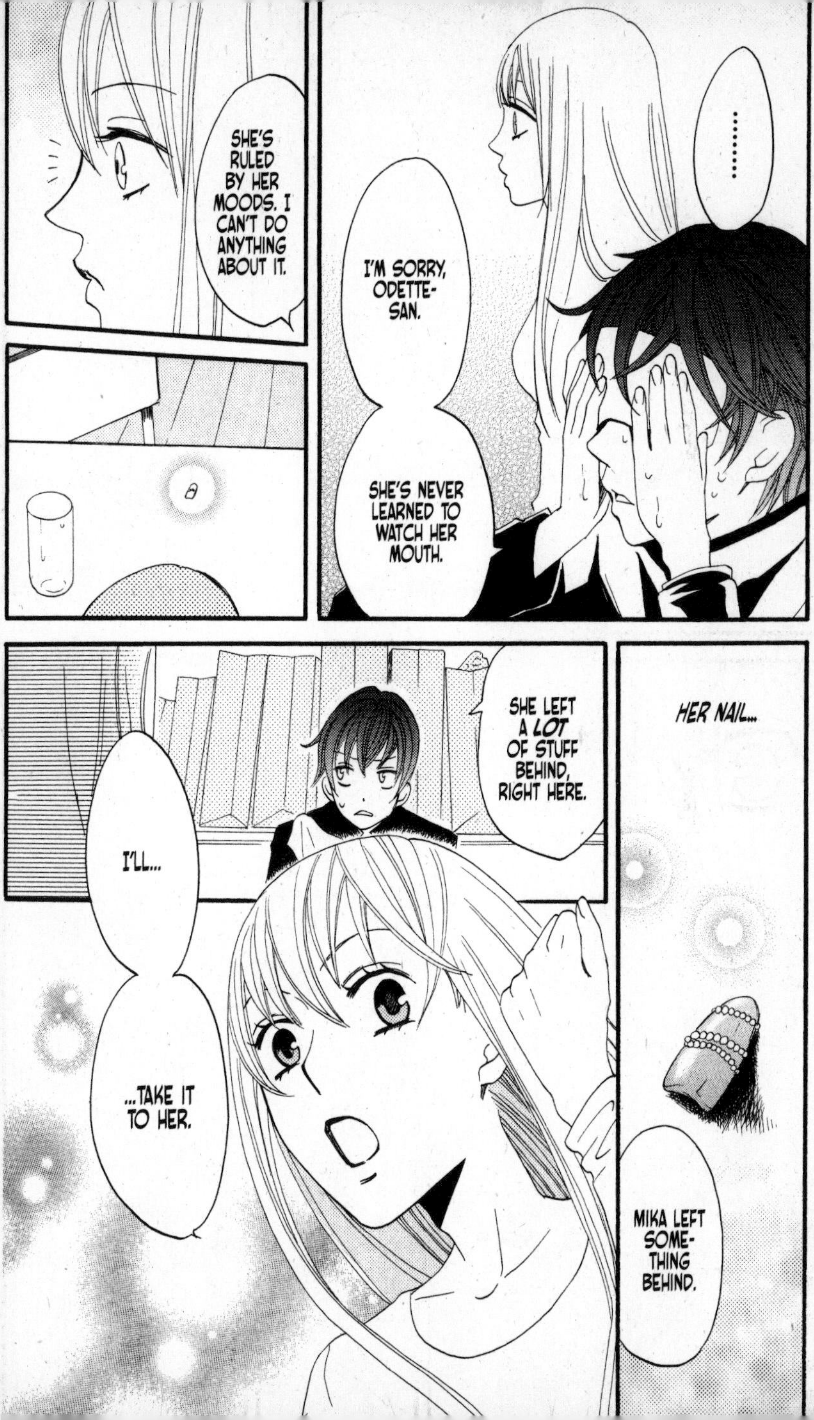
......
I'M SORRY, ODETTE-SAN.
SHE'S NEVER LEARNED TO WATCH HER MOUTH.
SHE'S RULED BY HER MOODS. I CAN'T DO ANYTHING ABOUT IT.
HER NAIL...
MIKA LEFT SOMETHING BEHIND.
SHE LEFT A *LOT* OF STUFF BEHIND, RIGHT HERE.
I'LL...
...TAKE IT TO HER.

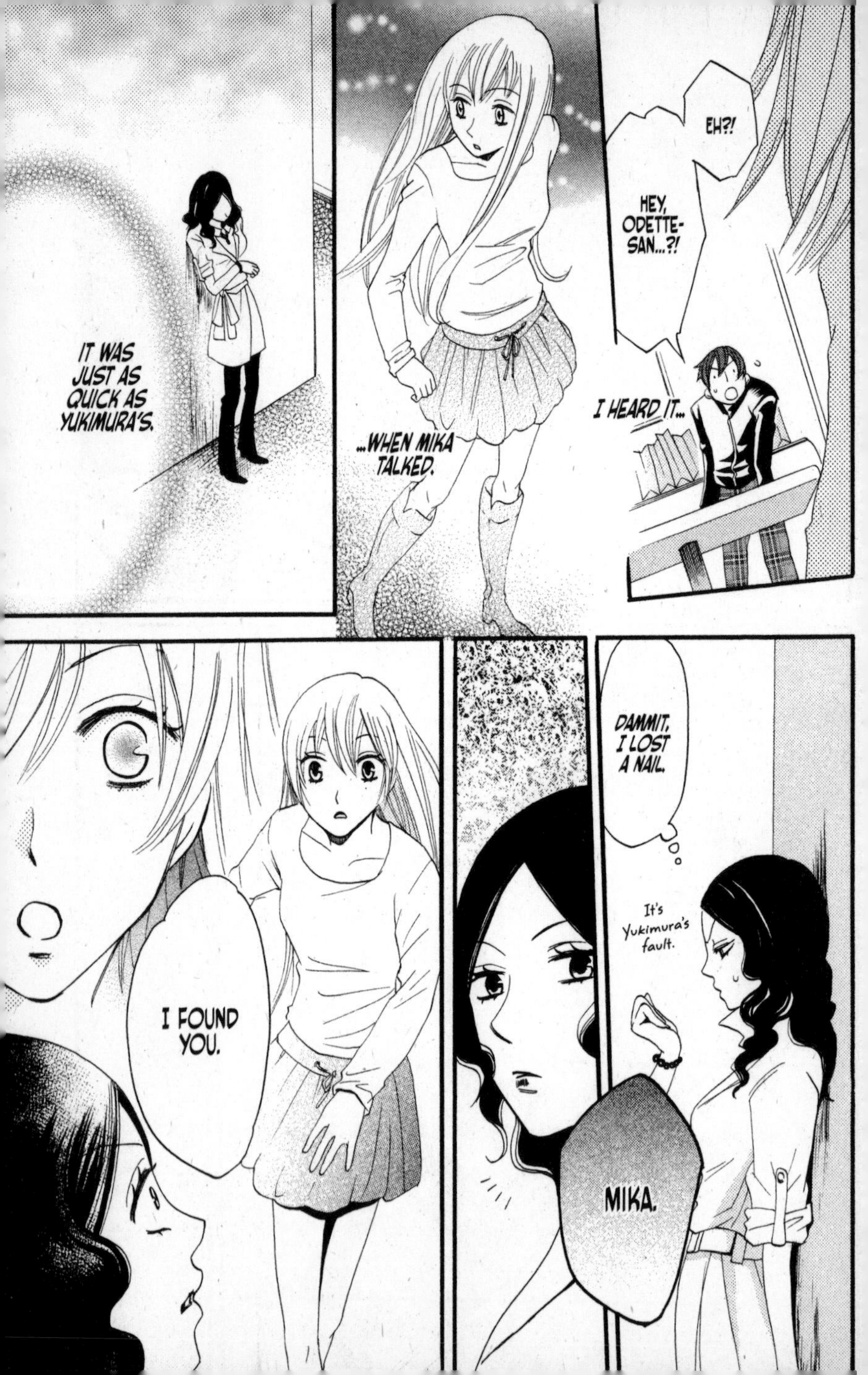
EH?!
HEY, ODETTE-SAN...?!
I HEARD IT...
...WHEN MIKA TALKED.
IT WAS JUST AS QUICK AS YUKIMURA'S.
DAMMIT, I LOST A NAIL.
It's Yukimura's fault.
MIKA.
I FOUND YOU.

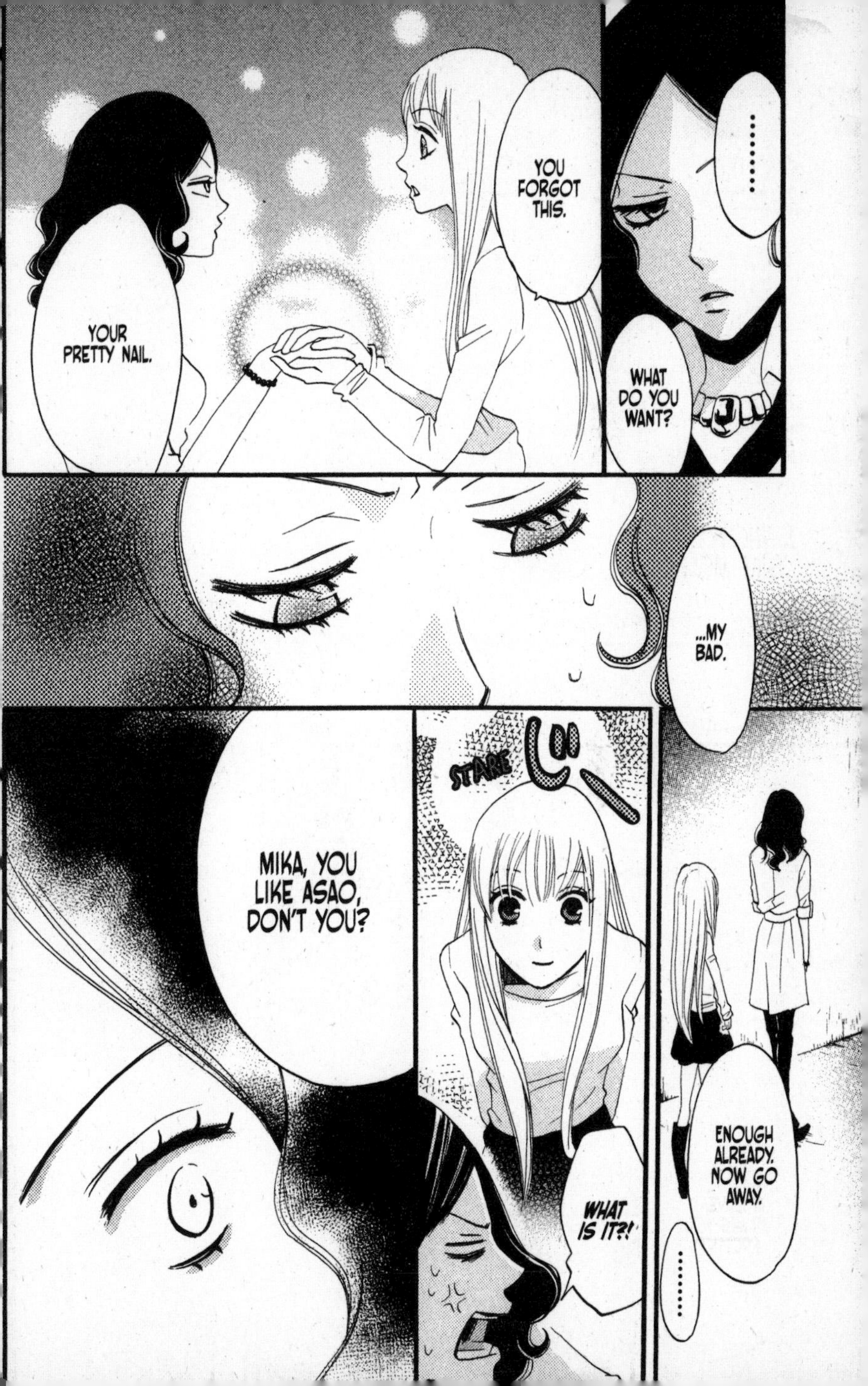
......
WHAT DO YOU WANT?
YOU FORGOT THIS.
YOUR PRETTY NAIL.
...MY BAD.
ENOUGH ALREADY. NOW GO AWAY.
......
STARE
WHAT IS IT?!
MIKA, YOU LIKE ASAO, DON'T YOU?

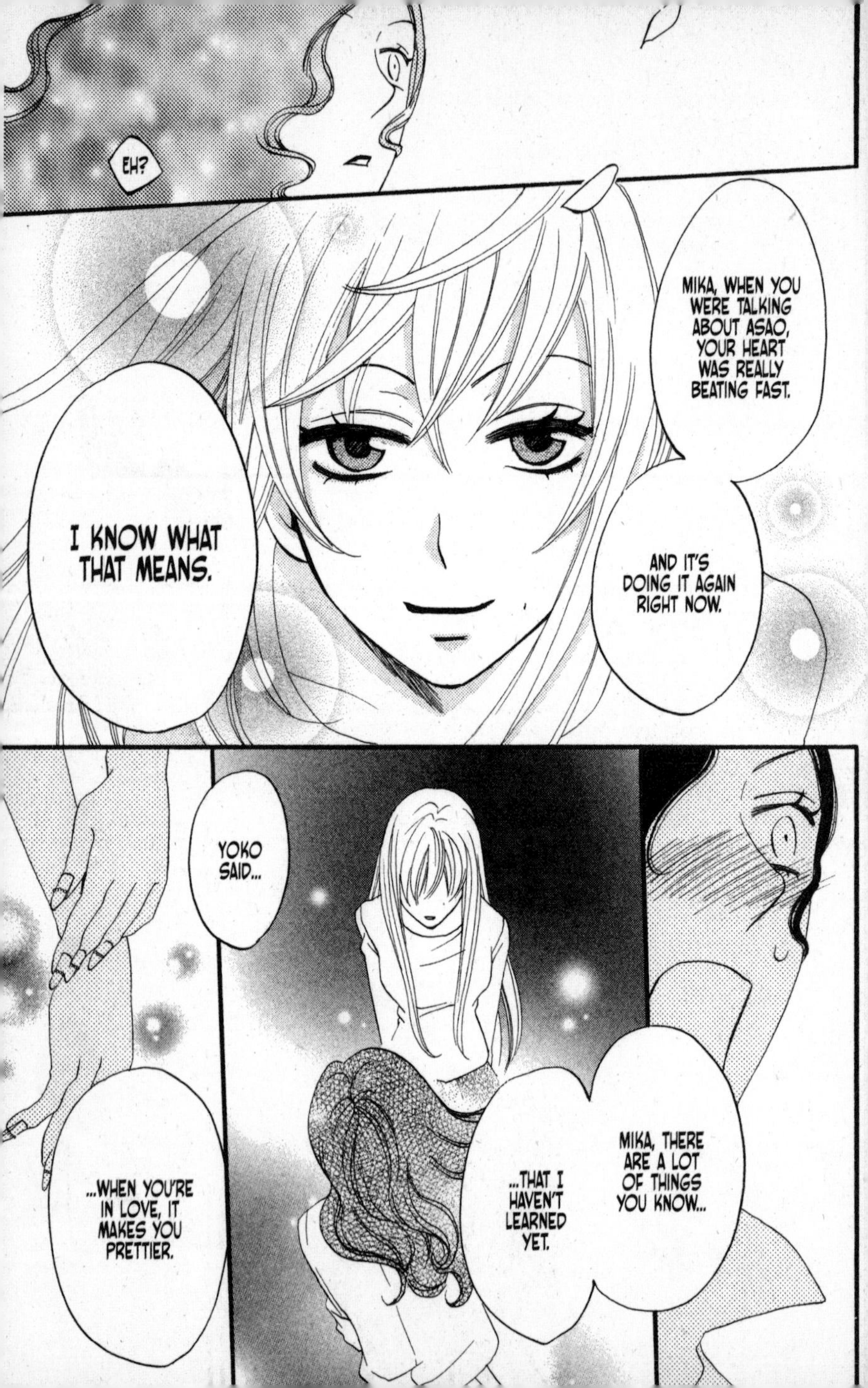
EH?
MIKA, WHEN YOU WERE TALKING ABOUT ASAO, YOUR HEART WAS REALLY BEATING FAST.
AND IT'S DOING IT AGAIN RIGHT NOW.
I KNOW WHAT THAT MEANS.
MIKA, THERE ARE A LOT OF THINGS YOU KNOW...
...THAT I HAVEN'T LEARNED YET.
YOKO SAID...
...WHEN YOU'RE IN LOVE, IT MAKES YOU PRETTIER.

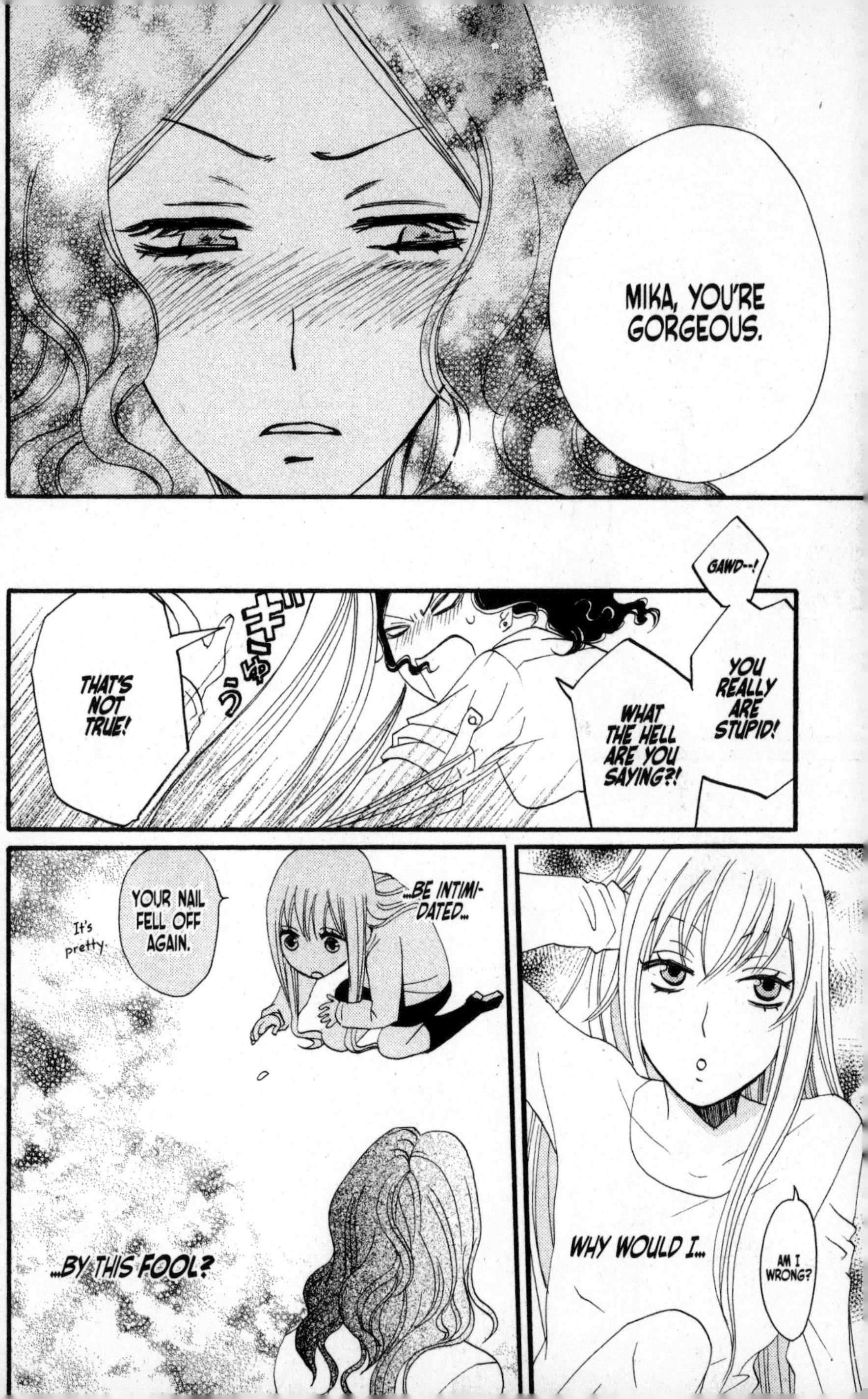
MIKA, YOU'RE GORGEOUS.
GAWD--!
YOU REALLY ARE STUPID!
WHAT THE HELL ARE YOU SAYING?!
THAT'S NOT TRUE!
AM I WRONG?
WHY WOULD I...
...BE INTIMI-DATED...
YOUR NAIL FELL OFF AGAIN.
It's pretty.
...BY THIS FOOL?

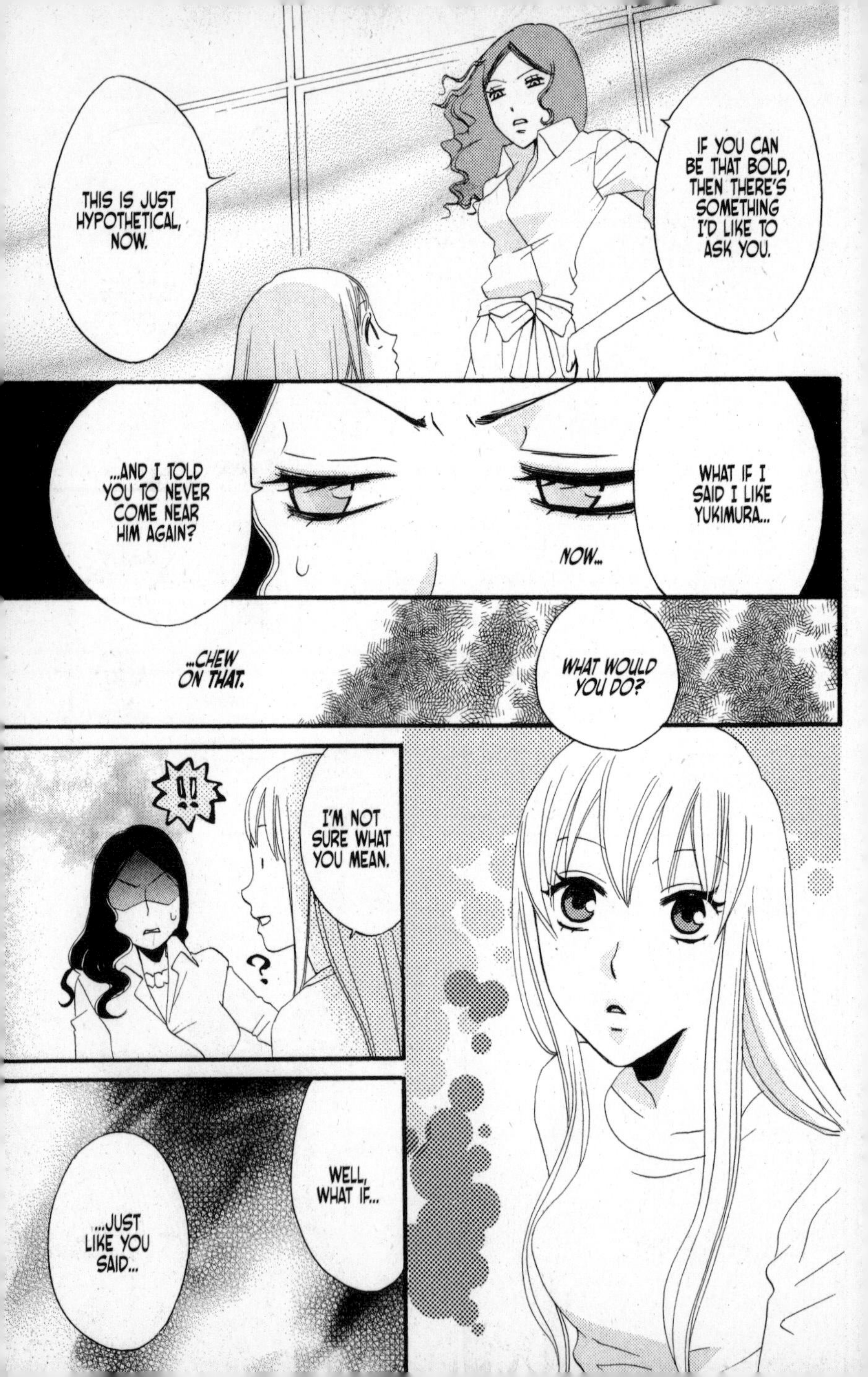
IF YOU CAN BE THAT BOLD, THEN THERE'S SOMETHING I'D LIKE TO ASK YOU.
THIS IS JUST HYPOTHETICAL, NOW.
WHAT IF I SAID I LIKE YUKIMURA...
NOW...
...AND I TOLD YOU TO NEVER COME NEAR HIM AGAIN?
WHAT WOULD YOU DO?
...CHEW ON THAT.
!!
I'M NOT SURE WHAT YOU MEAN.
?
WELL, WHAT IF...
...JUST LIKE YOU SAID...

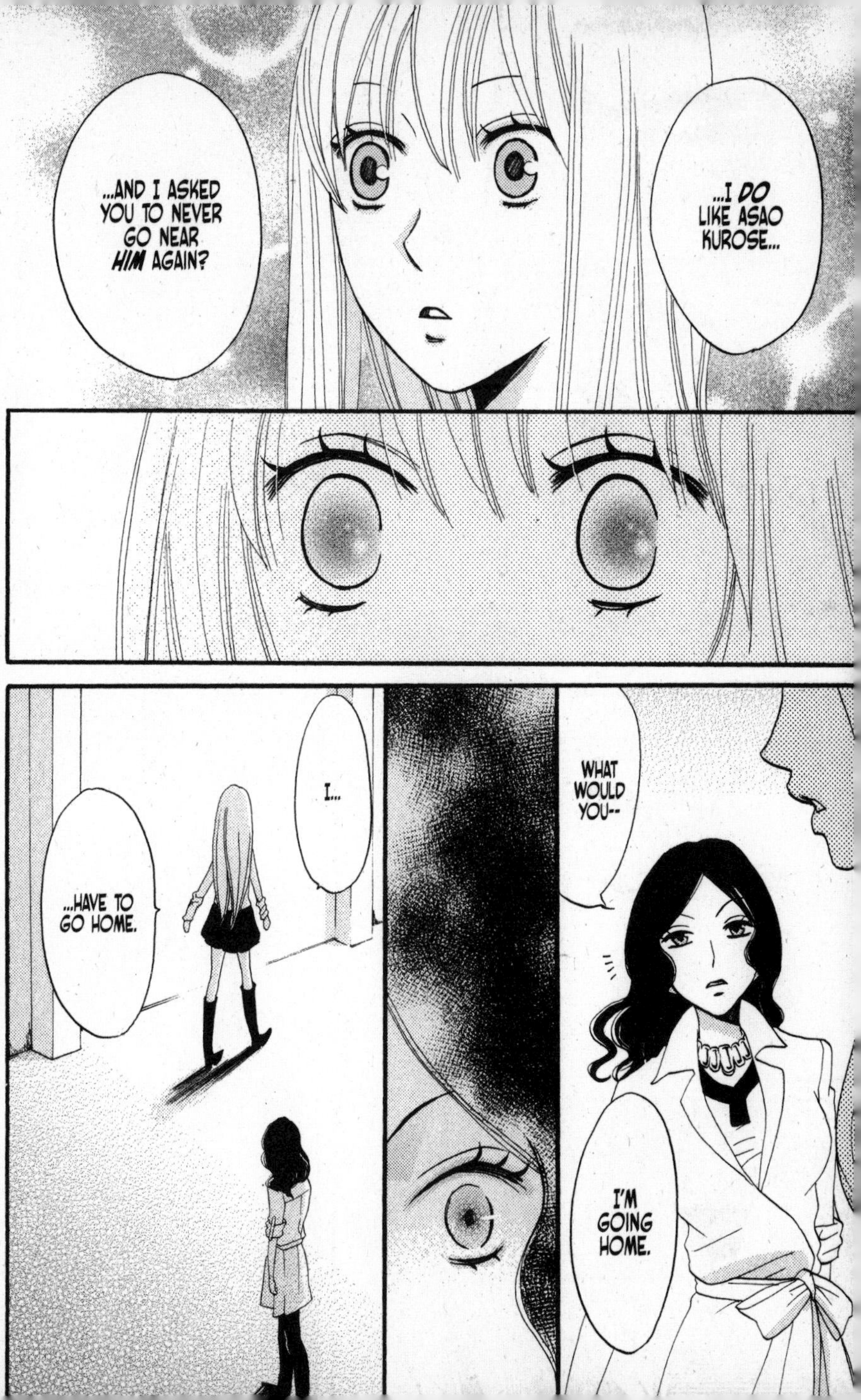
...I *DO* LIKE ASAO KUROSE...
...AND I ASKED YOU TO NEVER GO NEAR *HIM* AGAIN?
WHAT WOULD YOU--
I'M GOING HOME.
I...
...HAVE TO GO HOME.

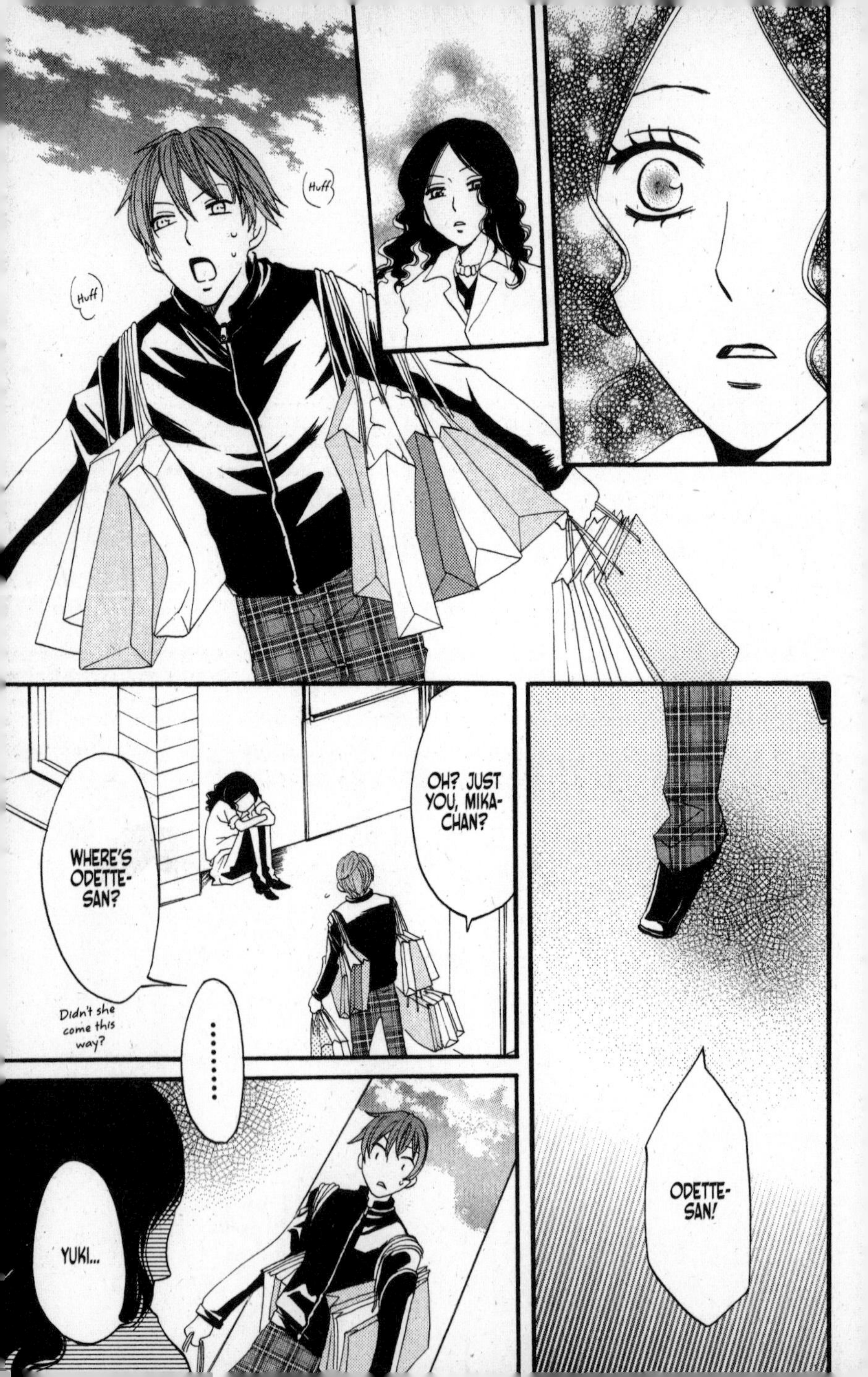
Huff
Huff
ODETTE-SAN!
OH? JUST YOU, MIKA-CHAN?
WHERE'S ODETTE-SAN?
Didn't she come this way?
....
YUKI...

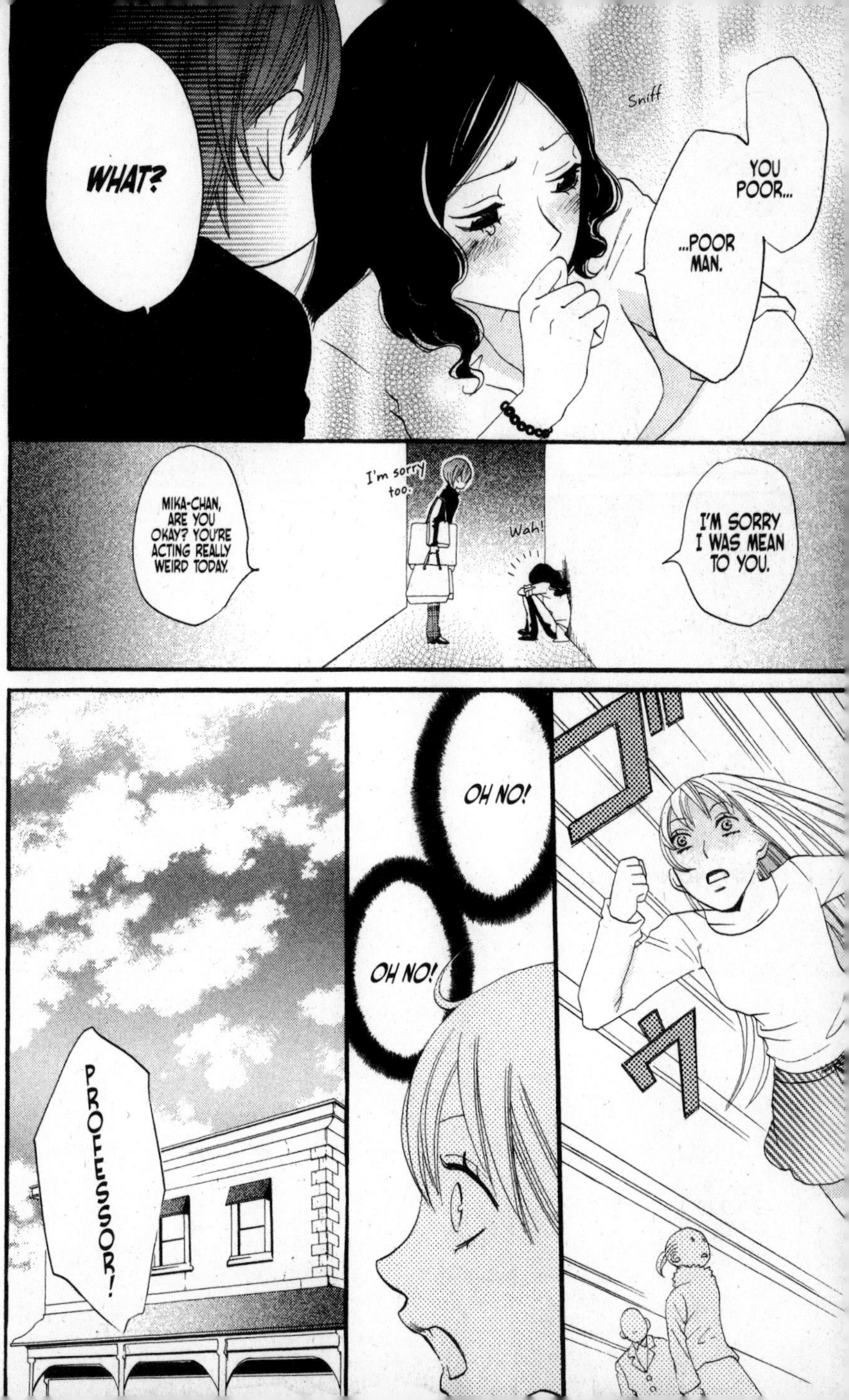
Sniff
YOU POOR...
...POOR MAN.
WHAT?
I'M SORRY I WAS MEAN TO YOU.
Wah!
I'm sorry too.
MIKA-CHAN, ARE YOU OKAY? YOU'RE ACTING REALLY WEIRD TODAY.
OH NO!
OH NO!
PROFESSOR!

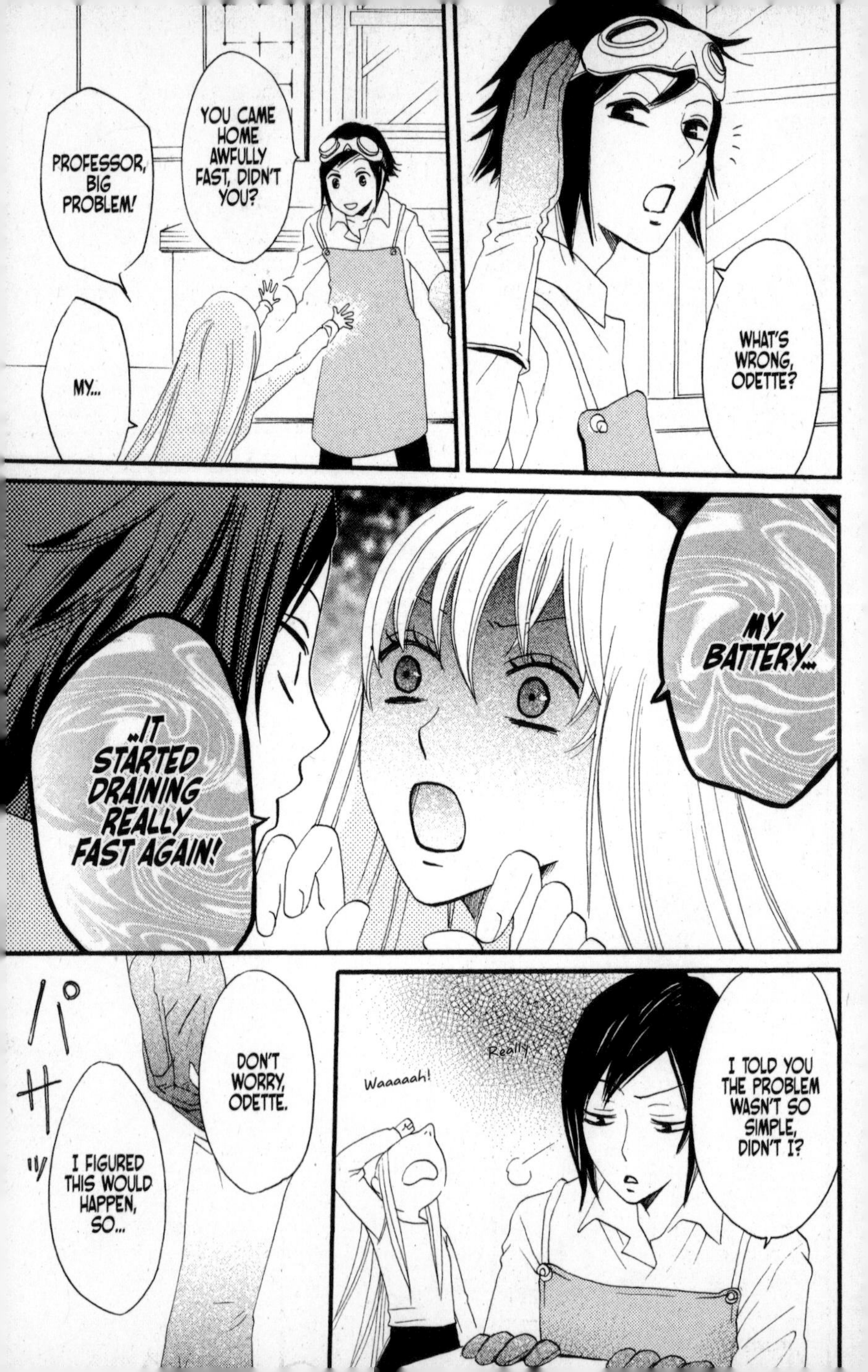
WHAT'S WRONG, ODETTE?
YOU CAME HOME AWFULLY FAST, DIDN'T YOU?
PROFESSOR, BIG PROBLEM!
MY...
MY BATTERY...
...IT STARTED DRAINING REALLY FAST AGAIN!
I TOLD YOU THE PROBLEM WASN'T SO SIMPLE, DIDN'T I?
Really...
Waaaaah!
DON'T WORRY, ODETTE.
I FIGURED THIS WOULD HAPPEN, SO...

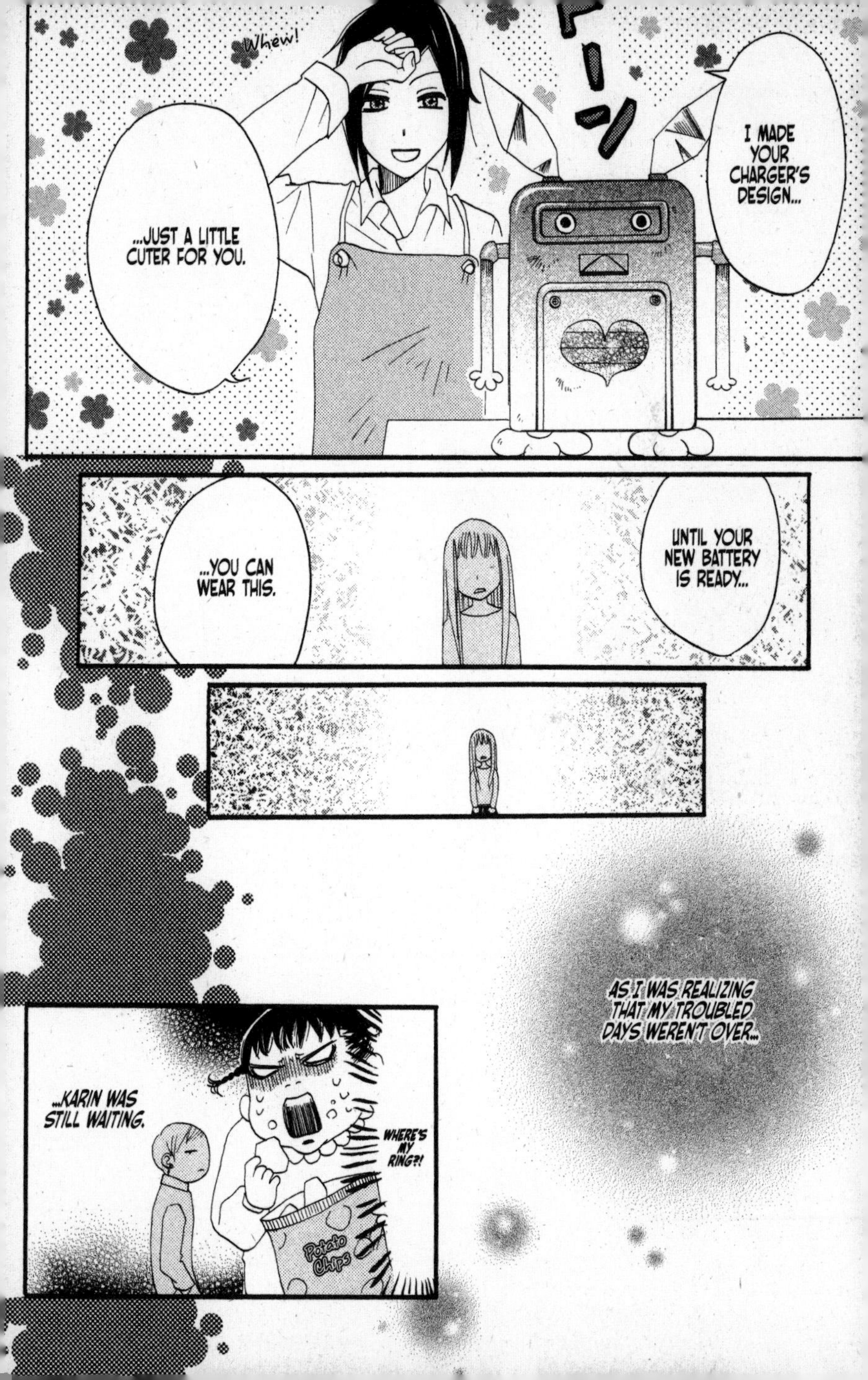
I MADE YOUR CHARGER'S DESIGN...
Whew!
...JUST A LITTLE CUTER FOR YOU.
UNTIL YOUR NEW BATTERY IS READY...
...YOU CAN WEAR THIS.
AS I WAS REALIZING THAT MY TROUBLED DAYS WEREN'T OVER...
...KARIN WAS STILL WAITING.
WHERE'S MY RING?!
Potato Chips

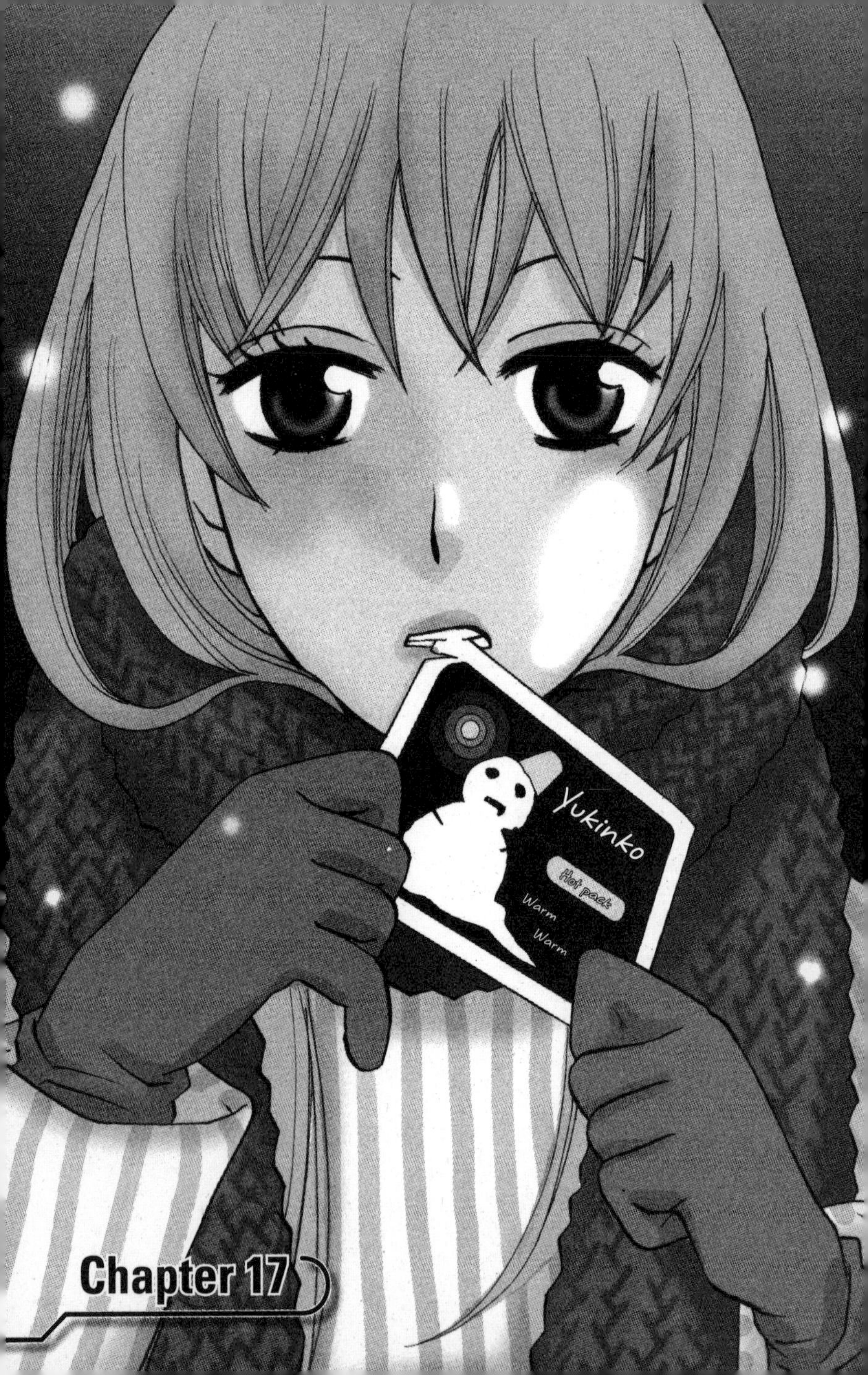
Yukinko
Hot pack
Warm
Warm
Chapter 17

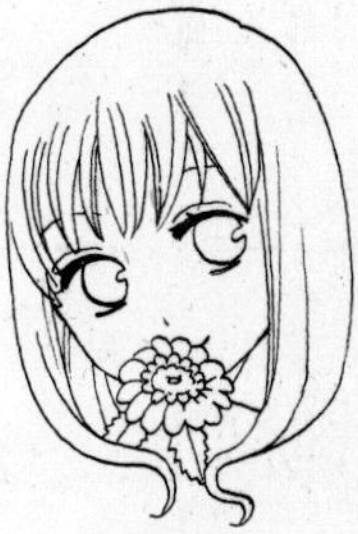
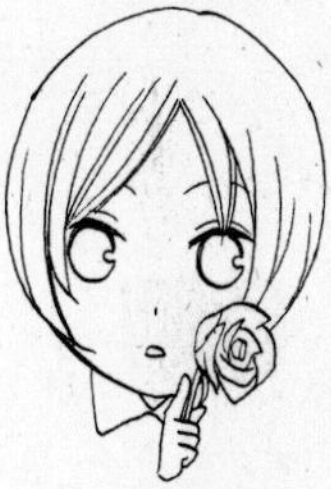
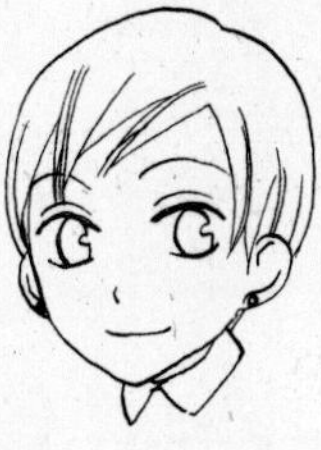

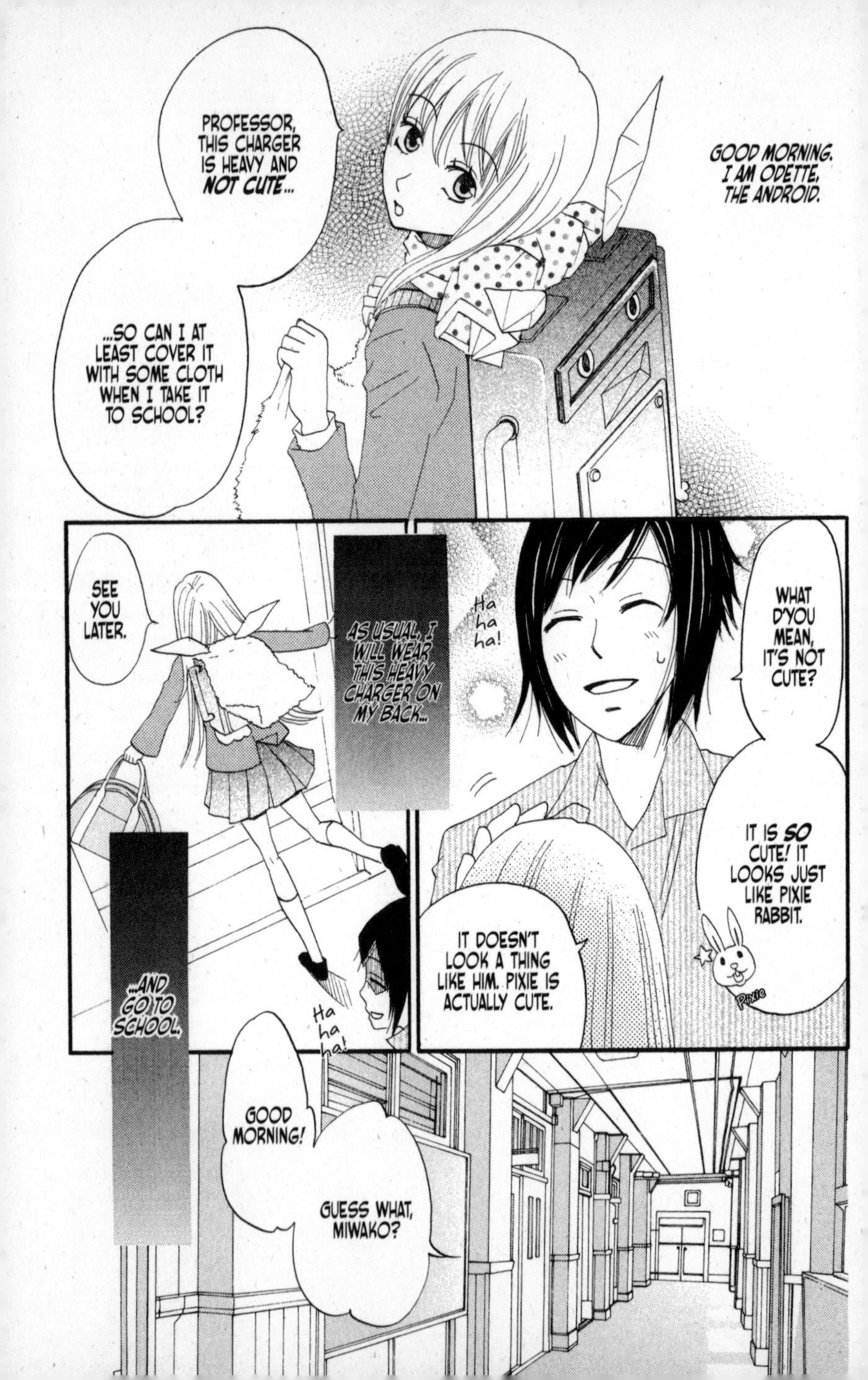
GOOD MORNING. I AM ODETTE, THE ANDROID.
PROFESSOR, THIS CHARGER IS HEAVY AND **NOT CUTE**...
...SO CAN I AT LEAST COVER IT WITH SOME CLOTH WHEN I TAKE IT TO SCHOOL?
WHAT D'YOU MEAN, IT'S NOT CUTE?
Ha ha ha!
IT IS *SO* CUTE! IT LOOKS JUST LIKE PIXIE RABBIT.
Pixie
IT DOESN'T LOOK A THING LIKE HIM. PIXIE IS ACTUALLY CUTE.
AS USUAL, I WILL WEAR THIS HEAVY CHARGER ON MY BACK...
SEE YOU LATER.
Ha ha ha!
...AND GO TO SCHOOL.
GOOD MORNING!
GUESS WHAT, MIWAKO?

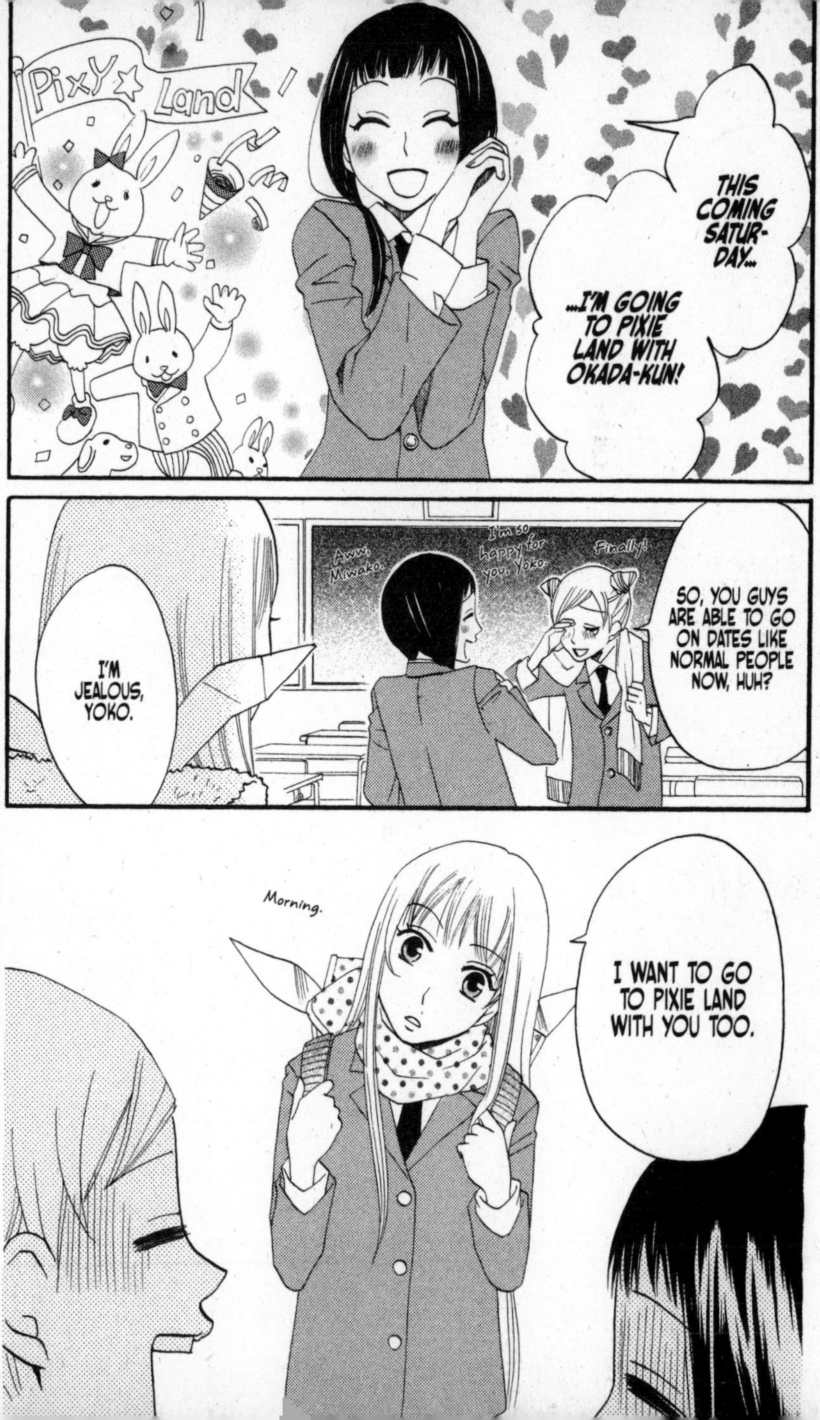
THIS COMING SATUR-DAY...
...I'M GOING TO PIXIE LAND WITH OKADA-KUN!
Pixy☆Land
SO, YOU GUYS ARE ABLE TO GO ON DATES LIKE NORMAL PEOPLE NOW, HUH?
Finally!
I'm so happy for you, Yoko.
Aww, Miwako.
I'M JEALOUS, YOKO.
I WANT TO GO TO PIXIE LAND WITH YOU TOO.
Morning.

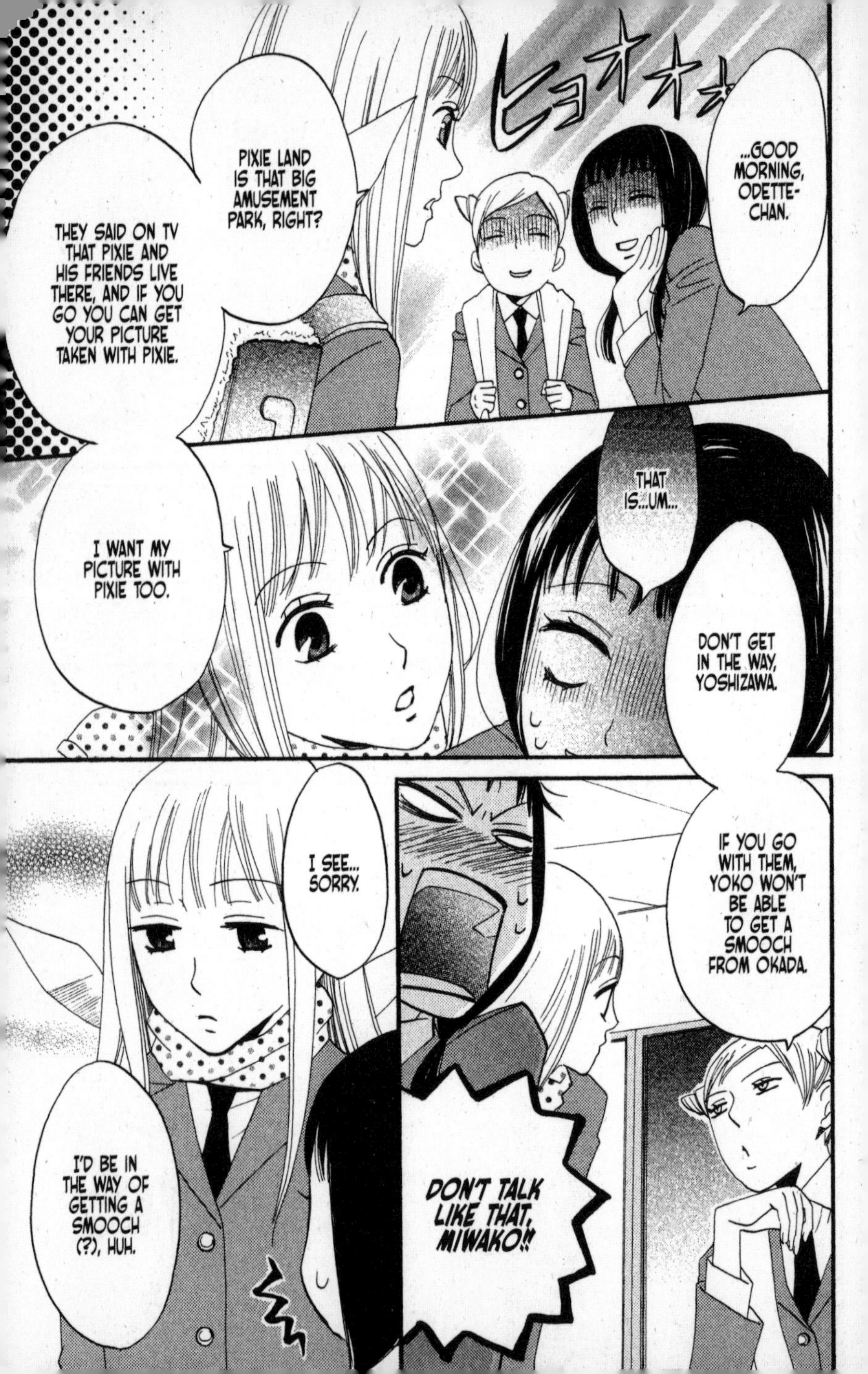
ヒョオオォ
...GOOD MORNING, ODETTE-CHAN.
PIXIE LAND IS THAT BIG AMUSEMENT PARK, RIGHT?
THEY SAID ON TV THAT PIXIE AND HIS FRIENDS LIVE THERE, AND IF YOU GO YOU CAN GET YOUR PICTURE TAKEN WITH PIXIE.
I WANT MY PICTURE WITH PIXIE TOO.
THAT IS...UM...
DON'T GET IN THE WAY, YOSHIZAWA.
IF YOU GO WITH THEM, YOKO WON'T BE ABLE TO GET A SMOOCH FROM OKADA.
DON'T TALK LIKE THAT, MIWAKO!!
I SEE... SORRY.
I'D BE IN THE WAY OF GETTING A SMOOCH (?), HUH.

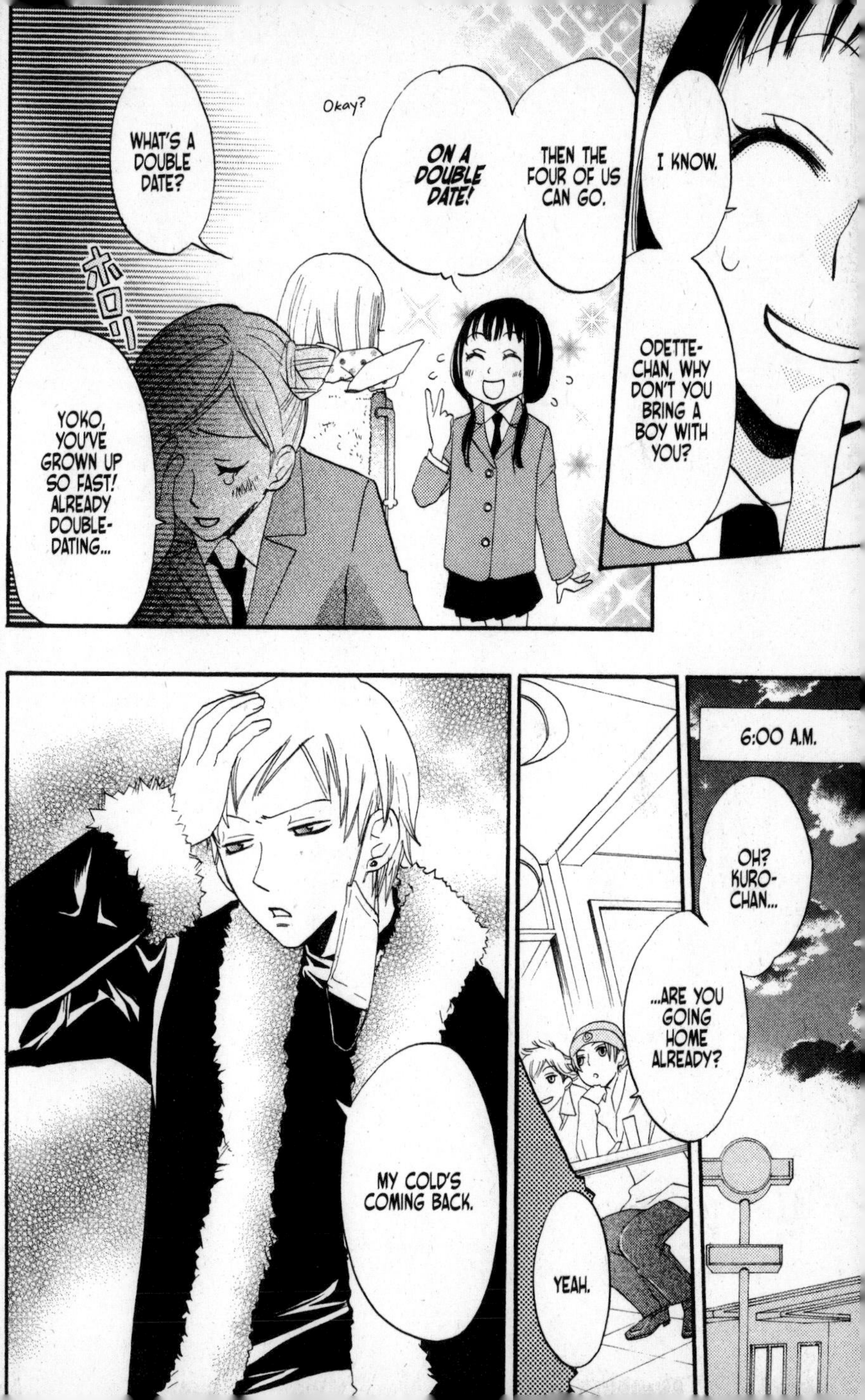
I KNOW.
ODETTE-CHAN, WHY DON'T YOU BRING A BOY WITH YOU?
THEN THE FOUR OF US CAN GO.
ON A DOUBLE DATE!
Okay?
WHAT'S A DOUBLE DATE?
ホロリ
YOKO, YOU'VE GROWN UP SO FAST! ALREADY DOUBLE-DATING...
6:00 A.M.
OH? KURO-CHAN...
...ARE YOU GOING HOME ALREADY?
YEAH.
MY COLD'S COMING BACK.

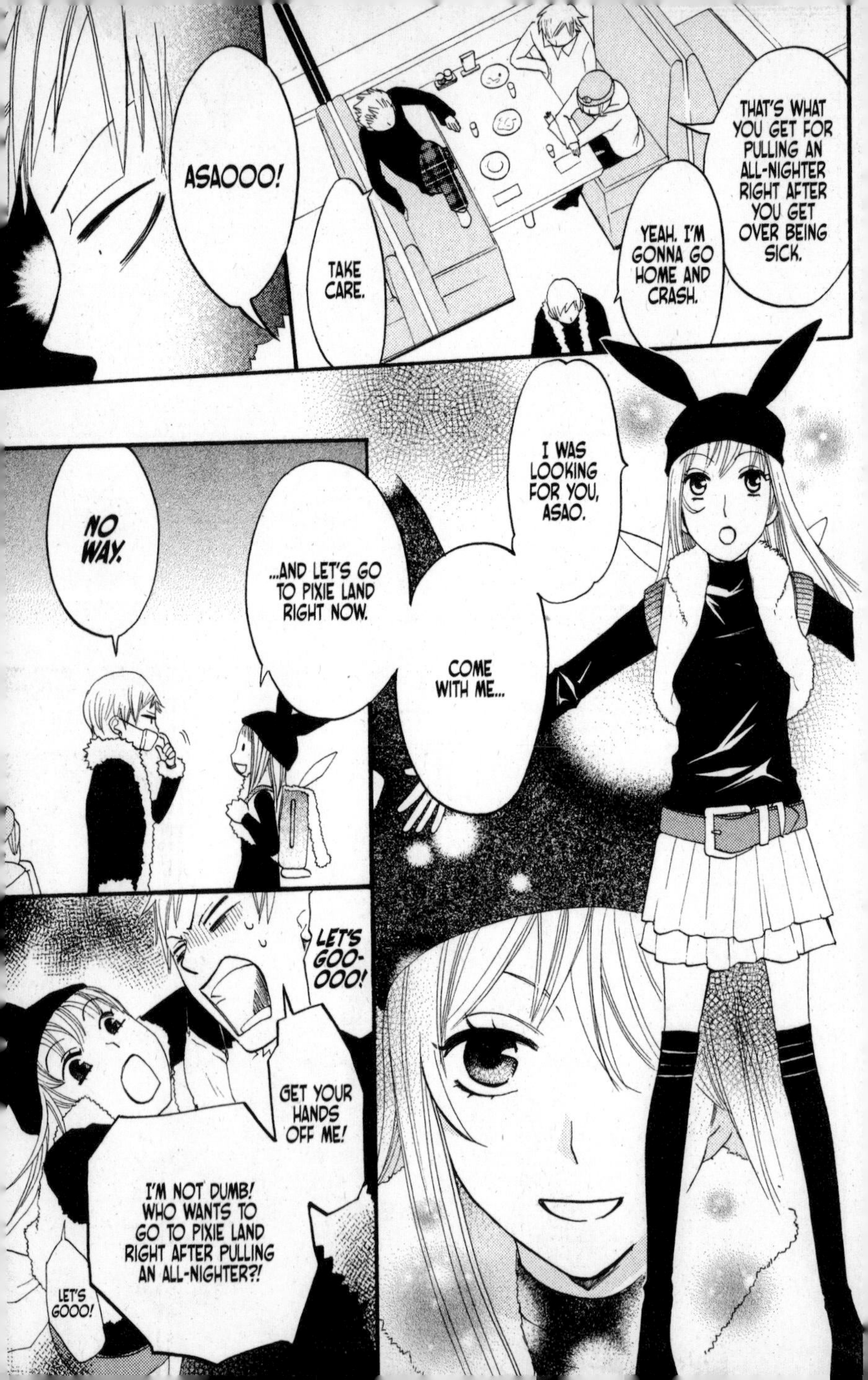
THAT'S WHAT YOU GET FOR PULLING AN ALL-NIGHTER RIGHT AFTER YOU GET OVER BEING SICK.
YEAH. I'M GONNA GO HOME AND CRASH.
TAKE CARE.
ASAOOO!
I WAS LOOKING FOR YOU, ASAO.
COME WITH ME...
...AND LET'S GO TO PIXIE LAND RIGHT NOW.
NO WAY.
LET'S GOO-OOO!
GET YOUR HANDS OFF ME!
I'M NOT DUMB! WHO WANTS TO GO TO PIXIE LAND RIGHT AFTER PULLING AN ALL-NIGHTER?!
LET'S GOOO!

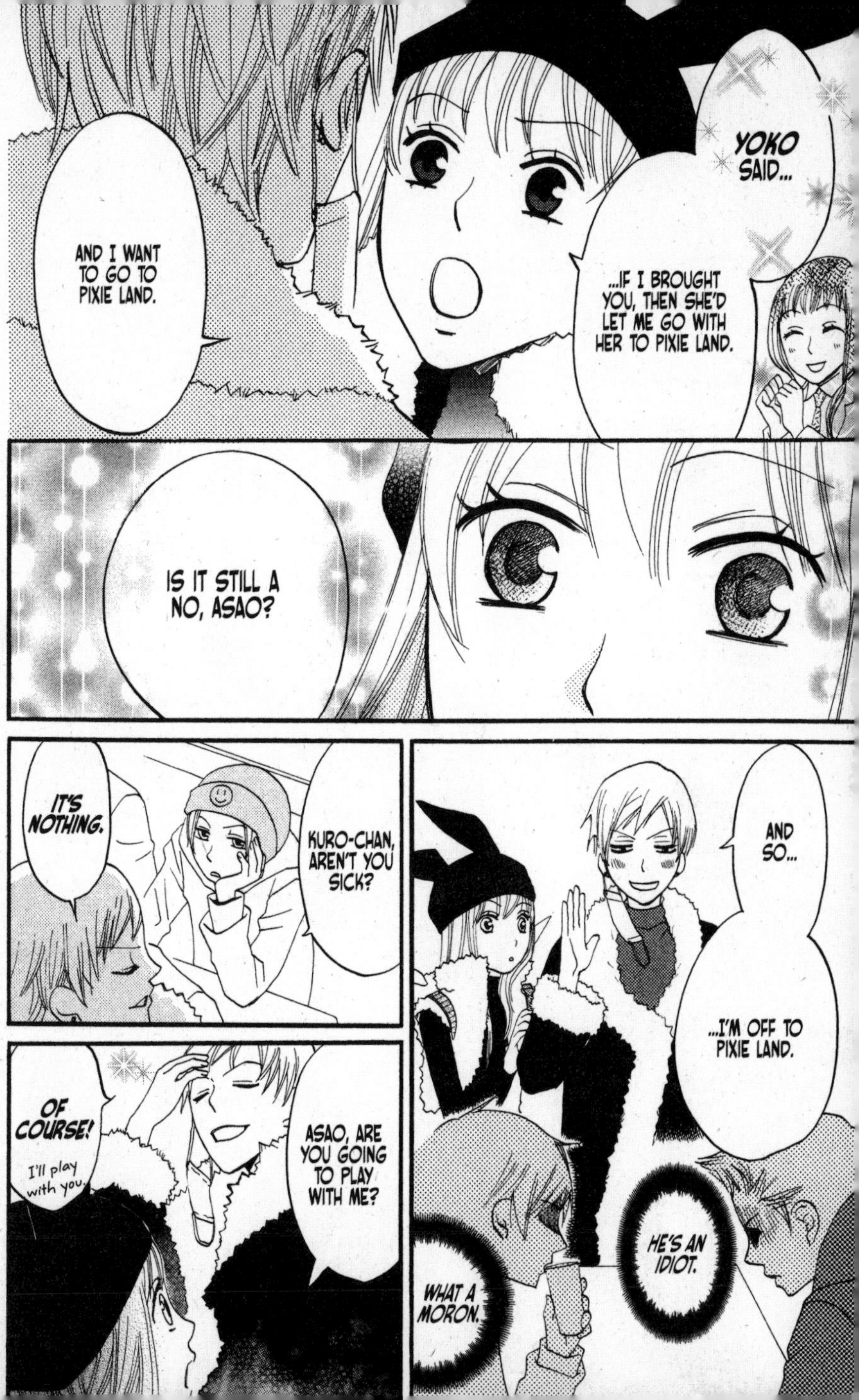
YOKO SAID...
...IF I BROUGHT YOU, THEN SHE'D LET ME GO WITH HER TO PIXIE LAND.
AND I WANT TO GO TO PIXIE LAND.
IS IT STILL A NO, ASAO?
AND SO...
...I'M OFF TO PIXIE LAND.
HE'S AN IDIOT.
WHAT A MORON.
KURO-CHAN, AREN'T YOU SICK?
IT'S NOTHING.
ASAO, ARE YOU GOING TO PLAY WITH ME?
OF COURSE!
I'll play with you.

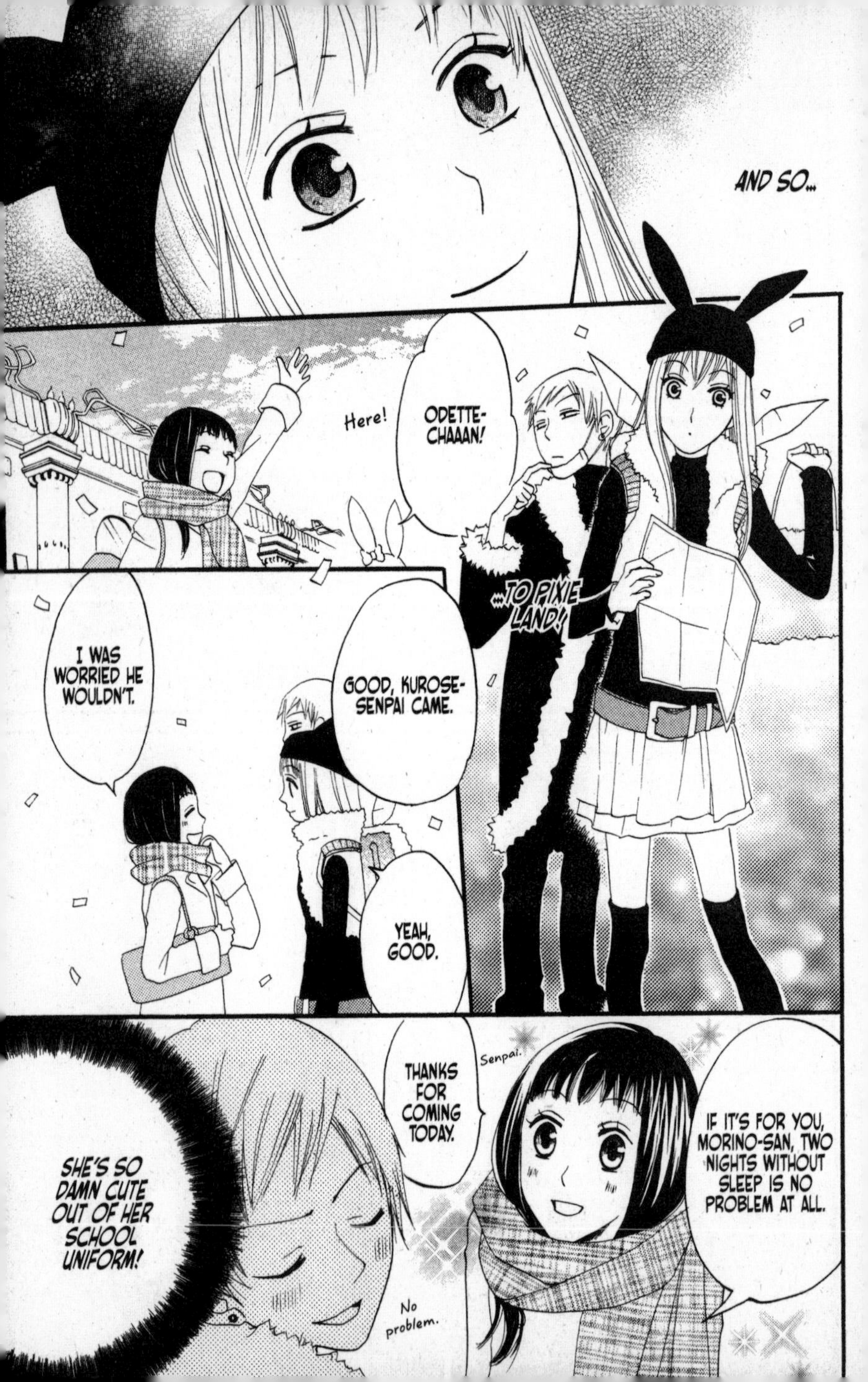
AND SO...
...TO PIXIE LAND!
ODETTE-CHAAAN!
Here!
GOOD, KUROSE-SENPAI CAME.
I WAS WORRIED HE WOULDN'T.
YEAH, GOOD.
Senpai.
THANKS FOR COMING TODAY.
IF IT'S FOR YOU, MORINO-SAN, TWO NIGHTS WITHOUT SLEEP IS NO PROBLEM AT ALL.
No problem.
SHE'S SO DAMN CUTE OUT OF HER SCHOOL UNIFORM!

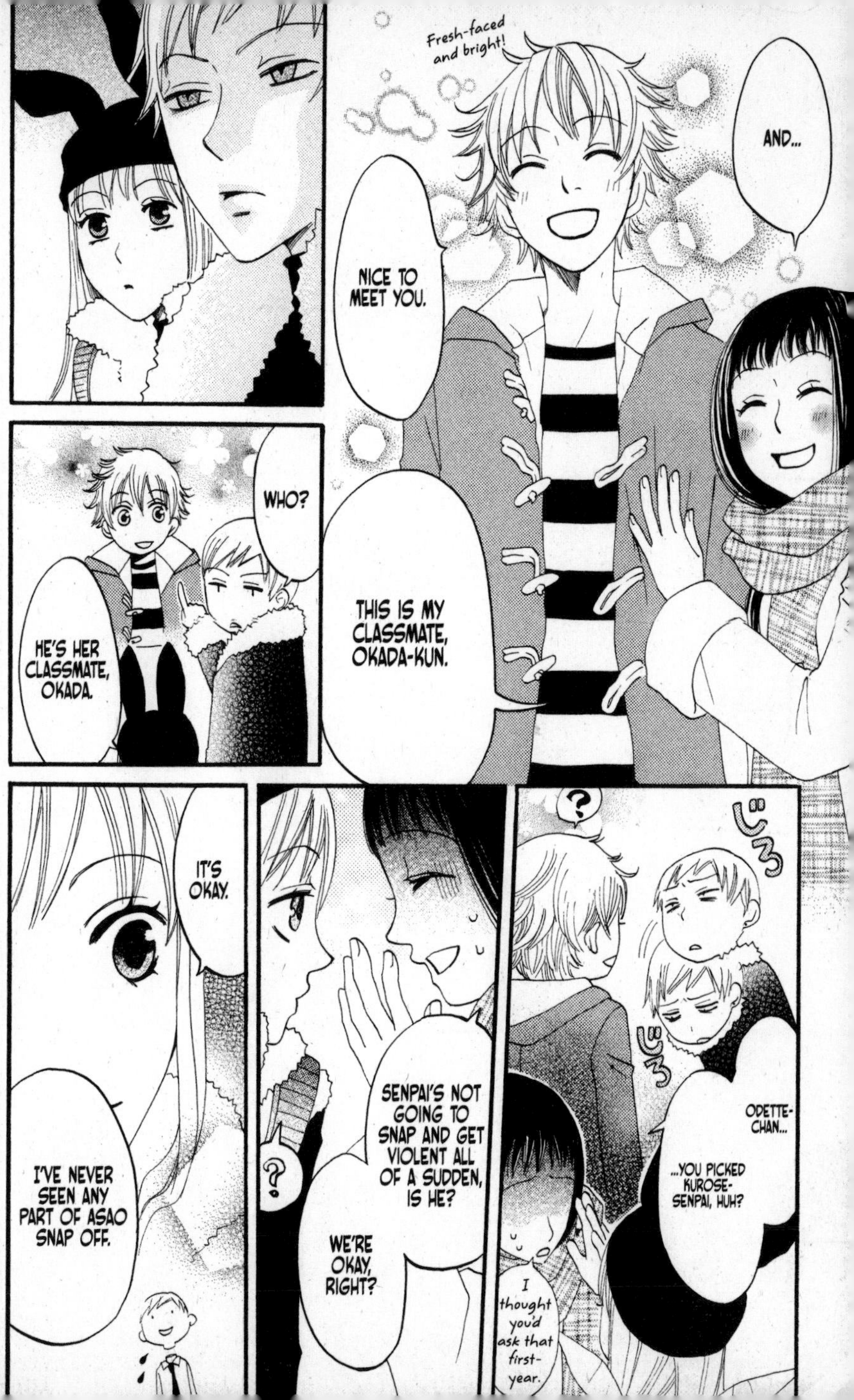
AND...
Fresh-faced and bright!
NICE TO MEET YOU.
THIS IS MY CLASSMATE, OKADA-KUN.
WHO?
HE'S HER CLASSMATE, OKADA.
?
じろ
じろ
ODETTE-CHAN...
...YOU PICKED KUROSE-SENPAI, HUH?
I thought you'd ask that first-year.
SENPAI'S NOT GOING TO SNAP AND GET VIOLENT ALL OF A SUDDEN, IS HE?
?
WE'RE OKAY, RIGHT?
IT'S OKAY.
I'VE NEVER SEEN ANY PART OF ASAO SNAP OFF.

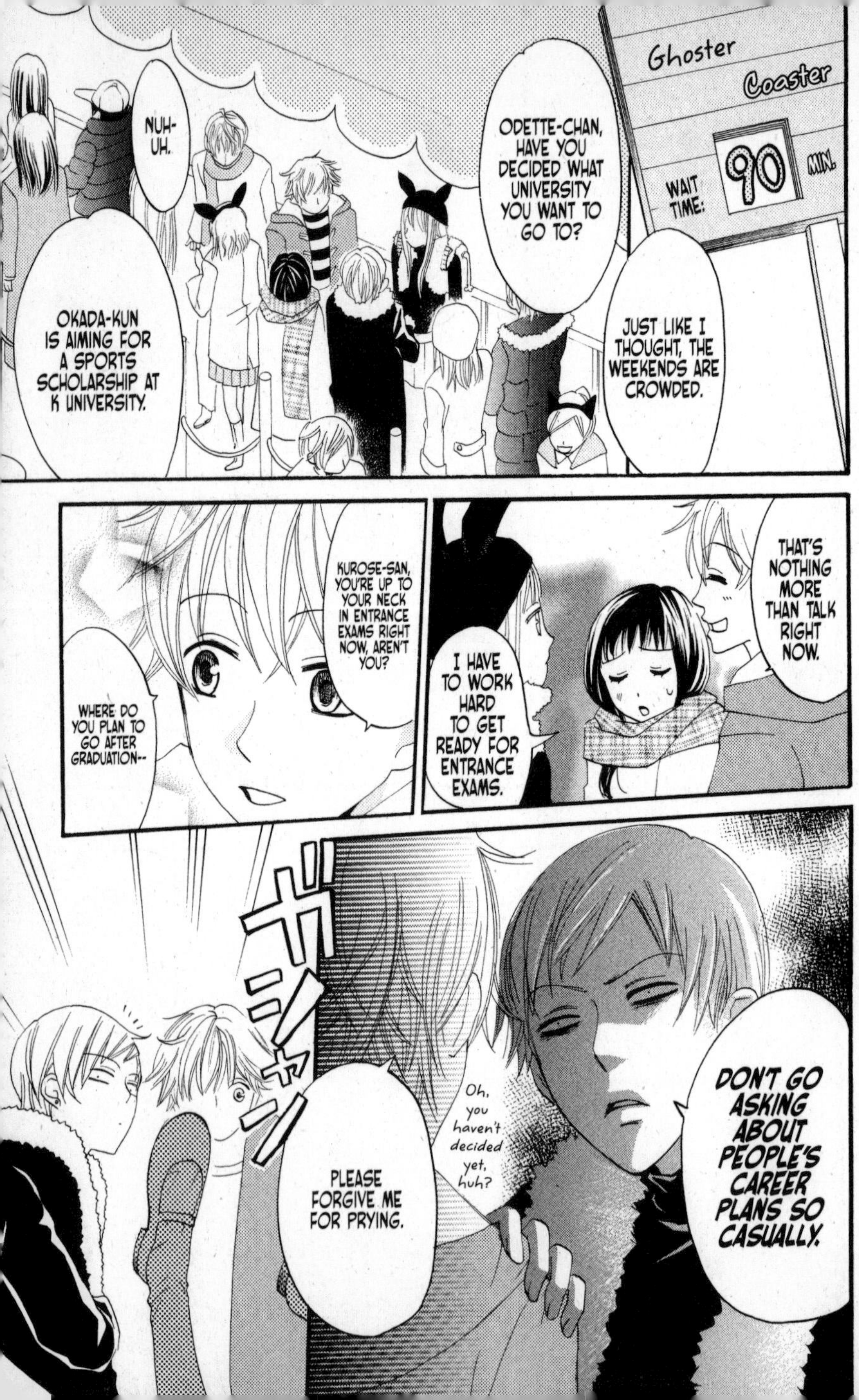
Ghoster Coaster
WAIT TIME: 90 MIN.
ODETTE-CHAN, HAVE YOU DECIDED WHAT UNIVERSITY YOU WANT TO GO TO?
JUST LIKE I THOUGHT, THE WEEKENDS ARE CROWDED.
NUH-UH.
OKADA-KUN IS AIMING FOR A SPORTS SCHOLARSHIP AT K UNIVERSITY.
THAT'S NOTHING MORE THAN TALK RIGHT NOW.
I HAVE TO WORK HARD TO GET READY FOR ENTRANCE EXAMS.
KUROSE-SAN, YOU'RE UP TO YOUR NECK IN ENTRANCE EXAMS RIGHT NOW, AREN'T YOU?
WHERE DO YOU PLAN TO GO AFTER GRADUATION--
DON'T GO ASKING ABOUT PEOPLE'S CAREER PLANS SO CASUALLY.
Oh, you haven't decided yet, huh?
ガシャー
PLEASE FORGIVE ME FOR PRYING.

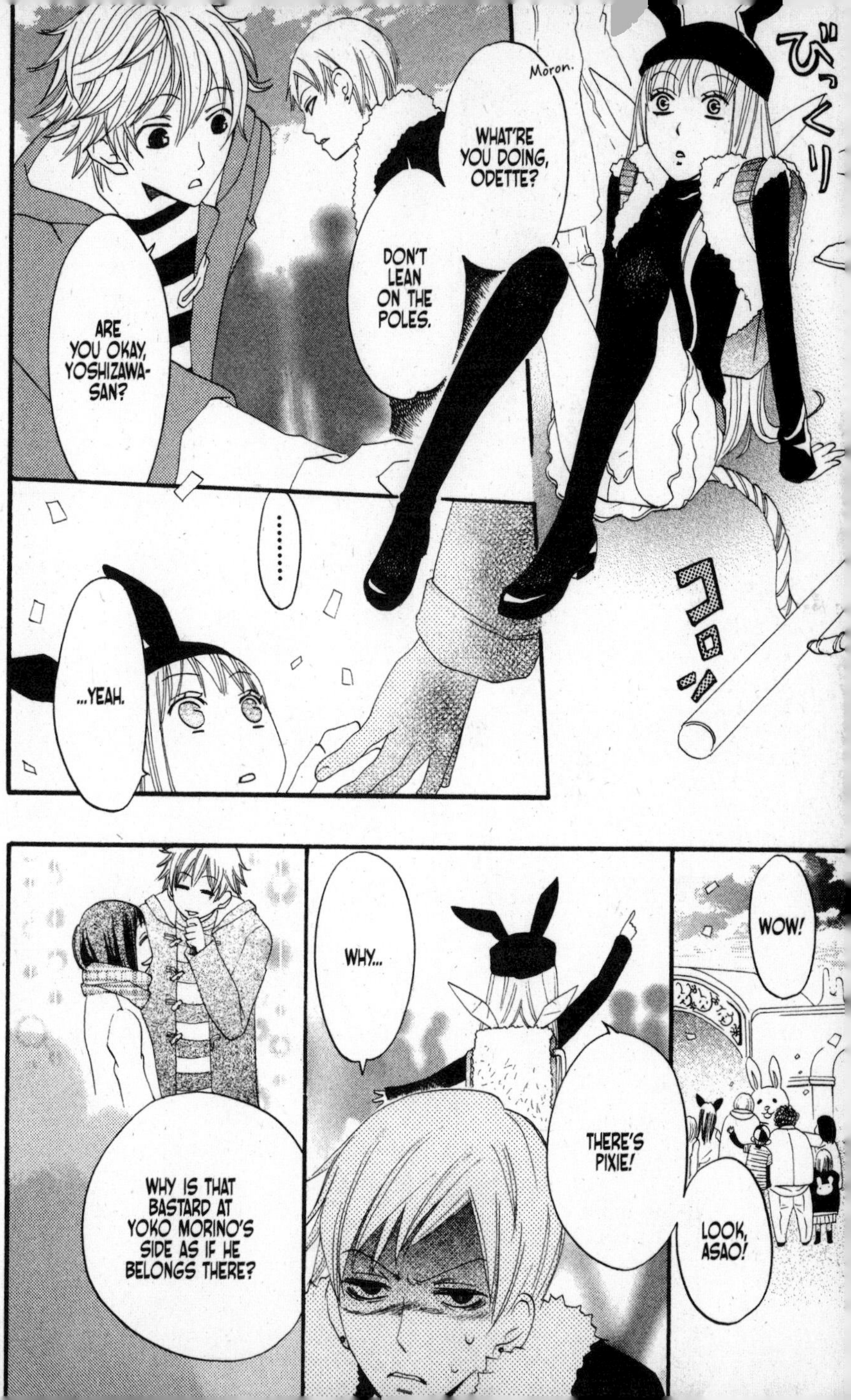
びっくり
Moron.
WHAT'RE YOU DOING, ODETTE?
DON'T LEAN ON THE POLES.
ARE YOU OKAY, YOSHIZAWA-SAN?
コロッ
....
...YEAH.
WOW!
LOOK, ASAO!
THERE'S PIXIE!
WHY...
WHY IS THAT BASTARD AT YOKO MORINO'S SIDE AS IF HE BELONGS THERE?

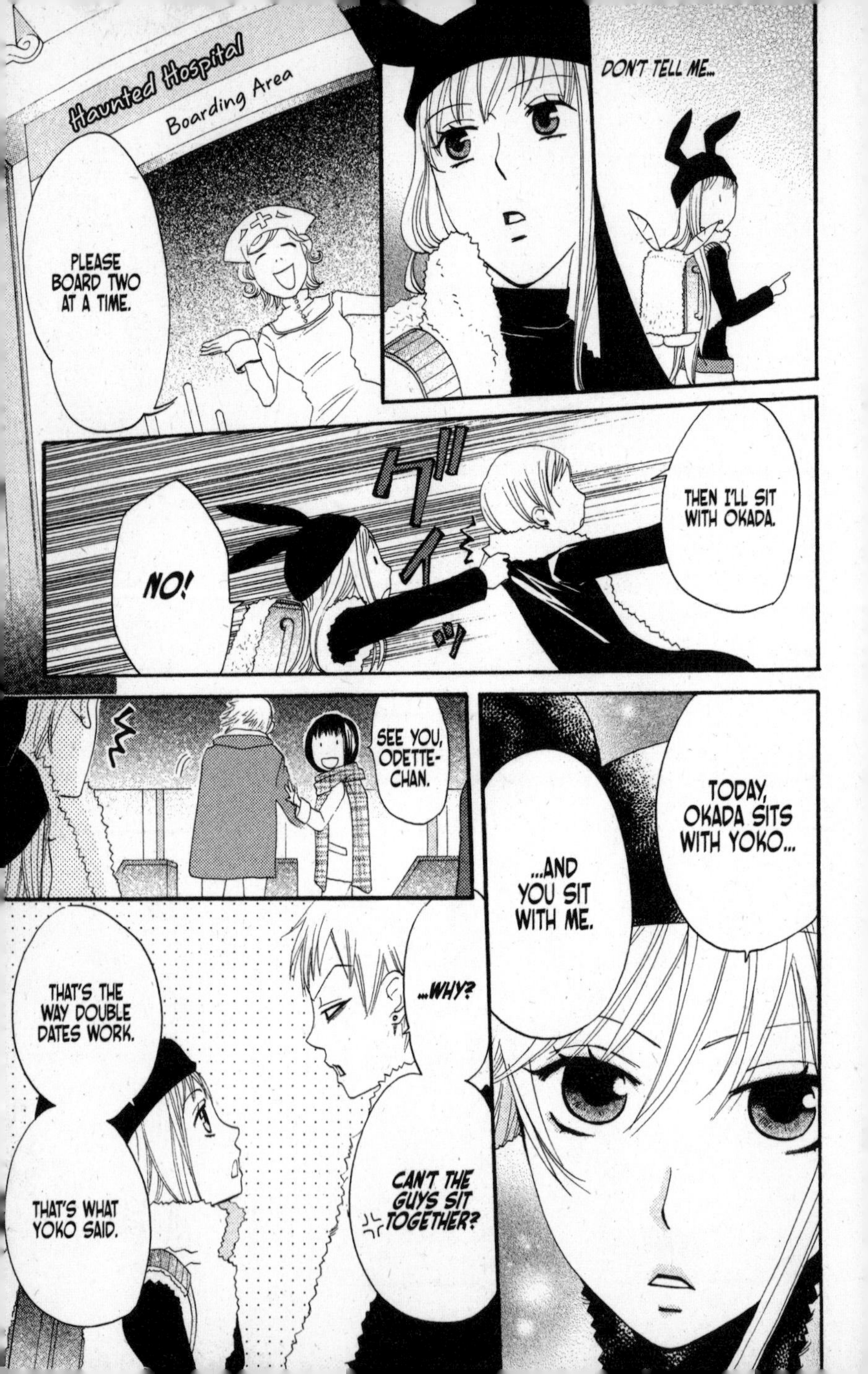
DON'T TELL ME...
Haunted Hospital
Boarding Area
PLEASE BOARD TWO AT A TIME.
THEN I'LL SIT WITH OKADA.
NO!
TODAY, OKADA SITS WITH YOKO...
...AND YOU SIT WITH ME.
SEE YOU, ODETTE-CHAN.
...WHY?
CAN'T THE GUYS SIT TOGETHER?
THAT'S THE WAY DOUBLE DATES WORK.
THAT'S WHAT YOKO SAID.

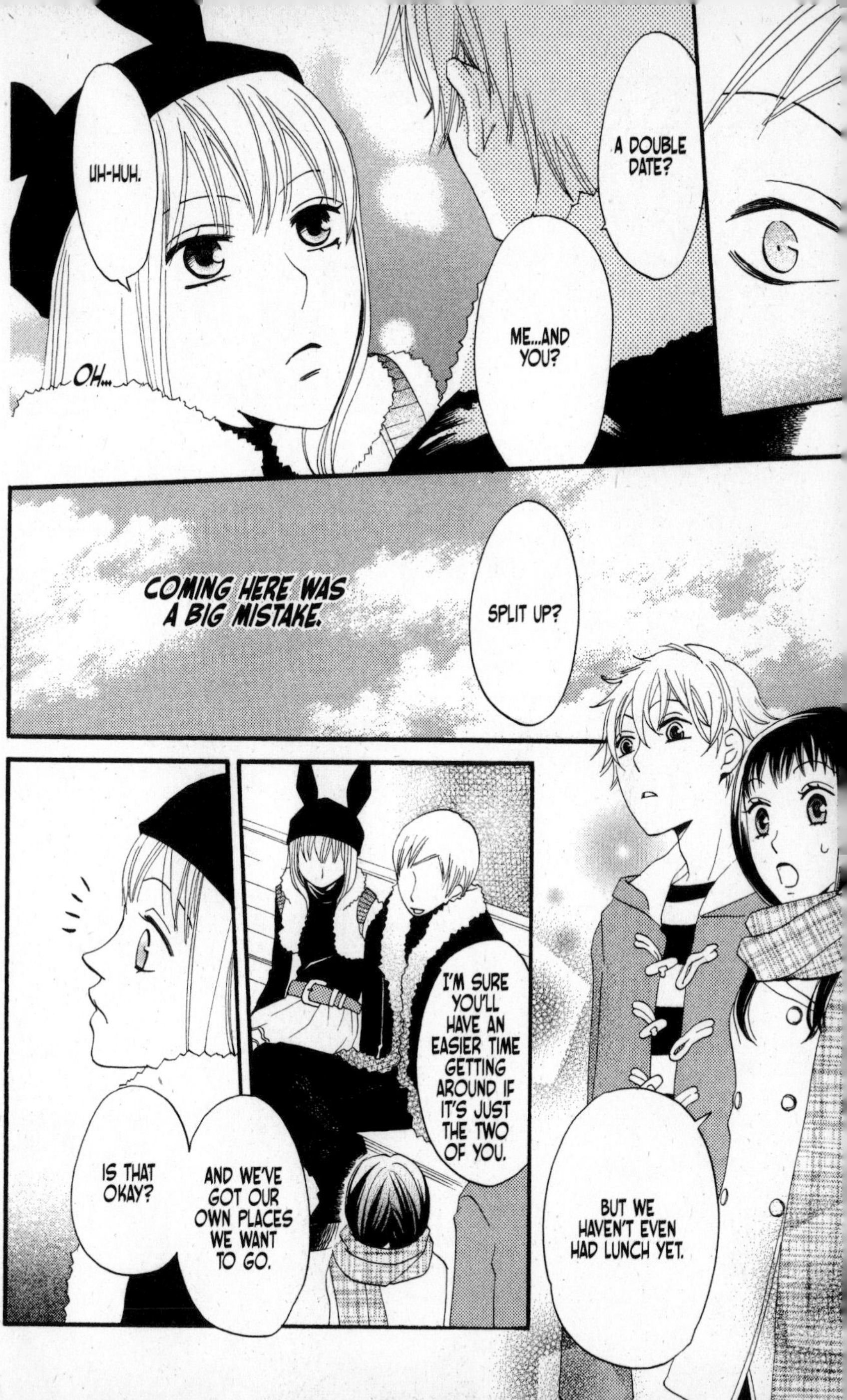

A DOUBLE DATE?
ME...AND YOU?
UH-HUH.
OH...
SPLIT UP?
COMING HERE WAS A BIG MISTAKE.
BUT WE HAVEN'T EVEN HAD LUNCH YET.
I'M SURE YOU'LL HAVE AN EASIER TIME GETTING AROUND IF IT'S JUST THE TWO OF YOU.
AND WE'VE GOT OUR OWN PLACES WE WANT TO GO.
IS THAT OKAY?

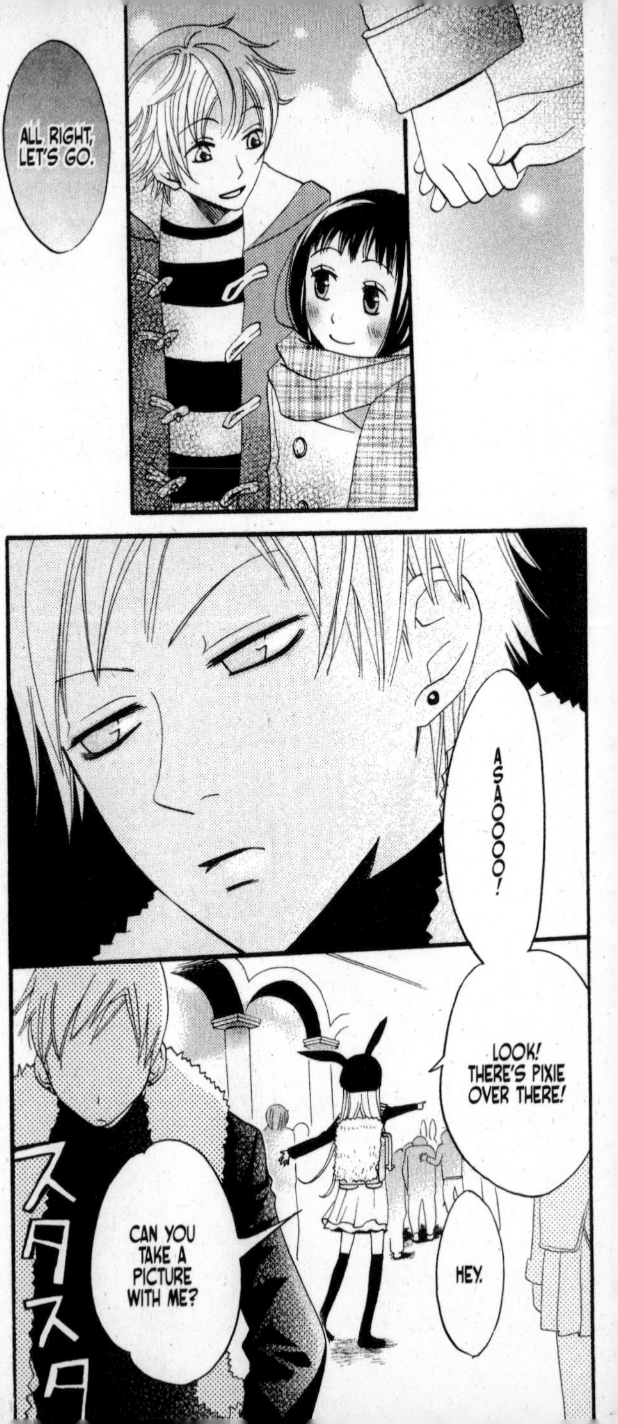
ALL RIGHT, LET'S GO.
ASAOOOO!
LOOK! THERE'S PIXIE OVER THERE!
HEY.
CAN YOU TAKE A PICTURE WITH ME?
スタスタ

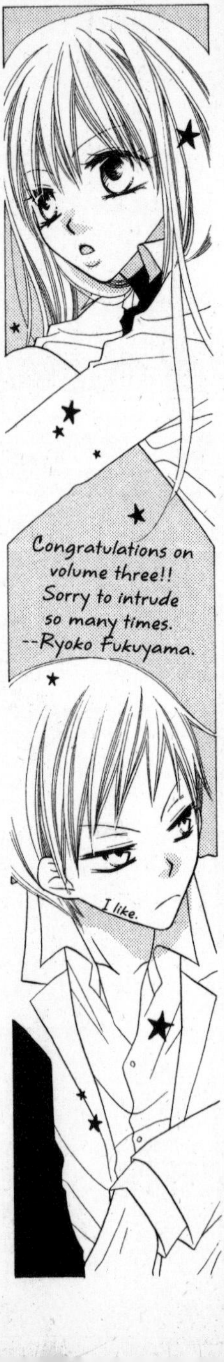
Congratulations on volume three!! Sorry to intrude so many times. --Ryoko Fukuyama.
I like.

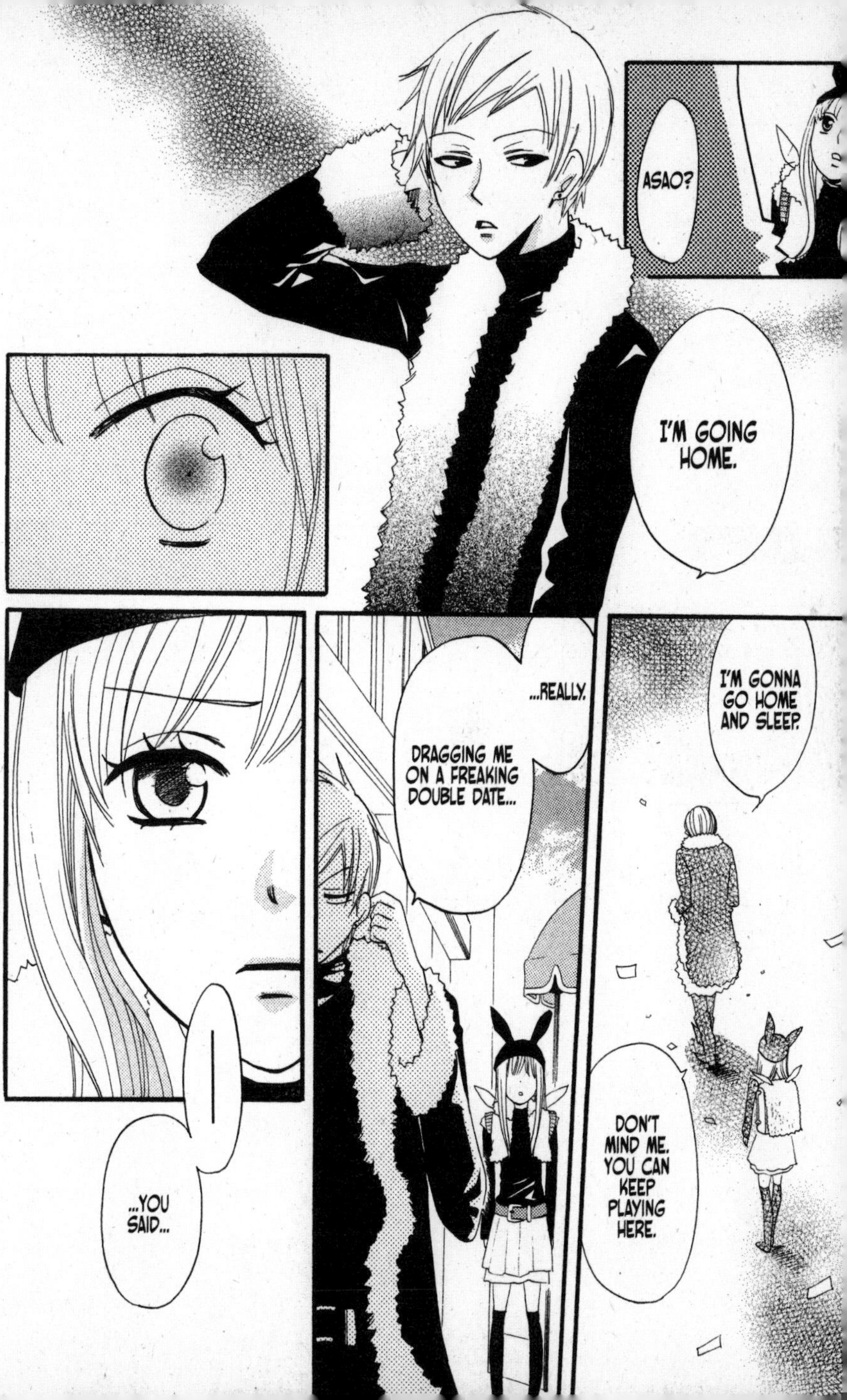
ASAO?
I'M GOING HOME.
I'M GONNA GO HOME AND SLEEP.
DON'T MIND ME. YOU CAN KEEP PLAYING HERE.
...REALLY.
DRAGGING ME ON A FREAKING DOUBLE DATE...
...YOU SAID...

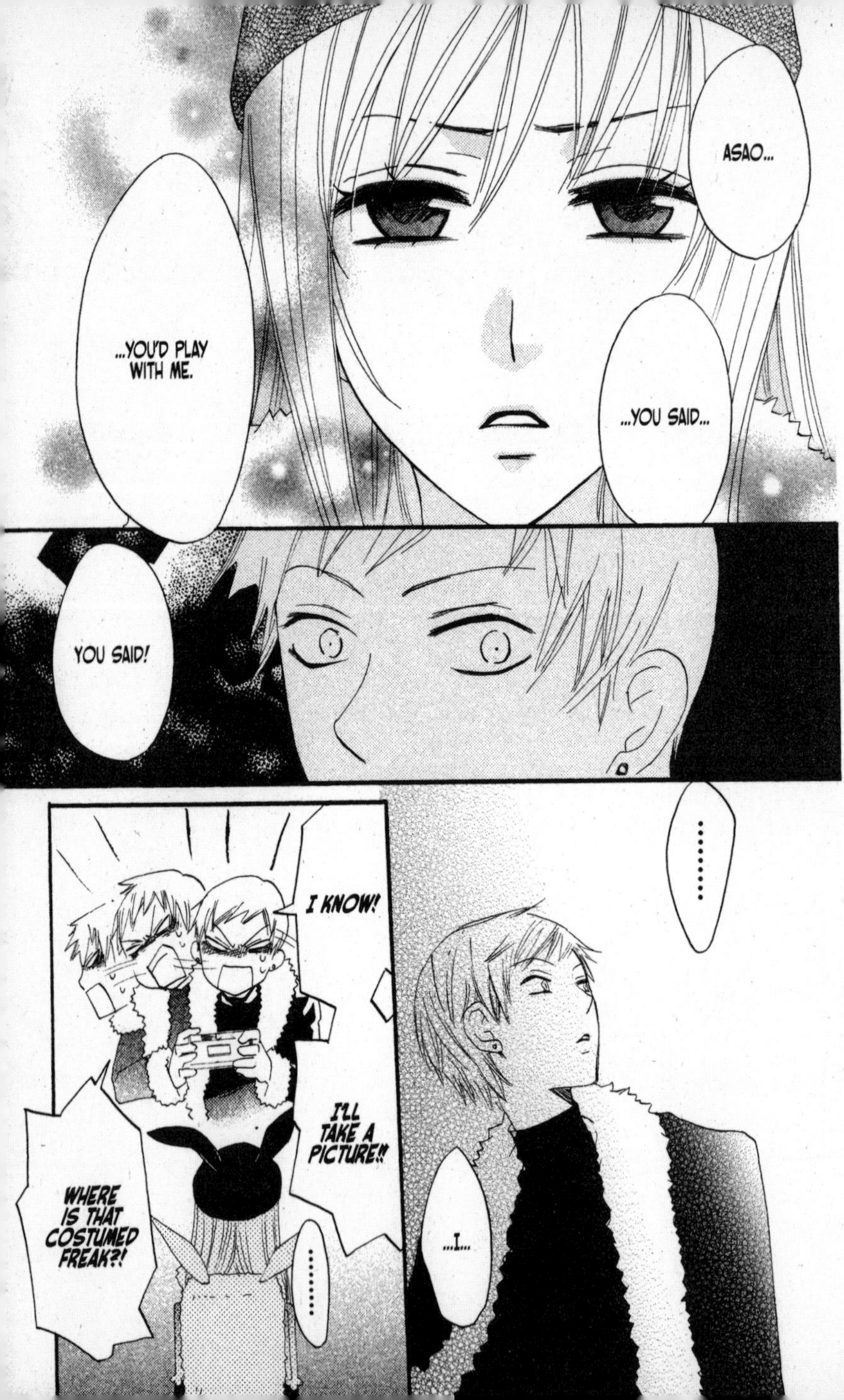
ASAO...
...YOU SAID...
...YOU'D PLAY WITH ME.
YOU SAID!
....
...I...
I KNOW!
I'LL TAKE A PICTURE!!
....
WHERE IS THAT COSTUMED FREAK?!

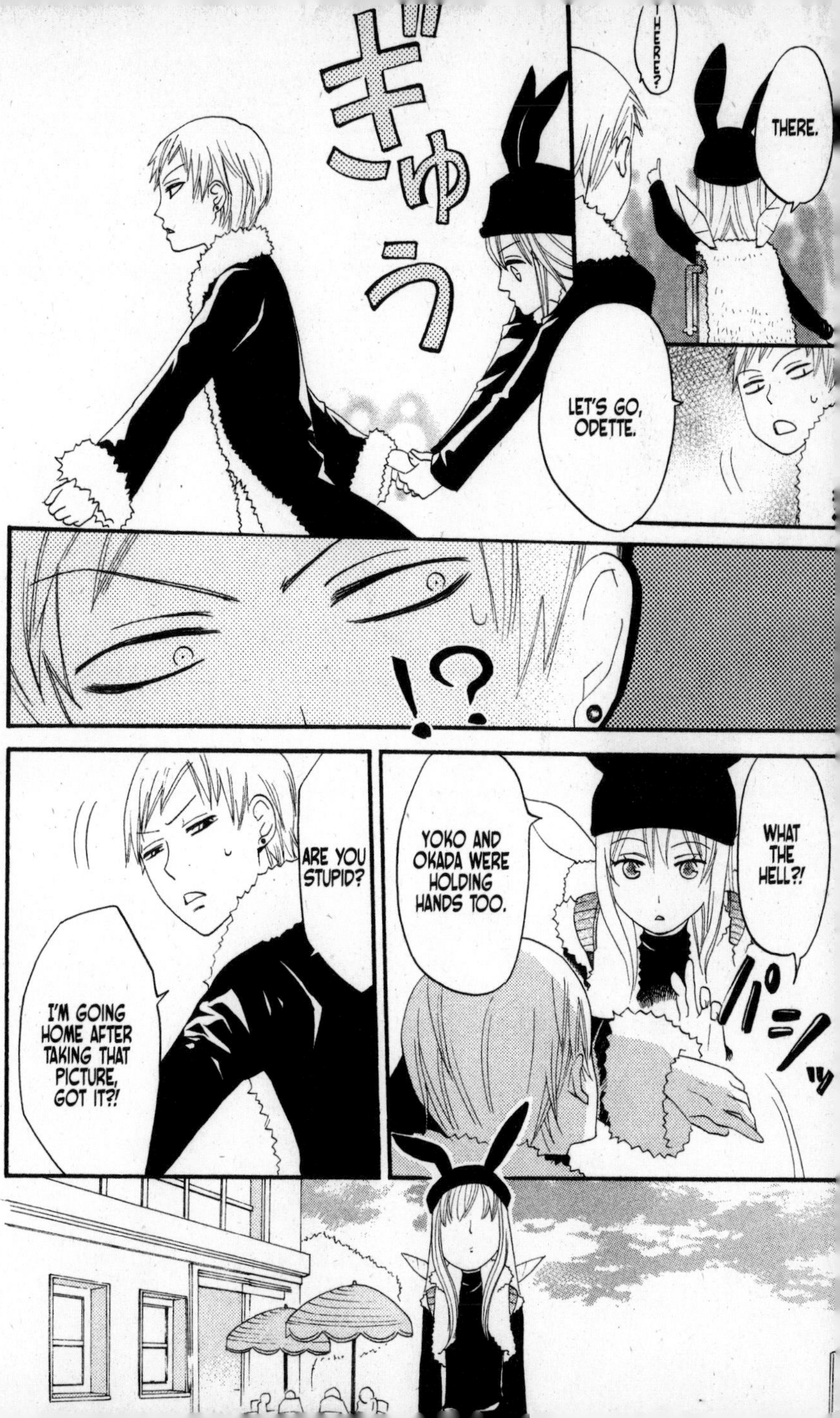
THERE.
THERE?
ぎゅう
LET'S GO, ODETTE.
!?
WHAT THE HELL?!
YOKO AND OKADA WERE HOLDING HANDS TOO.
パシッ
ARE YOU STUPID?
I'M GOING HOME AFTER TAKING THAT PICTURE, GOT IT?!

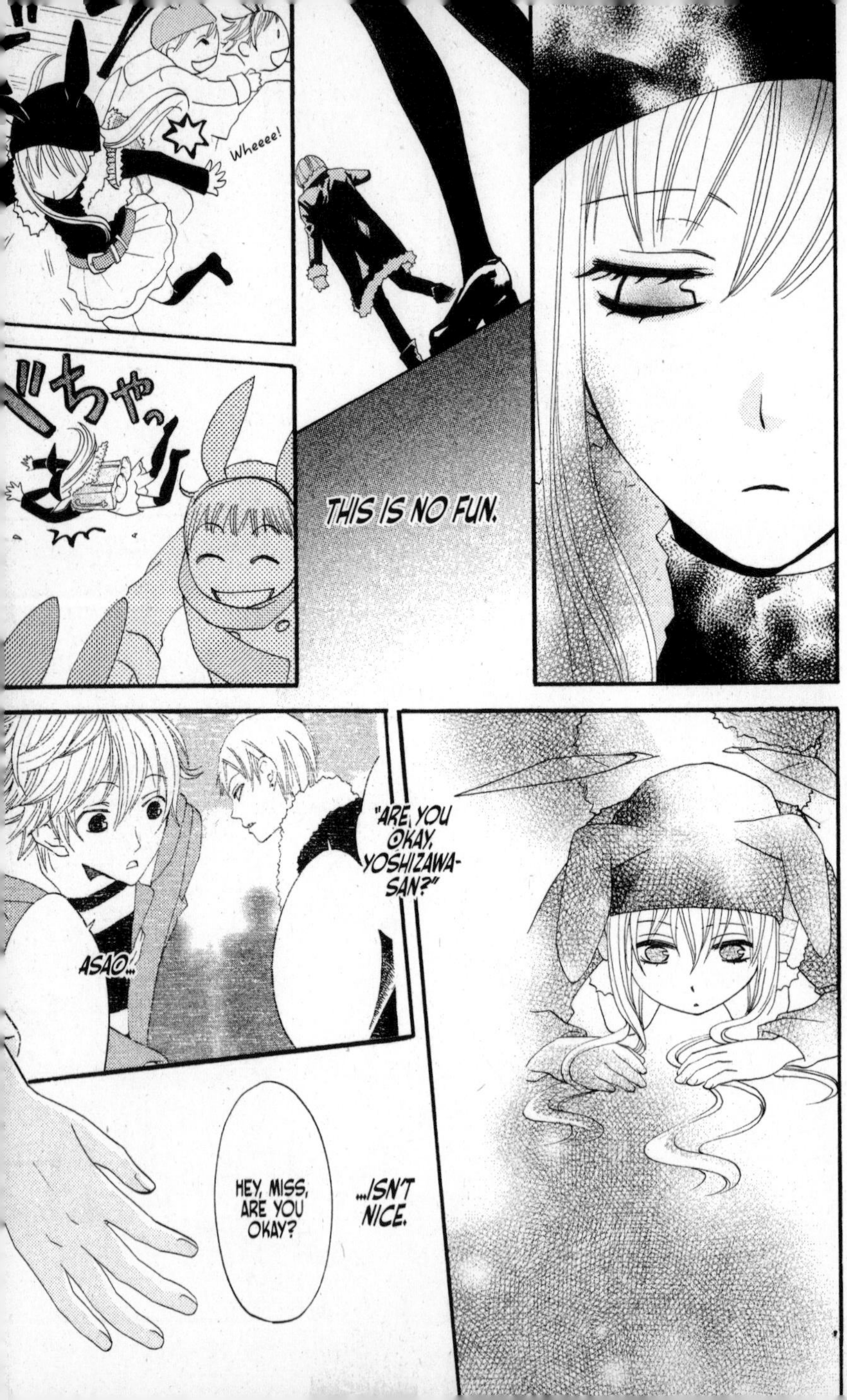
THIS IS NO FUN.
Wheeee!
ばちゃっ
"ARE YOU OKAY, YOSHIZAWA-SAN?"
ASAO...
...ISN'T NICE.
HEY, MISS, ARE YOU OKAY?

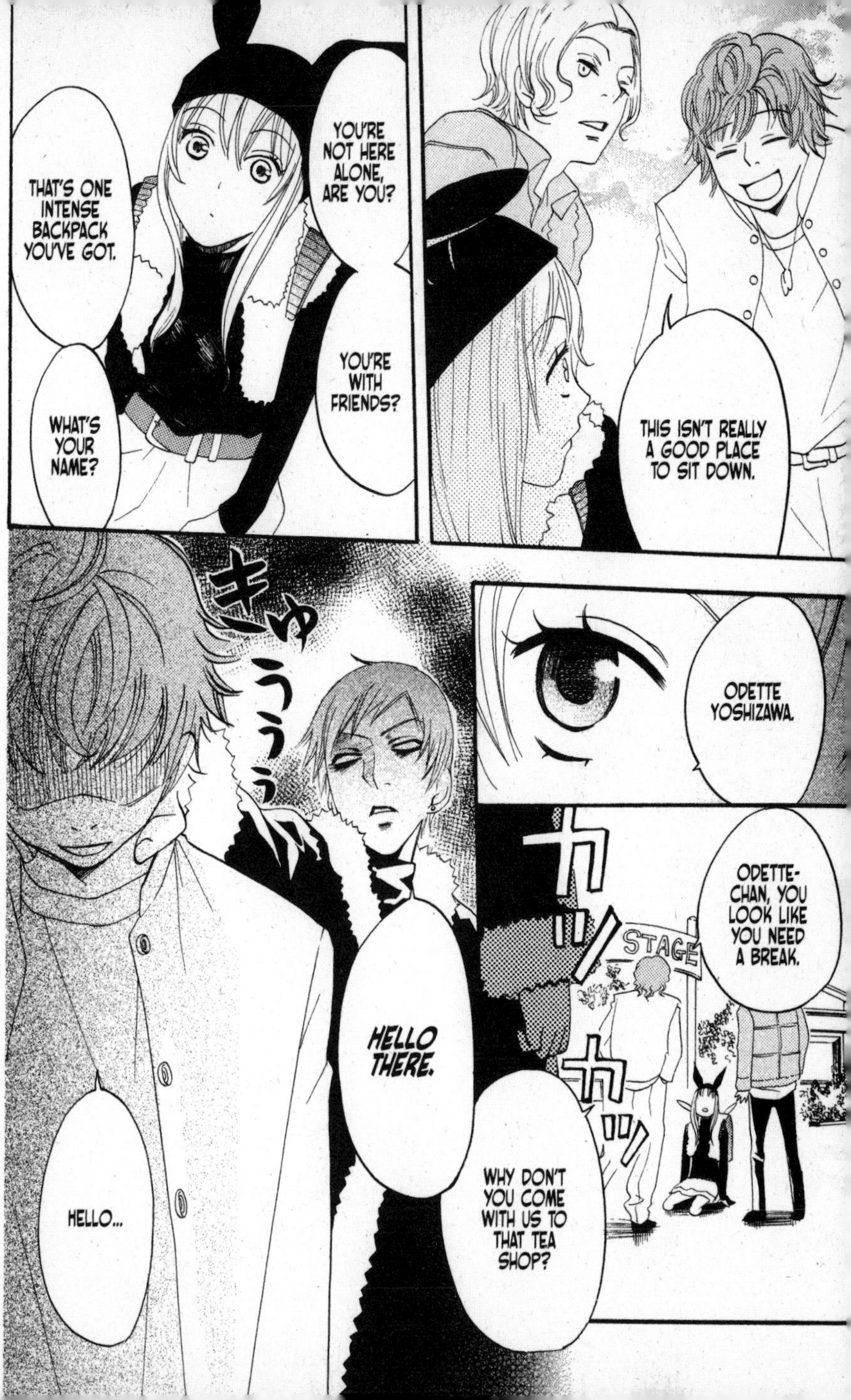
THIS ISN'T REALLY A GOOD PLACE TO SIT DOWN.
YOU'RE NOT HERE ALONE, ARE YOU?
THAT'S ONE INTENSE BACKPACK YOU'VE GOT.
YOU'RE WITH FRIENDS?
WHAT'S YOUR NAME?
ODETTE YOSHIZAWA.
ODETTE-CHAN, YOU LOOK LIKE YOU NEED A BREAK.
STAGE
WHY DON'T YOU COME WITH US TO THAT TEA SHOP?
きゅううう
HELLO THERE.
HELLO...

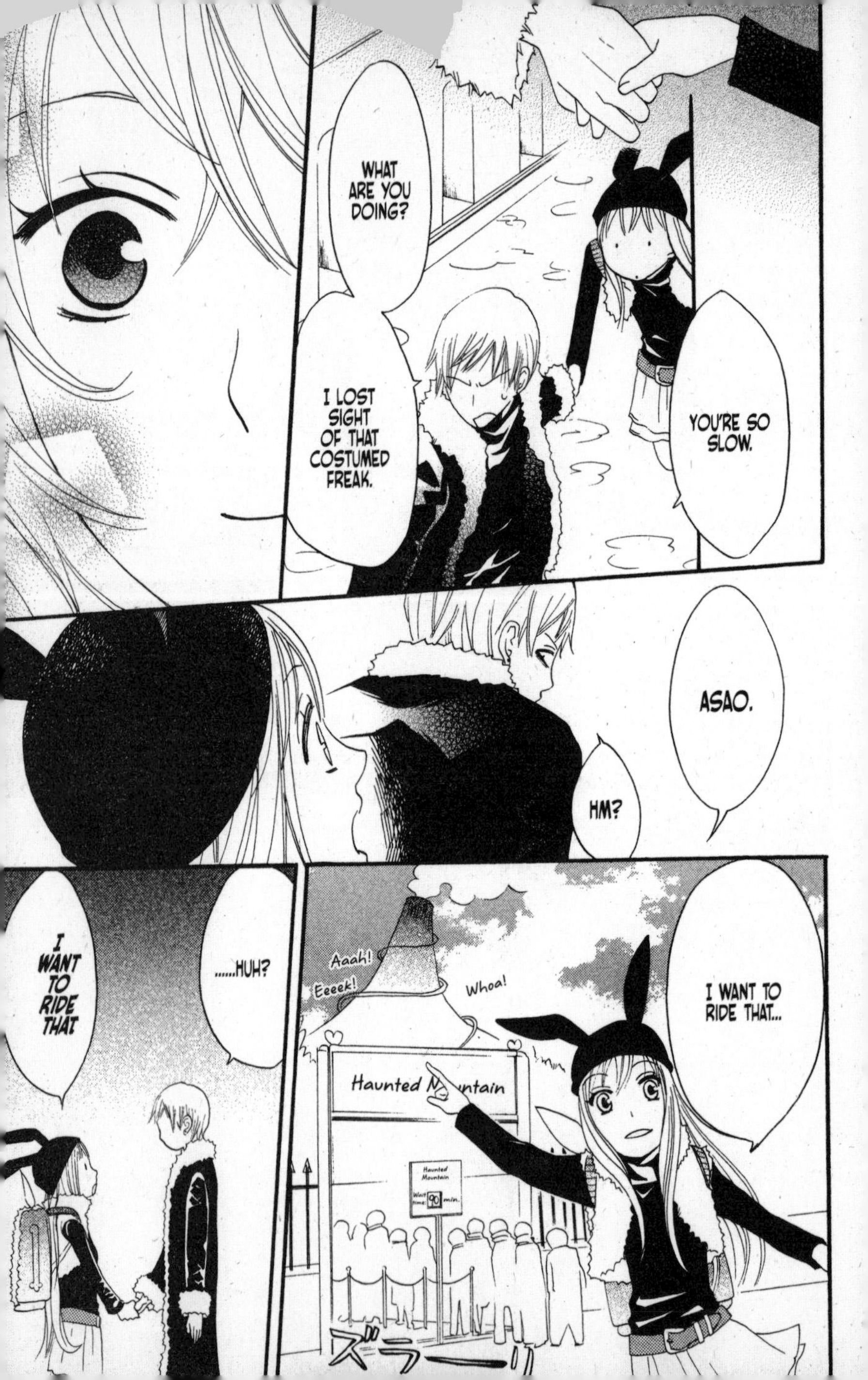
WHAT ARE YOU DOING?
I LOST SIGHT OF THAT COSTUMED FREAK.
YOU'RE SO SLOW.
ASAO.
HM?
I WANT TO RIDE THAT...
Aaah!
Eeeek!
Whoa!
Haunted Mountain
Haunted Mountain Wait time: 90 min.
ズラーッ
......HUH?
I WANT TO RIDE THAT.

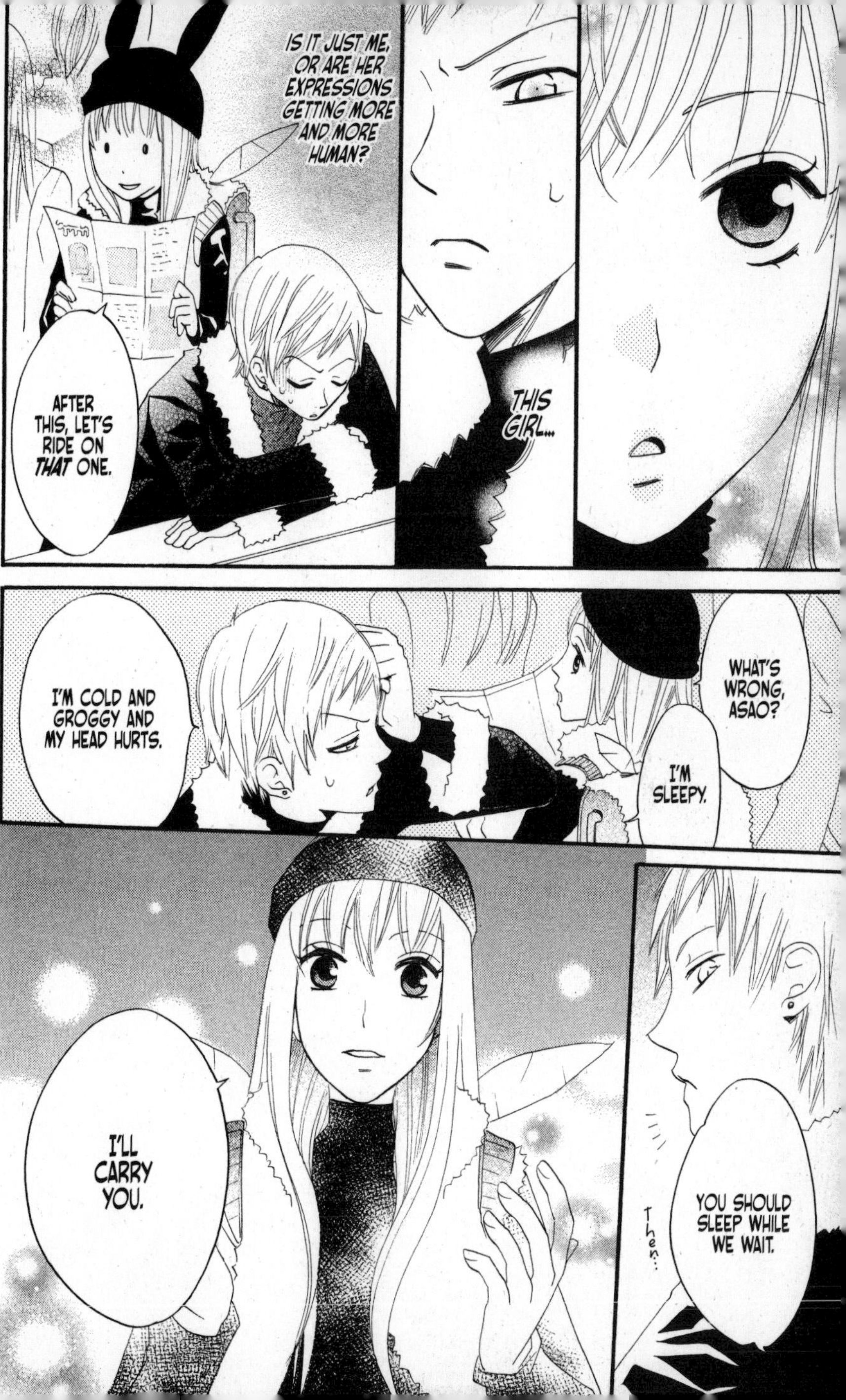
THIS GIRL...
IS IT JUST ME, OR ARE HER EXPRESSIONS GETTING MORE AND MORE HUMAN?
AFTER THIS, LET'S RIDE ON *THAT* ONE.
WHAT'S WRONG, ASAO?
I'M SLEEPY.
I'M COLD AND GROGGY AND MY HEAD HURTS.
YOU SHOULD SLEEP WHILE WE WAIT.
Then...
I'LL CARRY YOU.

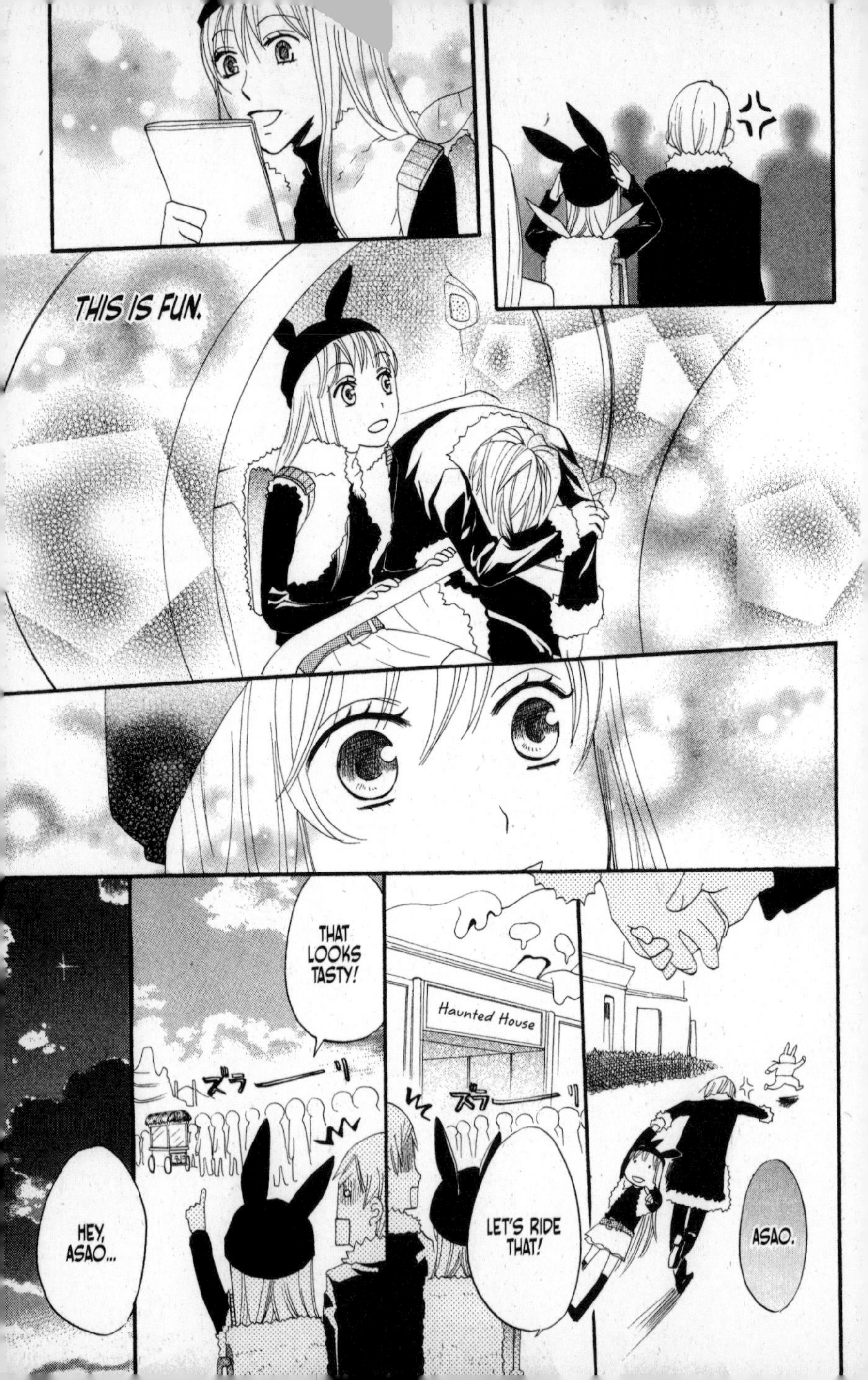
THIS IS FUN.
ASAO.
Haunted House
ズラーーリ
LET'S RIDE THAT!
THAT LOOKS TASTY!
ズラーーリ
HEY, ASAO...

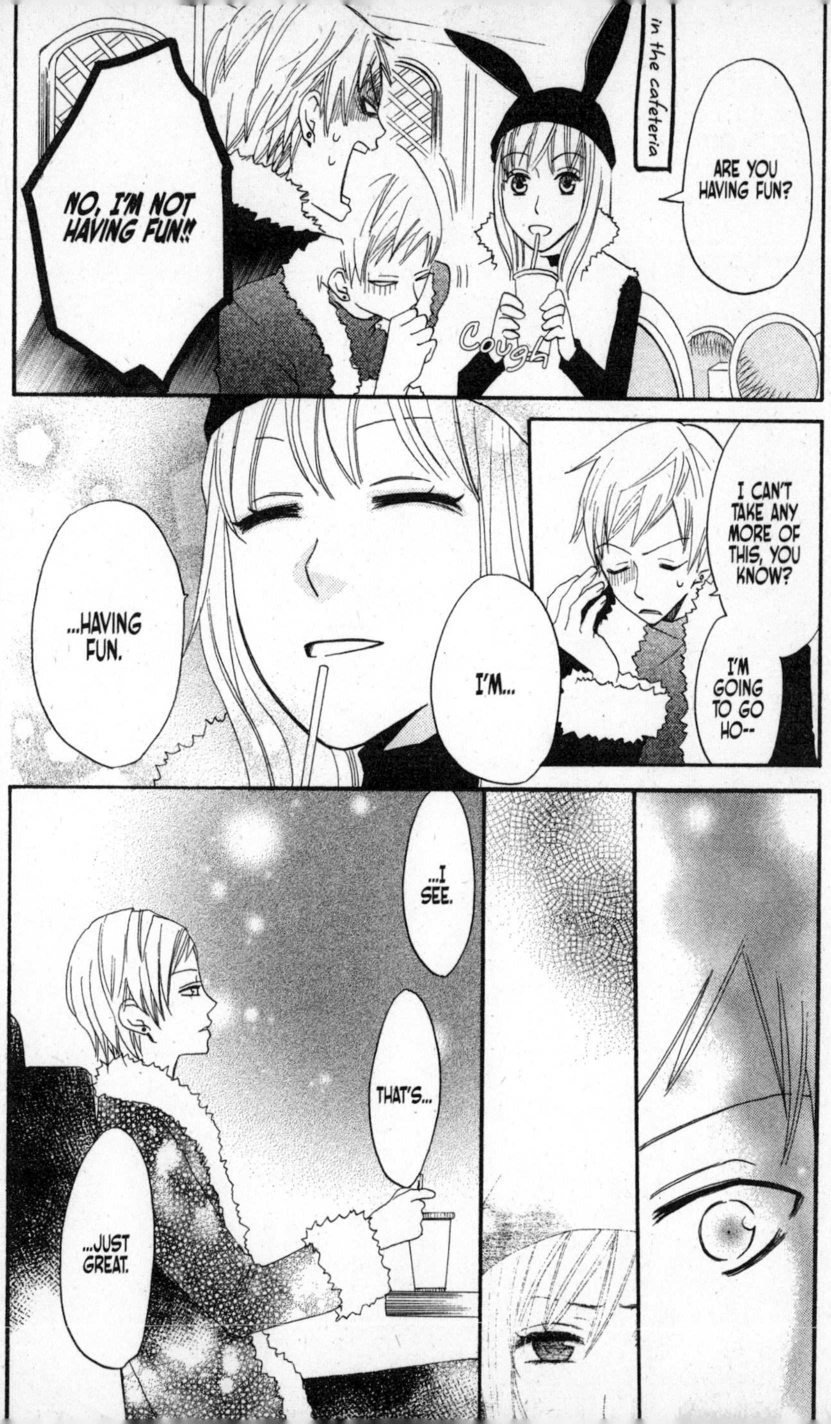
in the cafeteria
ARE YOU HAVING FUN?
Cough
NO, I'M NOT HAVING FUN!!
I CAN'T TAKE ANY MORE OF THIS, YOU KNOW?
I'M GOING TO GO HO--
I'M...
...HAVING FUN.
...I SEE.
THAT'S...
...JUST GREAT.

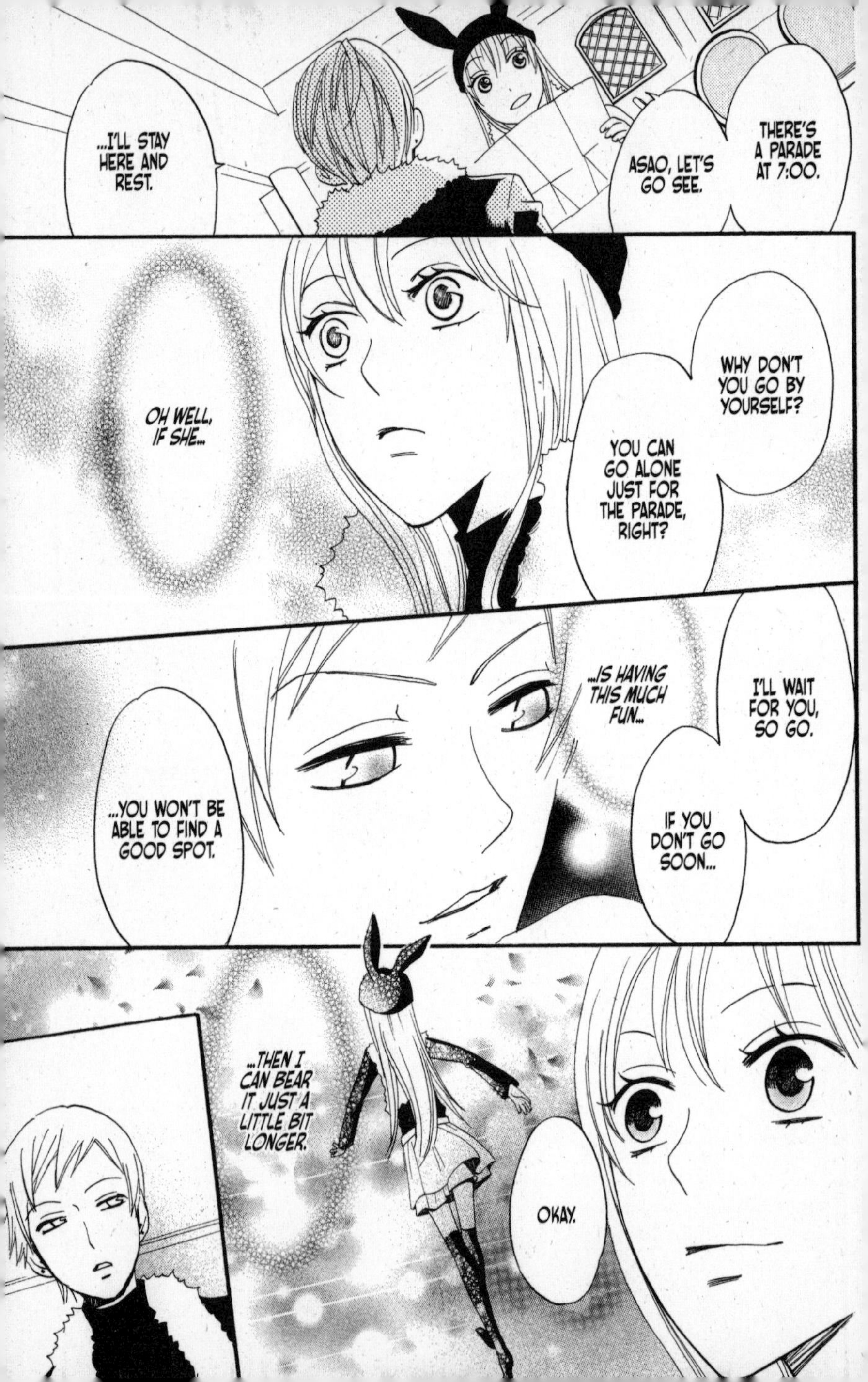
THERE'S A PARADE AT 7:00.
ASAO, LET'S GO SEE.
...I'LL STAY HERE AND REST.
WHY DON'T YOU GO BY YOURSELF?
YOU CAN GO ALONE JUST FOR THE PARADE, RIGHT?
OH WELL, IF SHE...
I'LL WAIT FOR YOU, SO GO.
...IS HAVING THIS MUCH FUN...
IF YOU DON'T GO SOON...
...YOU WON'T BE ABLE TO FIND A GOOD SPOT.
OKAY.
...THEN I CAN BEAR IT JUST A LITTLE BIT LONGER.

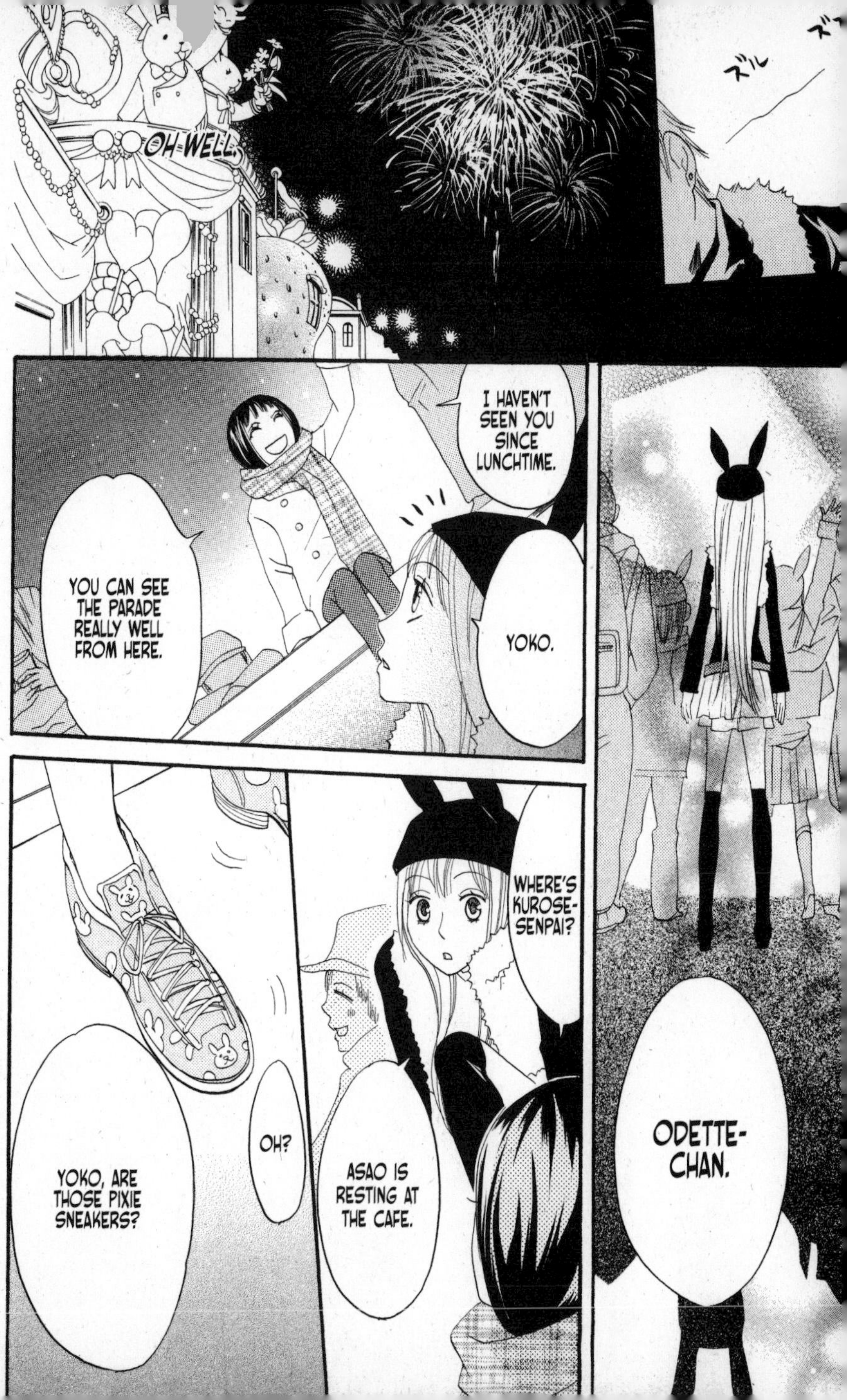
ズー
ズル
OH WELL.
ODETTE-CHAN.
YOKO.
I HAVEN'T SEEN YOU SINCE LUNCHTIME.
YOU CAN SEE THE PARADE REALLY WELL FROM HERE.
WHERE'S KUROSE-SENPAI?
ASAO IS RESTING AT THE CAFE.
OH?
YOKO, ARE THOSE PIXIE SNEAKERS?

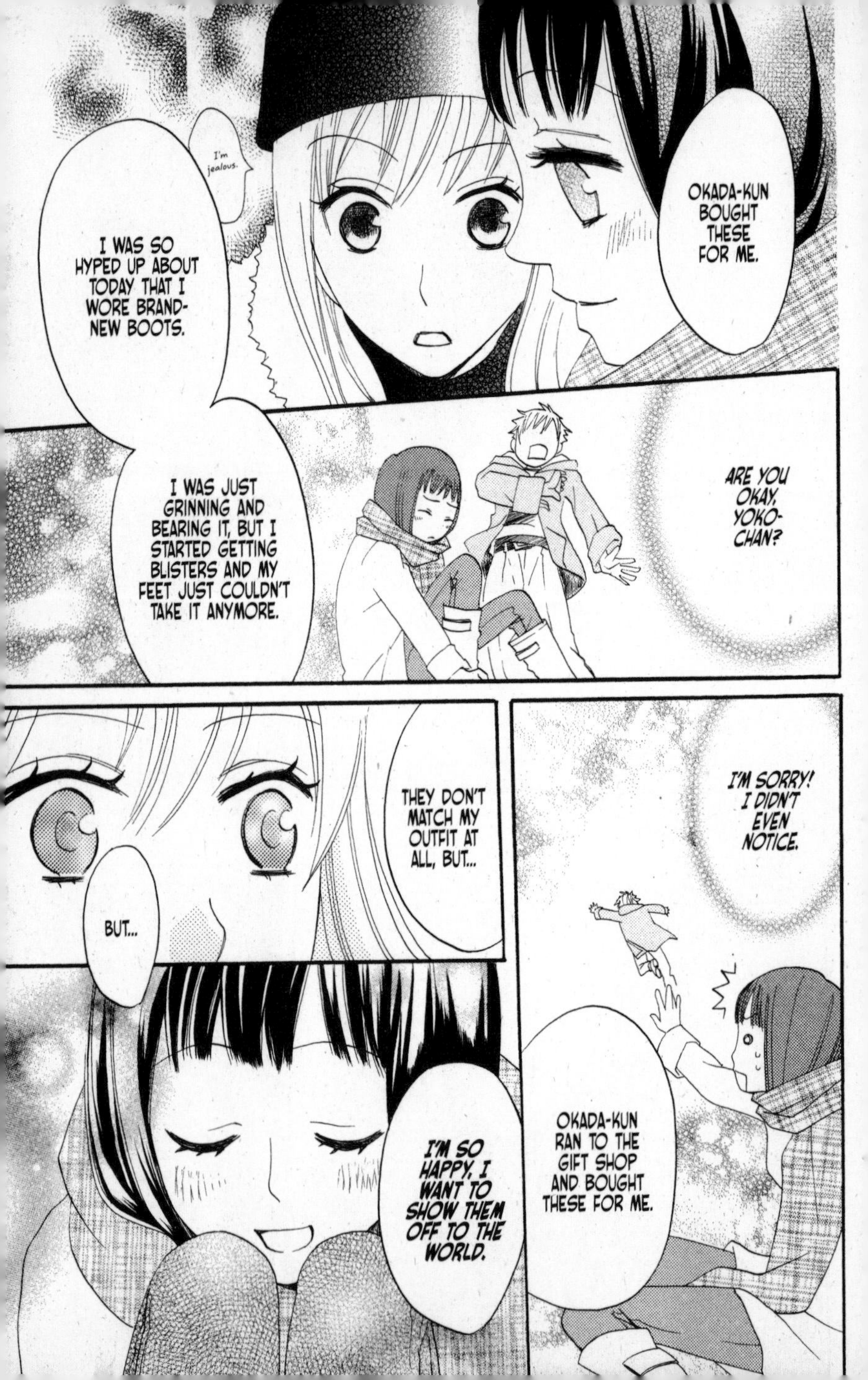
OKADA-KUN BOUGHT THESE FOR ME.
I'm jealous.
I WAS SO HYPED UP ABOUT TODAY THAT I WORE BRAND-NEW BOOTS.
ARE YOU OKAY, YOKO-CHAN?
I WAS JUST GRINNING AND BEARING IT, BUT I STARTED GETTING BLISTERS AND MY FEET JUST COULDN'T TAKE IT ANYMORE.
I'M SORRY! I DIDN'T EVEN NOTICE.
OKADA-KUN RAN TO THE GIFT SHOP AND BOUGHT THESE FOR ME.
THEY DON'T MATCH MY OUTFIT AT ALL, BUT...
BUT...
I'M SO HAPPY, I WANT TO SHOW THEM OFF TO THE WORLD.

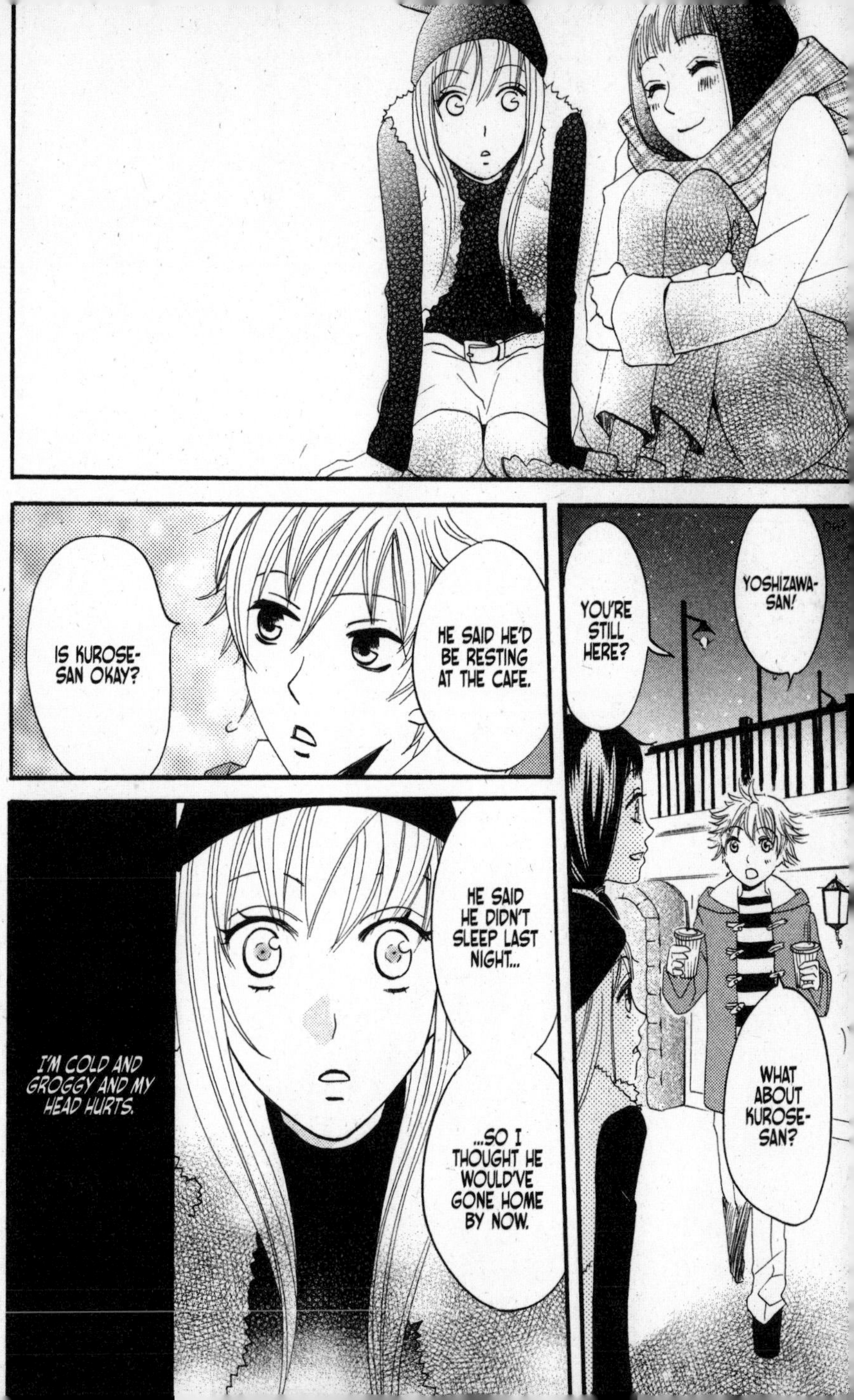
YOSHIZAWA-SAN!
YOU'RE STILL HERE?
WHAT ABOUT KUROSE-SAN?
HE SAID HE'D BE RESTING AT THE CAFE.
IS KUROSE-SAN OKAY?
HE SAID HE DIDN'T SLEEP LAST NIGHT...
...SO I THOUGHT HE WOULD'VE GONE HOME BY NOW.
I'M COLD AND GROGGY AND MY HEAD HURTS.

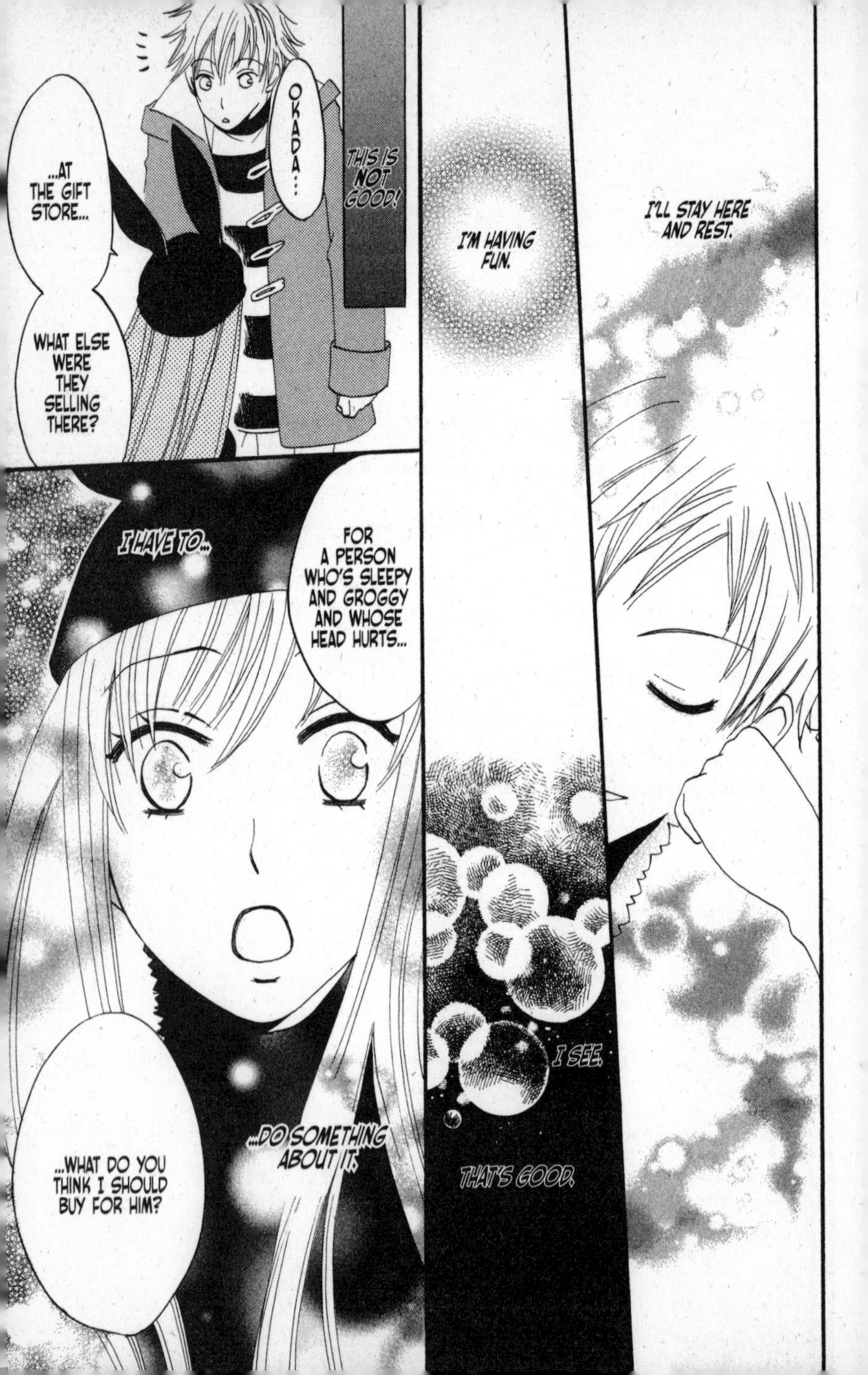
I'LL STAY HERE AND REST.
I'M HAVING FUN.
I SEE.
THAT'S GOOD.
OKADA...
THIS IS NOT GOOD!
...AT THE GIFT STORE...
WHAT ELSE WERE THEY SELLING THERE?
FOR A PERSON WHO'S SLEEPY AND GROGGY AND WHOSE HEAD HURTS...
I HAVE TO...
...WHAT DO YOU THINK I SHOULD BUY FOR HIM?
...DO SOMETHING ABOUT IT.

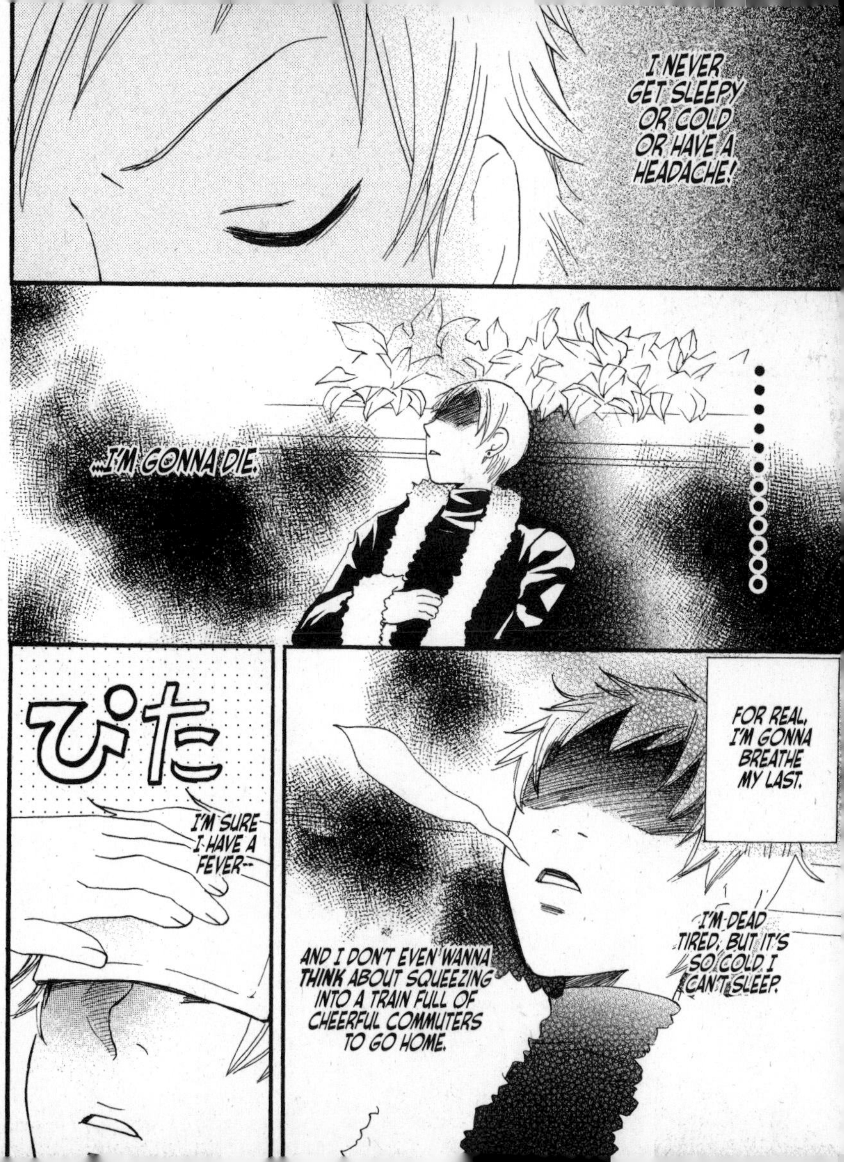
I NEVER GET SLEEPY OR COLD OR HAVE A HEADACHE!
...I'M GONNA DIE.
FOR REAL, I'M GONNA BREATHE MY LAST.
I'M DEAD TIRED, BUT IT'S SO COLD I CAN'T SLEEP.
AND I DON'T EVEN WANNA THINK ABOUT SQUEEZING INTO A TRAIN FULL OF CHEERFUL COMMUTERS TO GO HOME.
ぴた
I'M SURE I HAVE A FEVER--

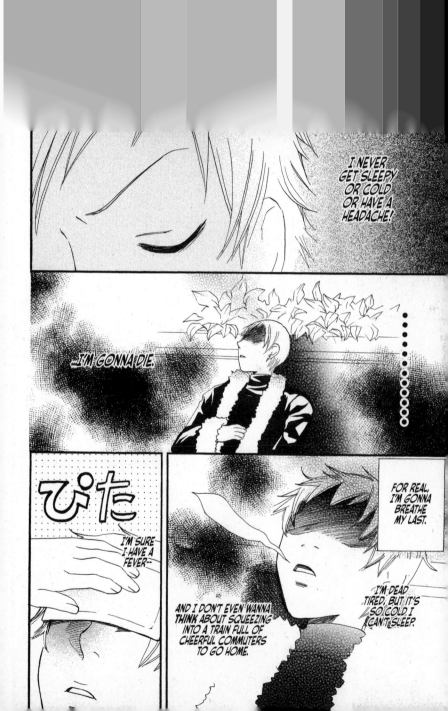

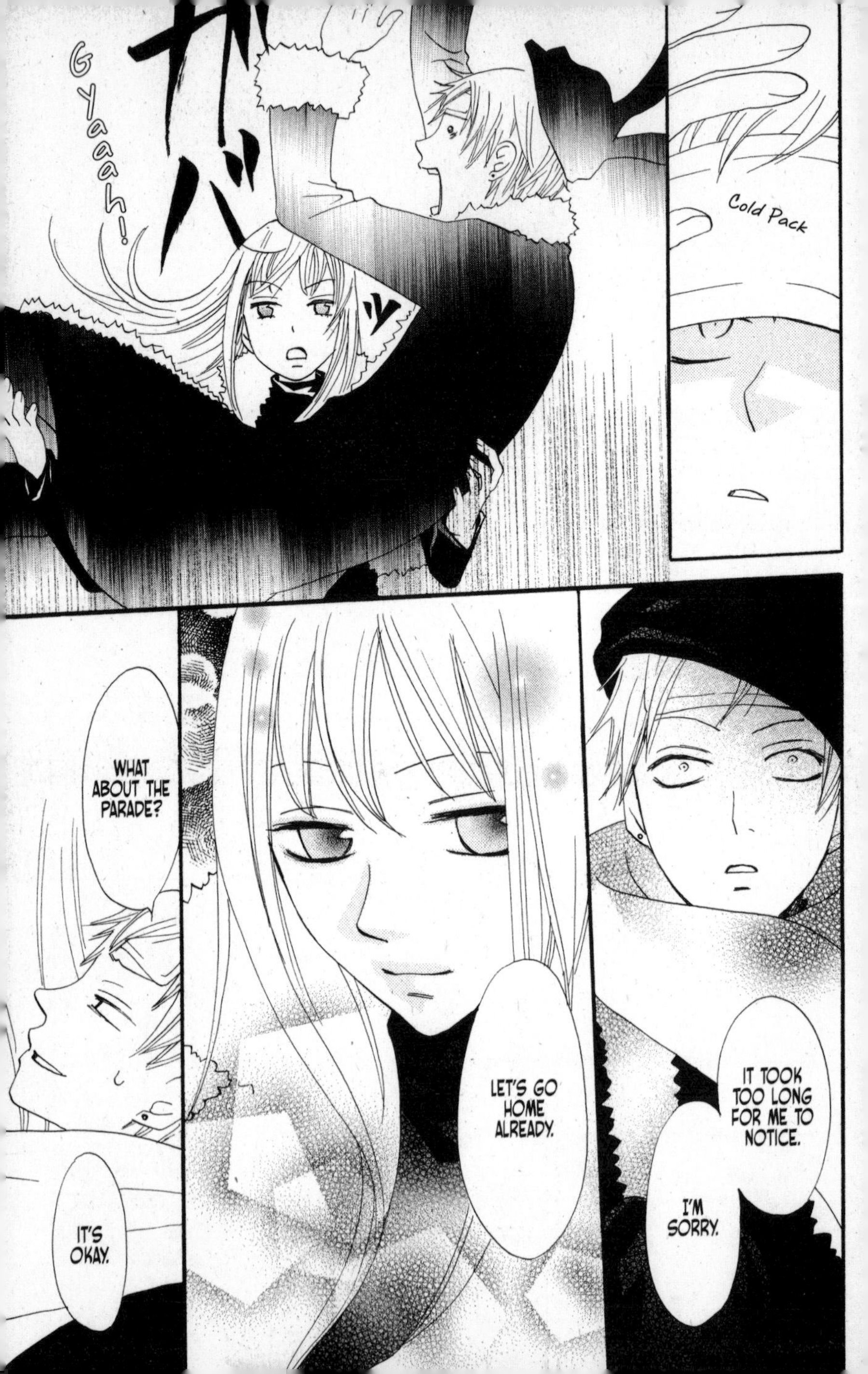
Cold Pack
Gyaaaah!
IT TOOK TOO LONG FOR ME TO NOTICE.
I'M SORRY.
LET'S GO HOME ALREADY.
WHAT ABOUT THE PARADE?
IT'S OKAY.

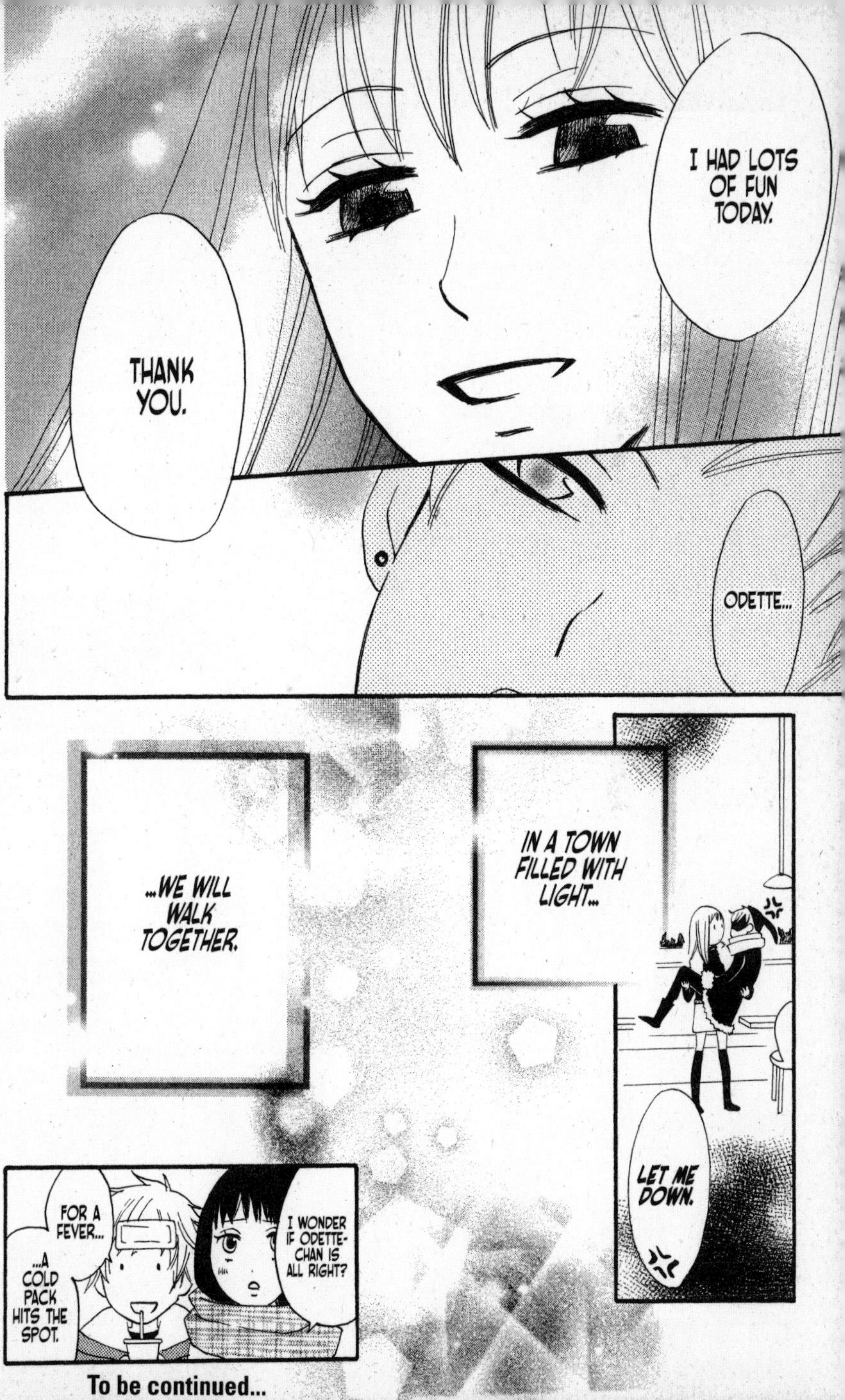
I HAD LOTS OF FUN TODAY.
THANK YOU.
ODETTE...
IN A TOWN FILLED WITH LIGHT...
LET ME DOWN.
...WE WILL WALK TOGETHER.
I WONDER IF ODETTE-CHAN IS ALL RIGHT?
FOR A FEVER...
...A COLD PACK HITS THE SPOT.

To be continued...

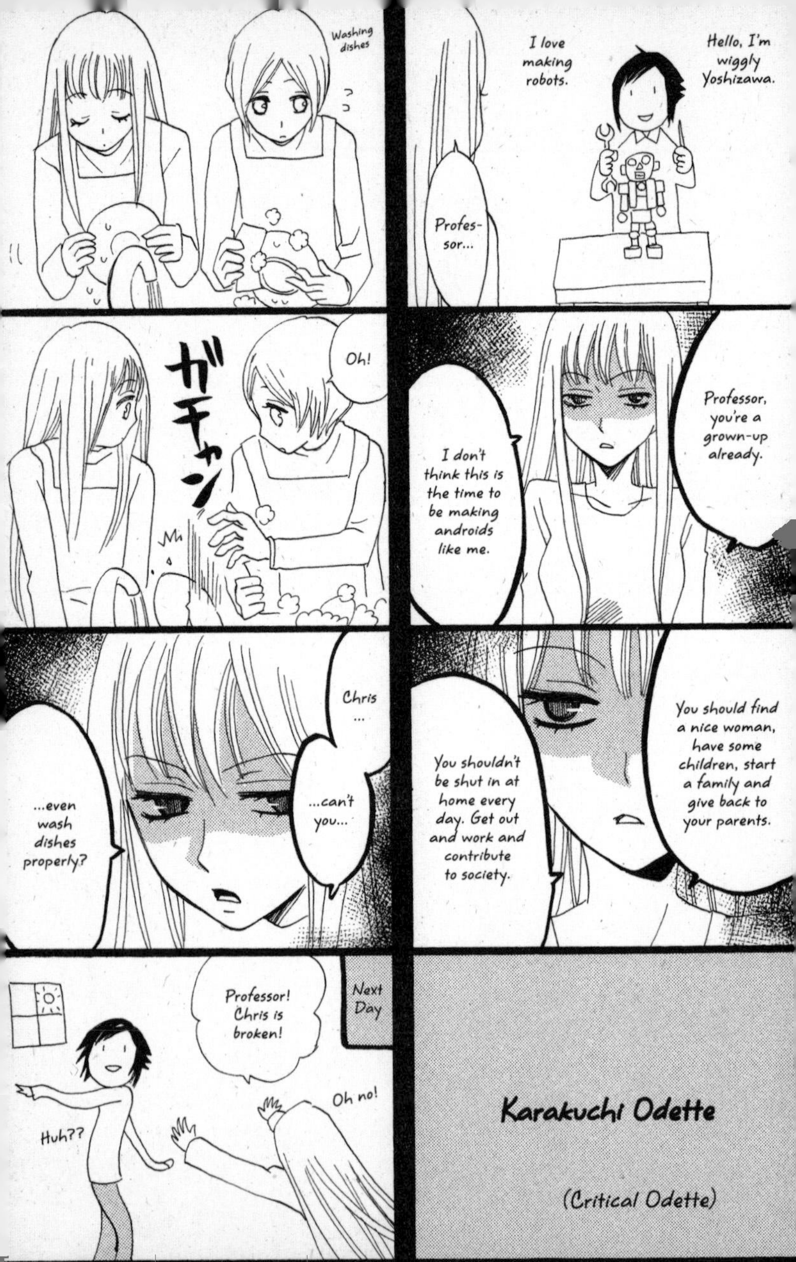
Hello, I'm wiggly Yoshizawa.
I love making robots.
Profes-sor...
Washing dishes
Professor, you're a grown-up already.
I don't think this is the time to be making androids like me.
Oh!
ガチャン
You should find a nice woman, have some children, start a family and give back to your parents.
You shouldn't be shut in at home every day. Get out and work and contribute to society.
Chris...
...can't you...
...even wash dishes properly?
Karakuchi Odette
(Critical Odette)
Next Day
Professor! Chris is broken!
Oh no!
Huh??

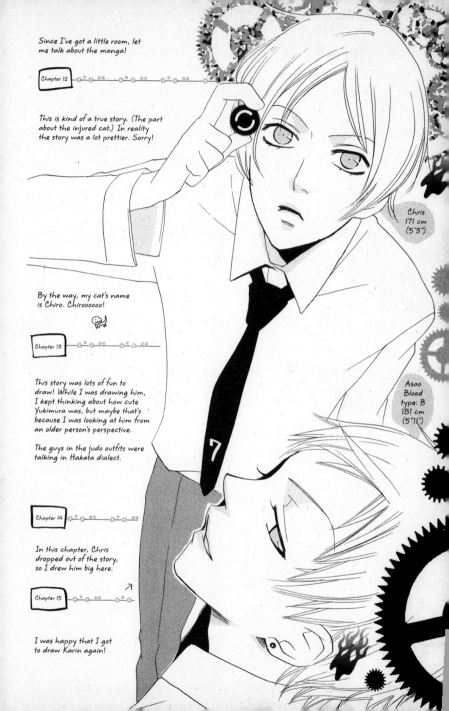

Since I've got a little room, let me talk about the manga!

Chapter 12

This is kind of a true story. (The part about the injured cat.) In reality the story was a lot prettier. Sorry!

By the way, my cat's name is Chiro. Chirooooo!

Chapter 13

This story was lots of fun to draw! While I was drawing him, I kept thinking about how cute Yukimura was, but maybe that's because I was looking at him from an older person's perspective.

The guys in the judo outfits were talking in Hakata dialect.

Chapter 14

In this chapter, Chris dropped out of the story, so I drew him big here.

Chapter 15

I was happy that I got to draw Karin again!

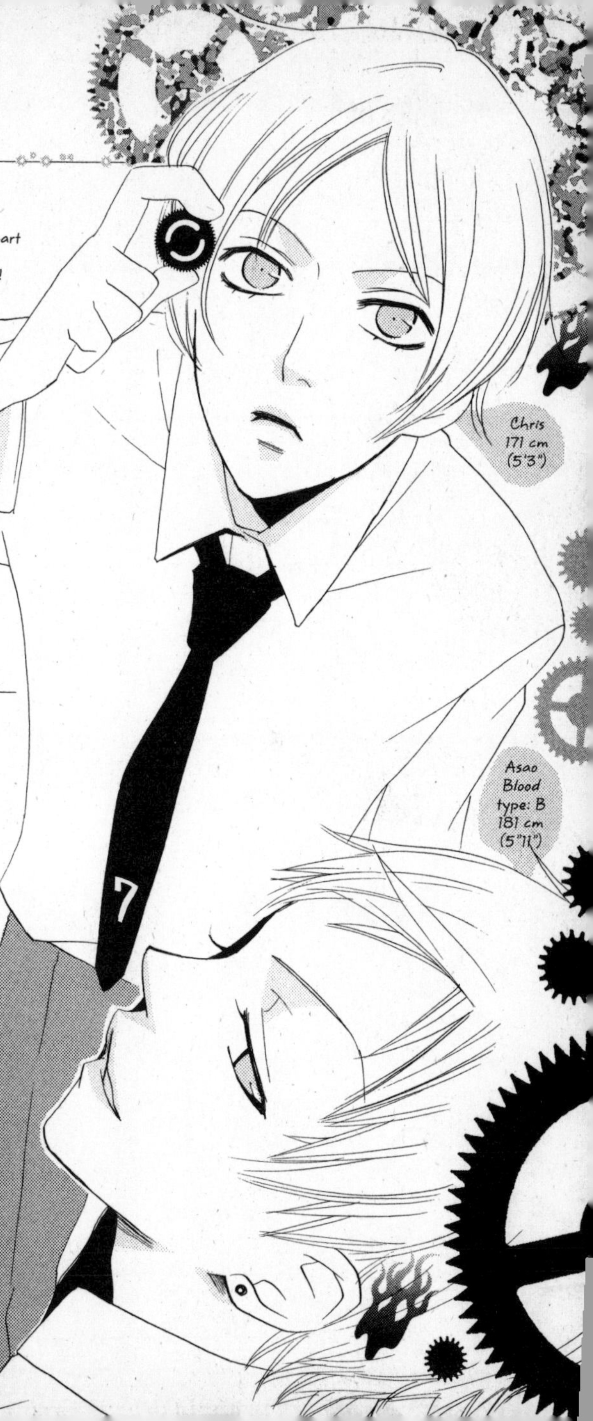

Chris 171 cm (5'3")
Asao Blood type: B 181 cm (5"11")

Chapter 16

I was happy to draw Karin (omitted)

Chapter 17

This was the first time I drew Okada in full. I thought about making him mean, but he turned out to be a nice guy.

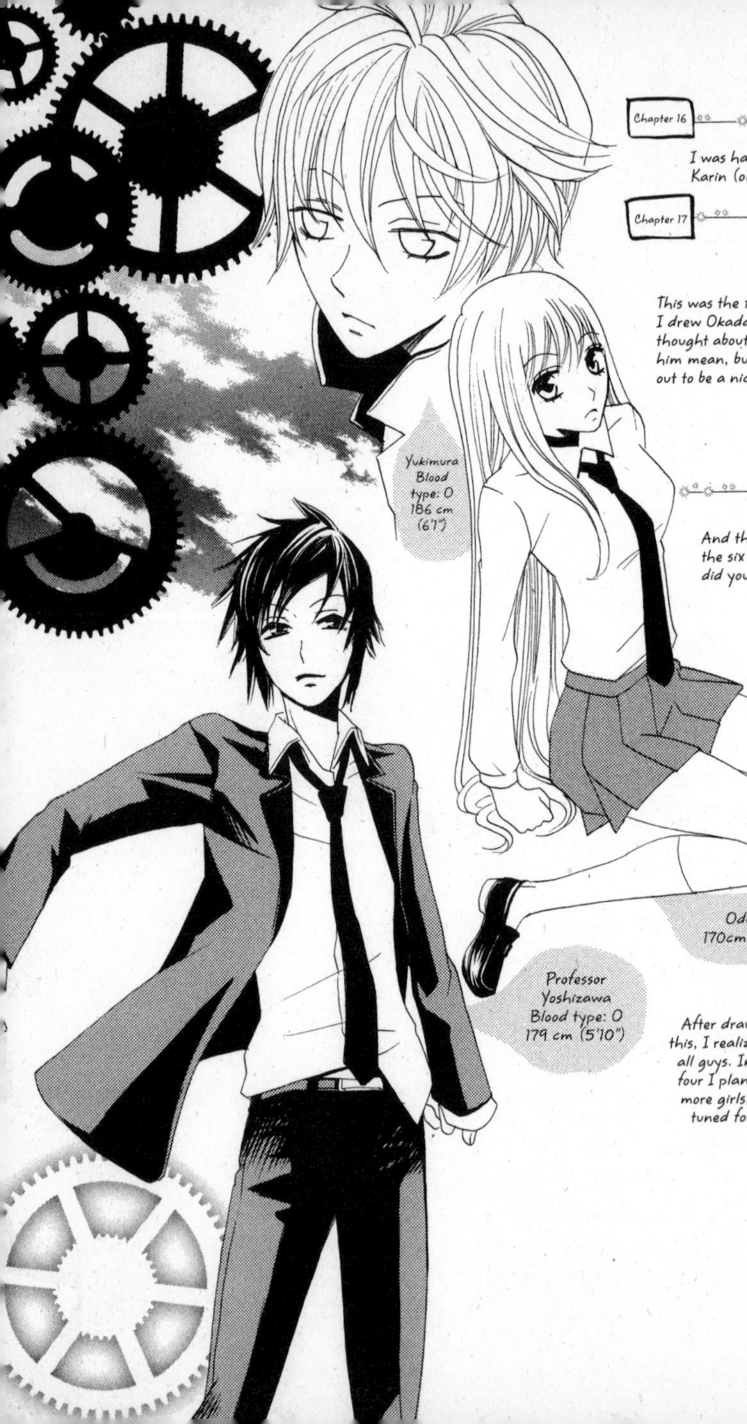
Yukimura Blood type: O 186 cm (6'1")
Odette 170cm (5'7")
Professor Yoshizawa Blood type: O 179 cm (5'10")

And there you have the six chapters. How did you like them?

After drawing all this, I realized it was all guys. In volume four I plan to have more girls, so stay tuned for that.

Thank you for sticking around! ❀
I already mentioned this in a
sidebar, but Karakuri Odette
reaching its third volume couldn't
have happened without the help
of so many people. Everyone who
encouraged me, people who came
by to help me, friends, my editor
who helped me and everyone who
was involved in the making of this
book... I thank you very much!

If you have any comments or
thoughts, please send them here:

Julietta Suzuki
c/o TOKYOPOP Editorial
5900 Wilshire Blvd. Ste. 2000
Los Angeles CA 90036

I started a website. Please
come and visit if you'd like. ❀

IN THE NEXT VOLUME OF...

KARAKURI ODETTE

カラクリ オデット

When the Professor sends Odette to deliver a new robot to a young girl, it turns into a surprising encounter for all concerned! Shirayuki has a mysterious ability that allows her to sense others' thoughts, but what will happen when she doesn't sense anything from Odette? And how will Odette relate to this new friend who is the first person to teach her the pain of loneliness?

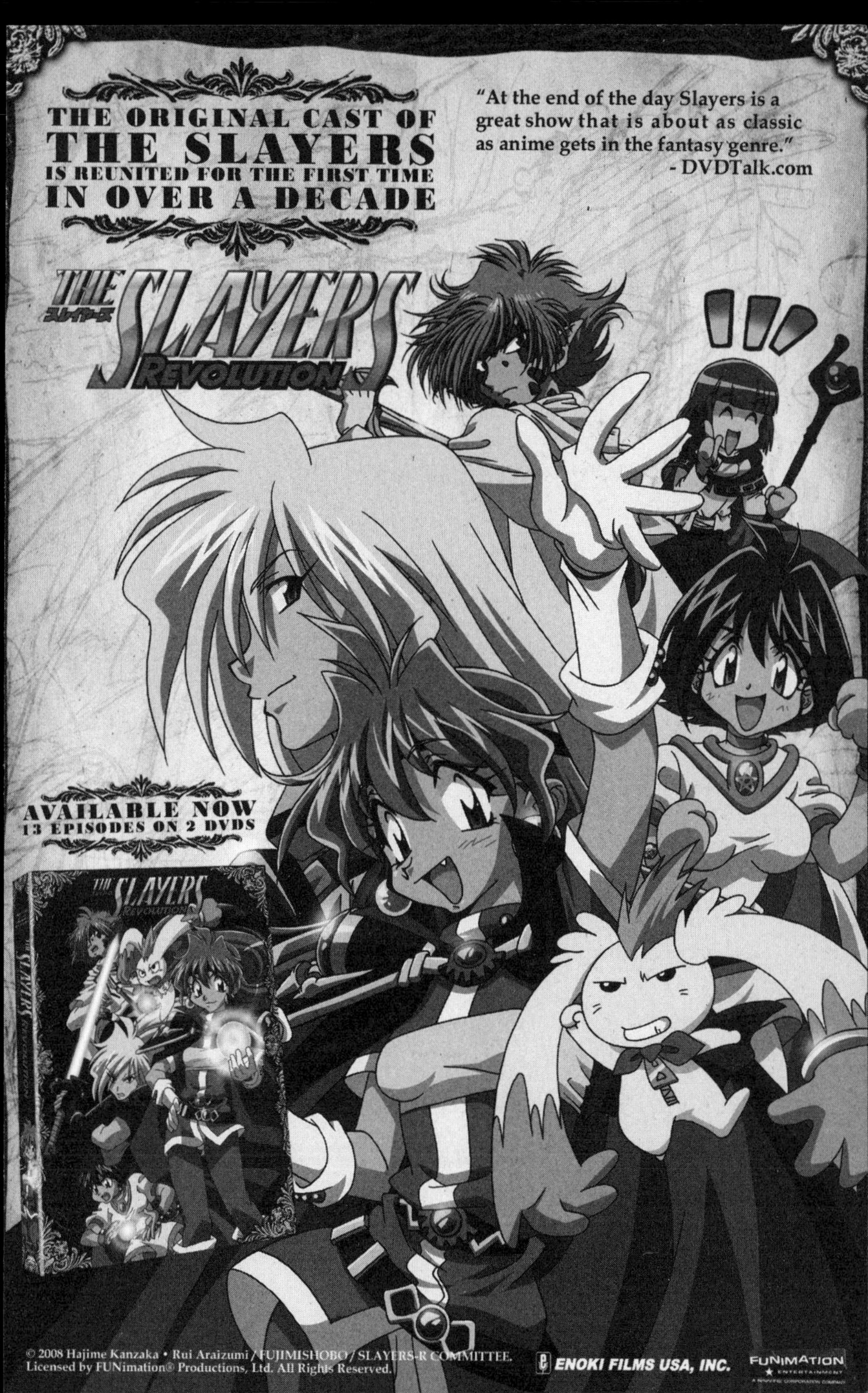

THE ORIGINAL CAST OF THE SLAYERS IS REUNITED FOR THE FIRST TIME IN OVER A DECADE
"At the end of the day Slayers is a great show that is about as classic as anime gets in the fantasy genre."
- DVDTalk.com
THE SLAYERS REVOLUTION
AVAILABLE NOW
13 EPISODES ON 2 DVDS
© 2008 Hajime Kanzaka • Rui Araizumi / FUJIMISHOBO / SLAYERS-R COMMITTEE.
Licensed by FUNimation® Productions, Ltd. All Rights Reserved.
ENOKI FILMS USA, INC.
FUNIMATION ENTERTAINMENT

The second epic trilogy continues!

Princess Ai: The Prism of Midnight Dawn

Princess Ai
The Prism of Midnight Dawn
Created by Courtney Love & Stuart "D.J. Milky" Levy
Story by Stuart "D.J. Milky" Levy Written by Christine Boylan Art by Misaho Kujiradou
2

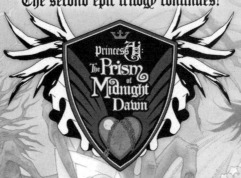

Ai fights to escape the clutches of her mysterious and malevolent captors, not knowing whether Kent, left behind on the Other Side, is even still alive. A frantic rescue mission commences, and in the end, even Ai's magical voice may not be enough to protect her from the trials of the Black Forest.

Dark secrets are revealed, and Ai must use all her strength and courage to face off against the new threat to Ai-Land. But will she ever see Kent again...?

"A very intriguing read that will satisfy old fans and create new fans, too."
– *Bookloons*

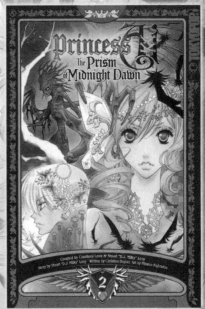

STO

This is the back of the book.
You wouldn't want to spoil a great ending!

This book is printed "manga-style," in the authentic Japanese right-to-left format. Since none of the artwork has been flipped or altered, readers get to experience the story just as the creator intended. You've been asking for it, so TOKYOPOP® delivered: authentic, hot-off-the-press, and far more fun!

1
2
3
4
5
6
7
8
9
10

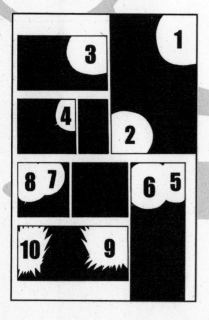

DIRECTIONS

If this is your first time reading manga-style, here's a quick guide to help you understand how it works.

It's easy... just start in the top right panel and follow the numbers. Have fun, and look for more 100% authentic manga from TOKYOPOP®!

THE MANGA REVOLUTION • LEADING THE MANGA REVOLUTION • LEADING

漫画革命

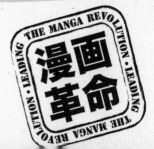